# Historical and Critical Matter the Tempest. Two Gentlemen of Verona. Merry Wives of Windsor
by William Shakespeare

Address:
HardPress
8345 NW 66TH ST #2561
MIAMI FL 33166-2626
USA
Email: info@hardpress.net

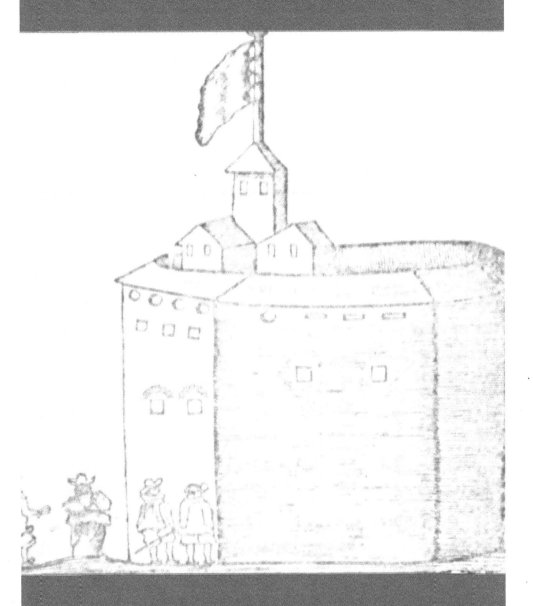

# The Plays of William Shakspeare: [Historical and ...

William Shakespeare, Alexander Chalmers,
George Steevens, Henry Fuseli

# THE

# PLAYS

## OF

# WILLIAM SHAKSPEARE.

C. Baldwin, Printer,
New Bridge-street, London.

W. SHAKSPEARE.

Published by J. Nichols and Son, October 30. 1810.

# THE
# PLAYS
## OF
# WILLIAM SHAKSPEARE,

Accurately printed from the Text of the corrected Copy left by the late
### GEORGE STEEVENS, Esq.

#### WITH
## A SERIES OF ENGRAVINGS,
### FROM ORIGINAL DESIGNS OF
## HENRY FUSELI, Esq. R.A. PROFESSOR OF PAINTING:

### AND A SELECTION
## OF EXPLANATORY AND HISTORICAL NOTES,
From the most eminent Commentators;
## *A History of the Stage, a Life of Shakspeare, &c.*
## BY ALEXANDER CHALMERS, A.M.

## A NEW EDITION.

## IN NINE VOLUMES.

## VOLUME I.

CONTAINING
### THE TEMPEST.
### TWO GENTLEMEN OF VERONA.
### MERRY WIVES OF WINDSOR.

## *LONDON:*
Printed for J. Nichols and Son; F. C. and J. Rivington; J. Stockdale;
W. Lowndes; G. Wilkie and J. Robinson; T. Egerton; J. Walker;
W. Clarke and Son; J. Barker; J. Cuthell; R. Lea; Lackington and
Co.; J. Deighton; J. White and Co.; B. Crosby and Co.; W. Earle;
J. Gray and Son; Longman and Co.; Cadell and Davies; J. Harding;
R. H. Evans; J. Booker; S. Bagster; J. Mawman; Black and Co.;
J. Richardson; J. Booth; Newman and Co.; R. Pheney; R. Scholey;
J. Asperne; J. Faulder; R. Baldwin; Cradock and Joy; J. Mackinlay; J. Johnson and Co.; Gale and Curtis; G. Robinson; and Wilson
and Son, York.

### 1811.

# PREFACE.

THE EDITOR's intentions, when this work was first suggested by the PROPRIETORS of Mr. STEEVENS's elaborate Edition, have been amply explained in the Prospectus which has accompanied every play; but with what success they have been carried into execution, it is impossible to conjecture. It is the first attempt that has been made to concentrate the information given in the copious notes of the various commentators within a moderate space, and with an attention rather to their conclusions than to their premises.

Mr. STEEVENS, in his Advertisement to the edition of 1793, after apologizing for the prolixity and number of his notes, seems to anticipate the time when " a judicious and frugal selection

# PREFACE.

" may be made from the labours of all" his coadjutors; but whether the present be either judicious or frugal, must be left to a decision over which the EDITOR can have no controul. He can only say that in the whole progress of his labours, he endeavoured to place himself in the situation of one who desires to understand his author at the smallest expence of time and thought, and who does not wish to have his attention diverted from a beauty, to be distracted by a contest. In thus assuming the character of a general reader, who is neither a scholar nor a critick, he found no difficulty; but it would have been arrogant, had it been possible, to measure the understandings of others by his own, and therefore from the opinions that he has given too much, or too little, he can have no appeal.

In selecting the notes, the names of the authors have seldom been retained, unless where they relate to contested points. Notes of criticism, however, have generally their author's names, and it is hoped that the preservation

# PREFACE.

of all Dr. JOHNSON's remarks of this kind will not be thought superfluous, since they are almost universally quoted as authorities. These and his celebrated Preface seem indispensable to every edition of SHAKSPEARE in which illustration is at all admitted. It is at his recommendation, likewise, that the EDITOR has prefixed Mr. POPE's Preface, " valuable alike for composition and " justness of remark, and containing a general " criticism on his author, so extensive that little " can be added, and so exact that little can be " disputed."

The HISTORY OF THE STAGE is merely an abridgement of Mr. MALONE's labours on that subject. Those who wish for farther information must wait the result of his present studies, and may wait with confidence. In the mean time, Mr. GEORGE CHALMERS' Apology and Supplement will valuably assist curious inquirers, and probably direct them to new means of research.

This Edition is accompanied by a LIFE of SHAKSPEARE, or rather an attempt, and the first of the kind, to collect the *disjecta membra* of his

## PREFACE.

biography scattered over the volumes of Johnson and Steevens. It may be useful as shewing the reader at one view all that is known of the personal history of our great bard, and it can pretend to no other merit.

ALEX<sup>R</sup>. CHALMERS.

Nov. 1804.

SKETCH

# SKETCH

## OF THE

# LIFE OF SHAKSPEARE.

WILLIAM SHAKSPEARE was born at Stratford-upon-Avon, in Warwickshire, on the
23d day of April, 1564. Of the rank of his family it is not easy to form an opinion. Mr. Rowe
says that by the register and certain publick writings relating to Stratford, it appears that his ancestors were " of good figure and fashion," in that
town, and are mentioned as " gentlemen," an
epithet which was more determinate then than at
present, when it has become an unlimited phrase
of courtesy. His father, JOHN SHAKSPEARE, was
a considerable dealer in wool, and had been an
officer and bailiff (probably high bailiff or mayor)
of the body corporate of Stratford. He held also
the office of justice of the peace, and at one
time, it is said, possessed lands and tenements to
the amount of £500, the reward of his grandfather's faithful and approved services to King

a

Henry VII. This, however, has been asserted upon very doubtful authority. Mr. Malone thinks " it is highly probable that he distinguished him- " self in Bosworth Field on the side of King " Henry, and that he was rewarded for his mili- " tary services by the bounty of that parsimo- " nious prince, though not with a grant of lands. " No such grant appears in the chapel of the " rolls from the beginning to the end of Henry's " reign." But whatever may have been his for- mer wealth, it appears to have been greatly reduced in the latter part of his life, as we find, from the books of the Corporation, that in 1579 he was excused the trifling weekly tax of four- pence levied on all the aldermen ; and that in 1586 another alderman was appointed in his room, in consequence of his declining to attend on the business of that office. It is even said by Aubrey,* a man sufficiently accurate in facts, although cre- dulous in superstitious narratives and traditions, that he followed for some time the occupation of a butcher, which Mr. Malone thinks not incon- sistent with probability. It must have been, how- ever, at this time, no inconsiderable addition to his difficulties that he had a family of ten children. His wife was the daughter and heiress of Robert

* MSS. Aubrey, Mus. Ashmol. Oxon, examined by Mr. Malone.

Arden of Wellingcote, in the county of Warwick, who is styled, "a gentleman of worship." The family of Arden is very ancient, Robert Arden of Bromich, Esq. being in the list of the gentry of this county returned by the commissioners in the twelfth year of King Henry VI. A. D. 1433. Edward Arden was Sheriff of the county in 1568. The woodland part of this county was anciently called *Ardern,* afterwards softened to *Arden;* and hence the name.

Our illustrious poet was the eldest son, and received his early education, however narrow or liberal, at a free-school, probably that founded at Stratford. From this he appears to have been soon removed, and placed, according to Mr. Malone's opinion, in the office of some country attorney, or the seneschal of some manor court, where it is highly probable he picked up those technical law phrases that so frequently occur in his plays, and could not have been in common use unless among professional men. Mr. Capell conjectures that his early marriage prevented his being sent to some university. It appears, however, as Dr. Farmer observes, that his early life was incompatible with a course of education, and it is certain that " his contemporaries, friends and foes, " nay and himself likewise, agree in his want of " what is usually termed literature." It is, indeed, a strong argument in favour of Shakspeare's illiterature, that it was maintained by all his contemporaries, many of whom have left upon record every merit they could bestow on him ; and by his successors, who lived nearest to his time, when " his memory was green ;" and that it has been denied only by Gildon, Sewell, and others down to Upton, who could have no means of ascertaining the truth.

In his eighteenth year, or perhaps a little sooner, he married ANNE HATHAWAY, who was eight years older than himself, the daughter of one HATHAWAY, who is said to have been a substantial yeoman in the neighbourhood of Stratford. Of his domestick economy, or professional occupation at this time, we have no information ; but it would appear that both were in a considerable degree neglected by his associating with a gang of deerstealers. Being detected with them in robbing the park of Sir Thomas Lucy of Charlecote, near Stratford, he was so rigorously prosecuted by that gentleman as to be obliged to leave his family and business, and take shelter in London. Sir Thomas, on this occasion, is said to have been exasperated by a ballad Shakspeare wrote, probably his first essay in poetry, of which the following stanza was communicated to Mr. Oldys :

" A parliemente member, a justice of peace,
" At home a poor scare-crowe, at London an asse,
" If lowsie is Lucy, as some volke miscalle it,
" Then Lucy is lowsie whatever befall it :
  " He thinks himself greate,
  " Yet an asse in his state
" We allowe by his ears but with asses to mate.
" If Lucy is lowsie, as some volke miscalle it,
" Sing lowsie Lucy, whatever befall it."

These lines, it must be confessed, do no great
honour to our poet ; and probably were unjust ; for
although some of his admirers have recorded Sir
Thomas as a " vain, weak, and vindictive magis-
" trate," he was certainly exerting no very violent
act of oppression, in protecting his property
against a man who was degrading the commonest
rank of life, and had at this time bespoke no indulgence by superior talents. The ballad, however, must have made some noise at Sir Thomas's
expence, as the author took care it should be affixed to his park-gates, and liberally circulated
among his neighbours.

On his arrival in London, which was probably
in 1586, when he was twenty-two years old, he
is said to have made his first acquaintance in the
play-house, to which idleness or taste may have
directed him, and where his necessities, if tradition may be credited, obliged him to accept the

office of call-boy, or prompter's attendant. This is a menial whose employment it is to give the performers notice to be ready to enter, as often as the business of the play requires their appearance on the stage. Pope, however, relates a story, communicated to him by Rowe, but which Rowe did not think deserving of a place in the life he wrote, that must a little retard the advancement of our poet to the office just mentioned. According to this story, Shakspeare's first employment was to wait at the door of the play-house, and hold the horses of those who had no servants, that they might be ready after the performance. But "I cannot," says his acute commentator, Mr. Steevens, " dismiss this anecdote without
" observing that it seems to want every mark of
" probability. Though Shakspeare quitted Strat-
" ford on account of a juvenile irregularity, we
" have no reason to suppose that he had forfeited
" the protection of his father who was engaged
" in a lucrative business, or the love of his wife
" who had already brought him two children, and
" was herself the daughter of a substantial yeo-
" man. It is unlikely, therefore, when he was
" beyond the reach of his prosecutor, that he
" should conceal his plan of life, or place of re-
" sidence, from those who, if he found himself
" distressed, could not fail to afford him such

" supplies as would have set him above the ne-
" cessity of *holding horses* for subsistence.    Mr.
" Malone has remarked in his " Attempt to ascer-
" tain the Order in which the Plays of Shakspeare
" were written, that he might have found an easy
" introduction to the stage : for Thomas Green,
" a celebrated comedian of that period, was his
" townsman, and perhaps his relation.    The ge-
" nius of our author prompted him to write
" poetry ; his connexion with a player might have
" given his productions a dramatic turn : or his
" own sagacity might have taught him that fame
" was not incompatible with profit, and that the'
" theatre was an avenue to both.    That it was
" once the general custom to ride on horseback
" to the play, I am likewise yet to learn.    The
" most popular of the theatres were on the Bank-
" side ; and we are told by the satirical pam-
" phleteers of that time, that the usual mode of
" conveyance to these places of amusement was
" by water, but not a single writer so much as
" hints at the custom of riding to them, or at
" the practice of having horses held during the
" hours of exhibition.    Some allusion to this
" usage, (if it had existed) must, I think, have
" been discovered in the course of our researches
" after contemporary fashions.    Let it be remem-
" bered too, that we receive this tale on no

" higher authority than that of Cibber's Lives of
" the Poets, Vol. I. p. 130.    Sir William Da-
" venant told it to Mr. Betterton, who commu-
" nicated it to Mr. Rowe, who, according to Dr.
" Johnson, related it to Mr. Pope."    Mr. Malone concurs in opinion that this story stands on
a very slender foundation, while he differs from
Mr. Steevens as to the fact of gentlemen going
to the theatre on horseback.    With respect likewise to Shakspeare's father being " engaged in a
" lucrative business," we may remark, that this
could not have been the case at the time our author came to London, if the preceding dates be
correct.    He is said to have arrived in London in
1586, the year in which his father resigned the
office of alderman, unless, indeed, we are permitted to conjecture that his resignation was not
the consequence of his necessities.

But in whatever situation he was first employed
at the theatre, he appears to have soon discovered
those talents which afterwards made him

" Th' applause! delight! the wonder of our stage!"

Some distinction he probably first acquired as
an actor, although Mr. Rowe has not been able
to discover any character in which he appeared to
more advantage than that of the ghost in Hamlet.
The instructions given to the player in that tra-

gedy, and other passages of his works, show an intimate acquaintance with the skill of acting, and such as is scarcely surpassed in our own days. He appears to have studied nature in acting as much as in writing. But all this might have been mere theory. Mr. Malone is of opinion he was no great actor. The distinction however, which he might obtain as an actor could only be in his own plays, in which he would be assisted by the novel appearance of author and actor combined. Before his time, it does not appear that any actor could avail himself of the wretched pieces represented on the stage.

Mr. Rowe regrets that he cannot inform us which was the first play he wrote. More skilful research has since found that Romeo and Juliet, and Richard II. and III. were printed in 1597, when he was thirty-three years old ; there is also some reason to think that he commenced a dramatic writer in 1592, and Mr. Malone even places his first play " First part of Henry VI." in 1589.* His plays, however, must have been not only popular, but approved by persons of the higher order, as we are certain that he enjoyed the gracious favour of Queen Elizabeth who was very fond of the stage : and the particular and affec-

* See the Lists of Mr. Malone and Mr. George Chalmers at the end of this Life.

tionate patronage of the Earl of Southampton, to whom he dedicated his poems of " Venus and Adonis," and his " Rape of Lucrece." On Sir William Davenant's authority, it has been asserted that this nobleman at one time gave him a thousand pounds to enable him to compleat a purchase. At the conclusion of the advertisement prefixed to Lintot's edition of Shakspeare's poems, it is said, " That most learned prince and great " patron of learning, King James the First, was " pleased with his own hand to write an amicable " letter to Mr. Shakspeare; which letter, though " now lost, remained long in the hands of Sir " William D'Avenant, as a credible person now " living can testify." Dr. Farmer with great probability supposes, that this letter was written by King James in return for the compliment paid to him in Macbeth. The relator of this anecdote was Sheffield, Duke of Buckingham.* These brief notices, meagre as they are, may show that our author enjoyed high favour in his day. Whatever we may think of King James as a " learned " prince," his patronage, as well as that of his predecessor, was sufficient to give celebrity to the founder of a new stage. It may be added that his uncommon merit, his candour, and good-

* Note by Mr. Malone to " Additional Anecdotes of William Shakspeare."

nature are supposed to have procured him the admiration and acquaintance of every person distinguished for such qualities. It is not difficult indeed, to suppose that Shakspeare was a man of humour and a social companion, and probably excelled in that species of minor wit not ill adapted to conversation, of which it could have been wished he had been more sparing in his writings.

How long he acted has not been discovered, but he continued to write till the year 1614. During his dramatic career he acquired a property in the theatre,* which he must have disposed of when he retired, as no mention of it occurs in his will. His connexion with Ben Jonson has been variously related. It is said that when Jonson was unknown to the world, he offered a play to the theatre, which was rejected after a very careless perusal, but that Shakspeare having accidentally cast his eye on it, conceived a favourable opinion of it, and afterwards recommended Jonson and his writings to the publick. For this candour he was repaid by Jonson, when the latter became a poet of note, with an envious disrespect. Jonson acquired reputation by the variety of his pieces, and endeavoured to arrogate the su-

* In 1603 he and several others obtained a licence from King James to exhibit comedies, tragedies, histories, &c. at the Globe Theatre and elsewhere.

12

premacy in dramatic genius. Like a French critick, he insinuated Shakspeare's incorrectness,
his careless manner of writing, and his want of
judgment, and, as he was a remarkable slow
writer himself, he could not endure the praise
frequently bestowed on Shakspeare of seldom al-
tering or blotting out what he had written. Mr.
Malone says, that " not long after the year
" 1600, a coolness arose between Shakspeare and
" him, which, however he may talk of his almost
" idolatrous affection, produced on his part, from
" that time to the death of our author, and for
" many years afterwards, much clumsy sarcasm
" and many malevolent reflections." But from
these, which are the commonly received opinions
on this subject, Dr. Farmer is inclined to depart,
and to think Jonson's hostility to Shakspeare absolutely groundless; so uncertain is every circumstance we attempt to recover of our great poet's life.
Jonson had only one advantage over Shakspeare,
that of superior learning, which might in certain
situations give him a superior rank, but could
never promote his rivalship with a man who at-
tained the highest excellence without it. Nor
will Shakspeare suffer by its being known that all
the dramatic poets before he appeared were
scholars. Greene, Lodge, Peele, Marlowe, Nashe,
Lily, and Kyd had all, says Mr. Malone, a regu-

lar university education, and, as scholars in our universities, frequently composed and acted plays on historical subjects.*

The latter part of Shakspeare's life was spent in ease, retirement, and the conversation of his friends. He had accumulated considerable property, which Gildon (in his "Letters and Essays" 1694) stated to amount to £300 *per annum*, a sum at least equal to £1000 in our days, but Mr. Malone doubts whether all his property amounted to much more than £200 *per ann.* which yet was a considerable fortune in those times, and it is supposed that he might have derived £200 *per ann.* from the theatre while he continued on the stage.

He retired some years before his death, to a house in Stratford, of which it has been thought important to give the history. It was built by Sir Hugh Clopton, a younger brother of an ancient family in that neighbourhood. Sir Hugh was Sheriff of London in the reign of Richard III. and Lord Mayor in the reign of Henry VII. By his will he bequeathed to his elder brother's son his manor of Clopton, &c. and his house by the

---

* This was the practice in Milton's days. " One of his objections to academical education, as it was then conducted, is, that men designed for orders in the church were permitted to act plays, &c." Johnson's Life of Milton.

name of the *Great House* in Stratford. A good part of the estate was in possession of Edward Clopton, Esq. and Sir Hugh Clopton, Knt. in 1733. The principal estate had been sold out of the Clopton family for above a century, at the time when Shakspeare became the purchaser; who having repaired and modelled it to his own mind, changed the name to *New Place*, which the mansion-house afterwards erected, in the room of the poet's house, retained for many years. The house and lands belonging to it continued in the possession of Shakspeare's descendants to the time of the restoration, when they were re-purchased by the Clopton family. Here in May 1742, when Mr. Garrick, Mr. Macklin, and Mr. Delane, visited Stratford, they were hospitably entertained under Shakspeare's mulberry-tree by Sir Hugh Clopton. He was a barrister at law, was knighted by King George I. and died in the 80th year of his age, in Dec. 1751. His executor, about the year 1752, sold *New Place* to the Rev. Mr. Gastrell, a man of large fortune, who resided in it but a few years in consequence of a disagreement with the inhabitants of Stratford. As he resided part of the year at Lichfield, he thought he was assessed too highly in the monthly rate towards the maintenance of the poor; but being very properly compelled by the magistrates of Stratford to pay the whole of what was levied on him, on the principle that his house was occupied by his servants in his absence, he peevishly declared, that *that* house should never be assessed again ; and soon afterwards pulled it down, sold the materials, and left the town. He had some time before cut down Shakspeare's mulberry tree,* to save himself the trouble of shewing it to those whose admiration of our great poet led them to visit the classic ground on which it stood. That Shakspeare planted this tree appears to be sufficiently authenticated. Where New Place stood is now a garden.—— Before concluding this history, it may be necessary to mention that the poet's house was once honoured by the temporary residence of Henrietta Maria, queen to Charles I. Theobald has given an inaccurate account of this, as if she had been obliged to take refuge in Stratford from the rebels ;

---

* " As the curiosity of this house and tree brought much fame, and more company and profit to the town, a certain man, on some disgust, has pulled the house down, so as not to leave one stone upon another, and cut down the tree, and piled it as a stack of firewood, to the great vexation, loss, and disappointment, of the inhabitants ; however, an honest silversmith bought the whole stack of wood, and makes many odd things of this wood for the curious." Letter in Annual Register. 1760. Of Mr. Gastrell and his Lady, see Boswell's Life of Dr. Johnson, Vol. II. p. 356. Edit. 1793.

but that was not the case.  She marched from
Newark, June 10, 1648, and entered Stratford
triumphantly about the 22d of the same month,
at the head of 3000 feet and 1500 horse, with
150 waggons and a train of artillery.  Here she
was met by Prince Rupert, accompanied by a large
body of troops.  She resided about three weeks at
our poet's house, which was then possessed by his
grand daughter Mrs. Nash, and her husband.

During Shakspeare's abode in this house, his
pleasurable wit, and good-nature, says Mr. Rowe,
engaged him the acquaintance, and entitled him
to the friendship of the gentlemen of the neighbourhood.  Among these Mr. Rowe tells a traditional story of a miser, or usurer, named Combe,
who, in conversation with Shakspeare, said he
fancied the poet intended to write his epitaph if
he should survive him, and desired to know what
he meant to say.  On this Shakspeare gave him
the following, probably extempore :

" Ten in the hundred lies here ingrav'd,
'Tis a hundred to ten his soul is not sav'd,
If any man ask, who lies in this tombe ?
Oh! ho! quoth the devil, 'tis my John-a-Combe."

The sharpness of the satire is said to have stung
the man so severely that he never forgave it.
These lines, however, or some which nearly re-

semble them, appeared in various collections both before and after the time they were said to have been composed; and the inquiries of Mr. Steevens and Mr. Malone satisfactorily prove that the whole story is a fabrication. Betterton is said to have heard it when he visited Warwickshire on purpose to collect anecdotes of our poet, and probably thought it of too much importance to be nicely examined.——We know not whether it be worth adding of a story which we have rejected, that a *usurer* in Shakspeare's time did not mean one who took exorbitant, but any interest or usance for money, and that ten in the hundred, or ten *per cent.* was then the ordinary interest of money.——It is of more consequence, however, to record the opinion of Mr. Malone, that Shakspeare, during his retirement, wrote the play of Twelfth Night.

He died on his birth-day, Tuesday, April 23, 1616, when he had exactly completed his fifty-second year,\* and was buried on the north side of the chancel, in the great church at Stratford, where a monument is placed in the wall, on which he is represented under an arch, in a sitting posture, a cushion spread before him, with a pen in

* The only notice we have of his person is from Aubrey, who says, " He was a handsome well-shaped man," and adds, " verie good company, and of a very ready, and pleasant and smooth wit."

his right hand, and his left rested on a scroll of
paper. The following Latin distich is engraved
under the cushion :

*Judicio Pylium, genio Socratem, arte Maronem,*
*Terra tegit, populus mæret, Olympus habet.*

" The first syllable in Socratem, says Mr.
" Steevens, is here made short, which cannot be
" allowed. Perhaps we should read Sophoclem.
" Shakspeare is then appositely compared with a
" dramatick author among the ancients : but still
" it should be remembered that the eulogium is
" lessened while the metre is reformed ; and it is
" well known that some of our early writers of
" Latin poetry were uncommonly negligent in
" their prosody, especially in proper names. The
" thought of this distich, as Mr. Tollet observes,
" might have been taken from The Faëry Queene
" of Spenser, B. II. c. ix. st. 48, and c. x. st. 3.
"   " To this Latin inscription on Shakspeare may
" be added the lines which are found underneath
" it on his monument :

" Stay, passenger, why dost thou go so fast ?
" Read, if thou canst, whom envious death hath plac'd
" Within this monument ; Shakspeare, with whom
" Quick nature dy'd ; whose name doth deck the tomb
" Far more than cost ; since all that he hath writ
" Leaves living art but page to serve his wit."
                " Obiit An°. Dni. 1616.
                æt. 53, die 23 April.

" It appears from the verses of Leonard Digges,
" that our author's monument was erected before
" the year 1623. It has been engraved by Vertue,
" and done in mezzotinto by Miller."

On his grave-stone underneath are these lines,
in an uncouth mixture of small and capital letters:

" Good Friend for Iesus SAKE forbeare
" To dica T-E Dust EncloAsed HERe
" Blese be T-E Man ᵼ spares T-Es Stones
" And curst be He ᵼ moves my Bones."

It is uncertain whether this request and impreca-
tion were written by Shakspeare, or by one of his
friends. They probably allude to the custom of
removing skeletons after a certain time, and de-
positing them in charnel-houses; and similar
execrations are found in many ancient Latin
epitaphs.

We have no account of the malady which at no
very advanced age closed the life and labours of
this unrivalled and incomparable genius.

His family consisted of two daughters, and a
son named Hamnet, who died in 1596, in the
twelfth year of his age. Susannah, the eldest
daughter, and her father's favourite, was married
to Dr. John Hall, a physician, who died Nov.
1635, aged 60. Mrs. Hall died July 11, 1649,
aged 66. They left only one child, Elizabeth,

b 2

born 1607-8, and married April 22, 1626, to Thomas Nashe, Esq. who died in 1647, and afterwards to Sir John Barnard, of Abington, in Northamptonshire, but died without issue by either husband.    Judith, Shakspeare's youngest daughter, was married to a Mr. Thomas Quiney, and died Feb. 1661-62, in her 77th year.    By Mr. Quiney she had three sons, Shakspeare, Richard, and Thomas, who all died unmarried. Sir Hugh Clopton, who was born two years after the death of Lady Barnard, which happened in 1669-70, related to Mr. Macklin, in 1742, an old tradition, that she had carried away with her from Stratford many of her grandfather's papers. On the death of Sir John Barnard, Mr. Malone thinks these must have fallen into the hands of Mr. Edward Bagley, Lady Barnard's executor, and if any descendant of that gentleman be now living, in his custody they probably remain.    To this account of Shakspeare's family we have now to add, that among Oldys's papers is another traditional gossip's story of his having been the father of Sir Wm. Davenant.  Oldys's relation is thus given.

    " If tradition may be trusted, Shakspeare often " baited at the Crown Inn or Tavern in Oxford, " in his journey to and from London.  The land– " lady was a woman of great beauty and sprightly

" wit, and her husband, Mr. John Davenant,
" (afterwards mayor of that city,) a grave melan-
" choly man ; who, as well as his wife, used much
" to delight in Shakspeare's pleasant company.
" Their son, young Will. Davenant, (afterwards
" Sir William) was then a little school-boy in the
" town, of about seven or eight years old, and
" so fond also of Shakspeare, that whenever he
" heard of his arrival, he would fly from school
" to see him. One day an old townsman ob-
" serving the boy running homeward almost out
" of breath, asked him whither he was posting
" in that heat and hurry. He answered, to see
" his *god*-father Shakspeare. There's a good
" boy, said the other, but have a care that you
" don't take *God's* name in vain. This story Mr.
" Pope told me at the Earl of Oxford's table,
" upon occasion of some discourse which arose
" about Shakspeare's monument then newly
" erected in Westminster Abbey."

This story appears to have originated with
Anthony Wood, and it has been thought a presumption of its being true that, after careful
examination, Mr. Thomas Warton was inclined
to believe it. Mr. Steevens, however, treats it
with the utmost contempt, but does not perhaps
argue with his usual attention to experience when
he brings Sir William Davenant's " heavy, vulgar,

unmeaning face," as a proof that he could not be Shakspeare's son.

In the year 1741, a monument was erected to our poet in Westminster-Abbey, by the direction of the Earl of Burlington, Dr. Mead, Mr. Pope, and Mr. Martyn. It was the work of Scheemaker, (who received £300 for it,) after a design of Kent, and was opened in January of that year. The performers of each of the London theatres gave a benefit to defray the expences, and the Dean and Chapter of Westminster took nothing for the ground. The money received by the performance at Drury-Lane theatre amounted to above £200, but the receipts at Covent-Garden did not exceed £100.

From these imperfect notices, which are all we have been able to collect from the labours of his biographers and commentators, our readers will perceive that less is known of Shakspeare than of almost any writer who has been considered as an object of laudable curiosity. Nothing could be more highly gratifying than an account of the early studies of this wonderful man, the progress of his pen, his moral and social qualities, his friendships, his failings, and whatever else constitutes personal history. But on all these topicks his contemporaries and his immediate successors have been equally silent, and if ought can be hereafter discovered, it must be by exploring sources which have hitherto escaped the anxious researches of those who have devoted their whole lives, and their most vigorous talents, to revive his memory and illustrate his writings. In the sketch we have given, if the dates of his birth and death be excepted, what is there on which the reader can depend, or for which, if he contend eagerly, he may not be involved in controversy, and perplexed with contradictory opinions and authorities?

It is usually said that the life of an author can be little else than a history of his works ; but this opinion is liable to many exceptions. If an author, indeed, has passed his days in retirement, his life can afford little more variety than that of any other man who has lived in retirement ; but if, as is generally the case with writers of great celebrity, he has acquired a pre-eminence over his contemporaries, if he has excited rival contentions, and defeated the attacks of criticism or of malignity, or if he has plunged into the controversies of his age, and performed the part either of a tyrant or a hero in literature, his history may be rendered as interesting as that of any other publick character. But whatever weight may be allowed to this remark, the decision will not be of much consequence in the case of Shakspeare.    Unfortunately we know as little of his writings as of his personal history.    The industry of his illustrators for the last thirty years has been such as probably never was surpassed in the annals of literary investigation, yet so far are we from information of the conclusive or satisfactory kind, that even the order in which his plays were written rests principally on conjecture, and of some plays usually printed among his works, it is not yet determined whether he wrote the whole, or any part.

Much of our ignorance of every thing which it would be desirable to know respecting Shakspeare's works, must be imputed to the author himself.    If we look merely at the state in which he left his productions, we should be apt to conclude, either that he was insensible of their value, or that while he was the greatest, he was at the same time the humblest writer the world ever produced ; " that he thought his works unworthy of " posterity, that he levied no ideal tribute upon " future times, nor had any further prospect, " than that of present popularity and present " profit."*    And such an opinion, although it apparently partakes of the ease and looseness of conjecture, may not be far from probability.    But

* Dr. Johnson's Preface.

before we allow it any higher merit, or attempt to decide upon the affection or neglect with which he reviewed his labours, it may be necessary to consider their precise nature, and certain circumstances in his situation which affected them ; and, above all, we must take into our account the character and predominant occupations of the times in which he lived, and of those which followed his decease.

With respect to himself, · it does not appear that he printed any one of his plays, and only eleven of them were printed in his life-time. The reason assigned for this is, that he wrote them for a particular theatre, sold them to the managers when only an actor, reserved them in manuscript when himself a manager, and when he disposed of his property in the theatre, they were still preserved in manuscript to prevent their being acted by the rival houses. Copies of some of them appear to have been surreptitiously obtained, and published in a very incorrect state, but we may suppose that it was wiser in the author or managers to overlook this fraud, than to publish a correct edition, and so destroy the exclusive property they enjoyed. It is clear therefore that any publication of his plays by himself would have interfered, at first with his own interest, and afterwards with the interest of those to whom he had made over his share in them. But even had this obstacle been removed, we are not sure that he would have gained much by publication. If he had no other copies but those belonging to the theatre, the business of correction for the press must have been a toil which we are afraid the taste of the publick at that time would have poorly rewarded. We know not the exact portion of fame he enjoyed: it was probably the highest which dramatic genius could confer, but dramatic genius was a new excellence, and not well understood. His claims were probably not heard out of the jurisdiction of the master of the revels, certainly not beyond the metropolis. Yet such was Shakspeare's reputation that we are told his name was put to pieces which he never wrote, and that he felt himself too confident in popular favour to undeceive the publick. This was singular resolution in a man who wrote so unequally, that at this day, the test of internal evidence must be applied to his doubtful productions with the greatest caution. But still how far his character would have been elevated by an examination of his plays in the closet, in an age when the refinements of criticism were not understood, and the sympathies of taste were seldom felt, may admit of a question. "His language," says Dr. Johnson, "*not being designed for the*

" *reader's desk,* was all that he desired it to be
" if it conveyed his meaning to the audience."

Shakspeare died in 1616, and seven years afterwards appeared the first edition of his plays, published at the charges of four booksellers; a circumstance from which Mr. Malone infers " that
" no single publisher was at that time willing to
" risk his money on a complete collection of our
" author's plays." This edition was printed from
the copies in the hands of his fellow-managers
Heminge and Condell, which had been in a series
of years frequently altered through convenience,
caprice, or ignorance. Heminge and Condell
had now retired from the stage, and, we may
suppose, were guilty of no injury to their successors, in printing what their own interest only
had formerly withheld. Of this, although we
have no documents amounting to demonstration, we may be convinced, by adverting to a
circumstance, which will, in our days, appear very
extraordinary, namely, the declension of Shakspeare's popularity. We have seen that the publication of his works was accounted a doubtful
speculation; and it is yet more certain, that so
much had the publick taste turned from him in
quest of variety, that for several years after his
death the plays of Fletcher were more frequently
acted than his, and during the whole of the

seventeenth century, they were made to give place to performances, the greater part of which cannot now be endured.    During the same period only four editions of his works were published, all in folio; and perhaps this unwieldy size of volume may be an additional proof that they were not popular; nor is it thought that the impressions were numerous.

These circumstances which attach to our author and to his works must be allowed a plausible weight in accounting for our deficiencies in his biography and literary career, but there were circumstances enough in the history of the times to suspend the progress of that more regular drama of which he had set the example, and may be considered as the founder.    If we wonder why we know so much less of Shakspeare than of his contemporaries, let us recollect that his genius, however highly and justly we now rate it, took a direction which was not calculated for permanent admiration either in the age in which he lived, or in that which followed.    Shakspeare was a writer of plays, a promoter of an amusement just emerging from barbarism; and an amusement which, although it has been classed among the schools of morality, has ever had such a strong tendency to deviate from moral purposes, that the force of law has in all ages been called in to preserve it within

the bounds of common decency. The church
has ever been unfriendly to the stage. A part of
the injunctions of Queen Elizabeth is particularly
directed against the printing of plays; and, according to an entry in the books of the Stationers
Company, in the 41st year of her reign, it is ordered, that no plays be printed except allowed by
persons in authority. Dr. Farmer also remarks,
that in that age poetry and novels were destroyed
publickly by the bishops, and privately by the
puritans. The main transactions, indeed, of that
period could not admit of much attention to
matters of amusement. The Reformation required
all the circumspection and policy of a long reign
to render it so firmly established in popular favour
as to brave the caprice of any succeeding sovereign. This was effected in a great measure by
the diffusion of religious controversy, which was
encouraged by the church, and especially by the
puritans who were the immediate teachers of the
lower classes, were listened to with veneration,
and usually inveighed against all publick amusements, as inconsistent with the Christian profession.
These controversies continued during the reign of
James I. and were in a considerable degree pro-
moted by him, although he, like Elizabeth, was
a favourer of the stage, as an appendage to the
grandeur and pleasures of the court. But the

commotions which followed in the unhappy reign
of Charles I. when the stage was totally abolished,
are sufficient to account for the oblivion thrown
on the history and works of our great bard.
From this time no inquiry was made, until it was
too late to obtain any information more satisfactory
than the few hearsay scraps and contested traditions above detailed. " How little," says Mr.
Steevens, " Shakspeare was once read, may be
" understood from Tate, who, in his dedication
" to the altered play of King Lear, speaks of the
" original as an obscure piece, recommended to
" his notice by a friend; and the author of the
" Tatler having occasion to quote a few lines out
" of Macbeth, was content to receive them from
" D'Avenant's alteration of that celebrated drama,
" in which almost every original beauty is either
" aukwardly disguised, or arbitrarily omitted." *

In fifty years after his death, Dryden mentions
that he was then become " a little obsolete." In
the beginning of the last century, Lord Shaftes-
bury complains of his " rude unpolished style,
and his antiquated phrase and wit." It is certain
that for nearly a hundred years after his death,
partly owing to the immediate revolution and
rebellion, and partly to the licentious taste en-

* Mr. Steevens's Advertisement to the Reader, first printed
in 1773.

couraged in Charles II's time, and perhaps partly
to the incorrect state of his works, he was almost
entirely neglected.　Mr. Malone has justly remarked, " that if he had been read, admired,
" studied, and imitated, in the same degree, as he
" is now, the enthusiasm of some one or other
" of his admirers in the last age would have in-
" duced him to make some inquiries concerning
" the history of his theatrical career, and the
" anecdotes of his private life." *

His admirers, however, if he had admirers in
that age, possessed no portion of such enthusiasm.
That curiosity, which in our days has raised biography to the rank of an independent study, was
scarcely known, and where known, confined
principally to the publick transactions of eminent
characters.　And if, in addition to the circumstances already stated, we consider how little is
known of the personal history of Shakspeare's
contemporaries, we may easily resolve the question,
why, of all men who have ever claimed admiration
by genius, wisdom, or valour, who have eminently contributed to enlarge the taste, promote
the happiness, or increase the reputation of their
country, we know the least of Shakspeare : and
why, of the few particulars which seem entitled

* Mr. Malone's Preface to his Edition, 1790.

to credit, when simply related, and in which there is no manifest violation of probability, or promise of importance, there is scarcely one which has not swelled into a controversy. After a careful examination of all that modern research has discovered, we know not how to trust our curiosity beyond the limits of those barren dates which afford no personal history. The nature of Shakspeare's writings prevents that appeal to internal evidence, which in other cases has been found to throw light on character. The purity of his morals, for example, if sought in his plays, must be measured against the licentiousness of his language, and the question will then be, how much did he write from conviction, and how much to gratify the taste of his hearers? How much did he add to the age, and how much did he borrow from it? Pope says, " he was obliged to please the lowest of the people, and to keep the worst of company ;" and Pope might have said more : for although we hope it was not true, we have no means of proving that it was false.

The only life which has been prefixed to all the editions of Shakspeare of the 18th century, is that drawn up by Mr. Rowe, and which he modestly calls " Some Account, &c." In this we have what Rowe could collect when every legitimate source of information was closed, a few traditions that were floating nearly a century after the author's death. Some inaccuracies in his account have been detected in the valuable notes of Mr. Steevens and Mr. Malone, who, in other parts of their respective editions have scattered a few brief notices which we have incorporated in the present sketch. The whole, however, is unsatisfactory. Shakspeare in his private character, in his friendships, in his amusements, in his closet, in his family, is no where before us: and such was the nature of the writings on which his fame depends, and of that employment in which he was engaged, that being in no important respect connected with the history of his age, it is in vain to look into the latter for any information concerning him.

Mr. Capell is of opinion that he wrote some prose works, because " it can hardly be supposed " that he, who had so considerable a share in " the confidence of the Earls of Essex and " Southampton, could be a mute spectator only " of controversies in which they were so much " interested." This editor, however, appears to have taken for granted a degree of confidence with these two statesmen which he ought first to have proved. Shakspeare might have enjoyed the confidence of their social hours, but it is mere conjecture that they admitted him into the confidence of their state affairs. Mr. Malone, whose opinions are entitled to a higher degree of credit, thinks that his prose compositions, if they should be discovered, would exhibit the same perspicuity, the same cadence, the same elegance and vigour, which we find in his plays. It is unfortunate, however, for all wishes and all conjectures, that not a line of Shakspeare's manuscript is known to exist, and his prose writings are no where hinted at. We have only printed copies of his plays and poems, and those so depraved by carelessness or ignorance that all the labour of all his commentators has not yet been able to restore them to a probable purity. Many of the greatest difficulties attending the perusal of them, yet remain, and will require, what it is scarcely possible to expect, greater sagacity and more happy conjecture than have hitherto been employed.

Of his POEMS, it is perhaps necessary that some notice should be taken, although they have never been favourites with the publick, and have seldom been reprinted with his plays. Shortly after his death, Mr. Malone informs us, a very incorrect impression of them was issued out, which in every subsequent edition was implicitly followed, until he published a correct edition in 1780 with illustrations, &c. But the peremptory decision of Mr. Steevens on the merits of these poems must be our apology for omitting them in the present abridgement of that critic's labours. " We have not reprinted the Sonnets, &c. of " Shakspeare, because the strongest act of par- " liament that could be framed would fail to " compel readers into their service. Had Shak- " speare produced no other works than these, his " name would have reached us with as little cele- " brity as time has conferred on that of Thomas " Watson, an older and much more elegant son- " netteer."

The elegant preface of Dr. Johnson gives an account of the attempts made in the early part of the last century to revive the memory and re- putation of our poet, by Rowe, Pope, Theobald, Hanmer, and Warburton, whose respective me- rits he has characterised with candour, and with singular felicity of expression. Shakspeare's works may be overloaded with criticism, for what writer has excited so much curiosity, and so many opi- nions ? but Johnson's preface is an accompani- ment worthy of the genius it celebrates.——His own edition followed in 1765, and a second, in con- junction with Mr. Steevens, 1773. The third edition of the joint editors appeared in 1785, the fourth in 1793, and the last and most complete, in 1803, in 21 volumes octavo. Mr.

Malone's edition was published in 1790 in 10 volumes crown octavo, and is now become exceedingly scarce. His original notes and improvements, however, are incorporated in the editions of 1793 and 1803 by Mr. Steevens. Mr. Malone says, that from the year 1716 to the date of his edition in 1790, that is, in seventy-four years, " above 30,000 copies of Shakspeare have been " dispersed through England." To this we may add with confidence, that since 1790 that number has been doubled. During last year no fewer than nine editions were in the press, belonging to the proprietors of this work; and if we add the editions printed by others, and those published in Scotland, Ireland, and America, we may surely fix the present as the highest æra of Shakspeare's popularity. Nor among the honours paid to his genius, ought we to forget the very magnificent edition undertaken by Messrs. Boydell. Still less ought it to be forgotten how much the reputation of Shakspeare was revived by the unrivalled excellence of Garrick's performance. His share in directing the publick taste towards the study of Shakspeare was perhaps greater than that of any individual in his time, and such was his zeal and such his success in this laudable attempt that he may readily be forgiven the foolish mummery of the Stratford Jubilee.

When publick opinion had begun to assign to Shakspeare the very high rank he was destined to hold, he became the promising object of fraud and imposture. This we have already observed, he did not wholly escape in his own time, and he had the spirit or policy to despise it.\* It was reserved for modern impostors, however, to avail themselves of the obscurity in which his history is involved. In 1751 a book was published, entitled " A Compendious or briefe examina-
" tion of certayne ordinary Complaints of diuers
" of our Countrymen in those our days: which
" although they are in some Parte unjust and
" frivolous, yet are they all by way of dialogue
" throughly debated and discussed by William
" Shakspeare, Gentleman." This had been originally published in 1581, but Dr. Farmer has clearly proved that *W. S. gent.* the only authority for attributing it to Shakspeare in the reprinted edition, meant *William Stafford, gent.*— Theobald, the same accurate critic informs us, was desirous of palming upon the world a play called " Double Falsehood," for a posthumous one of Shakspeare. In 1770 was reprinted at

---

\* Mr. Malone has given a list of 14 plays ascribed to Shakspeare, either by the editors of the two later folios, or by the compilers of ancient catalogues. Of these Pericles has found advocates for its admission into his works.

Feversham, an old play called " The Tragedy of Arden of Feversham and Black Will," with a preface attributing it to Shakspeare, without the smallest foundation.    But these were trifles compared to the atrocious attempt made in 1795-6, when, besides a vast mass of prose and verse, letters, &c. pretendedly in the hand-writing of Shakspeare and his correspondents, an entire play, entitled Vortigern, was not only brought forward for the astonishment of the admirers of Shakspeare, but actually performed on Drury-lane stage.    It would be unnecessary to expatiate on the merits of this play, which Mr. Steevens has very happily characterised as " the perform-" ance of a madman without a lucid interval," or to enter more at large into the nature of a fraud so recent, and so soon acknowledged by the authors of it.    It produced, however, an interesting controversy between Mr. Malone and Mr. George Chalmers, which, although mixed with some unpleasant asperities, was extended to inquiries into the history and antiquities of the stage from which future critics and historians may derive considerable information.

# SHAKSPEARE'S WILL,

FROM THE ORIGINAL

In the Office of the Prerogative Court of Canterbury.

---

*Vicesimo quinto die Martii,*[1] *Anno Regni Domini nostri Jacobi nunc Regis Angliæ, &c. decimo quarto, et Scotiæ quadragesimo nono. Anno Domini* 1616.

IN the name of God, Amen. I William Shakspeare of Stratford-upon-Avon, in the county of Warwick, gent. in perfect health and memory (God be praised!) do make and ordain this my last will and testament in manner and form following; that is to say:

*First,* I commend my soul into the hands of God my creator, hoping, and assuredly believing, through the only merits of Jesus Christ my Saviour, to be made partaker of life everlasting; and my body to the earth whereof it is made.

*Item,* I give and bequeath unto my daughter Judith, one hundred and fifty pounds of lawful English money, to be paid unto her in manner and form following; that is to say, one hundred pounds

---

[1] Our poet's will appears to have been drawn up in February, though not executed till the following month; for *February* was first written, and afterwards struck out, and *March* written over it. MALONE.

in discharge of her marriage portion within one year after my decease, with consideration after the rate of two shillings in the pound for so long time as the same shall be unpaid unto her after my decease; and the fifty pounds residue thereof, upon her surrendering of, or giving of such sufficient security as the overseers of this my will shall like of, to surrender or grant, all her estate and right that shall descend or come unto her after my decease, or that she now hath, of, in, or to, one copyhold tenement, with the appurtenances, lying and being in Stratford-upon-Avon aforesaid, in the said county of Warwick, being parcel or holden of the manor of Rowington, unto my daughter Susanna Hall, and her heirs for ever.

*Item,* I give and bequeath unto my said daughter Judith one hundred and fifty pounds more, if she, or any issue of her body, be living at the end of three years next ensuing the day of the date of this my will, during which time my executors to pay her consideration from my decease according to the rate aforesaid: and if she die within the said term without issue of her body, then my will is, and I do give and bequeath one hundred pounds thereof to my niece[a] Elizabeth Hall, and the fifty pounds to be set forth by my executors during the life of my sister Joan Hart, and the use and profit thereof coming, shall be paid to my said sister Joan, and after her decease the said fifty pounds shall remain amongst the children of my said sister, equally to be divided amongst them; but if my said daughter Judith be living at the end of the said three years, or any issue of her body, then my will is, and so I

---

[a] —— *to my niece* —] Elizabeth Hall was our poet's granddaughter. So, in *Othello*, Act I. sc. i. Iago says to Brabantio: " You'll have your *nephews* neigh to you;" meaning his grandchildren. MALONE.

devise and bequeath the said hundred and fifty pounds to be set out by my executors and overseers for the best benefit of her and her issue, and the stock not to be paid unto her so long as she shall be married and covert baron; but my will is, that she shall have the consideration yearly paid unto her during her life, and after her decease the said stock and consideration to be paid to her children, if she have any, and if not, to her executors or assigns, she living the said term after my decease: provided that if such husband as she shall at the end of the said three years be married unto, or at any [time] after, do sufficiently assure unto her, and the issue of her body, lands answerable to the portion by this my will given unto her, and to be adjudged so by my executors and overseers, then my will is, that the said hundred and fifty pounds shall be paid to such husband as shall make such assurance, to his own use.

*Item*, I give and bequeath unto my said sister Joan twenty pounds, and all my wearing apparel, to be paid and delivered within one year after my decease: and I do will and devise unto her the house, with the appurtenances, in Stratford, wherein she dwelleth, for her natural life, under the yearly rent of twelve-pence.

*Item*, I give and bequeath unto her three sons, William Hart, —— Hart,[3] and Michael Hart, five pounds apiece, to be paid within one year after my decease.

*Item*, I give and bequeath unto the said Elizabeth Hall all my plate, (except my broad silver and

---

[3] —— *Hart*,] It is singular that neither Shakspeare nor any of his family should have recollected the christian name of his nephew, who was born at Stratford but eleven years before the making of his will. His christian name was *Thomas*; and he was baptized in that town, July 24, 1605. MALONE.

gilt bowl,[4]) that I now have at the date of this my will.

*Item,* I give and bequeath unto the poor of Stratford aforesaid ten pounds; to Mr. Thomas Combe[5] my sword; to Thomas Russel, esq. five pounds; and to Francis Collins[6] of the borough of Warwick, in the county of Warwick, gent. thirteen pounds six shillings and eight-pence, to be paid within one year after my decease.

*Item,* I give and bequeath to Hamlet [*Hamnet*] Sadler[7] twenty-six shillings eight pence, to buy him a ring; to William Reynolds, gent. twenty-six shillings eight-pence, to buy him a ring; to my

---

[4] —— *except my broad silver and gilt* bowl.] This bowl, as we afterwards find, our poet bequeathed to his daughter Judith.

[5] —— *Mr. Thomas Combe,*] This gentleman was baptised at Stratford, Feb. 9, 1588-9, so that he was twenty-seven years old at the time of Shakspeare's death. He died at Stratford in July 1657, aged 68; and his elder brother William died at the same place, Jan. 30, 1666-7, aged 80. Mr. Thomas Combe by his will made June 20, 1656, directed his executors to convert all his personal property into money, and to lay it out in the purchase of lands, to be settled on William Combe, the eldest son of John Combe of Allchurch in the county of Worcester, Gent. and his heirs male; remainder to his two brothers successively. Where, therefore, our poet's sword has wandered, I have not been able to discover. I have taken the trouble to ascertain the ages of Shakspeare's friends and relations, and the time of their deaths, because we are thus enabled to judge how far the traditions concerning him which were communicated to Mr. Rowe in the beginning of this century, are worthy of credit. MALONE.

[6] —— *to Francis Collins* —] This gentleman, who was the son of Mr. Walter Collins, was baptized at Stratford, Dec. 24, 1582. I know not when he died. MALONE.

[7] —— *to Hamnet Sadler,*] This gentleman was godfather to Shakspeare's only son, who was called after him. Mr. Sadler, I believe, was born about the year 1550, and died at Stratford-upon-Avon, in October 1624. His wife, Judith Sadler, who was godmother to Shakspeare's youngest daughter, was buried there, March 23, 1613-14. Our poet probably was godfather to their son *William,* who was baptized at Stratford, Feb. 5, 1597-8. MALONE.

12

godson William Walker,[8] twenty shillings in gold; to Anthony Nash,[9] gent. twenty-six shillings eight-pence; and to Mr. John Nash,[1] twenty-six shillings eight-pence; and to my fellows, John Hemynge, Richard Burbage, and Henry Cundell,[2] twenty-six shillings eight-pence apiece, to buy them rings.

*Item*, I give, will, bequeath, and devise, unto my daughter Susanna Hall, for better enabling of her to perform this my will, and towards the performance thereof, all that capital messuage or tenement, with the appurtenances, in Stratford aforesaid, called The New Place, wherein I now dwell, and two messuages or tenements, with the appurtenances, situate, lying, and being in Henley-street, within the borough of Stratford aforesaid; and all my barns, stables, orchards, gardens, lands, tenements, and hereditaments whatsoever, situate, lying, and being, or to be had, received, perceived, or taken, within the towns, hamlets, villages, fields, and grounds of Stratford-upon-Avon, Old Stratford, Bishopton, and Welcombe,[3] or in any of them, in the said county

---

[8] *—— to my godson, William Walker,*] William, the son of Henry Walker, was baptized at Stratford, Oct. 16, 1608. I mention this circumstance, because it ascertains that our author was at his native town in the autumn of that year. Mr. William Walker was buried at Stratford, March 1, 1679-80. MALONE.

[9] *—— to Anthony Nash,*] He was father of Mr. Thomas Nash, who married our poet's grand-daughter, Elizabeth Hall. He lived, I believe, at Welcombe, where his estate lay; and was buried at Stratford, Nov. 18, 1622. MALONE.

[1] *=== to Mr. John Nash,*] This gentleman died at Stratford, and was buried there, Nov. 10, 1623. MALONE.

[2] *=== to my fellows, John Hemynge, Richard Burbage, and Henry Cundell,*] These our poet's *fellows* did not very long survive him. Burbage died in March, 1619; Cundell in December, 1627; and Heminge in October 1630. MALONE.

[3] *=== Old Stratford, Bishopton, and Welcombe,*] The lands of Old Stratford, Bishopton, and Welcombe, here devised, were in Shakspeare's time a continuation of one large field, all in the parish of Stratford. Bishopton is two miles from Stratford, and

ment, with the appurtenances, wherein one John
Robinson dwelleth, situate, lying, and being, in
the Blackfriars in London near the Wardrobe :[4] and
all other my lands, tenements, and hereditaments
whatsoever : to have and to hold all and singular the
said premises, with their appurtenances, unto the
said Susanna Hall, for and during the term of her
natural life ; and after her decease to the first son of
her body lawfully issuing, and to the heirs males of
the body of the said first son lawfully issuing ; and
for default of such issue, to the second son of her
body lawfully issuing, and to the heirs males of the
body of the said second son lawfully issuing ; and for
default of such heirs, to the third son of the body
of the said Susanna lawfully issuing, and to the heirs
males of the body of the said third son lawfully issuing ; and for default of such issue, the same so to

Welcombe one. For *Bishopton*, Mr. Theobald erroneously printed
*Bushaxton*, and the error has been continued in all the subsequent
editions. The word in Shakspeare's original will is spelt *Bushop-
ton*, the vulgar pronunciation of Bishopton.

I searched the Indexes in the Rolls chapel from the year 1589
to 1616, with the hope of finding an enrolment of the purchase-
deed of the estate here devised by our poet, and of ascertaining
its extent and value ; but it was not enrolled during that period,
nor could I find any inquisition taken after his death, by which
its value might have been ascertained. I suppose it was conveyed
by the former owner to Shakspeare, not by bargain and sale, but
by a deed of feoffment, which it was not necessary to enroll.
MALONE.

[4] —— *that messuage or tenement—in the Blackfriars in London
near* the Wardrobe ;] This was the house which was mortgaged to
Henry Walker.

By *the Wardrobe* is meant the King's Great Wardrobe, a royal
house, near Puddle-Wharf, purchased by King Edward the Third
from Sir John Beauchamp, who built it. King Richard III. was
lodged in this house, in the second year of his reign. See Stowe's
*Survey*, p. 693, edit. 1618. After the fire of London this office
was kept in the Savoy : but it is now abolished. MALONE.

be and remain to the fourth, fifth, sixth, and seventh sons of her body, lawfully issuing one after another, and to the heirs males of the bodies of the said fourth, fifth, sixth, and seventh sons lawfully issuing, in such manner as it is before limited to be and remain to the first, second, and third sons of her body, and to their heirs males; and for default of such issue, the said premises to be and remain to my said niece Hall, and the heirs males of her body lawfully issuing; and for default of such issue, to my daughter Judith, and the heirs males of her body lawfully issuing; and for default of such issue, to the right heirs of me the said William Shakspeare for ever.

*Item,* I give unto my wife my second best bed, with the furniture.[5]

*Item,* I give and bequeath to my said daughter Judith my broad silver gilt bowl. All the rest of my goods, chattels, leases, plate, jewels, and houshold stuff whatsoever, after my debts and legacies paid, and my funeral expences discharged, I give, devise, and bequeath to my son-in-law, John Hall, gent. and my daughter Susanna his wife, whom I ordain and make executors of this my last will and testament. And I do entreat and appoint the said Thomas Russell, esq. and Francis Collins, gent. to be overseers hereof. And do revoke all former wills,

---

[5] —— *my* second *best bed, with the furniture.*] Thus Shakspeare's original will.

It appears, in the original will of Shakspeare, (now in the Prerogative-office, Doctor's Commons,) that he had forgot his wife; the legacy to her being expressed by an interlineation, as well as those to Heminge, Burbage, and Condell.

The will is written on three sheets of paper, the last two of which are undoubtedly subscribed with Shakspeare's own hand. The first indeed has his name in the margin, but it differs somewhat in spelling as well as manner, from the two signatures that follow.

and publish this to be my last will and testament.
In witness whereof I have hereunto put my hand,
the day and year first above written.

> By me *William Shakspear*

*Witness to the publishing hereof,*

   Fra. Collyns,
   Julius Shaw,
   John Robinson,
   Hamnet Sadler,
   Robert Whatcott.


*Probatum fuit testamentum suprascriptum
apud London, coram Magistro William
Byrde, Legum Doctore, &c. vicesimo se-
cundo die mensis Junii, Anno Domini, 1616;
juramento Johannis Hall unius ex. cui, &c.
de bene, &c. jurat. reservata potestate, &c.
Susannæ Hall, alt. ex. &c. eam cum venerit,
&c. petitur. &c.*

# CHRONOLOGY OF SHAKSPEARE'S PLAYS.

The following is the order in which Mr. MALONE supposes the plays of Shakspeare to have been written:

Since the foregoing elaborate, and, for the most part, satisfactory result of a laborious enquiry was last published, the order of the plays of Shakspeare, as settled by Mr. Malone, has been controverted by Mr. Chalmers, who has formed a new arrangement; and in support of it has produced his evidence and assigned his reasons. To these (being too long to be here inserted) the reader is referred for farther satisfaction. On a subject which both parties admit does not pretend to the certainties of demonstration, a difference of opinion may be expected. Time, research, and accident, may yet bring to light evidence to confirm or confute either party's statement. The arrangement of Mr. Malone being already before the reader it will be necessary to add that of Mr. Chalmers; and that a judgment may be formed which claims the preference, both lists are subjoined. The first is by Mr. Chalmers, the second by Mr. Malone.

| | | | | |
|---|---|---|---|---|
| 1. | The Comedy of Errors | 1591 | .. | 1593 |
| 2. | Love's Labour's Lost | 1592 | .. | 1594 |
| 3. | Romeo and Juliet | 1592 | .. | 1595 |
| 4. | Henry VI. the First Part | 1593 | .. | 1589 |
| 5. | Henry VI. the Second Part | 1595 | .. | 1591 |
| 6. | Henry VI. the Third Part | 1595 | .. | 1591 |
| 7. | The Two Gentlemen of Verona | 1595 | .. | 1595 |
| 8. | Richard III | 1595 | .. | 1597 |
| 9. | Richard II | 1596 | .. | 1697 |
| 10. | The Merry Wives of Windsor | 1596 | .. | 1601 |
| 11. | Henry IV. the First Part | 1596 | .. | 1597 |
| 12. | Henry IV. the Second Part | 1597 | .. | 1598 |
| 13. | Henry V | 1597 | .. | 1597 |
| 14. | The Merchant of Venice | 1597 | .. | 1598 |
| 15. | Hamlet | 1597 | .. | 1596 |
| 16. | King John | 1598 | .. | 1596 |
| 17. | A Midsummer-Night's Dream | 1598 | .. | 1592 |
| 18. | The Taming of the Shrew | 1598 | .. | 1594 |
| 19. | All's Well that Ends Well | 1599 | .. | 1598 |
| 20. | Much Ado About Nothing | 1599 | .. | 1600 |
| 21. | As You Like It | 1599 | .. | 1600 |
| 22. | Troilus and Cressida | 1600 | .. | 1602 |
| 23. | Timon of Athens | 1601 | .. | 1609 |
| 24. | The Winter's Tale | 1601 | .. | 1604 |
| 25. | Measure for Measure | 1604 | .. | 1603 |
| 26. | Lear | 1605 | .. | 1605 |
| 27. | Cymbeline | 1606 | .. | 1605 |
| 28. | Macbeth | 1606 | .. | 1606 |
| 29. | Julius Cæsar | 1607 | .. | 1607 |
| 30. | Antony and Cleopatra | 1608 | .. | 1608 |
| 31. | Coriolanus | 1609 | .. | 1610 |
| 32. | The Tempest | 1613 | .. | 1612 |
| 33. | The Twelfth-Night | 1613 | .. | 1614 |
| 34. | Henry VIII | 1613 | .. | 1601 |
| 35. | Othello | 1614 | .. | 1611 |

See *Supplemental Apology for the Believers in the Shakspeare-Papers.* By George Chalmers, F. R. S. A. S. p. 266.

# DR. JOHNSON'S

# PREFACE.[1]

THAT praises are without reason lavished on the dead, and that the honours due only to excellence are paid to antiquity, is a complaint likely to be always continued by those, who, being able to add nothing to truth, hope for eminence from the heresies of paradox; or those, who, being forced by disappointment upon consolatory expedients, are willing to hope from posterity what the present age refuses, and flatter themselves that the regard which is yet denied by envy, will be at last bestowed by time.

Antiquity, like every other quality that attracts the notice of mankind, has undoubtedly votaries that reverence it, not from reason, but from prejudice. Some seem to admire indiscriminately whatever has been long preserved, without considering that time has sometimes co-operated with chance; all perhaps are more willing to honour past than present excellence; and the mind contemplates genius through the shades of age, as the eye surveys the sun through artificial opacity. The great contention of criticism is to find the faults of the moderns, and the beauties of the ancients. While an author is yet living, we estimate his powers by his worst performance; and when he is dead, we rate them by his best.

To works, however, of which the excellence is not absolute and definite, but gradual and comparative; to works not raised upon principles demonstrative and scientifick, but appealing wholly to observation and experience, no other test can be applied than length of duration and continuance of esteem. What mankind have long possessed they have often examined and compared, and if they persist to value the possession, it is because frequent comparisons have confirmed opinion in its favour. As among the works of nature

[1] First printed in 1765.

A

no man can properly call a river deep, or a mountain high, without the knowledge of many mountains, and many rivers; so in the productions of genius, nothing can be styled excellent till it has been compared with other works of the same kind. Demonstration immediately displays its power, and has nothing to hope or fear from the flux of years; but works tentative and experimental must be estimated by their proportion to the general and collective ability of man, as it is discovered in a long succession of endeavours. Of the first building that was raised, it might be with certainty determined that it was round or square; but whether it was spacious or lofty must have been referred to time. The Pythagorean scale of numbers was at once discovered to be perfect; but the poems of Homer we yet know not to transcend the common limits of human intelligence, but by remarking, that nation after nation, and century after century, has been able to do little more than transpose his incidents, new name his characters, and paraphrase his sentiments.

The reverence due to writings that have long subsisted arises therefore not from any credulous confidence in the superior wisdom of past ages, or gloomy persuasion of the degeneracy of mankind, but is the consequence of acknowledged and indubitable positions, that what has been longest known has been most considered, and what is most considered is best understood.

The poet, of whose works I have undertaken the revision, may now begin to assume the dignity of an ancient, and claim the privilege of established fame and prescriptive veneration. He has long outlived his century,[*] the term commonly fixed as the test of literary merit. Whatever advantages he might once derive from personal allusions, local customs, or temporary opinions, have for many years been lost; and every topick of merriment or motive of sorrow, which the modes of artificial life afforded him, now only obscure the scenes which they once illuminated. The effects of favour and competition are at an end; the tradition of his friendships and his enmities has perished; his works support no opinion with arguments, nor supply any faction with invectives; they can neither indulge vanity, nor gratify malignity; but are read without any other reason than the desire of pleasure, and are therefore praised only as pleasure is ob-

[*] " Est vetus atque probus, centum qui perficit annos."   *Hor.*
                                                        STEEVENS.

tained; yet, thus unassisted by interest or passion, they have past through variations of taste and changes of manners, and, as they devolved from one generation to another, have received new honours at every transmission.

But because human judgment, though it be gradually gaining upon certainty, never becomes infallible; and approbation, though long continued, may yet be only the approbation of prejudice or fashion; it is proper to inquire, by what peculiarities of excellence Shakspeare has gained and kept the favour of his countrymen.

Nothing can please many, and please long, but just representations of general nature. Particular manners can be known to few, and therefore few only can judge how nearly they are copied. The irregular combinations of fanciful invention may delight awhile, by that novelty of which the common satiety of life sends us all in quest; but the pleasures of sudden wonder are soon exhausted, and the mind can only repose on the stability of truth.

Shakspeare is above all writers, at least above all modern writers, the poet of nature; the poet that holds up to his readers a faithful mirror of manners and of life. His characters are not modified by the customs of particular places, unpractised by the rest of the world; by the peculiarities of studies or professions, which can operate but upon small numbers; or by the accidents of transient fashions or temporary opinions: they are the genuine progeny of common humanity, such as the world will always supply, and observation will always find. His persons act and speak by the influence of those general passions and principles by which all minds are agitated, and the whole system of life is continued in motion. In the writings of other poets a character is too often an individual; in those of Shakspeare it is commonly a species.

It is from this wide extension of design that so much instruction is derived. It is this which fills the plays of Shakspeare with practical axioms and domestick wisdom. It was said of Euripides, that every verse was a precept; and it may be said of Shakspeare, that from his works may be collected a system of civil and œconomical prudence. Yet his real power is not shown in the splendor of particular passages, but by the progress of his fable, and the tenor of his dialogue; and he that tries to recommend him by select quotations, will succeed like the pedant in Hierocles, who, when he offered his house to sale, carried a brick in his pocket as a specimen.

It will not easily be imagined how much Shakspeare excels in accommodating his sentiments to real life, but by comparing him with other authors. It was observed of the ancient schools of declamation, that the more diligently they were frequented, the more was the student disqualified for the world, because he found nothing there which he should ever meet in any other place. The same remark may be applied to every stage but that of Shakspeare. The theatre, when it is under any other direction, is peopled by such characters as were never seen, conversing in a language which was never heard, upon topicks which will never arise in the commerce of mankind. But the dialogue of this author is often so evidently determined by the incident which produces it, and is pursued with so much ease and simplicity, that it seems scarcely to claim the merit of fiction, but to have been gleaned by diligent selection out of common conversation, and common occurrences.

Upon every other stage the universal agent is love, by whose power all good and evil is distributed, and every action quickened or retarded. To bring a lover, a lady, and a rival into the fable; to entangle them in contradictory obligations, perplex them with oppositions of interest, and harass them with violence of desires inconsistent with each other; to make them meet in rapture, and part in agony; to fill their mouths with hyperbolical joy and outrageous sorrow; to distress them as nothing human ever was distressed; to deliver them as nothing human ever was delivered, is the business of a modern dramatist. For this, probability is violated, life is misrepresented, and language is depraved. But love is only one of many passions, and as it has no great influence upon the sum of life, it has little operation in the dramas of a poet, who caught his ideas from the living world, and exhibited only what he saw before him. He knew, that any other passion, as it was regular or exorbitant, was a cause of happiness or calamity.

Characters thus ample and general were not easily discriminated and preserved, yet perhaps no poet ever kept his personages more distinct from each other. I will not say with Pope, that every speech may be assigned to the proper speaker, because many speeches there are which have nothing characteristical; but, perhaps, though some may be equally adapted to every person, it will be difficult to find any that can be properly transferred from the present possessor to another claimant. The choice is right, when there is reason for choice.

Other dramatists can only gain attention by hyperbolical or aggravated characters, by fabulous and unexampled excellence or depravity, as the writers of barbarous romances invigorated the reader by a giant and a dwarf; and he that should form his expectation of human affairs from the play, or from the tale, would be equally deceived. Shakspeare has no heroes; his scenes are occupied only by men, who act and speak as the reader thinks that he should himself have spoken or acted on the same occasion: even where the agency is supernatural, the dialogue is level with life. Other writers disguise the most natural passions and most frequent incidents; so that he who contemplates them in the book will not know them in the world: Shakspeare approximates the remote, and familiarizes the wonderful; the event which he represents will not happen, but if it were possible, its effects would probably be such as he has assigned;[3] and it may be said, that he has not only shown human nature as it acts in real exigencies, but as it would be found in trials, to which it cannot be exposed.

This therefore is the praise of Shakspeare, that his drama is the mirror of life; that he who has mazed his imagination, in following the phantoms which other writers raise up before him, may here be cured of his delirious ecstasies, by reading human sentiments in human language; by scenes from which a hermit may estimate the transactions of the world, and a confessor predict the progress of the passions.

His adherence to general nature has exposed him to the censure of criticks, who form their judgments upon narrower principles. Dennis and Rymer think his Romans not sufficiently Roman, and Voltaire censures his kings as not completely royal. Dennis is offended, that Menenius, a senator of Rome, should play the buffoon; and Voltaire perhaps thinks decency violated when the Danish usurper is represented as a drunkard. But Shakspeare always makes nature predominate over accident; and if he preserves the essential character, is not very careful of distinctions superinduced and adventitious. His story requires Romans or kings, but he thinks only on men. He knew that Rome, like every other city, had men of all dispositions; and wanting a buffoon, he went into the senate-house for that which the senate-house would certainly have afforded him.

[3] " Quærit quod nusquam est gentium, reperit tamen,
" Facit illud verisimile quod mendacium est."
       Plauti. *Pseudolus*, Act I. sc. iv. STEEVENS.

He was inclined to show an usurper and a murderer not only odious, but despicable; he therefore added drunkenness to his other qualities, knowing that kings love wine like other men, and that wine exerts its natural power upon kings. These are the petty cavils of petty minds; a poet overlooks the casual distinction of country and condition, as a painter, satisfied with the figure, neglects the drapery.

The censure which he has incurred by mixing comick and tragick scenes, as it extends to all his works, deserves more consideration. Let the fact be first stated, and then examined.

Shakspeare's plays are not in the rigorous and critical sense either tragedies or comedies, but compositions of a distinct kind; exhibiting the real state of sublunary nature, which partakes of good and evil, joy and sorrow, mingled with endless variety of proportion and innumerable modes of combination; and expressing the course of the world, in which the loss of one is the gain of another; in which, at the same time, the reveller is hasting to his wine, and the mourner burying his friend; in which the malignity of one is sometimes defeated by the frolick of another: and many mischiefs and many benefits are done and hindered without design.

Out of this chaos of mingled purposes and casualties, the ancient poets, according to the laws which custom had prescribed, selected some the crimes of men, and some their absurdities: some the momentous vicissitudes of life, and some the lighter occurrences; some the terrors of distress, and some the gaieties of prosperity. Thus rose the two modes of imitation, known by the names of *tragedy* and *comedy*, compositions intended to promote different ends by contrary means, and considered as so little allied, that I do not recollect among the Greeks or Romans a single writer who attempted both.

Shakspeare has united the powers of exciting laughter and sorrow not only in one mind, but in one composition. Almost all his plays are divided between serious and ludicrous characters, and, in the successive evolutions of the design, sometimes produce seriousness and sorrow, and sometimes levity and laughter.

That this is a practice contrary to the rules of criticism will be readily allowed; but there is always an appeal open from criticism to nature. The end of writing is to instruct; the end of poetry is to instruct by pleasing. That the mingled drama may convey all the instruction of tragedy or comedy cannot be denied, because it includes both in its alternations of exhibition, and approaches nearer than either to the appearance of life, by showing how great machinations and slender designs may promote or obviate one another, and the high and the low co-operate in the general system by unavoidable concatenation.

It is objected, that by this change of scenes the passions are interrupted in their progression, and that the principal event, being not advanced by a due gradation of preparatory incidents, wants at last the power to move, which constitutes the perfection of dramatick poetry. This reasoning is so specious, that it is received as true even by those who in daily experience feel it to be false. The interchanges of mingled scenes seldom fail to produce the intended vicissitudes of passion. Fiction cannot move so much, but that the attention may be easily transferred; and though it must be allowed that pleasing melancholy be sometimes interrupted by unwelcome levity, yet let it be considered likewise, that melancholy is often not pleasing, and that the disturbance of one man may be the relief of another; that different auditors have different habitudes; and that, upon the whole, all pleasure consists in variety.

The players, who in their edition divided our author's works into comedies, histories, and tragedies, seem not to have distinguished the three kinds, by any very exact or definite ideas.

An action which ended happily to the principal persons, however serious or distressful through its intermediate incidents, in their opinion constituted a comedy. This idea of a comedy continued long amongst us, and plays were written, which, by changing the catastrophe, were tragedies to-day, and comedies to-morrow.

Tragedy was not in those times a poem of more general dignity or elevation than comedy; it required only a calamitous conclusion, with which the common criticism of that age was satisfied, whatever lighter pleasure it afforded in its progress.

History was a series of actions, with no other than chronological succession, independent on each other, and without any tendency to introduce and regulate the conclusion. It is not always very nicely distinguished from tragedy. There is not much nearer approach to unity of action in the tragedy of *Antony and Cleopatra*, than in the history of *Richard the Second*. But a history might be continued through many plays; as it had no plan, it had no limits.

Through all these denominations of the drama, Shakspeare's mode of composition is the same; an interchange of seriousness and merriment, by which the mind is softened at one time, and exhilarated at another. But whatever be his purpose, whether to gladden or depress, or to conduct the story, without vehemence or emotion, through tracts of easy and familiar dialogue, he never fails to attain his purpose; as he commands us, we laugh or mourn, or sit silent with quiet expectation, in tranquillity without indifference.

When Shakspeare's plan is understood, most of the criticisms of Rymer and Voltaire vanish away. The play of *Hamlet* is opened, without impropriety, by two centinels; Iago bellows at Brabantio's window, without injury to the scheme of the play, though in terms which a modern audience would not easily endure; the character of Polonius is seasonable and useful; and the Gravediggers themselves may be heard with applause.

Shakspeare engaged in dramatick poetry with the world open before him; the rules of the ancients were yet known to few; the publick judgment was unformed; he had no example of such fame as might force him upon imitation, nor criticks of such authority as might restrain his extravagance: he therefore indulged his natural disposition, and his disposition, as Rymer has remarked, led him to comedy. In tragedy he often writes with great appearance of toil and study, what is written at last with little felicity; but in his comick scenes, he seems to produce without labour, what no labour can improve. In tragedy he is always struggling after some occasion to be comick, but in comedy he seems to repose, or to luxuriate, as in a mode of thinking congenial to his nature. In his tragick scenes there is always something wanting, but his comedy often surpasses expectation or desire. His comedy pleases by the thoughts and the language, and his tragedy for the greater part by incident and action. His tragedy seems to be skill, his comedy to be instinct.

The force of his comick scenes has suffered little diminution from the changes made by a century and a half, in manners or in words. As his personages act upon principles arising from genuine passion, very little modified by particular forms, their pleasures and vexations are communicable to all times and to all places; they are natural, and therefore durable; the adventitious peculiarities of personal habits, are only superficial dies, bright and pleasing for a little while, yet soon fading to a dim tinct, without any remains of former lustre; but the discrimination of true passion are the colours of nature; they pervade the whole mass, and can only perish with the body that exhibits them. The accidental compositions of heterogeneous modes are dissolved by the chance that combined them; but the uniform simplicity of primitive qualities neither admits increase, nor suffers decay. The sand heaped by one flood is scattered by another, but the rock always continues in its place. The stream of time, which is continually washing the dissoluble fabricks of other poets, passes without injury by the adamant of Shakspeare.

If there be, what I believe there is, in every nation, a style which never becomes obsolete, a certain mode of phraseology so consonant and congenial to the analogy and principles of its respective language, as to remain settled and unaltered: this style is probably to be sought in the common intercourse of life, among those who speak only to be understood, without ambition of elegance. The polite are always catching modish innovations, and the learned depart from established forms of speech, in hope of finding or making better; those who wish for distinction forsake the vulgar, when the vulgar is right: but there is a conversation above grossness and below refinement, where propriety resides, and where this poet seems to have gathered his comick dialogue. He is therefore more agreeable to the ears of the present age than any other author equally remote, and among his other excellencies deserves to be studied as one of the original masters of our language.

These observations are to be considered not as unexceptionably constant, but as containing general and predominant truth. Shakspeare's familiar dialogue is affirmed to be smooth and clear, yet not wholly without ruggedness or difficulty: as a country may be eminently fruitful, though it has spots unfit for cultivation: his characters are praised as natural, though their sentiments are sometimes forced, and their actions improbable; as the earth upon the whole is spherical, though its surface is varied with protuberances and cavities.

Shakspeare with his excellencies has likewise faults, and faults sufficient to obscure and overwhelm any other merit. I shall show them in the proportion in which they appear to me, without envious malignity or superstitious veneration. No question can be more innocently discussed than a dead poet's pretensions to renown; and little regard is due to that bigotry which sets candour higher than truth.

His first defect is that to which may be imputed most of the evil in books or in men. He sacrifices virtue to convenience, and is so much more careful to please than to instruct, that he seems to write without any moral purpose. From his writings indeed a system of social duty may be selected, for he that thinks reasonably must think morally; but his precepts and axioms drop casually from him; he makes no just distribution of good or evil, nor is always careful to show in the virtuous a disapprobation of the wicked; he carries his persons indifferently through right and wrong, and at the close dismisses them without further care, and leaves their examples to operate by chance. This fault the barbarity of his age cannot extenuate; for it is always a writer's duty to make the world better, and justice is a virtue independent on time or place.

The plots are often so loosely formed, that a very slight consideration may improve them, and so carelessly pursued, that he seems not always fully to comprehend his own design. He omits opportunities of instructing or delighting, which the train of his story seems to force upon him, and apparently rejects those exhibitions which would be more affecting, for the sake of those which are more easy.

It may be observed, that in many of his plays the latter part is evidently neglected. When he found himself near the end of his work, and in view of his reward, he shortened the labour to snatch the profit. He therefore remits his efforts where he should most vigorously exert them, and his catastrophe is improbably produced or imperfectly represented.

He had no regard to distinction of time or place, but gives to one age or nation, without scruple, the customs, institutions, and opinions of another, at the expence not only of likelihood, but of possibility. These faults Pope has endeavoured, with more zeal than judgment, to transfer to his imagined interpolators. We need not to wonder to find Hector quoting Aristotle, when we see the loves of Theseus and Hippolyta combined with the Gothick mythology of fairies. Shakspeare, indeed, was not the only violator of chronology, for in the same age Sidney who wanted not the advantages of learning, has, in his *Arcadia*, confounded the pastoral with the feudal times, the days of innocence, quiet, and security, with those of turbulence, violence, and adventure.

In his comick scenes, he is seldom very successful, when he engages his characters in reciprocations of smartness and contests of sarcasm; their jests are commonly gross, and their pleasantry licentious ; neither his gentlemen nor his ladies have much delicacy, nor are sufficiently distinguished from his clowns by any appearance of refined manners. Whether he represented the real conversation of his time is not easy to determine ; the reign of Elizabeth is commonly supposed to have been a time of stateliness, formality, and reserve, yet perhaps the relaxations of that severity were not very elegant. There must, however, have been always some modes of gaiety preferable to others, and a writer ought to choose the best.

In tragedy his performance seems constantly to be worse, as his labour is more. The effusions of passion, which exigence forces out, are for the most part striking and energetick; but whenever he solicits his invention, or strains his faculties, the offspring of his throes is tumour, meanness, tediousness, and obscurity.

In narration he affects a disproportionate pomp of diction, and a wearisome train of circumlocution, and tells the incident imperfectly in many words, which might have been more plainly delivered in few. Narration in dramatick poetry is naturally tedious, as it is unanimated and inactive, and obstructs the progress of the action ; it should therefore always be rapid, and enlivened by frequent interruption. Shakspeare found it an incumbrance, and instead of lightening it by brevity, endeavoured to recommend it by dignity and splendor.

His declamations or set speeches are commonly cold and weak, for his power was the power of nature ; when he endeavoured, like other tragick writers, to catch opportunities of amplification, and instead of inquiring what the occasion demanded, to show how much his stores of knowledge could supply, he seldom escapes without the pity or resentment of his reader.

It is incident to him to be now and then entangled with an unwieldy sentiment, which he cannot well express, and will not reject ; he struggles with it a while, and if it continues stubborn, comprises it in words such as occur, and leaves it to be disentangled and evolved by those who have more leisure to bestow upon it.

Not that always where the language is intricate, the thought is subtle, or the image always great where the line is bulky ; the equality of words to things is very often neglected, and trivial sentiments and vulgar ideas disappoint the attention, to which they are recommended by sonorous epithets and swelling figures.

But the admirers of this great poet have most reason to complain when he approaches nearest to his highest excellence, and seems fully resolved to sink them in dejection and mollify them with tender emotions by the fall of greatness, the danger of innocence, or the crosses of love. What he does best, he soon ceases to do.* He is not long soft and pathetick without some idle conceit, or contemptible equivocation. He no sooner begins to move, than he counteracts himself; and terror and pity, as they are rising in the mind, are checked and blasted by sudden frigidity.

A quibble is to Shakspeare, what luminous vapours are to the traveller; he follows it at all adventures; it is sure to lead him out of his way, and sure to engulf him in the mire. It has some malignant power over his mind, and its fascinations are irresistible. Whatever be the dignity or profundity of his disquisitions, whether he be enlarging knowledge, or exalting affection, whether he be amusing attention with incidents, or enchanting it in suspense, let but a quibble spring up before him, and he leaves his work unfinished. A quibble is the golden apple for which he will always turn aside from his career, or stoop from his elevation. A quibble, poor and barren as it is, gave him such delight, that he was content to purchase it by the sacrifice of reason, propriety, and truth. A quibble was to him the fatal Cleopatra for which he lost the world, and was content to lose it.

It will be thought strange, that, in enumerating the defects of this writer, I have not yet mentioned his neglect of the unities; his violation of those laws which have been instituted and established by the joint authority of poets and of criticks.

For his other deviations from the art of writing, I resign him to critical justice, without making any other demand in his favour, than that which must be indulged to all human excellence; that his virtues be rated with his failings: but, from the censure which this irregularity may bring upon him, I shall, with due reverence to that learning which I must oppose, adventure to try how I can defend him.

His histories, being neither tragedies nor comedies, are

---

* "But the admirers of this great poet have never less reason to indulge their hopes of supreme excellence, than when he seems fully resolved to sink them in dejection, and mollify them with tender emotions by the fall of greatness, the danger of innocence, or the crosses of love. He is not long soft and pathetick, &c."

Orig. Edit. 1765.

not subject to any of their laws ; nothing more is necessary to all the praise which they expect, than that the changes of action be so prepared as to be understood, that the incidents be various and affecting, and the characters consistent, natural, and distinct. No other unity is intended, and therefore none is to be sought.

In his other works he has well enough preserved the unity of action. He has not, indeed, an intrigue regularly perplexed and regularly unravelled ; he does not endeavour to hide his design only to discover it, for this is seldom the order of real events, and Shakspeare is the poet of nature : but his plan has commonly what Aristotle requires, a beginning, a middle, and an end ; one event is concatenated with another, and the conclusion follows by easy consequence. There are perhaps some incidents that might be spared, as in other poets there is much talk that only fills up time upon the stage ; but the general system makes gradual advances, and the end of the play is the end of expectation.

To the unities of time and place he has shown no regard : and perhaps a nearer view of the principles on which they stand will diminish their value, and withdraw from them the veneration which, from the time of Corneille, they have very generally received, by discovering that they have given more trouble to the poet, than pleasure to the auditor.

The necessity of observing the unities of time and place arises from the supposed necessity of making the drama credible. The criticks hold it impossible, that an action of months or years can be possibly believed to pass in three hours ; or that the spectator can suppose himself to sit in the theatre, while ambassadors go and return between distant kings, while armies are levied and towns besieged, while an exile wanders and returns, or till he whom they saw courting his mistress, shall lament the untimely fall of his son. The mind revolts from evident falsehood, and fiction loses its force when it departs from the resemblance of reality.

From the narrow limitation of time necessarily arises the contraction of place. The spectator, who knows that he saw the first Act at Alexandria, cannot suppose that he sees the next at Rome, at a distance to which not the dragons of Medea could, in so short a time, have transported him ; he knows with certainty that he has not changed his place ; and he knows that place cannot change itself ; that what was a house cannot become a plain ; that what was Thebes can never be Persepolis.

Such is the triumphant language with which a critick

12

exults over the misery of an irregular poet, and exults commonly without resistance or reply. It is time therefore to tell him, by the authority of Shakspeare, that he assumes, as an unquestionable principle, a position, which, while his breath is forming it into words, his understanding pronounces to be false. It is false, that any representation is mistaken for reality; that any dramatick fable in its materiality was ever credible, or, for a single moment, was ever credited.

The objection arising from the impossibility of passing the first hour at Alexandria, and the next at Rome, supposes, that when the play opens, the spectator really imagines himself at Alexandria, and believes that his walk to the theatre has been a voyage to Egypt, and that he lives in the days of Antony and Cleopatra. Surely he that imagines this may imagine more. He that can take the stage at one time for the palace of the Ptolemies, may take it in half an hour for the promontory of Actium. Delusion, if delusion be admitted, has no certain limitation; if the spectator can be once persuaded, that his old acquaintance are Alexander and Cæsar, that a room illuminated with candles is the plain of Pharsalia, or the banks of Granicus, he is in a state of elevation above the reach of reason, or of truth, and from the heights of empyrean poetry, may despise the circumscriptions of terrestrial nature. There is no reason why a mind thus wandering in ecstasy should count the clock, or why an hour should not be a century in that calenture of the brains that can make the stage a field.

The truth is that the spectators are always in their senses, and know from the first Act to the last, that the stage is only a stage, and that the players are only players. They come to hear a certain number of lines recited with just gesture and elegant modulation. The lines relate to some action, and an action must be in some place; but the different actions that complete a story may be in places very remote from each other: and where is the absurdity of allowing that space to represent first Athens, and then Sicily, which was always known to be neither Sicily nor Athens, but a modern theatre?

By supposition, as place is introduced, time may be extended; the time required by the fable elapses for the most part between the acts; for, of so much of the action as is represented, the real and poetical duration is the same. If, in the first Act, preparations for war against Mithridates are represented to be made in Rome, the event of the war may, without absurdity, be represented, in the catastrophe, as happening in Pontus; we know that there is neither war, nor preparation for war; we know that we are neither in Rome nor Pontus: that neither Mithridates nor Lucullus are before us. The drama exhibits successive imitations of successive actions, and why may not the second imitation represent an action that happened years after the first; if it be so connected with it, that nothing but time can be supposed to intervene? Time is, of all modes of existence, most obsequious to the imagination; a lapse of years is as easily conceived as a passage of hours. In contemplation we easily contract the time of real actions, and therefore willingly permit it to be contracted when we only see their imitation.

It will be asked, how the drama moves, if it is not credited. It is credited with all the credit due to a drama. It is credited, whenever it moves, as a just picture of a real original; as representing to the auditor what he would himself feel, if he were to do or suffer what is there feigned to be suffered or to be done. The reflection that strikes the heart is not, that the evils before us are real evils, but that they are evils to which we ourselves may be exposed. If there be any fallacy, it is not that we fancy the players, but that we fancy ourselves unhappy for a moment; but we rather lament the possibility than suppose the presence of misery, as a mother weeps over her babe, when she remembers that death may take it from her. The delight of tragedy proceeds from our consciousness of fiction; if we thought murders and treasons real, they would please no more.

Imitations produce pain or pleasure, not because they are mistaken for realities, but because they bring realities to mind. When the imagination is recreated by a painted landscape, the trees are not supposed capable to give us shade, or the fountains coolness; but we consider, how we should be pleased with such fountains playing beside us, and such woods waving over us. We are agitated in reading the history of *Henry the Fifth*, yet no man takes his book for the field of Agincourt. A dramatick exhibition is a book recited with concomitants that increase or diminish its effect. Familiar comedy is often more powerful on the theatre, than in the page; imperial tragedy is always less. The humour of Petruchio may be heightened by grimace; but what voice or what gesture can hope to add dignity or force to the soliloquy of Cato?

9

A play read, affects the mind like a play acted. It is therefore evident, that the action is not supposed to be real; and it follows, that between the Acts a longer or shorter time may be allowed to pass, and that no more account of space or duration is to be taken by the auditor of a drama, than by the reader of a narrative, before whom may pass in an hour the life of a hero, or the revolutions of an empire.

Whether Shakspeare knew the unities, and rejected them by design, or deviated from them by happy ignorance, it is, I think, impossible to decide, and useless to inquire. We may reasonably suppose, that, when he rose to notice, he did not want the counsels and admonitions of scholars and criticks, and that he at last deliberately persisted in a practice, which he might have begun by chance. As nothing is essential to the fable, but unity of action, and as the unities of time and place arise evidently from false assumptions, and, by circumscribing the extent of the drama, lessen its variety, I cannot think it much to be lamented, that they were not known by him, or not observed: nor, if such another poet could arise, should I very vehemently reproach him, that his first Act passed at Venice, and his next in Cyprus. Such violations of rules merely positive, become the comprehensive genius of Shakspeare, and such censures are suitable to the minute and slender criticism of Voltaire:

" Non usque adeo permiscuit imis
" Longus summa dies, ut non, si voce Metelli
" Serventur leges, mallnt a Cæsare tolli."

Yet when I speak thus slightly of dramatick rules, I cannot but recollect how much wit and learning may be produced against me; before such authorities I am afraid to stand, not that I think the present question one of those that are to be decided by mere authority, but because it is to be suspected, that these precepts have not been so easily received, but for better reasons than I have yet been able to find. The result of my inquiries, in which it would be ludicrous to boast of impartiality, is, that the unities of time and place are not essential to a just drama; that though they may sometimes conduce to pleasure, they are always to be sacrificed to the nobler beauties of variety and instruction; and that a play, written with nice observation of critical rules, is to be contemplated as an elaborate curiosity, as the product of superfluous and ostentatious art, by which is shown, rather what is possible, than what is necessary.

He that, without diminution of any other excellence, shall preserve all the unities unbroken, deserves the like applause with the architect, who shall display all the orders of architecture in a citadel, without any deduction from its strength; but the principal beauty of a citadel is to exclude the enemy; and the greatest graces of a play are to copy nature, and instruct life.

Perhaps, what I have here not dogmatically but deliberately written, may recall the principles of the drama to a new examination. I am almost frighted at my own temerity; and when I estimate the fame and the strength of those that maintain the contrary opinion, am ready to sink down in reverential silence; as Æneas withdrew from the defence of Troy, when he saw Neptune shaking the wall, and Juno heading the besiegers.

Those whom my arguments cannot persuade to give their approbation to the judgment of Shakspeare, will easily, if they consider the condition of his life, make some allowance for his ignorance.

Every man's performances, to be rightly estimated, must be compared to the state of the age in which he lived, and with his own particular opportunities; and though to a reader a book be not worse or better for the circumstances of the author, yet as there is always a silent reference of human works to human abilities, and as the enquiry, how far man may extend his designs, or how high he may rate his native force, is of far greater dignity than in what rank we shall place any particular performance, curiosity is always busy to discover the instruments, as well as to survey the workmanship, to know how much is to be ascribed to original powers, and how much to casual and adventitious help. The palaces of Peru and Mexico were certainly mean and incommodious habitations, if compared to the houses of European monarchs; yet who could forbear to view them with astonishment, who remembered that they were built without the use of iron?

The English nation, in the time of Shakspeare, was yet struggling to emerge from barbarity. The philology of Italy had been transplanted hither in the reign of Henry the Eighth; and the learned languages had been successfully cultivated by Lilly, Linacre, and More; by Pole, Cheke, and Gardiner; and afterwards by Smith, Clerk, Haddon, and Ascham. Greek was now taught to boys in the principal schools; and those who united elegance with learning, read, with great diligence, the Italian and Spanish poets.

But literature was yet confined to professed scholars, or to men and women of high rank. The publick was gross and dark; and to be able to read and write, was an accomplishment still valued for its rarity.

Nations, like individuals, have their infancy. A people newly awakened to literary curiosity, being yet unacquainted with the true state of things, knows not how to judge of that which is proposed as its resemblance. Whatever is remote from common appearances is always welcome to vulgar, as to childish credulity; and of a country unenlightened by learning, the whole people is the vulgar. The study of those who then aspired to plebeian learning was laid out upon adventures, giants, dragons, and enchantments. *The Death of Arthur* was the favourite volume.

The mind, which has feasted on the luxurious wonders of fiction, has no taste of the insipidity of truth. A play which imitated only the common occurrences of the world, would, upon the admirers of *Palmerin* and *Guy of Warwick*, have made little impression; he that wrote for such an audience was under the necessity of looking round for strange events and fabulous transactions, and that incredibility, by which maturer knowledge is offended, was the chief recommendation of writings, to unskilful curiosity.

Our author's plots are generally borrowed from novels; and it is reasonable to suppose, that he chose the most popular, such as were read by many, and related by more; for his audience could not have followed him through the intricacies of the drama, had they not held the thread of the story in their hands.

The stories which we now find only in remoter authors, were in his time accessible and familiar. The fable of *As you like it*, which is supposed to be copied from Chaucer's *Gamelyn*, was a little pamphlet of those times; and old Mr. Cibber remembered the tale of *Hamlet* in plain English prose, which the criticks have now to seek in *Saxo Grammaticus.*

His English histories he took from English chronicles and English ballads; and as the ancient writers were made known to his countrymen by versions, they supplied him with new subjects; he dilated some of Plutarch's lives into plays, when they had been translated by North.

His plots, whether historical or fabulous, are always crouded with incidents, by which the attention of a rude people was more easily caught than by sentiment or argumentation; and such is the power of the marvellous, even over those who despise it, that every man finds his mind more strongly seized by the tragedies of Shakspeare than of any other writer; others please us by particular speeches, but he always makes us anxious for the event, and has perhaps excelled all but Homer in securing the first purpose of a writer, by exciting restless and unquenchable curiosity, and compelling him that reads his work to read it through.

The shows and bustle with which his plays abound have the same original. As knowledge advances, pleasure passes from the eye to the ear, but returns, as it declines, from the ear to the eye. Those to whom our author's labours were exhibited had more skill in pomps or processions than in poetical language, and perhaps wanted some visible and discriminated events, as comments on the dialogue. He knew how he should most please; and whether his practice is more agreeable to nature, or whether his example has prejudiced the nation, we still find that on our stage something must be done as well as said, and inactive declamation is very coldly heard, however musical or elegant, passionate or sublime.

Voltaire expresses his wonder, that our author's extravagancies are endured by a nation, which has seen the tragedy of *Cato*. Let him be answered, that Addison speaks the language of poets, and Shakspeare, of men. We find in *Cato* innumerable beauties which enamour us of its author, but we see nothing that acquaints us with human sentiments or human actions; we place it with the fairest and the noblest progeny which judgment propagates by conjunction with learning; but *Othello* is the vigorous and vivacious offspring of observation impregnated by genius. *Cato* affords a splendid exhibition of artificial and fictitious manners, and delivers just and noble sentiments, in diction easy, elevated, and harmonious, but its hopes and fears communicate no vibration to the heart; the composition refers us only to the writer; we pronounce the name of *Cato*, but we think on *Addison*.

The work of a correct and regular writer is a garden accurately formed and diligently planted, varied with shades, and scented with flowers; the composition of Shakspeare is a forest, in which oaks extend their branches, and pines tower in the air, interspersed sometimes with weeds and brambles, and sometimes giving shelter to myrtles and to roses; filling the eye with awful pomp, and gratifying the mind with endless diversity. Other poets display cabinets of precious rarities, minutely finished, wrought into shape, and polished into brightness. Shakspeare opens a mine which contains gold and diamonds in unexhaustible plenty, though clouded by incrustations, debased by impurities, and mingled with a mass of meaner minerals.

It has been much disputed, whether Shakspeare owed his excellence to his own native force, or whether he had the common helps of scholastick education, the precepts of critical science, and the examples of ancient authors.

There has always prevailed a tradition, that Shakspeare wanted learning, that he had no regular education, nor much skill in the dead languages. Jonson, his friend, affirms, that *he had small Latin, and less Greek*;* who, besides that he had no imaginable temptation to falsehood, wrote at a time when the character and acquisitions of Shakspeare were known to multitudes. His evidence ought therefore to decide the controversy, unless some testimony of equal force could be opposed.

Some have imagined, that they have discovered deep learning in many imitations of old writers; but the examples which I have known urged, were drawn from books translated in his time; or were such easy coincidencies of thought, as will happen to all who consider the same subjects; or such remarks on life or axioms of morality as float in conversation, and are transmitted through the world in proverbial sentences.

I have found it remarked, that, in this important sentence, *Go before, I'll follow*, we read a translation of, *I prae, sequar*. I have been told, that when Caliban, after a pleasing dream, says, *I cried to sleep again*, the author imitates Anacreon, who had, like every other man, the same wish on the same occasion.

There are a few passages which may pass for imitations, but so few, that the exception only confirms the rule; he obtained them from accidental quotations, or by oral com-

---

* " and *no* Greek." Orig. Edit. 1765. Dr. Farmer in his " Essay on the learning of Shakspeare," has the following note, alluding to this alteration. " This passage of Ben Jonson, so often quoted, is given us in the admirable preface to the late edition, with a various reading, " small Latin and *so* Greek," which hath been held up to the publick for a modern sophistication: yet whether an error or not, it was adopted above a century ago by W. Towers, in a panegyrick on Cartwright. His eulogy, with more than fifty others, on this now forgotten poet, was prefixed to the edit. 1651."

munication, and as he used what he had, would have used more if he had obtained it.

The *Comedy of Errors* is confessedly taken from the *Menæchmi of Plautus*; from the only play of Plautus which was then in English. What can be more probable, than that he who copied that, would have copied more ; but that those which were not translated were inaccessible ?

Whether he knew the modern languages is uncertain. That his plays have some French scenes proves but little ; he might easily procure them to be written, and probably, even though he had known the language in the common degree, he could not have written it without assistance. In the story of *Romeo and Juliet* he is observed to have followed the English translation, where it deviates from the Italian ; but this on the other part proves nothing against his knowledge of the original. He was to copy, not what he knew himself, but what was known to his audience.

It is most likely that he had learned Latin sufficiently to make him acquainted with construction, but that he never advanced to an easy perusal of the Roman authors. Concerning his skill in modern languages, I can find no sufficient ground of determination ; but as no imitations of French or Italian authors have been discovered, though the Italian poetry was then in high esteem, I am inclined to believe, that he read little more than English, and chose for his fables only such tales as he found translated.

That much knowledge is scattered over his works is very justly observed by Pope, but it is often such knowledge as books did not supply. He that will understand Shakspeare, must not be content to study him in the closet, he must look for his meaning sometimes among the sports of the field, and sometimes among the manufactures of the shop.

There is, however, proof enough that he was a very diligent reader, nor was our language then so indigent of books, but that he might very liberally indulge his curiosity without excursion into foreign literature. Many of the Roman authors were translated, and some of the Greek ; the Reformation had filled the kingdom with theological learning ; most of the topicks of human disquisition had found English writers ; and poetry had been cultivated, not only with diligence, but success. This was a stock of knowledge sufficient for a mind so capable of appropriating and improving it.

But the greater part of his excellence was the product of his own genius. He found the English stage in a state of the utmost rudeness; no essays either in tragedy or comedy had appeared, from which it could be discovered to what degree of delight either one or other might be carried. Neither character nor dialogue were yet understood. Shakspeare may be truly said to have introduced them both amongst us, and in some of his happier scenes to have carried them both to the utmost height.

By what gradations of improvement he proceeded, is not easily known; for the chronology of his works is yet unsettled. Rowe is of opinion, that *perhaps we are not to look for his beginning, like those of other writers, in his least perfect works; art had so little, and nature so large a share in what he did, that for aught I know*, says he, *the performances of his youth, as they were the most vigorous, were the best.* But the power of nature is only the power of using to any certain purpose the materials which diligence procures, or opportunity supplies. Nature gives no man knowledge, and when images are collected by study and experience, can only assist in combining or applying them. Shakspeare, however favoured by nature, could impart only what he had learned; and as he must encrease his ideas, like other mortals, by gradual acquisition, he, like them, grew wiser as he grew older, could display life better, as he knew it more, and instruct with more efficacy, as he was himself more amply instructed.

There is a vigilance of observation and accuracy of distinction which books and precepts cannot confer; from this almost all original and native excellence proceeds. Shakspeare must have looked upon mankind with perspicacity, in the highest degree curious and attentive. Other writers borrow their characters from preceding writers, and diversify them only by the accidental appendages of present manners; the dress is a little varied, but the body is the same. Our author had both matter and form to provide; for, except the characters of Chaucer, to whom I think he is not much indebted, there were no writers in English, and perhaps not many in other modern languages, which showed life in its native colours.

The contest about the original benevolence or malignity of man had not yet commenced. Speculation had not yet attempted to analyse the mind, to trace the passions to their sources, to unfold the seminal principles of vice and virtue, or sound the depths of the heart for the motives of action. All those enquiries, which from that time that human nature became the fashionable study, have been made sometimes with nice discernment, but often with idle subtilty, were yet unattempted. The tales, with which the infancy of learning was satisfied, exhibited only the superficial appearances of action, related the events, but omitted the causes, and were formed for such as delighted in wonders rather than in truth. Mankind was not then to be studied in the closet ; he that would know the world, was under the necessity of gleaning his own remarks, by mingling as he could in its business and amusements.

Boyle congratulated himself upon his high birth, because it favoured his curiosity, by facilitating his access. Shakspeare had no such advantage ; he came to London a needy adventurer, and lived for a time by very mean employments. Many works of genius and learning have been performed in states of life that appear very little favourable to thought or to enquiry ; so many, that he who considers them is inclined to think that he sees enterprize and perseverance predominating over all external agency, and bidding help and hindrance vanish before them. The genius of Shakspeare was not to be depressed by the weight of poverty, nor limited by the narrow conversation to which men in want are inevitably condemned ; the incumbrances of his fortune were shaken from his mind, *as dew drops from a lion's mane.*

Though he had so many difficulties to encounter, and so little assistance to surmount them, he has been able to obtain an exact knowledge of many modes of life, and many casts of native dispositions ; to vary them with great multiplicity ; to mark them by nice distinctions ; and to show them in full view by proper combinations. In this part of his performances he had none to imitate, but has himself been imitated by all succeeding writers ; and it may be doubted, whether from all his successors more maxims of theoretical knowledge, or more rules of practical prudence, can be collected, than he alone has given to his country.

Nor was his attention confined to the actions of men ; he was an exact surveyor of the inanimate world ; his descriptions have always some peculiarities, gathered by contemplating things as they really exist. It may be observed, that the oldest poets of many nations preserve their reputation, and that the following generations of wit, after a short celebrity, sink into oblivion. The first, whoever they be, must take their sentiments and descriptions immediately from knowledge ; the resemblance is therefore just, their descriptions are verified by every eye, and their sentiments acknowledged by every breast. Those whom their fame invites to the same studies, copy partly them, and partly nature, till the books of one age gain such authority, as to stand in the place of nature to another, and imitation, always deviating a little, becomes at last capricious and casual. Shakspeare, whether life or nature be his subject, shows plainly, that he has seen with his own eyes; he gives the image which he receives, not weakened or distorted by the intervention of any other mind ; the ignorant feel his representations to be just, and the learned see that they are complete.

Perhaps it would not be easy to find any author, except Homer, who invented so much as Shakspeare, who so much advanced the studies which he cultivated, or effused so much novelty upon his age or country. The form, the character, the language, and the shows of the English drama are his. *He seems, says Dennis, to have been the very original of our English tragical harmony, that is, the harmony of blank verse, diversified often by dissyllable and trissyllable terminations. For the diversity distinguishes it from heroick harmony, and by bringing it nearer to common use makes it more proper to gain attention, and more fit for action and dialogue. Such verse we make when we are writing prose; we make such verse in common conversation.*

I know not whether this praise is rigorously just. The dissyllable termination, which the critick rightly appropriates to the drama, is to be found, though, I think, not in *Gorboduc*, which is confessedly before our author; yet in *Hieronymo*, of which the date is not certain, but which there is reason to believe at least as old as his earliest plays. This however is certain, that he is the first who taught either tragedy or comedy to please, there being no theatrical piece of any older writer, of which the name is known, except to antiquaries and collectors of books, which are sought because they are scarce, and would not have been scarce, had they been much esteemed.

To him we must ascribe the praise, unless Spenser may divide it with him, of having first discovered to how much smoothness and harmony the English language could be softened. He has speeches, perhaps sometimes scenes, which have all the delicacy of Rowe, without his effeminacy. He endeavours indeed commonly to strike by the force and vigour of his dialogue, but he never executes his purpose better, than when he tries to sooth by softness.

Yet it must be at last confessed, that as we owe every thing to him, he owes something to us; that, if much of his praise is paid by perception and judgment, much is like-

wise given by custom and veneration.   We fix our eyes upon
his graces, and turn them from his deformities, and endure
in him what we should in another loath or despise.  If we
endured without praising, respect for the father of our drama
might excuse us; but I have seen, in the book of some modern critick, a collection of anomalies, which show that he
has corrupted language by every mode of depravation, but
which his admirer has accumulated as a monument of
honour.

He has scenes of undoubted and perpetual excellence, but
perhaps not one play, which, if it were now exhibited as
the work of a contemporary writer, would be heard to the
conclusion.   I am indeed far from thinking, that his works
were wrought to his own ideas of perfection; when they
were such as would satisfy the audience, they satisfied the
writer.   It is seldom that authors, though more studious of
fame than Shakspeare, rise much above the standard of their
own age; to add a little to what is best will always be sufficient for present praise, and those who find themselves
exalted into fame, are willing to credit their encomiasts, and
to spare the labour of contending with themselves.

It does not appear, that Shakspeare thought his works
worthy of posterity, that he levied any ideal tribute upon
future times, or had any further prospect, than of present
popularity and present profit.   When his plays had been
acted, his hope was at an end; he solicited no addition of
honour from the reader.   He therefore made no scruple to
repeat the same jests in many dialogues, or to entangle different plots by the same knot of perplexity, which may be at
least forgiven him, by those who recollect, that of Congreve's
four comedies, two are concluded by a marriage in a mask,
by a deception, which perhaps never happened, and which,
whether likely or not, he did not invent.

So careless was this great poet of future fame, that, though
he retired to ease and plenty, while he was yet little *declined
into the vale of years*, before he could be disgusted with fa-
tigue, or disabled by infirmity, he made no collection of
his works, nor desired to rescue those that had been already
published from the depravations that obscured them, or secure to the rest a better destiny, by giving them to the world
in their genuine state.

Of the plays which bear the name of Shakspeare in the
late editions, the greater part were not published till about
seven years after his death, and the few which appeared in
his life are apparently thrust into the world without the

care of the author, and therefore probably without his knowledge.

Of all the publishers, clandestine or professed, the negligence and unskilfulness has by the late revisers been sufficiently shown. The faults of all are indeed numerous and gross, and have not only corrupted many passages perhaps beyond recovery, but have brought others into suspicion, which are only obscured by obsolete phraseology, or by the writer's unskilfulness and affectation. To alter is more easy than to explain, and temerity is a more common quality than diligence. Those who saw that they must employ conjecture to a certain degree, were willing to indulge it a little further. Had the author published his own works, we should have sat quietly down to disentangle his intricacies, and clear his obscurities; but now we tear what we cannot loose, and eject what we happen not to understand.

The faults are more than could have happened without the concurrence of many causes. The style of Shakspeare was in itself ungrammatical, perplexed, and obscure; his works were transcribed for the players by those who may be supposed to have seldom understood them; they were transmitted by copiers equally unskilful, who still multiplied errors; they were perhaps sometimes mutilated by the actors, for the sake of shortening the speeches; and were at last printed without correction of the press.

In this state they remained, not as Dr. Warburton supposes, because they were unregarded, but because the editor's art was not yet applied to modern languages, and our ancestors were accustomed to so much negligence of English printers, that they could very patiently endure it. At last an edition was undertaken by Rowe; not because a poet was to be published by a poet, for Rowe seems to have thought very little on correction or explanation, but that our author's works might appear like those of his fraternity, with the appendages of a life and recommendatory preface. Rowe has been clamorously blamed for not performing what he did not undertake, and it is time that justice be done him, by confessing, that though he seems to have had no thought of corruption beyond the printer's errors, yet he has made many emendations, if they were not made before, which his successors have received without acknowledgment, and which, if they had produced them, would have filled pages and pages with censures of the stupidity by which the faults were committed, with displays of the absurdities which they involved, with ostentatious expositions of the new reading, and self-congratulations on the happiness of discovering it.

As of the other editors I have preserved the prefaces, I have likewise borrowed the author's life from Rowe,* though not written with much elegance or spirit; it relates, however, what is now to be known, and therefore deserves to pass through all succeeding publications.

The nation had been for many years content enough with Mr. Rowe's performance; when Mr. Pope made them acquainted with the true state of Shakspeare's text, showed that it was extremely corrupt, and gave reason to hope that there were means of reforming it. He collated the old copies, which none had thought to examine before, and restored many lines to their integrity; but by a very compendious criticism, he rejected whatever he disliked, and thought more of amputation than of cure.

I know not why he is commended by Dr. Warburton for distinguishing the genuine from the spurious plays. In this choice he exerted no judgment of his own; the plays which he received, were given by Hemings and Condel, the first editors; and those which he rejected, though, according to the licentiousness of the press in those times, they were printed during Shakspeare's life, with his name, had been omitted by his friends, and were never added to his works before the edition of 1664, from which they were copied by the latter printers.

This was a work which Pope seems to have thought unworthy of his abilities, being not able to suppress his contempt of *the dull duty of an editor.* He understood but half his undertaking. The duty of a collator is indeed dull, yet, like other tedious tasks, is very necessary; but an emendatory critick would ill discharge his duty, without qualities very different from dulness. In perusing a corrupted piece, he must have before him all possibilities of meaning, with all possibilities of expression. Such must be his comprehension of thought, and such his copiousness of language. Out of many readings possible, he must be able to select that which bests suits with the state, opinions, and modes of language prevailing in every age, and with his author's particular cast of thought, and turn of expression. Such must be his knowledge, and such his taste. Conjectural criticism demands more than humanity possesses, and he that exercises

* " Of Rowe, as of all the editors, I have preserved the preface, and have likewise retained the author's life." Orig. Edit. 1765.

it with most praise, has very frequent need of indulgence. Let us now be told no more of the dull duty of an editor.

Confidence is the common consequence of success. They whose excellence of any kind has been loudly celebrated, are ready to conclude, that their powers are universal. Pope's edition fell below his own expectations, and he was so much offended, when he was found to have left any thing for others to do, that he passed the latter part of his life in a state of hostility with verbal criticism.

I have retained all his notes, that no fragment of so great a writer may be lost; his preface, valuable alike for elegance of composition and justness of remark, and containing a general criticism on his author, so extensive that little can be added, and so exact, that little can be disputed, every editor has an interest to suppress, but that every reader would demand its insertion.

Pope was succeeded by Theobald, a man of narrow comprehension, and small acquisitions, with no native and intrinsick splendor of genius, with little of the artificial light of learning, but zealous for minute accuracy, and not negligent in pursuing it. He collated the ancient copies, and rectified many errors. A man so anxiously scrupulous might have been expected to do more, but what little he did was commonly right.

In his reports of copies and editions he is not to be trusted without examination. He speaks sometimes indefinitely of copies, when he has only one. In his enumeration of editions, he mentions the two first folios as of high, and the third folio as of middle authority; but the truth is, that the first is equivalent to all others, and that the rest only deviate from it by the printer's negligence. Whoever has any of the folios has all, excepting those diversities which mere reiteration of editions will produce. I collated them all at the beginning, but afterwards used only the first.

Of his notes I have generally retained those which he retained himself in his second edition, except when they were confuted by subsequent annotators, or were too minute to merit preservation. I have sometimes adopted his restoration of a comma, without inserting the panegyrick in which he celebrated himself for his achievement. The exuberant excrescence of his diction I have often lopped, his triumphant exultations over Pope and Rowe I have sometimes suppressed, and his contemptible ostentation I have frequently concealed; but I have in some places shown him, as he would have shown himself, for the reader's diversion, that the inflated emptiness of some notes may justify or excuse the contraction of the rest.

Theobald, thus weak and ignorant, thus mean and faithless, thus petulant and ostentatious, by the good luck of having Pope for his enemy, has escaped, and escaped alone, with reputation, from this undertaking. So willingly does the world support those who solicit favour, against those who command reverence; and so easily is he praised, whom no man can envy.

Our author fell then into the hands of Sir Thomas Hanmer, the Oxford editor, a man, in my opinion, eminently qualified by nature for such studies. He had, what is the first requisite to emendatory criticism, that intuition by which the poet's intention is immediately discovered, and that dexterity of intellect which despatches its work by the easiest means. He had undoubtedly read much: his acquaintance with customs, opinions, and traditions, seems to have been large; and he is often learned without show. He seldom passes what he does not understand, without an attempt to find or to make a meaning, and sometimes hastily makes what a little more attention would have found. He is solicitous to reduce to grammar, what he could not be sure that his author intended to be grammatical. Shakspeare regarded more the series of ideas, than of words; and his language, not being designed for the reader's desk, was all that he desired it to be, if it conveyed his meaning to the audience.

Hanmer's care of the metre has been too violently censured. He found the measure reformed in so many passages, by the silent labours of some editors, with the silent acquiescence of the rest, that he thought himself allowed to extend a little further the licence, which had already been carried so far without reprehension; and of his corrections in general, it must be confessed, that they are often just, and made commonly with the least possible violation of the text.

But, by inserting his emendations, whether invented or borrowed, into the page, without any notice of varying copies, he has appropriated the labour of his predecessors, and made his own edition of little authority. His confidence, indeed, both in himself and others, was too great; he supposes all to be right that was done by Pope and Theobald; he seems not to suspect a critick of fallibility, and it was but reasonable that he should claim what he so liberally granted.

As he never writes without careful enquiry and diligent consideration, I have received all his notes, and believe that every reader will wish for more.

Of the last editor it is more difficult to speak. Respect is due to high place, tenderness to living reputation, and veneration to genius and learning; but he cannot be justly offended at that liberty of which he has himself so frequently given an example, nor very solicitous what is thought of notes which he ought never to have considered as part of his serious employments, and which, I suppose, since the ardour of composition is remitted, he no longer numbers among his happy effusions.

The original and predominant error of his commentary, is acquiescence in his first thoughts; that precipitation which is produced by consciousness of quick discernment; and that confidence which presumes to do, by surveying the surface, what labour only can perform, by penetrating the bottom. His notes exhibit sometimes perverse interpretations, and sometimes improbable conjectures; he at one time gives the author more profundity of meaning than the sentence admits, and at another discovers absurdities, where the sense is plain to every other reader. But his emendations are likewise often happy and just: and his interpretation of obscure passages learned and sagacious.

Of his notes, I have commonly rejected those, against which the general voice of the publick has exclaimed, or which their own incongruity immediately condemns, and which I suppose the author himself would desire to be forgotten. Of the rest, to part I have given the highest approbation, by inserting the offered reading in the text; part I have left to the judgment of the reader, as doubtful, though specious; and part I have censured without reserve, but I am sure without bitterness of malice, and, I hope, without wantonness of insult.

It is no pleasure to me, in revising my volumes, to observe how much paper is wasted in confutation. Whoever considers the revolutions of learning, and the various questions of greater or less importance, upon which wit and reason have exercised their powers, must lament the unsuccessfulness of enquiry, and the slow advances of truth, when he reflects, that great part of the labour of every writer is only the destruction of those that went before him. The first care of the builder of a new system is to demolish the fabricks which are standing. The chief desire of him that comments an author, is to show how much other commentators have corrupted and obscured him. The opinions prevalent in one age, as truths above the reach of controversy, are confuted and rejected in another, and rise again to reception in remoter times. Thus the human mind is kept in motion without progress. Thus sometimes truth and error, and sometimes contrarieties of error, take each other's place by reciprocal invasion. The tide of seeming knowledge which is poured over one generation, retires and leaves another naked and barren; the sudden meteors of intelligence, which for a while appear to shoot their beams into the regions of obscurity, on a sudden withdraw their lustre, and leave mortals again to grope their way.

These elevations and depressions of renown, and the contradictions to which all improvers of knowledge must for ever be exposed, since they are not escaped by the highest and brightest of mankind, may surely be endured with patience by criticks and annotators, who can rank themselves but as the satellites of their authors. How canst thou beg for life, says Homer's hero* to his captive, when thou knowest that thou art now to suffer only what must another day be suffered by Achilles?

Dr. Warburton had a name sufficient to confer celebrity on those who could exalt themselves into antagonists, and his notes have raised a clamour too loud to be distinct. His chief assailants are the authors of *The Canons of Criticism*, and of *The Revisal of Shakspeare's Text*; of whom one ridicules his errors with airy petulance, suitable enough to the levity of the controversy; the other attacks them with gloomy malignity, as if he were dragging to justice an assassin or incendiary. The one stings like a fly, sucks a little blood, takes a gay flutter, and returns for more; the other bites like a viper, and would be glad to leave inflammations and gangrene behind him. When I think on one, with his confederates, I remember the danger of Coriolanus, who was afraid that *girls with spits, and boys with stones, should slay him in puny battle*; when the other crosses my imagination, I remember the prodigy in *Macbeth* :

> " A falcon tow'ring in his pride of place,
> " Was by a mousing owl hawk'd at and kill'd."

Let me however do them justice. One is a wit, and one a scholar. They have both shown acuteness sufficient in the discovery of faults, and have both advanced some probable

* " Achilles." Orig. Edit. 1765.

interpretations of obscure passages; but when they aspire to conjecture and emendation, it appears how falsely we all estimate our own abilities, and the little which they have been able to perform might have taught them more candour to the endeavours of others.

Before Dr. Warburton's edition, *Critical Observations on Shakspeare* had been published by Mr. Upton, a man skilled in languages, and acquainted with books, but who seems to have had no great vigour of genius or nicety of taste. Many of his explanations are curious and useful, but he likewise, though he professed to oppose the licentious confidence of editors, and adhere to the old copies, is unable to restrain the rage of emendation, though his ardour is ill seconded by his skill. Every cold empirick, when his heart is expanded by a successful experiment, swells into a theorist, and the laborious collator at some unlucky moment frolicks in conjecture.

*Critical, historical, and explanatory Notes* have been likewise published upon Shakspeare by Dr. Grey, whose diligent perusal of the old English writers has enabled him to make some useful observations. What he undertook he has well enough performed, but as he neither attempts judicial nor emendatory criticism, he employs rather his memory than his sagacity. It were to be wished that all would endeavour to imitate his modesty, who have not been able to surpass his knowledge.

I can say with great sincerity of all my predecessors, what I hope will hereafter be said of me, that not one has left Shakspeare without improvement, nor is there one to whom I have not been indebted for assistance and information. Whatever I have taken from them, it was my intention to refer to its original author, and it is certain, that what I have not given to another, I believed when I wrote it to be my own. In some perhaps I have been anticipated; but if I am ever found to encroach upon the remarks of any other commentator, I am willing that the honour, be it more or less, should be transferred to the first claimant, for his right, and his alone, stands above dispute; the second can prove his pretensions only to himself, nor can himself always distinguish invention, with sufficient certainty, from recollection.

They have all been treated by me with candour, which they have not been careful of observing to one another. It is not easy to discover from what cause the acrimony of a scholiast can naturally proceed. The subjects to be discussed by him are of very small importance; they involve neither property nor liberty; nor favour the interest of sect or party. The various readings of copies, and different interpretations of a passage, seem to be questions that might exercise the wit, without engaging the passions. But whether it be, that *small things make mean men proud*, and vanity catches small occasions; or that all contrariety of opinion, even in those that can defend it no longer, makes proud men angry; there is often found in commentaries a spontaneous strain of invective and contempt, more eager and venomous than is vented by the most furious controvertist in politicks against those whom he is hired to defame.

Perhaps the lightness of the matter may conduce to the vehemence of the agency; when the truth to be investigated is so near to inexistence, as to escape attention, its bulk is to be enlarged by rage and exclamation: that to which all would be indifferent in its original state, may attract notice when the fate of a name is appended to it. A commentator has indeed great temptations to supply by turbulence what he wants of dignity, to beat his little gold to a spacious surface, to work that to foam which no art or diligence can exalt to spirit.

The notes which I have borrowed or written are either illustrative, by which difficulties are explained; or judicial, by which faults and beauties are remarked; or emendatory, by which depravations are corrected.

The explanations transcribed from others, if I do not subjoin any other interpretation, I suppose commonly to be right, at least I intend by acquiescence to confess, that I have nothing better to propose.

After the labours of all the editors, I found many passages which appeared to me likely to obstruct the greater number of readers, and thought it my duty to facilitate their passage. It is impossible for an expositor not to write too little for some, and too much for others. He can only judge what is necessary by his own experience; and how long soever he may deliberate, will at last explain many lines which the learned will think impossible to be mistaken, and omit many for which the ignorant will want his help. These are censures merely relative, and must be quietly endured. I have endeavoured to be neither superfluously copious, nor scrupulously reserved, and hope that I have made my author's meaning accessible to many, who before were frighted from perusing him, and contributed something to the publick, by diffusing innocent and rational pleasure.

The complete explanation of an author not systematick,

VOL. I.                    c

and consequential, but desultory and vagrant, abounding in casual allusions and light hints, is not to be expected from any single scholiast. All personal reflections, when names are suppressed, must be in a few years irrecoverably obliterated; and customs, too minute to attract the notice of law, such as modes of dress, formalities of conversation, rules of visits, disposition of furniture, and practices of ceremony, which naturally find places in familiar dialogue, are so fugitive and unsubstantial, that they are not easily retained or recovered. What can be known will be collected by chance, from the recesses of obscure and obsolete papers, perused commonly with some other view. Of this knowledge every man has some, and none has much; but when an author has engaged the publick attention, those who can add any thing to his illustration, communicate their discoveries, and time produces what had eluded diligence.

To time I have been obliged to resign many passages, which, though I did not understand them, will perhaps hereafter be explained, having, I hope, illustrated some, which others have neglected or mistaken, sometimes by short remarks, or marginal directions, such as every editor has added at his will, and often by comments more laborious than the matter will seem to deserve; but that which is most difficult is not always most important, and to an editor nothing is a trifle by which his author is obscured.

The poetical beauties or defects I have not been very diligent to observe. Some plays have more, and some fewer judicial observations, not in proportion to their difference of merit, but because I give this part of my design to chance and to caprice. The reader, I believe, is seldom pleased to find his opinion anticipated; it is natural to delight more in what we find or make, than in what we receive. Judgment, like other faculties, is improved by practice, and its advancement is hindered by submission to dictatorial decisions, as the memory grows torpid by the use of a table-book. Some initiation is however necessary; of all skill, part is infused by precept, and part is obtained by habit; I have therefore shown so much as may enable the candidate of criticism to discover the rest.

To the end of most plays I have added short strictures, containing a general censure of faults, or praise of excellence; in which I know not how much I have concurred with the current opinion; but I have not, by any affectation of singularity, deviated from it. Nothing is minutely and particularly examined, and therefore it is to be supposed, that in the plays which are condemned there is much to be praised, and in these which are praised much to be condemned.

The part of criticism in which the whole succession of editors has laboured with the greatest diligence, which has occasioned the most arrogant ostentation, and excited the keenest acrimony, is the emendation of corrupted passages, to which the publick attention having been first drawn by the violence of the contention between Pope and Theobald, has been continued by the persecution, which, with a kind of conspiracy, has been since raised against all the publishers of Shakspeare.

That many passages have passed in a state of depravation through all the editions is indubitably certain; of these, the restoration is only to be attempted by collation of copies, or sagacity of conjecture. The collator's province is safe and easy, the conjecturer's perilous and difficult. Yet as the greater part of the plays are extant only in one copy, the peril must not be avoided, nor the difficulty refused.

Of the readings which this emulation of amendment has hitherto produced, some from the labours of every publisher I have advanced into the text; those are to be considered as in my opinion sufficiently supported; some I have rejected without mention, as evidently erroneous; some I have left in the notes without censure or approbation, as resting in equipoise between objection and defence; and some, which seemed specious but not right, I have inserted with a subsequent animadversion.

Having classed the observations of others, I was at last to try what I could substitute for their mistakes, and how I could supply their omissions. I collated such copies as I could procure, and wished for more, but have not found the collectors of these rarities very communicative. Of the editions which chance or kindness put into my hands I have given an enumeration, that I may not be blamed for neglecting what I had not the power to do.

By examining the old copies, I soon found that the later publishers, with all their boasts of diligence, suffered many passages to stand unauthorized, and contented themselves with Rowe's regulation of the text, even where they knew it to be arbitrary, and with a little consideration might have found it to be wrong. Some of these alterations are only the ejection of a word for one that appeared to him more elegant or more intelligible. These corruptions I have often silently rectified; for the history of our language, and the

c 2

true force of our words, can only be preserved, by keeping the text of authors free from adulteration. Others, and those very frequent, smoothed the cadence, or regulated the measure; on these I have not exercised the same rigour; if only a word was transposed, or a particle inserted or omitted, I have sometimes suffered the line to stand; for the inconstancy of the copies is such, as that some liberties may be easily permitted. But this practice I have not suffered to proceed far, having restored the primitive diction wherever it could for any reason be preferred.

The emendations, which comparison of copies supplied, I have inserted in the text; sometimes, where the improvement was slight, without notice, and sometimes with an account of the reasons of the change.

Conjecture, though it be sometimes unavoidable, I have not wantonly nor licentiously indulged. It has been my settled principle, that the reading of the ancient books is probably true, and therefore is not to be disturbed for the sake of elegance, perspicuity, or mere improvement of the sense. For though much credit is not due to the fidelity, nor any to the judgment of the first publishers, yet they who had the copy before their eyes were more likely to read it right, than we who read it only by imagination. But it is evident that they have often made strange mistakes by ignorance or negligence, and that therefore something may be properly attempted by criticism, keeping the middle way between presumption and timidity.

Such criticism I have attempted to practise, and where any passage appeared inextricably perplexed, have endeavoured to discover how it may be recalled to sense, with least violence. But my first labour is, always to turn the old text on every side, and try if there be any interstice, through which light can find its way; nor would Huetius himself condemn me, as refusing the trouble of research, for the ambition of alternation. In this modest industry, I have not been unsuccessful. I have rescued many lines from the violations of temerity, and secured many scenes from the inroads of correction. I have adopted the Roman sentiment, that it is more honourable to save a citizen, than to kill an enemy, and have been more careful to protect than to attack.

I have preserved the common distribution of the plays into acts, though I believe it to be in almost all the plays void of authority. Some of those which are divided in the later editions have no division in the first folio, and some that are divided in the folio have no division in the preceding copies. The settled mode of the theatre requires four intervals in the play, but few, if any, of our author's compositions can be properly distributed in that manner. An act is so much of the drama as passes without intervention of time, or change of place. A pause makes a new act. In every real, and therefore in every imitative action, the intervals may be more or fewer. the restriction of five acts being accidental and arbitrary. This Shakspeare knew, and this he practised; his plays were written, and at first printed in one unbroken continuity, and ought now to be exhibited with short pauses, interposed as often as the scene is changed, or any considerable time is required to pass. This method would at once quell a thousand absurdities.

In restoring the author's works to their integrity, I have considered the punctuation as wholly in my power; for what could be their care of colons and commas, who corrupted words and sentences. Whatever could be done by adjusting points, is therefore silently performed, in some plays with much diligence, in others with less; it is hard to keep a busy eye steadily fixed upon evanescent atoms, or a discursive mind upon evanescent truth.

The same liberty has been taken with a few particles, or other words of slight effect. I have sometimes inserted or omitted them without notice. I have done that sometimes, which the other editors have done always, and which indeed the state of the text may sufficiently justify.

The greater part of readers, instead of blaming us for passing trifles, will wonder that on mere trifles so much labour is expended, with such importance of debate, and such solemnity of diction. To these I answer with confidence, that they are judging of an art which they do not understand; yet cannot much reproach them with their ignorance, nor promise that they would become in general, by learning criticism, more useful, happier, or wiser.

As I practised conjecture more, I learned to trust it less; and after I had printed a few plays, resolved to insert none of my own readings in the text. Upon this caution I now congratulate myself, for every day encreases my doubt of my emendations.

Since I have confined my imagination to the margin, it must not be considered as very reprehensible, if I have suffered it to play some freaks in its own dominion. There is no danger in conjecture, if it be proposed as conjecture; and while the text remains uninjured, those changes may be safely offered, which are not considered even by him that offers them as necessary or safe.

If my readings are of little value, they have not been ostentatiously displayed or importunately obtruded. I could have written longer notes, for the art of writing notes is not of difficult attainment. The work is performed, first by railing at the stupidity, negligence, ignorance, and asinine tastelessness of the former editors, showing, from all that goes before and all that follows, the inelegance and absurdity of the old reading; then by proposing something, which to superficial readers would seem specious, but which the editor rejects with indignation; then by producing the true reading, with a long paraphrase, and concluding with loud acclamations on the discovery, and a sober wish for the advancement and prosperity of genuine criticism.

All this may be done, and perhaps done sometimes without impropriety. But I have always suspected that the reading is right, which requires many words to prove it wrong; and the emendation wrong, that cannot without so much labour appear to be right. The justness of a happy restoration strikes at once, and the moral precept may be well applied to criticism, *quod dubitas ne feceris.*

To dread the shore which he sees spread with wrecks, is natural to the sailor. I had before my eye, so many critical adventures ended in miscarriage, that caution was forced upon me. I encountered in every page wit struggling with its own sophistry, and learning confused by the multiplicity of its views. I was forced to censure those whom I admired, and could not but reflect, while I was dispossessing their emendations, how soon the same fate might happen to my own, and how many of the readings which I have corrected may be by some other editor defended and established.

> " Criticks I saw, that others' names efface,
> " And fix their own, with labour, in the place:
> " Their own, like others, soon their place resign'd,
> " Or disappear'd, and left the first behind."   Pope.

That a conjectural critick should often be mistaken, cannot be wonderful, either to others, or himself, if it be considered, that in his art there is no system, no principal and axiomatical truth that regulates subordinate positions. His chance of error is renewed at every attempt; an oblique view of the passage, a slight misapprehension of a phrase, a casual inattention to the parts connected, is sufficient to make

12

him not only fail, but fail ridiculously ; and when he succeeds best, he produces perhaps but one reading of many probable, and he that suggests another will always be able to dispute his claims.

It is an unhappy state, in which danger is hid under pleasure. The allurements of emendation are scarcely resistible. Conjecture has all the joy and all the pride of invention, and he that has once started a happy change, is too much delighted to consider what objections may rise against it.

Yet conjectural criticism has been of great use in the learned world ; nor is it my intention to depreciate a study, that has exercised so many mighty minds, from the revival of learning to our own age, from the Bishop of Aleria to English Bentley. The criticks on ancient authors have, in the exercise of their sagacity, many assistances, which the editor of Shakspeare is condemned to want. They are employed upon grammatical and settled languages, whose construction contributes so much to perspicuity, that Homer has fewer passages unintelligible than Chaucer. The words have not only a known regimen, but invariable quantities, which direct and confine the choice. There are commonly more manuscripts than one ; and they do not often conspire in the same mistakes. Yet Scaliger could confess to Salmasius how little satisfaction his emendations gave him. *Illudunt nobis conjecturæ, quarum nos pudet, posteaquam in meliores codices incidimus.* And Lipsius could complain, that criticks were making faults, by trying to remove them, *Ut olim vitiis, ita nunc remediis laboratur.* And indeed, when mere conjecture is to be used, the emendations of Scaliger and Lipsius, notwithstanding their wonderful sagacity and erudition, are often vague and disputable, like mine or Theobald's.

Perhaps I may not be more censured for doing wrong, than for doing little ; for raising in the publick expectations, which at last I have not answered. The expectation of ignorance is indefinite, and that of knowledge is often tyrannical. It is hard to satisfy those who know not what to demand, or those who demand by design what they think impossible to be done. I have indeed disappointed no opinion more than my own ; yet I have endeavoured to perform my task with no slight solicitude. Not a single passage in the whole work has appeared to me corrupt, which I have not attempted to restore ; or obscure, which I have not endeavoured to illustrate. In many I have failed like others ; and from many, after all my efforts, I have retreated, and

confessed the repulse. I have not passed over, with affected
superiority, what is equally difficult to the reader and to myself, but where I could not instruct him, have owned my
ignorance. I might easily have accumulated a mass of
seeming learning upon easy scenes; but it ought not to be
imputed to negligence, that, where nothing was necessary,
nothing has been done, or that, where others have said
enough, I have said no more.

.Notes are often necessary, but they are necessary evils.
Let him, that is yet unacquainted with the powers of Shakspeare, and who desires to feel the highest pleasure that the
drama can give, read every play, from the first scene to the
last, with utter negligence of all his commentators. When
his fancy is once on the wing, let it not stoop at correction
or explanation. When his attention is strongly engaged, let
it disdain alike to turn aside to the name of Theobald and of
Pope. Let him read on through brightness and obscurity,
through integrity and corruption; let him preserve his comprehension of the dialogue and his interest in the fable. And
when the pleasures of novelty have ceased, let him attempt
exactness, and read the commentators.

Particular passages are cleared by notes, but the general
effect of the work is weakened. The mind is refrigerated by
interruption; the thoughts are diverted from the principal
subject; the reader is weary, he suspects not why; and at
last throws away the book which he has too diligently
studied.

.Parts are not to be examined till the whole has been sur-
veyed; there is a kind of intellectual remoteness necessary
for the comprehension of any great work in its full design
and in its true proportions; a close approach shows the
smaller niceties, but the beauty of the whole is discerned no
longer.

It is not very grateful to consider how little the succession
of editors has added to this author's power of pleasing. He
was read, admired, studied, and imitated, while he was yet
deformed with all the improprieties which ignorance and
neglect could accumulate upon him; while the reading was
yet not rectified, nor his allusions understood; yet then did
Dryden pronounce, " that Shakspeare was the man, who,
of all modern and perhaps ancient poets, had the largest and
most comprehensive soul. All the images of nature were
still present to him, and he drew them not laboriously, but
luckily: when he describes any thing, you more than see it,
you feel it too. Those, who accuse him to have wanted

learning, give him the greater commendation; he was naturally learned; he needed not the spectacles of books to read nature; he looked inwards, and found her there. I cannot say he is every where alike; were he so, I should do him injury to compare him with the greatest of mankind. He is many times flat and insipid; his comick wit degenerating into clenches, his serious swelling into bombast. But he is always great, when some great occasion is presented to him; no man can say, he ever had a fit subject for his wit, and did not then raise himself as high above the rest of poets,

" Quantum lenta solent inter viburna cupressi."

It is to be lamented, that such a writer should want a commentary; that his language should become obsolete, or his sentiments obscure.    But it is vain to carry wishes beyond the condition of human things; that which must happen to all, has happened to Shakspeare, by accident and time; and more than has been suffered by any other writer since the use of types, has been suffered by him through his own negligence of fame, or perhaps by that superiority of mind, which despised its own performances, when it compared them with its powers, and judged those works unworthy to be preserved, which the criticks of following ages were to contend for the fame of restoring and explaining.

Among these candidates of inferior fame, I am now to stand the judgment of the publick; and wish that I could confidently produce my commentary as equal to the encouragement which I have had the honour of receiving.    Every work of this kind is by its nature deficient, and I should feel little solicitude about the sentence, were it to be pronounced only by the skilful and the learned.

AN

# HISTORICAL ACCOUNT

OF

# THE ENGLISH STAGE:

## BY MR. MALONE.

THE drama before the time of Shakspeare was so little cultivated, or so ill understood, that to many it may appear unnecessary to carry our theatrical researches higher than that period. Dryden has truly observed, that he " found not, but created first the stage ;" of which no one can doubt, who considers, that of all the plays issued from the press antecedent to the year 1592, when there is reason to believe he commenced a dramatick writer, the titles are scarcely known, except to antiquaries ; nor is there one of them that will bear a second perusal. Yet these, contemptible and few as they are, we may suppose to have been the most popular productions of the time, and the best that had been exhibited before the appearance of Shakspeare.

A minute investigation, therefore, of the origin and progress of the drama in England, will scarcely repay the labour of the inquiry. However, as the best introduction to an account of the internal economy and usages of the English theatres in the time of Shakspeare, (the principal object of this dissertation,) I shall take a cursory view of our most ancient dramatick exhibitions, though I fear I can add but little to the researches which have already been made on that subject.

Mr. Warton in his elegant and ingenious *History of English Poetry* has given so accurate an account of our earliest dramatick performances, that I shall make no apology for extracting from various parts of his valuable work, such particulars as suit my present purpose.

The earliest dramatick entertainments exhibited in England, as well as every other part of Europe, were of a religious kind. So early as in the beginning of the twelfth century, it was customary in England on holy festivals to represent, in or near the churches, either the lives and miracles of saints, or the more mysterious parts of holy writ, such as the incarnation, passion, and resurrection of Christ, these scriptural plays were denominated *Miracles*, or *Mysteries*. At what period of time they were first exhibited in this country, I am unable to ascertain. Undoubtedly, however, they are of very great antiquity; and Riccoboni, who has contended that the Italian theatre is the most ancient in Europe, has claimed for his country an honour to which it is not entitled. The era of the earliest representation in Italy, founded on holy writ, he has placed in the year 1264, when the fraternity *del Gonfalone* was established; but we had similar exhibitions in England above 150 years before that time. In the year 1110, as Dr. Percy and Mr. Warton have observed, the Miracle-play of *Saint Catharine*, written by Geoffrey, a learned Norman, (afterwards Abbot of St. Alban's) was acted, probably by his scholars, in the abbey of Dunstable; perhaps the first spectacle of this kind exhibited in England. William Fitz-Stephen, a monk of Canterbury, who according to the best accounts composed his very curious work in 1174, about four years after the murder of his patron Archbishop Becket, and in the twenty-first year of the reign of King Henry the Second, mentions, that " London, for its theatrical exhibitions, has religious plays, either the representations of miracles wrought by holy confessors, or the sufferings of martyrs."

Mr. Warton has remarked, that " in the time of Chaucer, Plays of Miracles appear to have been the common resort of idle gossips in Lent.

" And in Pierce Plowman's Creed, a piece perhaps prior to Chaucer, a friar Minorite mentions these Miracles as not less frequented than market-towns and fairs :

' We haunten no taverns, ne hobelen about,
' At markets and Miracles we meddle us never."

The elegant writer, whose words I have just quoted, has given the following ingenious account of the origin of this rude species of dramatick entertainment :

" About the eighth century trade was principally carried on by means of fairs, which lasted several days. Charlemagne established many great marts of this sort in France, as did William the Conqueror, and his Norman successors in England. The merchants who frequented these fairs in numerous caravans or companies, employed every art to draw the people together. They were therefore accompanied by jugglers, minstrels, and buffoons; who were no less interested in giving their attendance, and exerting all their skill on these occasions. As now but few large towns existed, no publick spectacles or popular amusements were established : and as the sedentary pleasures of domestick life and private society were yet unknown, the fair-time was the season for diversion. In proportion as these shews were attended and encouraged, they began to be set off with new decorations and improvements : and the arts of buffoonery being rendered still more attractive, by extending their circle of exhibition, acquired an importance in the eyes of the people. By degrees the clergy observing that the entertainments of dancing, musick, and mimickry, exhibited at these protracted annual celebrities, made the people less religious, by promoting idleness and a love of festivity, proscribed these sports, and excommunicated the performers. But finding that no regard was paid to their censures, they changed their plan, and determined to take these recreations into their own hands. They turned actors ; and instead of profane mummeries, presented stories taken from legends or the Bible. This was the origin of sacred comedy. The death of Saint Catharine, acted by the monks of Saint Dennis, rivalled the popularity of the professed players. Musick was admitted into the churches, which served as theatres for the representation of holy farces. The festivals among the French, called *La Fete de Foux*, *de l'Ane*, and *des Innocens*, at length became greater favourites, as they certainly were more capricious and absurd, than the interludes of the buffoons at the fairs. These are the ideas of a judicious French writer now living, who has investigated the history of human manners with great comprehension and sagacity."

" Voltaire's theory on this subject is also very ingenious, and quite new. Religious plays, he supposes, came originally from Constantinople ; where the old Grecian stage continued to flourish in some degree, and the tragedies of Sophocles and Euripides were represented, till the fourth century. About that period, Gregory Nazianzen, an Archbishop, a poet, and one of the fathers of the church, banished Pagan plays from the stage at Constantinople, and introduced stories from the Old and New Testament. As the ancient Greek tragedy was a religious spectacle, a transition was made on the same plan ; and the chorusses were turned into Christian hymns. Gregory wrote many sacred dramas for this purpose, which have not survived those inimitable compositions over which they triumphed for a time : one, however, his tragedy called Χριστος πασχων, or *Christ's Passion*, is still extant. In the prologue it is said to be an imitation of Euripides, and that this is the first time the Virgin Mary had been introduced on the stage. The fashion of acting spiritual dramas, in which at first a due degree of method and decorum was preserved, was at length adopted from Constantinople by the Italians ; who framed, in the depth of the dark ages, on this foundation, that barbarous species of theatrical representation called MYSTERIES, or sacred comedies, and which were soon after received in France. This opinion will acquire probability, if we consider the early commercial intercourse between Italy and Constantinople : and although the Italians, at the time when they may be supposed to have imported plays of this nature, did not understand the Greek language, yet they could understand, and consequently could imitate, what they saw."

" In defence of Voltaire's hypothesis, it may be further observed, that *The Feast of Fools*, and of *the Ass*, with other religious farces of that sort, so common in Europe, originated at Constantinople. They were instituted, although perhaps under other names, in the Greek church, about the year 990, by Theophylact, patriarch of Constantinople, probably with a better design than is imagined by the ecclesiastical annalists ; that of weaning the minds of the people from the pagan ceremonies, by the substitution of christian spectacles partaking of the same spirit of licentiousness.—To those who are accustomed to contemplate the great picture of human follies, which the unpolished ages of Europe hold up to our view, it will not appear surprising, that the people who were forbidden to read the events of the sacred history in the Bible, in which they were faithfully and beautifully related, should at the same time be permitted to see them represented on the stage, disgraced with the grossest improprieties, corrupted with inventions and additions of the most ridiculous kind, sullied with impurities, and expressed in the language of the lowest farce."

" On the whole, the *Mysteries* appear to have originated among the ecclesiasticks : and were most probably first acted with any degree of form by the monks. This was certainly the case in the English monasteries. I have already mentioned the play of Saint Catharine, performed at Dunstable Abbey, by the novices in the eleventh century, under the superintendance of Geoffrey a Parisian ecclesiastick : and the exhibition of the *Passion* by the mendicant friers of

Coventry and other places. Instances have been given of the like practice among the French. The only persons who could now read were in the religious societies; and various circumstances, peculiarly arising from their situation, profession, and institution, enabled the monks to be the sole performers of these representations."

" As learning encreased, and was more widely disseminated, from the monasteries, by a natural and easy transition, the practice migrated to schools and universities, which were formed on the monastick plan, and in many respects resembled the ecclesiastical bodies."

*Candlemas-day*, or *The Slaughter of the Innocents*, written by Ihan Parfre, in 1512, *Mary Magdalene*, produced in the same year, and *The Promises of God*, written by John Bale, and printed in 1538, are curious specimens of this early species of drama. But the most ancient as well as most complete collection of this kind is, *The Chester Mysteries*, which were written by Ralph Higden, a monk of the Abbey of Chester, about the year 1328;[1] of which a particular account will be found below.

[1] MSS. Harl. 2013, &c. " Exhibited at Chester in the year 1327, at the expence of the different trading companies of that city. *The fall of Lucifer*, by the Tanners. *The Creation*, by the Drapers. *The Deluge*, by the Dyers. *Abraham, Melchisedeck*, and *Lot*, by the Barbers. *Moses, Balak*, and *Balaam*, by the Cappers. *The Salutation* and *Nativity*, by the Wrightes. *The Shepherds feeding their Flocks by Night*, by the Painters and Glaziers. *The three Kings*, by the Vintners. *The Oblation of the three Kings*, by the Mercers. *The killing of the Innocents*, by the Goldsmiths. *The Purification*, by the Blacksmiths. *The Temptation*, by the Butchers. *The last Supper*, by the Bakers. *The blind Men and Lazarus*, by the Glovers. *Jesus and the Lepers*, by the Corvesarys. *Christ's Passion*, by the Bowyers, Fletchers, and Ironmongers. *Descent into Hell*, by the Cooks and Innkeepers. *The Resurrection*, by the Skinners. *The Ascension*, by the Taylors. *The Election of S. Mathias, sending of the Holy Ghost*, &c. by the Fishmongers. *Antichrist*, by the Clothiers. *Day of Judgment*, by the Websters. The reader will perhaps smile at some of these combinations. This is the substance and order of the former part of the play. God enters creating the world; he breathes life into Adam, leads him into Paradise, and opens his side while sleeping. Adam and Eve appear naked, and *not ashamed*, and the old serpent enters lamenting his fall. He converses with Eve. She eats of the forbidden fruit, and gives part to Adam. They propose, according to the stage-direction, to make themselves *subligacula a foliis quibus tegamus pudenda*.

Many licentious pleasantries, as Mr. Warton has observed, were sometimes introduced into these religious representations. " This might imperceptibly lead the way to subjects entirely profane, and to comedy ; and perhaps earlier than is imagined. In a Mystery of *The Massacre of the Holy Innocents*, part of the subject of a sacred drama given by the English fathers at the famous Council of Constance, in the year 1417, a low buffoon of Herod's court is introduced, desiring of his lord to be dubbed a knight, that he might be properly qualified to *go on the adventure* of killing the mothers of the children of Bethlehem. This tragical business is treated with the most ridiculous levity. The good women of Bethlehem attack our knight-errant with their spinning-wheels, break his head with their distaffs, abuse him as a coward and a disgrace to chivalry, and send him to Herod as a recreant champion with much ignominy. ——It is certain that our ancestors intended no sort of impiety by these monstrous and unnatural mixtures. Neither the writers nor the spectators saw the impropriety, nor paid a separate attention to the comick and the serious part of these motly scenes ; at least they were persuaded that the solemnity of the subject covered or excused all incongruities. They had no just idea of decorum, consequently but little sense of the ridiculous : what appears to us to be the highest burlesque, on them would have made no sort of impression. We must not wonder at this, in an age when courage, devotion, and ignorance, composed the character of European manners ; when the knight going to a tournament, first invoked his God, then his mistress, and afterwards proceeded with a safe conscience and great resolution to engage his antagonist. In these Mysteries I have sometimes seen gross and open obscenities. In a play of *The Old and New Testament*, Adam and Eve are both exhibited on the stage naked, and conversing about their nakedness ; this very pertinently introduces the next scene ; in which they have coverings of fig leaves. This extraordinary spectacle was beheld by a numerous assembly of both sexes with great

Cover their nakedness with leaves, and converse with God. God's curse. The serpent *exit* hissing. They are driven from Paradise by four angels and the cherubim with a flaming sword. Adam appears digging the ground, and Eve spinning. Their children Cain and Abel enter : the former kills his brother. Adam's lamentation. Cain is banished," &c. Warton's *History of English Poetry*, Vol. I. p. 243.

composure : they had the authority of scripture for such a representation, and they gave matters just as they found them in the third chapter of *Genesis.* It would have been absolute heresy to have departed from the sacred text in personating the primitive appearance of our first parents, whom the spectators so nearly resembled in simplicity; and if this had not been the case, the dramatists were ignorant what to reject and what to retain."

" I must not omit," adds Mr. Warton, " an anecdote entirely new, with regard to the mode of playing the *Mysteries* at this period, [the latter part of the fifteenth century,] which yet is perhaps of much higher antiquity. In the year 1487, while Henry the Seventh kept his residence at the castle of Winchester, on occasion of the birth of prince Arthur, on a Sunday, during the time of dinner, he was entertained with a religious drama called *Christi Descensus ad inferos,* or *Christ's Descent into Hell.* It was represented by the *Pueri Eleemosynarii,* or choir-boys, of Hyde Abbey, and Saint Swithin's Priory, two large monasteries at Winchester. This is the only proof I have ever seen of choir-boys acting the old *Mysteries :* nor do I recollect any other instance of a royal dinner, even on a festival, accompanied with this species of diversion. The story of this interlude, in which the chief characters were Christ, Adam, Eve, Abraham, and John the Baptist, was not uncommon in the ancient religious drama, and I believe made a part of what is called the LUDUS PASCHALIS, or *Easter Play.* It occurs in the Coventry Plays acted on Corpus Christi day, and in the Whitsun-plays at Chester, where it is called the HARROWING OF HELL. The representation is, Christ entering hell triumphantly, delivering our first parents, and the most sacred characters of the old and new testaments, from the dominion of Satan, and conveying them into paradise.—The composers of the Mysteries did not think the plain and probable events of the new testament sufficiently marvellous for an audience who wanted only to be surprised. They frequently selected their materials from books which had more of the air of romance. The subject of the Mysteries just mentioned was borrowed from the *Pseudo-Evangelium,* or the *fabulous Gospel,* ascribed to Nicodemus : a book, which together with the numerous apocryphal narratives, containing infinite innovations of the evangelical history, and forged at Constantinople by the early writers of the Greek church, gave birth to an endless variety of legends concerning the life of Christ and his

apostles ; and which, in the barbarous ages, was better esteemed than the genuine gospel, on account of its improbabilities
and absurdities."

" But whatsoever was the source of these exhibitions,
they were thought to contribute so much to the information
and instruction of the people on the most important subjects
of religion, that one of the popes granted a pardon of one
thousand days to every person who resorted peaceably to the
plays performed in the Whitsun week at Chester, beginning
with the creation, and ending with the general judgment ;
and this indulgence was seconded by the bishop of the diocese, who granted forty days of pardon : the pope at the
same time denouncing the sentence of damnation on all
these incorrigible sinners who presumed to interrupt the due
celebration of these pious sports. It is certain that they
had their use, not only in teaching the great truths of
scripture to men who could not read the Bible, but in abo-
lishing the barbarous attachment to military games, and the
bloody contentions of the tournament, which had so long
prevailed as the sole species of popular amusement. Rude
and even ridiculous as they were, they softened the manners
of the people, by diverting the public attention to spectacles
in which the mind was concerned, and by creating a regard
for other arts than those of bodily strength and savage
valour."

I may add, that these representations were so far from
being considered as indecent or profane, that even a supreme
pontiff, Pope Pius the Second, about the year 1416, composed and caused to be acted before him on Corpus Christi
day, a Mystery, in which was represented the *court of the
king of heaven.*

These religious dramas were usually represented on holy
festivals in or near churches. " In several of our old scriptural plays," says Mr. Warton, " we see some of the
scenes directed to be represented *cum cantu et organis*, a
common rubrick in a missal. That is, because they were
performed in a church where the choir assisted. There is a
curious passage in Lambarde's *Topographical Dictionary,*
written about the year 1570, much to our purpose, which I
am therefore tempted to transcribe. ' In the dayes of cere-
monial religion, they used at Wytney (in Oxfordshire) to
set fourthe yearly in maner of a shew or interlude, the resurrection of our Lord, &c. For the which purposes, and the
more lyvely hereby to exhibite to the eye the hole action of
the resurrection, the priestes garnished out certain small

puppettes, representing the persons of Christ, the Watch-man, Marie, and others ; amongest the which, one bore the parte of a waking watchman, who espiinge Christe to arrise, made a continuall noyce, like to the sound that is caused· by the metynge of two stickes, and was therefore commonly called *Jack Snacker of Wytney*. The like toye I myself, beinge then a childe, once saw in Powles Church, at London, at a feast of Whitsuntyde ; wheare the comynge downe of the Holy Ghost was set forthe by a white pigeon, that was let to fly out of a hole that yet is to be sene in the mydst of the roofe of the great ile, and by a longe censer which descend-inge out of the same place almost to the verie grounde, was swinged up and downe at such a lengthe, that it reached with thone sweepe, almost to the west-gate of the churche, and with the other to the quyre staires of the same ; breathinge out over the whole churche and companie a most pleasant perfume of such swete thinges as burned therein. With the like doome-shews they used everie where to furnish sondrye parts of theire church service, as by their spectacles of the na-tivitie, passion, and ascension," &c.

In a preceding passage Mr. Warton has mentioned that the singing boys of Hyde Abbey and St. Swithin's Priory at Winchester, performed a Mystery before King Henry the Seventh in 1487 ; adding, that this is the only instance he has met with of choir-boys performing in Mysteries ; but it appears from the accompts of various monasteries that this was a very ancient practice, probably coeval with the earliest attempts at dramatick representations. In the year 1378, the scholars, or choristers of Saint Paul's cathedral, presented a petition to King Richard the Second, praying his Majesty to prohibit some ignorant and unexperienced persons from act-ing the HISTORY OF THE OLD TESTAMENT, to the great pre-judice of the clergy of the church, who had expended consi-derable sums for a publick presentation of that play at the ensuing Christmas. About twelve years afterwards, the Pa-rish Clerks of London, as Stowe informs us, performed spiri-tual plays at Skinner's Well for three days successively, in the presence of the King, Queen, and nobles of the realm. And in 1409, the tenth year of King Henry IV. they acted at Clerkenwell for eight days successively a play, which " was matter from the creation of the world," and probably con-cluded with the day of judgment, in the presence of most of the nobility and gentry of England. -

We are indebted to Mr. Warton for some curious circum-stances relative to these Miracle-plays, which " appear in a roll of the Churchwardens of Bassingborne, in Cambridge-shire, which is an accompt of the expences and receptions for acting the play of SAINT GEORGE at Bassingborne, on the feast of Saint Margaret, in the year 1511. They collected upwards of four pounds in twenty-seven neighbouring parishes for furnishing the play. They disbursed about two pounds in the representation. These disbursements are to four minstrels, or waits, of Cambridge, for three days, vs. vjd. To the players, in bread and ale, iijs. ijd. To the *garnement-man* for *garnements* and *propyrts*, that is, for dresses, decorations, and implements, and for play-books, xxs. To John Hobard, *brotherhoode preeste*, that is, a priest of the guild in the church, for the *play book*, ijs. viiid. For the *crofte*, or field in which the play was exhibited, js. For *propyrte-making*, or furniture, js. ivd. For fish and bread, and to setting up the stages, ivd. For painting three *fanchoms* and four *tormenters*, words which I do not understand, but perhaps *fantoms* and devils - - - -. The rest was expended for a feast on the occasion, in which are recited ' Four chicken for the gentilmen, ivd.' It appears by the manuscript of the Coventry plays, that a temporary scaffold only was erected for these performances."

In the ancient religious plays the Devil was very frequently introduced. He was usually represented with horns, a very wide mouth, (by means of a mask,) staring eyes, a large nose, a red beard, cloven feet, and a tail. His constant attendant was the Vice, (the buffoon of the piece,) whose principal employment was to belabour the ·Devil with his wooden dagger, and to make him roar for the entertainment of the populace.

As the *Mysteries* or *Miracle-plays* " frequently required the introduction of allegorical characters, such as Charity, Sin, Death, Hope, Faith, or the like, and as the common poetry of the times, especially among the French, began to deal much in allegory, at length plays were formed entirely consisting of such personifications. These were called MORALITIES. The *Miracle-plays* or MYSTERIES were totally destitute of invention and plan : they tamely represented stories, according to the letter of the scripture, or the respective legend. But the MORALITIES indicate dawnings of the dramatick art : they contain some rudiments of a plot, and even attempt to delineate characters, and to paint manners. From hence the gradual transition to real historical personages was natural and obvious."

Dr. Percy, in his Account of the English Stage, has

D 2

given an Analysis of two ancient Moralities, entitled *Every Man*, and *Lusty Juventus*, from which a perfect notion of this kind of drama may be obtained. *Every Man* was written in the reign of King Henry the Eighth, and *Lusty Juventus* in that of King Edward the Sixth. As Dr. Percy's curious and valuable collection of ancient English Poetry is in the hands of every scholar, I shall content myself with merely referring to it. Many other Moralities are yet extant, of some of which I shall give titles below.[a] Of one, which is not now extant, we have a curious account in a book entitled, *Mount Tabor, or Private Exercises of a Penitent Sinner, by* R. W. [R. Willis,] *Esqr. published in the year of his age 75, Anno Domini*, 1639; an extract from which will give the reader a more accurate notion of the old Moralities than a long dissertation on the subject.

"*Upon a stage-play which i saw when i was a child.*

"In the city of Gloucester the manner is, (as I think it is in other like corporations,) that when players of enterludes come to towne, they first attend the Mayor, to enforme him what noblemans servants they are, and so to get licence for their publike playing; and if the Mayor like the actors, or would shew respect to their lord and master, he appoints them to play their first play before himself, and the Alderman and Common-Counsell of the city; and that is called *the Mayor's play*: where every one that will, comes in without money, the Mayor giving the players a reward as hee thinks fit to shew respect unto them. At such a play, my father tooke me with him and made me stand between his leggs, as he sate upon one of the benches, where we saw and heard very well. The play was called *The Cradle of Security*, wherein was personated a king or some great prince, with his courtiers of several kinds, among which three ladies were in special grace with him; and they keeping him in delights

---

[a] *Magnificence*, written by John *Skelton*; *Impatient Poverty*, 1560; *The Life and Repentance of Marie Magdalene*, 1567; *The Trial of Treasure*, 1567; *The Nice Wanton*, 1568; *The Disobedient Child*, no date; *The Marriage of Wit and Science*, 1570; *The Interlude of Youth*, no date; *The longer thou livest, the more Fool thou art*, no date; *The interlude of Wealth and Health*, no date; *All for Money*, 1578; *The Conflict of Conscience*, 1581; *The Three Ladies of London*, 1584; *The Three Lords of London*, 1590; *Tom Tyler and his Wife*, &c.

and pleasures, drew him from his graver counsellors, hearing of sermons, and listening to good councell and admonitions, that in the end they got him to lye down in a cradle upon the stage, where these three ladies joyning in a sweet song, rocked him asleepe, that he snorted againe; and in the mean time closely conveyed under the cloaths wherewithall he was covered, a vizard, like a swines snout, upon his face, with three wire chains fastened thereunto, the other end whereof being holden severally by those three ladies; who fall to singing againe, and then discovered his face that the spectators might see how they had transformed him, going on with their singing. Whilst all this was acting, there came forth of another doore at the farthest end of the stage, two old men; the one in blew, with a serjeant at armes his mace on his shoulder; the other in red, with a drawn sword in his hand, and leaning with the other hand upon the others shoulder; and so they went along with a soft pace round about by the skirt of the stage, till at last they came to the cradle, when all the court was in the greatest jollity; and then the foremost old man with his mace stroke a fearfull blow upon the cradle; wherewith all the courtiers, with the three ladies, and the vizard, all vanished; and the desolate prince starting up bare-faced, and finding himself thus sent for to judgement, made a lamentable complaint of his miserable case, and so was carried away by wicked spirits. This prince did personate in the Morall, the wicked of the world; the three ladies, Pride, Covetousness, and Luxury; the two old men, the end of the world, and the last judgement. This sight took such impression in me, that when I came towards mans estate, it was as fresh in my memory, as if I had seen it newly acted."

The writer of this book appears to have been born in the same year with our great poet (1564). Supposing him to have been seven or eight years old when he saw this interlude, the exhibition must have been in 1571 or 1572.

I am unable to ascertain when the first Morality appeared, but incline to think not sooner than the reign of King Edward the Fourth (1460). The publick pageants of the reign of King Henry the Sixth were uncommonly splendid; and being then first enlivened by the introduction of speaking allegorical personages properly and characteristically habited, they naturally led the way to those personifications by which Moralities were distinguished from the simpler religious dramas called Mysteries. We must not, however, suppose, that, after Moralities were introduced, Mysteries ceased to be exhibited. We have already seen that a Mystery was represented before King Henry the Seventh, at Winchester, in 1487. Sixteen years afterwards, on the first Sunday after the marriage of his daughter with King James of Scotland, a Morality was performed. In the early part of the reign of King Henry the Eighth, they were perhaps performed indiscriminately; but Mysteries were probably seldom represented after the statute 34 and 35 Henry VIII. c. 1, which was made, as the preamble informs us, with a view that the kingdom should be purged and cleansed of all *religious plays, interludes*, rhymes, ballads, and songs, which are equally *pestiferous* and *noysome* to the commonweal. At this time both Moralities and Mysteries were made the vehicle of religious controversy; Bale's *Comedy of the three Laws of Nature*, printed in 1538, (which in fact is a Mystery,) being a disguised satire against popery; as the Morality of *Lusty Juventus* was written expressly with the same view in the reign of King Edward the Sixth. In that of his successor Queen Mary, Mysteries were again revived, as appendages to the papistical worship. "In the year 1556," says Mr. Warton, "*a goodly stage-play* of the *Passion of Christ* was presented at the Grey-friars in London, on Corpus-Christi day, before the Lord-Mayor, the Privy-council, and many great estates of the realm. Strype also mentions, under the year 1577, a stage-play at the Grey-friars, of the Passion of Christ, on the day that war was proclaimed in London against France, and in honour of that occasion. On Saint Olave's day in the same year, the holiday of the church in Silver-street, which is dedicated to that saint, was kept with great solemnity. At eight of the clock at night, began a stage-play of *goodly matter*, being the miraculous history of the life of that saint, which continued four hours, and concluded with many religious songs." No Mysteries, I believe, were represented during the reign of Elizabeth, except such as were occasionally performed by those who were favourers of the popish religion, and those already mentioned, known by the name of the Chester Mysteries, which had been originally composed in 1328, were revived in the time of King Henry the Eighth, (1533,) and again performed at Chester in the year 1600. The last Mystery, I believe, ever represented in England, was that of *Christ's Passion*, in the reign of King James the First, which Prynne tells us was " performed at Elie-House in Holborne, when Gundomar lay there, on Good-friday at night, at which there were thousands present."

In France the representation of Mysteries was forbid in the year 1548, when the fraternity associated under the name of *The Actors of our Saviour's Passion*, who had received letters patent from King Charles the Sixth, in 1402, and had for near 150 years exhibited religious plays, built their new theatre on the site of the Duke of Burgundy's house; and were authorised by an arret of parliament to act, on condition that " they should meddle with none but profane subjects, such as are lawful and honest, and not represent any sacred Mysteries." Representations founded on holy writ continued to be exhibited in Italy till the year 1660, and the Mystery of *Christ's Passion* was represented at Vienna so lately as the early part of the present century.

Having thus occasionally mentioned foreign theatres, I take this opportunity to observe, that the stages of France so lately as in the beginning of Queen Elizabeth's reign were entirely unfurnished with scenery or any kind of decoration, and that the performers at that time remained on the stage the whole time of the exhibition; in which mode perhaps our Mysteries in England were represented. For this information we are indebted to the elder Scaliger, in whose *Poeticks* is the following curious passage: " At present in France [about the year 1556] plays are represented in such a manner, that nothing is withdrawn from the view of the spectator. The whole apparatus of the theatre consists of some high seats ranged in proper order. The persons of the scene never depart during the representation: he who ceases to speak, is considered as if he were no longer on the stage. But in truth it is extremely ridiculous, that the spectator should see the actor listening, and yet he himself should not hear what one of his fellow-actors says concerning him, though in his own presence and within his hearing: as if he were absent, while he is present. It is the great object of the dramatick poet to keep the mind in a constant state of suspence and expectation. But in our theatres, there can be no novelty, no surprise: insomuch that the spectator is more likely to be satiated with what he has already seen, than to have any appetite for what is to come. Upon this ground it was, that Euripides objected to Æschylus, in The Frogs of Aristophanes, for having introduced Niobe and Achilles as mutes upon the scene, with a covering which entirely concealed their heads from the spectators."

Another practice, equally extraordinary, is mentioned by Bulenger in his treatise on the Grecian and Roman theatres. In his time, so late as in the year 1600, all the actors em-

12

ployed in a dramatick piece came on the stage in a troop, before the play began, and presented themselves to the spectators, in order, says he, to raise the expectation of the audience. I know not whether this was ever practised in England. Instead of raising, it should seem more likely to repress, expectation. I suppose, however, this writer conceived the audience would be animated by the *number* of the characters, and that this display would operate on the gaping spectators like some of our modern enormous play-bills; in which the length of the show sometimes constitutes the principal merit of the entertainment.

Mr. Warton observes that Moralities were become so fashionable a spectacle about the close of the reign of Henry the Seventh, that " John Rastall, a learned typographer, brother-in-law to Sir Thomas More, extended its province, which had been hitherto confined either to moral allegory, or to religion blended with buffoonery, and conceived a design of making it the vehicle of science and philosophy. With this view he published *A new* INTERLUDE *and a mery, of the nature of the iiij Elements, declaring many proper points of philosophy naturall, and dyvers straunge landys, &c.* In the cosmographical part of the play, in which the poet professes to treat of *dyvers straunge landys, and of the new-found landys,* the tracts of America recently discovered, and the manners of the natives are described. The characters are, a Messenger, who speaks the prologue, Nature, Humanity, Studious Desire, Sensual Appetite, a Taverner, Experience, and Ignorance."

As it is uncertain at what period of time the ancient Mysteries ceased to be represented as an ordinary spectacle for the amusement of the people, and Moralities were substituted in their room, it is equally difficult to ascertain the precise time when the latter gave way to a more legitimate theatrical exhibition. We know that Moralities were exhibited *occasionally* during the whole of the reign of Queen Elizabeth, and even in that of her successor, long after regular dramas had been presented on the scene; but I suspect that about the year 1570 (the 13th year of Queen Elizabeth) this species of drama began to lose much of its attraction, and gave way to something that had more the appearance of comedy and tragedy. *Gammer Gurton's Needle,* which was written by Mr. Still, (afterwards Bishop of Bath and Wells,) in the 23d year of his age, and acted at Christ's College, Cambridge, in 1566, is pointed out by the ingenious writer of the tract entitled *Historia Histrionica,* as the first piece

" that looks like a regular comedy ;" that is, the first play that was neither Mystery nor Morality, and in which some humour and discrimination of character may be found. In 1561-2, Thomas Sackville, Lord Buckhurst, and Thomas Norton, joined in writing the tragedy of *Ferrex and Porrex*, which was exhibited on the 18th of January in that year, by the Students of the Inner Temple, before Queen Elizabeth, at Whitehall. Neither of these pieces appears to have been acted on a publick theatre, nor was there at that time any building in London constructed solely for the purpose of representing plays. Of the latter piece, which, as Mr. Warton has observed, is perhaps " the first specimen in our language of an heroick tale written in verse, and divided into acts and scenes, and cloathed in all the formalities of a regular tragedy," a correct analysis may be found in THE HISTORY OF ENGLISH POETRY, and the play itself within these few years has been accurately reprinted.

It has been justly remarked by the same judicious writer, that the early practice of performing plays in schools and universities greatly contributed to the improvement of our drama. " While the people were amused with Skelton's *Trial of Simony*, Bale's *God's Promises, and Christ's Descent into Hell*, the scholars of the times were composing and acting plays on historical subjects, and in imitation of Plautus and Terence. Hence ideas of legitimate fable must have been imperceptibly derived to the popular and vernacular drama."

In confirmation of what has been suggested, it may be observed, that the principal dramatick writers, before Shakspeare appeared, were scholars. Greene, Lodge, Peele, Marlowe, Nashe, Lily, and Kyd, had all a regular university education. From whatever cause it may have arisen, the dramatick poetry about this period certainly assumed a better, though still an exceptionable, form. The example which had been furnished by Sackville, was quickly followed, and a great number of tragedies and historical plays was produced between the years 1570 and 1590 ; some of which are still extant, though by far the greater part is lost. This, I apprehend, was the great era of those bloody and bombastick pieces, which afforded subsequent writers perpetual topicks of ridicule : and during the same period were exhibited many *Histories*, or historical dramas, formed on our English Chronicles, and representing a series of events simply in the order of time in which they happened. Some have supposed that Shakspeare was the first dramatick poet

9

that introduced this species of drama ; but this is an undoubted error. I have elsewhere observed that every one of the
subjects on which he constructed his historical plays, appears
to have been dramatized, and brought upon the scene, before
his time. The historical drama is by an elegant modern writer supposed to have owed its rise to the publication of *The
Mirrour for Magistrates*, in which many of the most distinguished characters in English history are introduced, giving a
poetical narrative of their own misfortunes. Of this book
three editions, with various alterations and improvements,
were printed between 1563 and 1587.

At length (about the year 1591) the great luminary of the
dramatick world blazed out, and our poet produced those
plays which have now for two hundred years been the boast
and admiration of his countrymen.

Our earliest dramas, as we have seen, were represented in
churches or near them by ecclesiasticks : but at a very early
period, I believe, we had regular and established players,
who obtained a livelihood by their art. So early as in the
year 1378, as has been already noticed, the singing-boys of
St. Paul's represented to the King, that they had been at a
considerable expence in preparing a stage representation at
Christmas. These, however, cannot properly be called comedians, nor am I able to point out the time when the
profession of a player became common and established. It
has been supposed that the license granted by Queen Elizabeth to James Burbage and others, in 1574, was the first
regular license ever granted to comedians in England ; but
this is a mistake, for Heywood informs us that similar li-
censes had been granted by her father King Henry the
Eighth, King Edward the Sixth, and Queen Mary. Stowe
records, that " when King Edward the Fourth would shew
himself in state to the view of the people, he repaired to his
palace at St. John's, where he was accustomed to see the
*City Actors.*" In two books in the Remembrancer's office
in the Exchequer, containing an account of the daily expences
of King Henry the Seventh, are many articles ; from which it
appears, that at that time players, both French and English,
made a part of the appendages of the court, and were supported by regal establishment.

And it appears that there was then not only a regular
troop of players in London, but also a royal company. The
intimate knowledge of the French language and manners
which Henry must have acquired during his long sojourn in

foreign courts, (from 1471 to 1485,) accounts for the article relative to the company of French players.

In a manuscript in the Cottonian Library in the Museum, a narrative is given of the shews and ceremonies exhibited at Christmas in the fifth year of this king's reign, 1490 : " This Cristmass I saw no disgysyngs, and but *right few plays*; but ther was an abbot of mis-rule, that made muche sport, and did right well his office.—On Candell Mass day, the king, the the qwen, my ladye the king's moder, with the substance of al the lordes temporell present at the parlement, &c. wenten a procession from the chapell into the hall, and soo into Westmynster Hall :—The kynge was that daye in a riche gowne of purple, pirled withe gold, furred wythe sabuls :—At nyght the king, the qwene, and my ladye the kyngs moder, came into the Whit hall, and ther had *a pley.*"—On New-yeeres day at nyght, (says the same writer, speaking of the year 1488,) ther was a goodly disgysyng, and also this Crist-mass ther wer *many and dyvers playes.*"

A proclamation which was issued out in the year 1547 by King Edward the Sixth, to prohibit for about two months the exhibition of " any kind of interlude, play, dialogue, or other matter set forth in the form of a play, in the English tongue," describes plays as a familiar entertainment, both in London and in the country, and the profession of an actor as common and established. " For as much as great number of those that be *common players of interludes and playes*, as well within the city of London as elsewhere within the realme, doe for the most part play such interludes as contain matter tending to sedition," &c. By *common* players of interludes here mentioned, I apprehend, were meant the players of the city, as contradistinguished from the king's own servants. In a manuscript which I saw some years ago, and which is now in the library of the Marquis of Lansdown, are sundry charges for the players belonging to King Edward the Sixth ; but I have not preserved the articles. And in the house-hold book of Queen Mary, in the Library of the Antiquarian Society, is an entry which shows that she also had a theatrical establishment : " Eight players of interludes, each 66s. 8d.—26l. 13s. 4d.

It has already been mentioned that originally plays were performed in churches. Though Bonner Bishop of London issued a proclamation to the clergy of his diocese in 1542, prohibiting " all manner of common plays, games, or in-terludes, to be played, set forth, or declared within their churches, chappels," &c. the practice seems to have been continued occasionally during the reign of Queen Elizabeth; for the author of *The Third Blast of Retrait from Plays and Players* complains, in 1580, that " the players are permitted to publish their mammetrie in every temple of God, and that throughout England;" &c. and this abuse is taken notice of in one of the Canons of King James the First, given soon after his accession in the year 1603. Early, however, in Queen Elizabeth's reign, the established players of London began to act in temporary theatres constructed in the yards of inns; and about the year 1570, I imagine, one or two regular playhouses were erected. Both the theatre in Blackfriars and that in Whitefriars were certainly built before 1580; for we learn from a puritanical pamphlet published in the last century, that soon after that year, " many goodly citizens and well disposed gentlemen of London, considering that playhouses and dicing-houses were traps for young gentlemen, and others, and perceiving that many inconveniencies and great damage would ensue upon the long suffering of the same,—acquainted some pious magistrates therewith,—who thereupon made humble suite to Queene Elizabeth and her privy-councell, and obtained leave from her majesty to thrust the players out of the citty, and to pull down all playhouses and dicing-houses within their liberties; which accordingly was effected, and the playhouses in Gracious-street, Bishopsgate-street, that nigh Paul's, that on Ludgate-hill, and the White-friers, were quite pulled down and suppressed by the care of these religious senators." The theatre in Blackfriars, not being within the liberties of the city of London, escaped the fury of these fanaticks. Elizabeth, however, though she yielded in this instance to the frenzy of the time, was during the whole course of her reign a favourer of the stage, and a frequent attendant upon plays. So early as in the year 1569, as we learn from another puritanical writer, the children of her chapel, (who are described as " her majesty's unfledged minions,") " flaunted it in their silkes and sattens," and acted plays on profane subjects in the chapel-royal. In 1574 she granted a licence to James Burbage, probably the father of the celebrated tragedian, and four others, servants to the Earl of Leicester, to exhibit all kinds of stage-plays, during pleasure, in any part of England, " as well for the recreation of her loving subjects, as for her own solace and pleasure when she should think good to see them;" and in the year 1583, soon after a furious attack had been made on the stage by the puritans, twelve of the principal comedians of that time, at the earnest request of Sir Francis Walsingham, were selected from the companies then subsisting, under the licence and protection of various noblemen, and were sworn her majesty's servants. Eight of them had an annual stipend of 3l. 6s. 8d. each. At that time there were eight companies of comedians, each of which performed twice or thrice a week.

King James the First appears to have patronized the stage with as much warmth as his predecessor. In 1599, while he was yet in Scotland, he solicited Queen Elizabeth (if we may believe a modern historian) to send a company of English comedians to Edinburgh; and very soon after his accession to the throne, granted a licence to the company at the Globe, which is found in Rymer's *Fœdera*.

---

HAVING now, as concisely as I could, traced the History of the English Stage, from its first rude state to the period of its maturity and greatest splendor, I shall endeavour to exhibit as accurate a delineation of the internal form and economy of our ancient theatres, as the distance at which we stand, and the obscurity of the subject, will permit.

The most ancient English playhouses of which I have found any account, are, the playhouse in *Blackfriars*, that in *Whitefriars*, the *Theatre*, of which I am unable to ascertain the situation, and *The Curtain*, in Shoreditch. The *Theatre*, from its name, was probably the first building erected in or near the metropolis purposely for scenick exhibitions.

In the time of Shakspeare there were seven principal theatres: three private houses, namely, that in *Blackfriars*, that in *Whitefriars*, and *The Cockpit* or *Phœnix*, in Drury Lane; and four that were called publick theatres; viz. *The Globe* on the Bankside, *The Curtain* in Shoreditch, *The Red Bull*, at the upper end of St. John's Street, and *The Fortune* in Whitecross Street. The last two were chiefly frequented by citizens. There were, however, but six companies of comedians; for the playhouse in Blackfriars, and the Globe, belonged to the same troop. Beside these seven theatres, there were for some time on the Bankside three other publick theatres; *The Swan, The Rose,* and *The Hope:* but *The Hope* being used chiefly as a bear-garden, and *The Swan* and *The Rose* having fallen to decay early in King James's reign, they ought not to be enumerated with the other regular theatres.

All the established theatres that were open in 1598, were either without the city of London or its liberties.

It appears from the office-book of Sir Henry Herbert, Master of the Revels to King James the First, and the two succeeding kings, that very soon after our poet's death, in the year 1622, there were but five principal companies of comedians in London; the King's Servants, who performed at the Globe and in Blackfriars; the Prince's Servants, who performed then at the Curtain; the Palsgrave's Servants, who had possession of the Fortune; the players of the Revels, who acted at the Red Bull; and the Lady Elizabeth's Servants, or, as they are sometimes denominated, the Queen of Bohemia's players, who performed at the Cockpit in Drury Lane.

When Prynne published his *Histriomastix*, (1633,) there were six playhouses open; the theatre in Blackfriars; the Globe; the Fortune; the Red Bull; the Cockpit or Phoenix, and a theatre in Salisbury Court, Whitefriars.

All the plays of Shakspeare appear to have been performed either at *The Globe*, or the theatre in *Blackfriars*. I shall therefore confine my inquiries principally to those two. They belonged, as I have already observed, to the same company of comedians, namely, his Majesty's servants, which title they obtained after a licence had been granted to them by King James in 1603; having before that time, I apprehend, been called the servants of the Lord Chamberlain. Like the other servants of the household, the performers enrolled into this company were sworn into office, and each of them was allowed four yards of bastard scarlet for a cloak, and a quarter of a yard of velvet for the cape, every second year.

The theatre in Blackfriars was situated near the present Apothecaries' Hall, in the neighbourhood of which there is yet *Playhouse Yard*, not far from which the theatre probably stood. It was, as has been mentioned, a private house; but what were the distinguishing marks of a private playhouse, it is not easy to ascertain. We know only that it was smaller than those which were called publick theatres; and that in the private theatres plays were usually presented by candle-light.

In this theatre, which was a very ancient one, the children of the Revels occasionally performed.

It is said in Camden's Annals of the reign of King James

the First, that the theatre in Blackfriars fell down in the year 1623, and that above eighty persons were killed by the accident; but he was misinformed. The room which gave way was in a private house, and appropriated to the service of religion.

I am unable to ascertain at what time the Globe theatre was built. Hentzner has alluded to it as existing in 1598, though he does not expressly mention it. I believe it was not built long before the year 1596. It was situated on the Bankside, (the southern side of the river Thames,) nearly opposite to Friday Street, Cheapside. It was an hexagonal wooden building, partly open to the weather, and partly thatched.[*] When Hentzner wrote, all the other theatres as well as this were composed of wood.

[*] In the long Antwerp View of London in the Pepysian Library at Cambridge, is a representation of the Globe theatre, from which a drawing was made by the Rev. Mr. Henley, and transmitted to Mr. Steevens. From that drawing this cut was made.

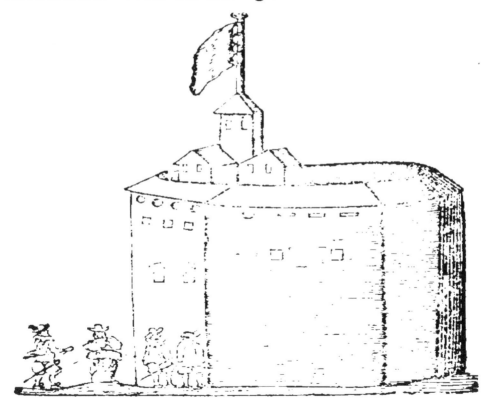

The Globe was a publick theatre, and of considerable size, and there they always acted by day-light. On the roof of this and the other publick theatres a pole was erected, to which a flag was affixed. These flags were probably displayed only during the hours of exhibition; and it should seem from one of the old comedies that they were taken down in Lent, in which time, during the early part of King James's reign, plays were not allowed to be represented, though at a subsequent period this prohibition was dispensed with.

I formerly conjectured that *The Globe*, though hexagonal at the outside, was perhaps a rotunda within, and that it might have derived its name from its circular form. But, though the part appropriated to the audience was probably circular, I now believe that the house was denominated only from its sign; which was a figure of Hercules supporting the Globe, under which was written, *Totus mundus agit histrionem.* This theatre was burnt down on the 29th of June, 1613; but it was rebuilt in the following year, and decorated with more ornament than had been originally bestowed upon it.

The exhibitions at *the Globe* seem to have been calculated chiefly for the lower class of people; those at *Blackfriars,* for a more select and judicious audience. This appears from the following prologue to Shirley's *Doubtful Heir,* which is inserted among his poems, printed in 1646, with this title:

" Prologue at *the* GLOBE, to his Comedy called *The Doubtful Heir,* which should have been presented at *the Blackfriars.*

    " Gentlemen, I am only sent to say,
    " Our author did not calculate his play
    " For *this* meridian. The *Bankside,* he knows,
    " Is far more skilful at the ebbs and flows
    " Of water than of wit; he did not mean
    " For the elevation of your poles, this scene.
    " No shows,—no dance,—and what you most delight in,
    " Grave understanders, here's no target-fighting
    " Upon the stage; all work for cutler's barr'd;
    " No bawdry, nor no ballads;—this goes hard;
    " But language clean, and, what affects you not,
    " Without impossibilities the plot;
    " No clown, no squibs, no devil in't.—Oh now,
    " You squirrels that want nuts, what will you do?
    " Pray do not crack the benches, and we may
    " Hereafter fit your palates with a play.

" But you that can contract yourselves, and sit,
" As you were now in the *Blackfriars* pit,
" And will not deaf us with lewd noise and tongues,
" Because we have no heart to break our lungs,
" Will pardon our *vast* stage, and not disgrace
" This play, meant for your persons, not the place."

The superior discernment of the *Blackfriars* audience may be likewise collected from a passage in the preface prefixed by Hemings and Condell to the first folio edition of our author's works : " And though you be *a magistrate of wit*, and sit on the stage at *Blackfriers*, or the Cockpit, to arraigne plays dailie, know these plays have had their trial already, and stood out all appeales."

A writer already quoted informs us that one of these theatres was a winter, and the other a summer, house. As *the Globe* was partly exposed to the weather, and they acted there usually by day-light, it appeared to me probable (when this Essay was originally published) that this was the summer theatre ; and I have lately found my conjecture confirmed by Sir Henry Herbert's Manuscript. The king's company usually began to play at the Globe in the month of May. The exhibitions here seem to have been more frequent than at *Blackfriars*, till the year 1604, or 1605, when the *Bankside* appears to have become less fashionable, and less frequented than it formerly had been.

Many of our ancient dramatick pieces (as has been already observed) were performed in the yards of carriers' inns, in which, in the beginning of Queen Elizabeth's reign, the comedians, who then first united themselves in companies, erected an occasional stage. The form of these temporary playhouses seems to be preserved in our modern theatre. The galleries, in both, are ranged over each other on three sides of the building. The small rooms under the lowest of these galleries answer to our present boxes; and it is observable that these, even in theatres which were built in a subsequent period expressly for dramatick exhibitions, still retained their old name, and are frequently called *rooms*, by our ancient writers. The yard bears a sufficient resemblance to the pit, as at present in use. We may suppose the stage to have been raised in this area, on the fourth side, with its back to the gateway of the inn, at which the money for admission was taken. Thus, in fine weather, a playhouse not incommodious might have been formed.

Hence, in the middle of *the Globe*, and I suppose of the

other *publick* theatres, in the time of Shakspeare, there was an open yard or area, where the common people stood to see the exhibition: from which circumstance they are called by our author *groundlings*, and by Ben Jonson " the *understanding* gentlemen of the *ground*."

The galleries, or *scaffolds*, as they are sometimes called, and that part of the house which in private theatres was named the pit, seem to have been at the same price; and probably in houses of reputation, such as *the Globe*, and that in *Blackfriars*, the price of admission into those parts of the theatre was sixpence, while in some meaner play-houses it was only a penny, in others twopence. The price of admission into the best *rooms* or boxes, was, I believe, in our author's time, a shilling; though afterwards it appears to have risen to two shillings, and half a crown. At the Blackfriars theatre the price of the boxes was, I imagine, higher than at the Globe.

From several passages in our old plays we learn, that spectators were admitted on the stage, and that the criticks and wits of the time usually sat there. Some were placed on the ground; others sat on stools, of which the price was either sixpence, or a shilling, according, I suppose, to the commodiousness of the situation. And they were attended by pages, who furnished them with pipes and tobacco, which was smoked here as well as in other parts of the house. Yet it should seem that persons were suffered to sit on the stage only in the private playhouses, (such as *Blackfriars*, &c.) where the audience was more select, and of a higher class; and that in *the Globe* and the other publick theatres, no such licence was permitted.

The stage was strewed with rushes, which, we learn from Hentzner and Caius de Ephemera, was in the time of Shak-speare the usual covering of floors in England. On some occasions it was entirely matted over; but this was probably very rare. The curtain which hangs in the front of the present stage, drawn up by lines and pullies, though not a modern invention, (for it was used by Inigo Jones in the masques at court,) was yet an apparatus to which the simple mechanism of our ancient theatres had not arrived; for in them the curtains opened in the middle, and were drawn backwards and forwards on an iron rod. In some play-houses they were woollen, in others, made of silk. Towards the rear of the stage there appears to have been a balcony, or upper stage; the platform of which was probably eight or nine feet from the ground. I suppose it to have been supported by pillars. From hence, in many of our old plays, part of the dialogue was spoken; and in the front of it curtains likewise were hung, so as occasionally to conceal the persons in it from the view of the audience. At each side of this balcony was a box, very inconveniently situated which sometimes was called the *private box*. In these boxes, which were at a lower price, some persons sate, either from economy or singularity.

How little the imaginations of the audience were assisted by scenical deception, and how much necessity our author had to call on them to " piece out imperfections with their thoughts," may be collected from Sir Philip Sidney, who, describing the state of the drama and the stage, in his time, (about the year 1583,) says, " Now you shall have three ladies walk to gather flowers, and then we must beleeve the stage to be a garden. By and by we heare news of shipwrack in the same place; then we are to blame, if we accept it not for a rock. Upon the back of that, comes out a hidious monster with fire and smoke; and then the miserable beholders are bound to take it for a cave; while in the mean time two armies fly in, represented with four swords and bucklers, and then what hard hart wil not receive it for a pitched field."

The first notice that I have found of any thing like moveable scenes being used in England, is in the narrative of the entertainment given to King James at Oxford, in August, 1605, when three plays were performed in the hall of Christ Church, of which we have the following account by a contemporary writer. " The stage" (he tells us) " was built close to the upper end of the hall, as it seemed at the first sight; but indeed it was but a false wall faire painted, and adorned with stately pillars, which pillars would turn about; by reason whereof, with the help of other *painted clothes*, their stage did vary three times in the acting of one tragedy:" that is, in other words, there were three scenes employed in the exhibition of the piece. The scenery was contrived by Inigo Jones, who is described as *a great traveller*, and who undertook to " further his employers much, and furnish them with rare devices, but produced very little to that which was expected."

It is observable, that the writer of this account was not acquainted even with the term, *scene*, having used *painted clothes* instead of it; nor indeed is this surprising, it not be-

E 2

ing then found in this sense in any dictionary or vocabulary, English or foreign, that I have met with. Had the common stages been furnished with them, neither this writer, nor the makers of dictionaries, could have been ignorant of it. To effect even what was done at Christ-Church, the University found it necessary to employ two of the king's carpenters, and to have the advice of the controller of his works. The Queen's Masque, which was exhibited in the preceding January, was not much more successful, though above 3000l. was expended upon it. " At night," says Sir Dudley Carleton, " we had the Queen's Maske in the Banqueting-house, or rather her Pageant. There was a great engine at the lower end of the room, which had motion, and in it were the images of sea-horses, (with other terrible fishes,) which were ridden by the Moors. The indecorum was, that there was all fish and no water. At the further end was a great shell in form of a skallop, wherein were four seats ; on the lowest sat the queen with my lady Bedford ; on the rest were placed the ladies Suffolk, Darby," &c. Such were most of the Masques in the time of James the First : triumphal cars, castles, rocks, caves, pillars, temples, clouds, rivers, tritons, &c. composed the principal part of their decoration. In the courtly masques given by his successor during the first fifteen years of his reign, and in some of the plays exhibited at court, the art of scenery seems to have been somewhat improved. In 1636 a piece written by Thomas Heywood, called *Love's Mistress or the Queen's Masque*, was represented at Denmark House before their Majesties. " For the rare decorements" (says Heywood in his preface) " which new apparelled it, when it came the second time to the royal view, (her gracious majesty then entertaining his highness at *Denmark House* upon his birth-day,) I cannot pretermit to give a due character to that admirable artist Mr. Inigo Jones, master surveyor of the king's worke, &c. who to *every act*, nay *almost* to every *scene*, by his excellent inventions gave such an extraordinary lustre ; upon every occasion *changing the stage*, to the admiration of all the spectators." Here, as on a former occasion, we may remark, the term *scene* is not used : the *stage was changed*, to the admiration of all the spectators.

In August, 1636, *The Royal Slave*, written by a very popular poet, William Cartwright, was acted at Oxford before the king and queen, and afterwards at Hampton-Court. Wood informs us, that the scenery was an exquisite and uncommon piece of machinery, contrived by Inigo Jones. The play was printed in 1639; and yet even at that late period, the term *scene*, in the sense now affixed to it, was unknown to the author; for describing the various scenes employed in this court-exhibition, he denominates them thus: " The first *Appearance*, a temple of the sun.—Second *Appearance*, a city in the front, and a prison at the side," &c. The three other *Appearances* in this play were, a wood, a palace, and a castle.

In every disquisition of this kind much trouble and many words might be saved, by defining the subject of dispute. Before therefore I proceed further in this inquiry, I think it proper to say, that by a *scene*, I mean, *A* painting *in* perspective *on a cloth fastened to a wooden frame or roller*; and that I do *not* mean by this term, " a coffin, or a tomb, or a gilt chair, or a fair chain of pearl, or a crucifix;" and I am the rather induced to make this declaration, because a writer, who obliquely alluded to the position which I am now maintaining, soon after the first edition of this Essay was published, has mentioned exhibitions of this kind as a proof of the *scenery* of our old plays; and taking it for granted that the point is completely established by this *decisive* argument, triumphantly adds, " Let us for the future no more be told of the want of proper *scenes* and dresses in our ancient theatres."

A passage which has been produced from one of the old comedies, proves that the common theatres were furnished with some rude pieces of *machinery*, which were used when it was necessary to exhibit the descent of some god or saint; but it is manifest from what has been already stated, as well as from all the contemporary accounts, that the mechanism of our ancient theatres seldom went beyond a tomb, a painted chair, a sinking cauldron, or a trap-door, and that none of them had moveable scenes. When King Henry VIII. is to be discovered by the Dukes of Suffolk and Norfolk, reading in his study, the scenical direction in the first folio, 1623, (which was printed apparently from playhouse copies,) is, " *The King draws the curtain*, [i. e. draws it open] *and sits reading pensively*;" for, beside the principal curtains that hung in the front of the stage, they used others as substitutes for scenes, which were denominated *traverses*. If a bedchamber is to be represented, no change of scene is mentioned; but the property-man is simply ordered *to thrust forth a bed*, or, the curtains being opened, a bed is exhibited.

So, in the old play on which Shakspeare formed his *King Henry VI. P. II.* when Cardinal Beaufort is exhibited dying, the stage-direction is—" Enter King and Salisbury, and then *the curtaines be drawn*, [i. e. drawn open,] and the Cardinal is·discovered in his bed, raving and staring as if he were mad." When the fable requires the Roman capitol to be represented, we find two officers enter, " to lay cushions, *as it were* in the capitol." So, in *King Richard II.* Act IV. sc. 1; " Bolingbroke, &c. enter *as* to the parliament." Again, in *Sir John Oldcastle*, 1600; " Enter Cambridge, Scroop, and Gray, *as* in a chamber." When the citizens of Angiers are to appear on the walls of their town, and young Arthur to leap from the battlements, I suppose our ancestors were contented with seeing them in the balcony already described; or perhaps a few boards were tacked together, and painted so as to resemble the rude discoloured walls of an old town, behind which a platform might have been placed near the top, on which the citizens stood : but surely this can scarcely be called a *scene*. Though undoubtedly our poet's company were furnished with some wooden fabrick sufficiently resembling a tomb, for which they must have had occasion in several plays, yet some doubt may be entertained, whether in *Romeo and Juliet* any exhibition of Juliet's monument was given on the stage. Romeo perhaps only opened with his mattock one of the stage trap=doors, (which might have represented a tomb-stone,) by which he descended to a vault beneath the stage, where Juliet was deposited; and this notion is countenanced by a passage in the play, and by the poem on which the drama was founded.

In all the old copies of the play last-mentioned we find the following stage-direction : " *They march about the stage, and serving-men come forth with their napkins.*" A more decisive proof than this, that the stage was not furnished with scenes, cannot be produced. Romeo, Mercutio, &c. with their torch-bearers and attendants, are the persons who march about the stage. They are in the street, on their way to Capulet's house, where a masquerade is given; but Capulet's servants who come forth with their napkins, are supposed to be in a hall or saloon of their master's house : yet both the masquers *without* and the servants *within* appear on the same spot. In like manner in *King Henry VIII.* the very same spot is at once the outside and inside of the Council-Chamber.

It is not, however, necessary to insist either upon the

term itself, in the sense of a painting in perspective on cloth or canvas, being unknown to our early writers, or upon the various stage-directions which are found in the plays of our poet and his contemporaries, and which afford the strongest presumptive evidence that the stage in his time was not furnished with scenes: because we have to the same point the concurrent testimony of Shakspeare himself, of Ben Jonson, of every writer of the last age who has had occasion to mention this subject, and even of the very person who first introduced scenes on the publick stage.

In the year 1629 Jonson's comedy intitled *The New Inn* was performed at the Blackfriars theatre, and deservedly damned. Ben was so much incensed at the town for condemning his piece, that in 1631 he published it with the following title: " *The New Inne, or the light Heart,* a comedy ; as it was never acted, but most negligently played, by some, the kings servants, and more squeamishly beheld and censured by others, the kings subjects, 1629 : And how at last set at liberty to the readers, his Ma.<sup>ties</sup> servants and subjects, to be judged, 1631." In the Dedication to this piece, the author, after expressing his profound contempt for the spectators, who were at the first representation of this play, says, " What did they come for then, thou wilt ask me. I will as punctually answer : to see and to be seene. To make a general muster of themselves in their clothes of credit, and possesse the stage against the playe : to dislike all, but marke nothing : and by their confidence of rising between the actes in oblique lines, make affidavit to the whole house of their not understanding one scene. Arm'd with this prejudice, as *the stage furniture or arras clothes,* they were there ; as spectators away ; for *the faces in the hangings* and they beheld alike."

The exhibition of plays being forbidden some time before the death of Charles I. Sir William D'Avenant in 1656 invented a new species of entertainment, which was exhibited at Rutland House, at the upper end of Aldersgate Street. The title of the piece, which was printed in the same year, is, *The Siege of Rhodes, made a Representation by the Art of prospective in Scenes; and the Story sung in recitative Musick.* " The original of this musick," says Dryden, " and of the *scenes* which adorned his work, he had from the Italian operas; but he heightened his characters (as I may probably imagine) from the examples of Corneille and some French poets." If sixty years before, the exhibition of the plays of Shakspeare had been aided on the common stage by the advantage of moveable scenes, or if the term *scene* had been familiar to D'Avenant's audience, can we suppose that he would have found it necessary to use a periphrastick description, and to promise that his representation should be assisted by *the art of prospective in scenes?* " It has been often wished," says he, in his Address to the Reader, " that our *scenes* (we having obliged ourselves to the variety of *five changes*, according to the ancient dramatick distinctions made for time,) had not been confined to about eleven feet in the height and about fifteen in depth, including the places of passage reserved for the musick." From these words we learn that he had in that piece five scenes. In 1658 he exhibited at the old theatre called the Cockpit in Drury Lane, *The Cruelty of the Spaniards in Peru, express'd by vocal and instrumental Musick, and by Art of* perspective *in* Scenes. In spring 1662, having obtained a patent from King Charles the Second, and built a new playhouse in Lincoln's Inn Fields, he opened his theatre with *The First Part of the Siege of Rhodes,* which since its first exhibition he had enlarged. He afterwards in the same year exhibited, *The Second Part of the Siege of Rhodes,* and his comedy called *The Wits;* " these plays," says Downes, who himself acted in *The Siege of Rhodes,* " having new *scenes* and decorations, being *the first* that ever were introduced in England." Scenes had certainly been used before in the masques at Court, and in a few private exhibitions, and by D'Avenant himself in his attempts at theatrical entertainments shortly before the death of Cromwell: Downes, therefore, who is extremely inaccurate in his language in every part of his book, must have meant—the first ever exhibited in a *regular drama, on a public theatre.*

I have said that I could produce the testimony of Sir William D'Avenant himself on this subject. His prologue to *The Wits,* which was exhibited in the spring of the year 1662, soon after the opening of his theatre in Lincoln's Inn Fields, if every other document had perished, would prove decisively that our author's play had not the assistance of painted scenes. " There are some," says D'Avenant,

" —— who would the world persuade,
" That gold is better when the stamp is bad;
" And that an *ugly ragged* piece of eight
" Is ever true in metal and in weight;
" As if a guinny and louís had less
" Intrinsick value for their handsomeness.

" So diverse, who outlive the former age,
" Allow the coarseness of the *plain old stage*,
" And think rich vests and *scenes* are only fit
" Disguises for the want of art and wit."

And no less decisive is the different language of the licence for erecting a theatre, granted to him by King Charles I. in 1639, and the letters patent which he obtained from his son in 1662. In the former, after he is authorized " to entertain, govern, privilege, and keep such and so many players to exercise action, musical presentments, scenes, dancing, and the like, as he the said William Davenant shall think fit and approve for the said house, and such persons to permit and continue at and during the pleasure of the said W. D. to act plays in such house so to be by him erected, and exercise musick, musical presentments, scenes, dancing, or other the like, at the same or other hours, or times, or after plays are ended,"—the clause which empowers him to take certain prices from those who should resort to his theatre runs thus :

" And that it shall and may be lawful to and for the said W. D. &c. to take and receive of such our subjects as shall resort to see or hear any such *plays, scenes, and entertainments* whatsoever, such sum or sums of money, as is or hereafter from time to time shall be accustomed to be given or taken in other playhouses and places for the like plays, scenes, presentments, and entertainments."

Here we see that when the theatre was fitted up in the usual way of that time without the decoration of scenery, (for *scenes* in the foregoing passages mean, not paintings, but short stage-representations or presentments,) the usual prices were authorized to be taken : but after the Restoration, when Sir W. D'Avenant furnished his new theatre with scenery, he took care that the letters patent which he then obtained, should speak a different language, for there the corresponding clause is as follows :

" And that it shall and may be lawful to and for the said Sir William D'Avenant, his heirs, and assigns, to take and receive of such of our subjects as shall resort to see or hear any such plays, scenes, and entertainments whatsoever, such sum or sums of money, as either have accustomably been given and taken in the like kind, or as shall be thought reasonable by him or them, in regard of the great expences of SCENES, musick, and such new decorations *as have not been formerly used.*"

Here for the first time in these letters patent the word *scene* is used in that sense in which Sir William had employed it in the printed title-pages of his musical entertainments exhibited a few years before. In the former letters patent granted in 1639, the word in that sense does not once occur.

To the testimony of D'Avenant himself may be added that of Dryden, both in the passage already quoted, and in his prologue to *The Rival Ladies*, performed at the King's theatre in 1664 :

> " ――――― in former days
> " Good prologues were as scarce as now good plays—
> " You now have habits, dances, *scenes*, and rhymes ;
> " High language often, ay, and sense sometimes."

And still more express is that of the author of *The Generous Enemies*, exhibited at the King's Theatre in 1672 :

> " I cannot choose but laugh, when I look back and see
> " The strange vicissitudes of poetrie.
> " Your aged fathers came to plays for wit,
> " And sat knee-deep in nutshells in the pit :
> " *Coarse hangings then, instead of scenes were worn,*
> " *And Kidderminster did the stage adorn :*
> " But you, their wiser offspring, did advance
> " To plot of jig, and to dramatick dance," &c.

These are not the speculations of scholars concerning a custom of a former age, but the testimony of persons who were either spectators of what they describe, or daily conversed with those who had trod our ancient stage : for D'Avenant's first play, *The Cruel Brother*, was acted at the Blackfriars in January, 1626–7, and Mohun, and Hart, who had themselves acted before the civil wars, were employed in that company, by whose immediate successors *The Generous Enemies* was exhibited : I mean the King's Servants. Major Mohun acted in the piece before which the lines last quoted were spoken.

I may add also, that Mr. Wright, the author of *Historia Histrionica*, whose father had been a spectator of several plays before the breaking out of the civil wars, expressly says, that the theatre had *no scenes*.

But, says Mr. Steevens, (who differs with me in opinion on the subject before us,) " how happened it, that Shakspeare himself should have mentioned the act of *shifting*

12

scenes, if in his time there were no scenes capable of being shifted? Thus, in the Chorus to *King Henry V* :

'Unto Southampton do we *shift our scene.*'

" This phrase" (he adds) " was hardly more ancient than the custom it describes."

Who does not see, that Shakspeare in the passage here quoted uses the word *scene* in the same sense in which it was used two thousand years before he was born; that is, for the place of action represented by the stage; and not for that moveable hanging or painted cloth, strained on a wooden frame, or rolled round a cylinder, which is now called a SCENE? If the smallest doubt could be entertained of his meaning, the following lines in the same play would remove it:

" The king is set from London, and the *scene*
" Is now *transported* to Southampton."

This, and this only, was the *shifting* that was meant; a movement from one place to another in the progress of the drama; nor is there found a single passage in his plays in which the word *scene* is used in the sense required to support the argument of those who suppose that the common stages were furnished with moveable scenes in his time. He constantly uses the word either for a stage-exhibition in general, or the component part of a play, or the place of action represented by the stage:

" For all my life has been but as a *scene*
" Acting that argument."    *King Henry IV*. Part II.

" At your industrious *scenes* and acts of death."
                                        *King John.*

" What *scene* of death hath Roscius now to act ?"
                                *King Henry VI*. Part III.

" Thus with imagin'd wing our swift *scene* flies,——."
                                        *King Henry V.*

" To give our *scene* such growing,——."        *Ibid.*

" And so our *scene* must to the battle fly,——."    *Ibid.*

" That he might play the woman in the *scene*."
                                        *Coriolanus.*

" A queen in jest, only to fill the *scene*."
                                *King Richard III.*

I shall add but one more instance from *All's well that ends well:*

> " Our *scene* is alter'd from a serious thing,
> " And now *chang'd* to the Beggar and the King."

from which lines it might, I conceive, be as reasonably inferred that *scenes* were *changed* in Shakspeare's time, as from the passage relied on in *King Henry V.* and perhaps by the same mode of reasoning it might be proved, from a line above quoted from the same play, that the technical modern term, *wings,* or side-scenes, was not unknown to our great poet.

The various circumstances which I have stated, and the accounts of the contemporary writers, furnish us, in my apprehension, with decisive and incontrovertible proofs, that the stage of Shakspeare was not furnished with *moveable painted scenes,* but merely decorated with curtains, and arras or tapestry hangings, which, when decayed, appear to have been sometimes ornamented with pictures; and some passages in our old dramas incline me to think, that when tragedies were performed, the stage was hung with black.

In the early part, at least, of our author's acquaintance with the theatre, the want of scenery seems to have been supplied by the simple expedient of writing the names of the different places where the scene was laid in the progress of the play, which were disposed in such a manner as to be visible to the audience.

Though the apparatus for theatrick exhibitions was thus scanty, and the machinery of the simplest kind, the invention of trap-doors appears not to be modern; for in an old Morality, entitled, *All for Money,* we find a marginal direction, which implies that they were very early in use.

We learn from Heywood's *Apology for Actors,* that the covering, or internal roof, of the stage, was anciently termed *the heavens.* It was probably painted of a sky-blue colour; or perhaps pieces of drapery tinged with blue were suspended across the stage, to represent the heavens.

It appears from the stage-directions given in *The Spanish Tragedy,* that when a play was exhibited within a play, (if I may so express myself,) as is the case in that piece and in *Hamlet,* the court or audience before whom the interlude was performed sat in the balcony, or upper stage already described; and a curtain or traverse being hung across the stage *for the nonce,* the performers entered between that curtain and the general audience, and on its being drawn, began their piece, addressing themselves to the balcony, and regardless of the spectators in the theatre, to whom their backs must have been turned during the whole of the performance.

From a plate prefixed to Kirkman's *Drolls*, printed in 1672, in which there is a view of a theatrical booth, it should seem that the stage was formerly lighted by two large branches, of a form similar to those now hung in churches; and from Beaumont's Verses prefixed to Fletcher's *Faithful Shepherdess*, which was acted before the year 1611, we find that wax lights were used.

These branches having been found incommodious, as they obstructed the sight of the spectators, gave place at a subsequent period to small circular wooden frames, furnished with candles, eight of which were hung on the stage, four at either side; and these within a few years were wholly removed by Mr. Garrick, who, on his return from France in 1765, first introduced the present commodious method of illuminating the stage by lights not visible to the audience.

The body of the house was illuminated by cressets, or large open lanterns of nearly the same size with those which are fixed in the poop of a ship.

If all the players whose names are enumerated in the first folio edition of our author's works, belonged to the same theatre, they composed a numerous company; but it is doubtful whether they all performed at the same period, or always continued in the same house. Many of the companies, in the infancy of the stage, certainly were so thin, that the same person played two or three parts; and a battle on which the fate of an empire was supposed to depend, was decided by half a dozen combatants. It appears to have been a common practice in their mock engagements, to discharge small pieces of ordnance on or behind the stage.

Before the exhibition began, three flourishes were played, or, in the ancient language, there were three soundings. Musick was likewise played between the acts. The instruments chiefly used, were trumpets, cornets, hautboys, lutes, recorders, viols, and organs. The band, which, I believe, did not consist of more than eight or ten performers, sat (as I have been told by a very ancient stage-veteran, who had his information from Bowman, the contemporary of Betterton,) in an upper balcony, over what is now called the stage-box.

From Sir Henry Herbert's Manuscript I learn, that the

musicians belonging to Shakspeare's company were obliged to pay the Master of the Revels an annual fee for a licence to play in the theatre.

Not very long after our poet's death the Blackfriars' band was more numerous; and their reputation was so high as to be noticed by Sir Bulstrode Whitelocke, in an account which he has left of the splendid Masque given by the four Inns of Court on the second of February, 1633-4, entitled *The Triumph of Peace*, and intended, as he himself informs us, " to manifest the difference of their opinion from Mr. Prynne's new learning, and to confute his *Histriomastix* against interludes."

A very particular account of this masque is found in his *Memorials*; but that which Dr. Burney has lately given in his very curious and elegant *History of Musick*, from a manuscript in the possession of Dr. Moreton, of the British Museum, contains some minute particulars not noticed in the former printed account, and among others an eulogy on our poet's band of musicians.

" For the Musicke," says Whitelocke, " which was particularly committed to my charge, I gave to Mr. Ives, and to Mr. Lawes, 100l. a piece for their rewards; for the four French gentlemen, the queen's servants, I thought that a handsome and liberall gratifying of them would be made known to the queen, their mistris, and well taken by her. I therefore invited them one morning to a collation att St. Dunstan's taverne, in the great room, the Oracle of Apollo, where each of them had his plate lay'd by him, covered, and the napkin by it, and when they opened their plates, they found in each of them forty pieces of gould, of their master's coyne, for the first dish, and they had cause to be much pleased with this surprisall.

" The rest of the musitians had rewards answearable to their parts and qualities; and the whole charge of the musicke came to about one thousand pounds. The clothes of the horsemen reckoned one with another at £100 a suit, att the least, amounted to £10,000.—The charges of all the rest of the masque, which were borne by the societies, were accounted to be above twenty thousand pounds.

" I was so conversant with the musitians, and so willing to gain their favour, especially at this time, that I composed an aier my selfe, with the assistance of Mr. Ives, and called it *Whitelock's Coranto*; which being cried up, was first played publiquely by the Blackefryars Musicke, *who*

*were then esteemed the best of common musitians in London.*
Whenever I came to that house, (as I did sometimes in those
dayes, though not often,) to see a play, the musitians would
presently play *Whitelocke's Coranto:* and it was so often called
for, that they would have it played twice or thrice in an af-
ternoone. The queen hearing it, would not be persuaded that
it was made by an Englishman, bicause she said it was fuller
of life and spirit than the English aiers used to be; butt she
honoured the *Coranto* and the maker of it with her majestyes
royall commendation. It grew to that request, that all the
common musitians in this towne, and all over the kingdome,
gott the composition of itt, and played it publiquely in all
places for above thirtie years after."

The stage, in Shakspeare's time seems to have been sepa-
rated from the pit only by pales. Soon after the Restoration,
the band, I imagine, took the station which they have kept
ever since, in an orchestra placed between the stage and the
pit.

The person who spoke the prologue, who entered immediately after the third sounding, usually wore a long black
velvet cloak, which, I suppose, was considered as best suited
to a supplicatory address. Of this custom, whatever may
have been its origin, some traces remained till very lately; a
black coat having been, if I mistake not, within these few
years, the constant stage-habiliment of our modern prologue-
speakers. The complete dress of the ancient prologue-
speaker is still retained in the play exhibited in *Hamlet*, before
the king and court of Denmark.

An epilogue does not appear to have been a regular appendage to a play in Shakspeare's time; for many of his dramas
had none; at least, they have not been preserved. In *All's
well that ends well*, *A Midsummer-Night's Dream*, *As you
like it*, *Troilus and Cressida*, and *The Tempest*, the epilogue
is spoken by one of the persons of the drama, and adapted to
the character of the speaker; a circumstance that I have not
observed in the epilogues of any other author of that age.
The epilogue was not always spoken by one of the performers
in the piece; for that subjoined to *The Second Part of King
Henry IV.* appears to have been delivered by a dancer.

The performers of male characters frequently wore periwigs which in the age of Shakspeare were not in common
use. It appears from a passage in Puttenham's *Arte of
English Poesie*, 1589, that vizards were on some occasions
used by the actors of those days; and it may be inferred from

a scene in one of our author's comedies, that they were some-times worn in his time, by those who performed female cha-racters. But this, I imagine, was very rare. Some of the female part of the audience likewise appeared in masks.

Both the prompter, or book-holder, as he was sometimes called, and the property-man, appear to have been regular appendages of our ancient theatres.

The stage-dresses, it is reasonable to suppose, were much more costly in some playhouses than others. Yet the ward-robe of even the king's servants at *The Globe* and *Blackfriars* was, we find, but scantily furnished; and our author's dramas derived very little aid from the splendour of exhi-bition.

It is well known, that in the time of Shakspeare, and for many years afterwards, female characters were represented solely by boys or young men. Nashe in a pamphlet pub-lished in 1592, speaking in defence of the English stage, *boasts* that the players of his time were " not as the players beyond sea, a sort of squirting bawdie comedians, that have whores and common curtizans to play women's parts." What Nashe considered as an high eulogy on his country, Prynne has made one of his principal charges against the English stage; having employed several pages in his bulky volume, and quoted many hundred authorities, to prove that " those playes wherein any men act women's parts in woman's apparell must needs be sinful, yea, abominable unto christians." The grand basis of his argument is a text in scripture; *Deuteronomy*, xxii. 5; " The woman shall not wear that which pertaineth unto man, neither shall a man put on a woman's garment:" a precept, which Sir Richard Baker has justly remarked, is no part of the moral law, and ought not to be understood literally. " Where," says Sir Richard, " finds he this precept? Even in the same place where he finds also that we must not weare cloaths of linsey-woolsey: and seeing we lawfully now wear cloathes of linsey-woolsey, why may it not be as lawful for men to put on women's garments?"

It may perhaps be supposed, that Prynne, having thus vehemently inveighed against men's representing female cha-racters on the stage, would not have been averse to the in-troduction of women in the scene; but sinful as this zealot thought it in *men* to assume the garments of the other sex, he considered it as not less abominable in *women* to tread the stage in their own proper dress: for he informs us, " that some Frenchwomen, or *monsters* rather, in Michaelmas term, 1629, attempted to act a French play at the playhouse in Blackfriers," which he represents as " an impudent, shameful, unwomanish, graceless, if not more than *whorish* attempt."

Soon after the period he speaks of, a regular French theatre was established in London, where without doubt women acted. They had long before appeared on the Italian as well as the French stage. When Coryate was at Venice, [July, 1608,] he tells us, he was at one of their playhouses, and saw a comedy acted. " The house (he adds) is very beggarly and base, in comparison of our stately playhouses in England; neither can their actors compare with us for apparell, shewes, and musicke. Here I observed certaine things that I never saw before; for I saw women act, a thing that I never saw before, though I have heard that it hath been some times used in London; and they performed it with as good a grace, action, gesture, and whatsoever convenient for a player, as ever I saw any masculine actor."

The practice of men's performing the parts of women in the scene is of the highest antiquity. On the Grecian stage no woman certainly ever *acted*. From Plutarch's Life of Phocian, we learn, that in his time (about three hundred and eighteen years before the Christian era) the performance of a tragedy at Athens was interrupted for some time by one of the actors, who was to personate a *queen*, refusing to come on the stage, because he had not a suitable mask and dress, and a train of attendants richly habited; and Demosthenes in one of his orations, mentions Theodorus and Aristodemus as having often represented the Antigone of Sophocles. This fact is also ascertained by an anecdote preserved by Aulus Gellius. A very celebrated actor, whose name was Polus, was appointed to perform the part of Electra in Sophocles's play; who in the progress of the drama appears with an urn in her hands, containing, as she supposes, the ashes of Orestes. The actor having some time before been deprived by death of a beloved son, to indulge his grief, as it it should seem, procured the urn which contained the ashes of his child, to be brought from his tomb; which affected him so much, that when he appeared with it on the scene, he embraced it with unfeigned sorrow, and burst into tears.

That on the Roman stage also female parts were represented by men in tragedy, is ascertained by one of Cicero's letters to Atticus, in which he speaks of Antipho, who performed the part of Andromache; and by a passage in Horace, who informs us, that Fusius Phocæus being to perform the part of Ilione, the wife of Polymnestor, in a tragedy written either by Accius or Pacuvius, and being in the course of the play to be awakened out of sleep by the cries of the shade of Polydorus, got so drunk, that he fell into a real and profound sleep, from which no noise could rouse him.

Horace indeed mentions a female performer, called Arbuscula; but as we find from his own authority that men personated women on the Roman stage, she probably was only an *embollaria*, who performed in the interludes and dances exhibited between the acts and at the end of the play. Servius calls her *mima*, but that may mean nothing more than one who acted in the *mimes*, or danced in the pantomime dances; and this seems the more probable from the manner in which she is mentioned by Cicero, from whom we learn that the part of Andromache was performed by a male actor on that very day when Arbuscula exhibited with the highest applause.

The same practice prevailed in the time of the emperors; for in the list of parts which Nero, with a preposterous ambition, acted in the publick theatre, we find that of Canace, who was represented in labour on the stage.

In the interludes exhibited between the acts undoubtedly women appeared. The elder Pliny informs us, that a female named Lucceïa acted in these interludes for an hundred years; and Galeria Copiola for above ninety years; having been first introduced on the scene in the fourteenth year of her age, in the year of Rome 672, when Caius Marius the younger, and Cuelus Carbo were consuls, and having performed in the 104th year of her age, six years before the death of Augustus, in the consulate of C. Poppæus and Quintus Sulpicius, A. U. C. 762.

Eunuchs also sometimes represented women on the Roman stage, as they do at this day in Italy; for we find that Spórus, who made so conspicuous a figure in the time of Nero, being appointed in the year 70, [A. U. C. 823] to personate a nymph, who, in an interlude exhibited before Vitellius, was to be carried off by a ravisher, rather than endure the indignity of wearing a female dress on the stage, put himself to death: a singular end for one, who about ten years before had been publickly espoused to Nero, in the hymeneal veil, and had been carried through one of the streets of Rome by the side of that monster, in the imperial robes of the empresses, ornamented with a profusion of jewels.

Thus ancient was the usage, which, though not adopted in the neighbouring countries of France and Italy, prevailed in England from the infancy of the stage. The prejudice against women appearing on the scene continued so strong, that till near the time of the Restoration, boys constantly performed female characters: and, strange as it may now appear, the old practice was not deserted without many apologies for the *indecorum* of the novel usage. In 1659, or 1660, in imitation of the foreign theatres, women were first introduced on the scene. In 1656, indeed, Mrs. Coleman, the wife of Mr. Edward Coleman, represented *Ianthe* in the First Part of D'Avenant's *Siege of Rhodes*; but the little she had to say was spoken in recitative. The first woman that appeared in any regular drama on a publick stage, performed the part of Desdemona; but who the lady was, I am unable to ascertain. The play of *Othello* is enumerated by Downes as one of the stock-plays of the king's company on their opening their theatre in Drury Lane in April, 1663; and it appears from a paper found with Sir Henry Herbert's Office-book, and indorsed by him, that it was one of the stock-plays of the same company from the time they began to play without a patent at the Red Bull in St. John Street. Mrs. Hughs performed the part of Desdemona in 1663, when the company removed to Drury Lane, and obtained the title of the king's servants; but whether she performed with them while they played at the Red Bull, or in Vere Street, near Clare Market, has not been ascertained. Perhaps Mrs. Saunderson made her first essay there, though she afterwards was enlisted in D'Avenant's company. The received tradition is, that she was the first English actress. The verses which were spoken by way of introducing a female to the audience, were written by Thomas Jordan, and being only found in a very scarce miscellany, I shall here transcribe them:

" *A Prologue, to introduce the first woman that came to act
on the stage, in the tragedy called* The Moor of Venice.

 " I come, unknown to any of the rest,
 " To tell you news ; I saw the lady drest :
 " The woman plays to-day : mistake me not,
 " No man in gown, or page in petticoat :
 " A woman to my knowledge ; yet I can't,
 " If I should die, make affidavit on't.
 " Do you not twitter, gentlemen ? I know
 " You will be censuring : do it fairly though.
 " 'Tis *possible* a virtuous woman may
 " Abhor all sorts of looseness, and yet play :
 " Play on the stage,—where all eyes are upon her :—
 " Shall we count that a crime, France counts an honour :
 " In other kingdoms husbands safely trust 'em ;
 " The difference lies only in the custom.
 " And let it be our custom, I advise ;
 " I'm sure this custom's better than th' excise,
 " And may procure *us* custom : hearts of flint
 " Will melt in passion, when a woman's in't.

  " But gentlemen, you that as judges sit
 " In the star-chamber of the house, the pit,
 " Have modest thoughts of her ; pray, do not run
 " To give her visits when the play is done,
 " With ' *damn me, your most humble servant, lady ;*'
 " She knows these things as well as you, it may be :
 " Not a bit there, dear gallants, she doth know
 " Her own deserts,—and your temptations too.—
 " But to the point :—In this reforming age
 " We have intents to civilize the stage.
 " Our women are defective, and so siz'd,
 " You'd think they were some of the guard disguis'd :
 " For, to speak truth, men act, that are between
 " Forty and fifty, wenches of fifteen ;
 " With bone so large, and nerve so incompliant,
 " When you call DESDEMONA, enter GIANT.—
 " We shall purge every thing that is unclean,
 " Lascivious, scurrilous, impious, or obscene ;
 " And when we've put all things in this fair way,
 " BAREBONES himself may come to see a play."

The Epilogue, which consists of but twelve lines, is in the same strain of apology:

> " And how do you like her ? Come, what is't ye drive at ?
> " She's the same thing in publick as in private ;
> " As far from being what you call a whore ;
> " As Desdemona, injur'd by the Moor :
> " Then he that censures her in such a case,
> " Hath a soul blacker than Othello's face.
> " But, ladies, what think *you* ? for if you tax
> " Her freedom with dishonour to your sex,
> " She means to act no more, and this shall be
> " No other play but her own tragedy.
> " She will submit to none but your commands,
> " And take commission only from your hands."

From a paper in Sir Henry Herbert's hand-writing, I find that *Othello* was performed by the Red Bull company, (afterwards his Majesties servants,) at their new theatre in Vere Street, near Clare Market, on Saturday, December 8, 1660, for the first time that winter. On that day therefore it is probable an actress first appeared on the English stage. This theatre was opened on Thursday, November 8, with the play of *King Henry the Fourth.* Most of Jordan's prologues and epilogues appear to have been written for that company.

It is certain, however, that for some time after the Restoration men also acted female parts ; and Mr. Kynaston, even after women had assumed their proper rank on the stage, was not only endured, but admired ; if we may believe a contemporary writer ; who assures us, " that being then very young, he made a complete stage beauty, performing his parts so well, (particularly *Arthiope* and *Auglaura,)* that it has since been disputable among the judicious, whether any woman that succeeded him, touched the audience so sensibly as he."

In D'Avenant's company, the first actress that appeared was probably Mrs. Saunderson, who performed *Ianthe* in *The Siege of Rhodes,* on the opening of his new theatre in Lincoln's Inn Fields, in April, 1662. It does not appear from Downes's account, that while D'Avenant's company performed at the Cockpit in Drury Lane during the years 1659, 1660, and 1661, they had any female performer among them : or that *Othello* was acted by them at that period.

In the infancy of the English stage it was customary in every piece to introduce a Clown, " by his mimick gestures to breed in the less capable mirth and laughter." The privileges of the Clown were very extensive; for, between the acts, and sometimes between the scenes, he claimed a right to enter on the stage, and to excite merriment by any species of buffoonery that struck him. Like the Harlequin of the Italian comedy, his wit was often extemporal, and he sometimes entered into a contest of raillery and sarcasm with some of the audience. He generally threw his thoughts into hobbling doggrel verses, which he made shorter or longer as he found convenient; but, however irregular his metre might be, or whatever the length of his verses, he always took care to tag them with words of corresponding sound : like Dryden's DOEG,

> " He fagotted his notions as they fell,
> " And if they rhym'd and rattled, all was well."

Thomas Wilson and Richard Tarleton, both sworn servants to Queen Elizabeth, were the most popular performers of that time in this department of the drama, and are highly praised by the Continuator of Stowe's Annals, for " their wondrous plentiful, pleasant, and *extemporal* wit." Tarleton, whose comick powers were so great, that, according to Sir Richard Baker, " he delighted the spectators before he had spoken a word," is thus described in a very rare old pamphlet : " The next, by his sute of russet, his buttoned cap, his taber, his standing on the toe, and other tricks, I knew to be either the body or resemblance of Tarleton, who living, for his pleasant conceits was of all men liked, and, dying, for mirth left not his like." In 1611 was published a book entitled his *Jeasts*, in which some specimens are given of the extempore wit which our ancestors thought so excellent. As he was performing some part " at the Bull in Bishops-gate-street, where the Queenes players oftentimes played," while he was " kneeling down to aske his father's blessing," a fellow in the gallery threw an apple at him, which hit him on the cheek. He immediately took up the apple, and advancing to the audience, addressed them in these lines :

> " Gentlemen, this fellow, with his face of mapple,
> " Instead of a pippin hath throwne me an apple ;
> " But as for an apple he hath cast a crab,
> " So instead of an honest woman God hath sent him a
>     drab."

" The people," says the relater, " laughed heartily ; for the fellow had a quean to his wife."

Another of these stories, which I shall give in the author's own words, establishes what I have already mentioned, that it was customary for the Clown to talk to the audience or the actors *ad libitum.*

" At the Bull at Bishops-gate, was a play of *Henry the V.* [the performance which preceded Shakspeare's,] wherein the judge was to take a box on the eare ; and because *he* was absent that should take the blow, Tarlton himselfe ever forward to please, tooke upon him to play the same judge, besides his own part of the clowne; and Knel, then playing Henry the Fifth, hit Tarleton a sound box indeed, which made the people laugh the more, because it was he : but anon the judge goes in, and immediately Tarleton in his clownes cloathes comes out, and asks the actors, *What news ?* O, saith one, had'st thou been here, thou shouldest have seen Prince Henry hit the judge a terrible box on the eare. What, man, said Tarlton, strike a judge ! It is true, i'faith, said the other. No other like, said Tarlton, and it could not be but terrible to the judge, when the report so terrifies me, that methinks the blowe remaines still on my cheeke, that it burnes againe. The people laught at this mightily, and to this day I have heard it commended for rare; but no marvell, for he had many of these. But I would see *our clownes in these days* do the like. No, I warrant ye ; and yet they thinke well of themselves too."

The last words show that this practice was not discontinued in the time of Shakspeare, and we here see that he had abundant reason for his precept in *Hamlet :* " Let those that play your *clowns, speak no more than is set down for them ;* for there be of them, that will of themselves laugh, to set on some quantity of barren spectators to laugh too ; though *in the mean time some necessary question of the play be then to be considered.*"

This practice was undoubtedly coeval with the English stage ; for we are told that Sir Thomas More, while he lived as a page with Archbishop Moreton, (about the year 1490,) as the Christmas plays were going on in the palace, would sometimes suddenly step upon the stage, " without studying for the matter," and exhibit a part of his own, which gave the audience much more entertainment than the whole performance besides.

But the peculiar province of the Clown was to entertain

the audience after the play was finished, at which time *themes* were sometimes given to him by some of the spectators, to descant upon; but more commonly the audience were entertained by a *jig*. A jig was a ludicrous metrical composition, often in rhyme, which was sung by the Clown, who likewise, I believe, occasionally danced, and was always accompanied by a tabor and pipe. In these jigs more persons than one were sometimes introduced. The original of the entertainment which this buffoon afforded our ancestors between the acts and after the play, may be traced to the satyrical interludes of Greece, and the Attellans and Mimes of the Roman stage. The *Exodiarii* and *Embollariæ* of the Mimes are undoubtedly the remote progenitors of the Vice and Clown of our ancient dramas.

No writer that I have met with, intimates that in the time of Shakspeare it was customary to exhibit more than a single dramatick piece on one day. Had any shorter pieces, of the same kind with our modern farces, (beside the *jigs* already mentioned,) been presented after the principal performance, some of them probably would have been printed; but there are none of them extant of an earlier date than the time of the Restoration. The practice therefore of exhibiting two dramas successively in the same afternoon, we may be assured, was not established before that period. But though our ancient audiences were not gratified by the representation of more than one drama in the same day, the entertainment in the middle of the reign of Elizabeth was diversified, and the populace diverted, by vaulting, tumbling, slight of hand, and morrice-dancing; and in the time of Shakspeare, by the extemporaneous buffoonery of the Clown, whenever he chose to solicit the attention of the audience: by singing and dancing between the acts, and either a song or the metrical jig already described at the end of the piece: a mixture not more heterogeneous than that with which we are now daily presented, a tragedy and a farce. In the dances, I believe, not only men, but boys in women's dresses, were introduced: a practice which prevailed on the Grecian stage, and in France till late in the last century.

The amusements of our ancestors, before the commencement of the play, were of various kinds. While some part of the audience entertained themselves with reading, or playing at cards, others were employed in less refined occupations; in drinking ale, or smoking tobacco: with these and nuts and apples they were furnished by male attendants, of whose clamour a satirical writer of the time of James I. loudly complains. In 1633, when Prynne published his *Histriomastix*, women smoked tobacco in the playhouses as well as men.

It was a common practice to carry table-books to the theatre, and either from curiosity, or enmity to the author, or some other motive, to write down passages of the play that was represented ; and there is reason to believe that the imperfect and mutilated copies of one or two of Shakspeare's dramas, which are yet extant, were taken down by the ear or in short-hand during the exhibition.

At the end of the piece, the actors, in noblemen's houses and in taverns, where plays were frequently performed, prayed for the health and prosperity of their patrons ; and in the publick theatres, for the king and queen. This prayer sometimes made part of the epilogue. Hence, probably, as Mr. Steevens has observed, the addition of *Vivant rex et regina*, to the modern play-bills.

Plays in the time of our author, began at one o'clock in the afternoon ; and the exhibition was sometimes finished in two hours. Even in 1667, they commenced at three o'clock. About thirty years afterwards, (in 1696) theatrical entertainments began an hour later.

We have seen that in the infancy of our stage, Mysteries were usually acted in churches ; and the practice of exhibiting religious dramas in buildings appropriated to the service of religion on the Lord's-day certainly continued after the Reformation.

During the reign of Queen Elizabeth plays were exhibited in the publick theatres on Sundays, as well as on other days of the week. The licence granted by that queen to James Burbage in 1574, which has been already printed in a former page, shows that they were then represented on that day *out of the hours of prayer*.

We are told indeed by John Field in his *Declaration of God's Judgment at Paris Garden*, that in the year 1580 " the magistrates of the city of London obtained from Queene Elizabeth, that all heathenish playes and enterludes should be banished upon sabbath dayes." This prohibition, however, probably lasted but a short time ; for her majesty, when she visited Oxford in 1592, did not scruple to be present at a theatrical exhibition on Sunday night, the 24th of September in that year. During the reign of James the First, though dramatick entertainments were performed at

9

court on Sundays, I believe, no plays were *publickly* represented on that day; and by the statute 3 Car. I. c. 1. their exhibition on the Sabbath day was absolutely prohibited: yet, notwithstanding this act of parliament, both plays and masques were performed at court on Sundays, during the first sixteen years of the reign of that king, and certainly in private houses, if not on the publick stage.

It has been a question, whether it was formerly a common practice to ride on horseback to the playhouse; a circumstance that would scarcely deserve consideration, if it were not in some sort connected with our author's history, a plausible story having been built on this foundation, relative to his first introduction to the stage.

The modes of conveyance to the theatre, anciently, as at present, seem to have been various; some going in coaches, others on horseback, and many by water. To *the Globe* playhouse the company probably were conveyed by water: to that in *Blackfriars*, the gentry went either in coaches, or on horseback; and the common people on foot.

Plays in the time of King James the First, (and probably afterwards,) appear to have been performed every day at each theatre during the winter season, except in the time of Lent, when they were not permitted on the sermon days, as they were called, that is, on Wednesday and Friday; nor on the other days of the week, except by special licence; which however was obtained by a fee paid to the Master of the Revels. In the summer season the stage exhibitions were continued, but during the long vacation they were less frequently repeated. However, it appears from Sir Henry Herbert's Manuscript, that the king's company usually brought out two or three new plays at the Globe every summer.

Though, from the want of newspapers and other periodical publications, intelligence was not so speedily circulated in former times as at present, our ancient theatres do not appear to have laboured under any disadvantage in this respect; for the players printed and exposed accounts of the pieces that they intended to exhibit, which, however, did not contain a list of the characters, or the names of the actors by whom they were represented.

The long and whimsical titles which are prefixed to the quarto copies of our author's plays, were undoubtedly either written by booksellers, or transcribed from the play-bills of the time. They were equally calculated to attract the notice of the idle gazer in the walks at St. Paul's, or to draw a croud about some vociferous Autolycus, who perhaps was hired by the players thus to raise the expectations of the multitude. It is indeed absurd to suppose, that the modest Shakspeare, who has more than once apologized for his *untutored lines*, should in his manuscripts have entitled any of his dramas *most excellent and pleasant* performances.

It is uncertain at what time the usage of giving authors a benefit on the third day of the exhibition of their piece, commenced. Mr. Oldys, in one of his manuscripts, intimates that dramatick poets had anciently their benefit on the first day that a new play was represented; a regulation which would have been very favourable to some of the ephemeral productions of modern times. I have found no authority which proves this to have been the case in the time of Shakspeare; but at the beginning of the present century it appears to have been customary in Lent for the *players* of the theatre in Drury Lane to divide the profits of the first representation of a new play among them.

From D'Avenant, indeed, we learn, that in the latter part of the reign of Queen Elizabeth, the poet had his benefit on the second day. As it was a general practice, in the time of Shakspeare, to sell the copy of the play to the theatre, I imagine, in such cases, an author derived no other advantage from his piece, than what arose from the sale of it. Sometimes, however, he found it more beneficial to retain the copy-right in his own hands; and when he did so, I suppose he had a benefit. It is certain that the giving authors the profits of the third exhibition of their play, which seems to have been the usual mode during a great part of the last century, was an established custom in the year 1612; for Decker, in the prologue to one of his comedies, printed in that year, speaks of the poet's *third day.*

The unfortunate Otway had no more than one benefit on the production of a new play; and this too, it seems, he was sometimes forced to mortgage, before the piece was acted. Southerne was the first dramatick writer who obtained the emoluments arising from two representations; and to Farquhar, in the year 1700, the benefit of a third was granted; but this appears to have been a particular favour to that gentleman; for for several years afterwards dramatick poets had only the benefit of the third and sixth performance.

The profit of three representations did not become the established right of authors till after the year 1720.

To the honour of Mr. Addison, it should be remembered, that he first discontinued the ancient, but humiliating, practice of distributing tickets, and soliciting company to attend at the theatre, on the poet's nights.

When an author sold his piece to the sharers or proprietors of a theatre, it could not be performed by any other company, and remained for several years unpublished; but, when that was not the case, he printed it for sale, to which many seem to have been induced from an apprehension that an imperfect copy might be issued from the press without their consent. The customary price of the copy of a play, in the time of Shakspeare, appears to have been twenty nobles, or six pounds thirteen shillings and four-pence. The play when printed was sold for sixpence; and the usual present from a patron, in return for a dedication, was forty shillings.

On the first day of exhibiting a new play, the prices of admission appear to have been raised, sometimes to double, sometimes to treble, prices; and this seems to have been occasionally practised on the benefit-nights of authors, and on the representation of expensive plays, to the year 1726 in the present century.

Dramatick poets in ancient times, as at present, were admitted gratis into the theatre.

It appears from Sir Henry Herbert's Office-book that the king's company between the years 1622 and 1641 produced either at Blackfriars or the Globe at least four new plays every year. Every play, before it was represented on the stage, was licensed by the Master of the Revels, for which he received in the time of Queen Elizabeth, but a noble, though at a subsequent period the stated fee on this occasion rose to two pounds.

Neither Queen Elizabeth, nor King James the First, nor Charles the First, I believe, ever went to the publick theatre; but they frequently ordered plays to be performed at court, which were represented in the royal theatre called the Cockpit, in Whitehall: and the actors of the king's company were sometimes commanded to attend his majesty in his summer's progress, to perform before him in the country. Queen Henrietta Maria, however, went sometimes o the publick theatre at Blackfriars. I find from the Council-books that in the time of Elizabeth ten pounds was the payment for a play performed before her; that is, twenty nobles, or six pounds, thirteen shillings, and four-pence, as the regular and stated fee ; and three pounds, six shillings, and eight-pence, by way of bounty or reward. The same sum, as I learn from the manuscript notes of Lord Stanhope, Treasurer of the Chamber to King James the First, continued to be paid during his reign : and this was the stated payment during the reign of his successor also. Plays at court were usually performed at night, by which means they did not interfere with the regular exhibition at the publick theatres, which was early in the afternoon ; and thus the royal bounty was for so much a clear profit to the company : but when a play was commanded to be performed at any of the royal palaces in the neighbourhood of London, by which the actors were prevented from deriving any profit from a publick exhibition on the same day, the fee, as appears from a manuscript in the Lord Chamberlain's office, was, in the year 1630, and probably in Shakspeare's time also, twenty pounds; and this circumstance I formerly stated, as strongly indicating that the sum last mentioned was a very considerable produce on any one representation at the Blackfriars or Globe playhouse. The office-book which I have so often quoted, has fully confirmed my conjecture.

The custom of passing a final censure on plays at their first exhibition, is as ancient as the time of our author; for no less than three plays of his rival, Ben Jonson, appear to have been deservedly damned ; and Fletcher's *Faithful Shepherdess,* and *The Knight of the burning Pestle,* written by him and Beaumont, underwent the same fate.

· It is not easy to ascertain what were the emoluments of a successful actor in the time of Shakspeare. They had not then annual benefits, as at present. The clear emoluments of the theatre, after deducting the nightly expences for lights, men occasionally hired for the evening, &c. which in Shakspeare's house was but forty-five shillings, were divided into shares, of which part belonged to the proprietors, who were called housekeepers, and the remainder was divided among the actors, according to their rank and merit. I suspect that the whole clear receipt was divided into forty shares, of which perhaps the housekeepers or proprietors had fifteen, the actors twenty-two, and three were devoted to the purchase of new plays, dresses, &c. From Ben Jonson's *Poetaster,* it should seem that one of the performers had seven shares and a half; but of what integral sum is not mentioned. The person alluded to, (if any person was alluded to, which is not certain,) must, I think, have been a proprietor, as well as a principal actor. Our poet in his *Hamlet* speaks of a *whole share*, as no contemptible emolument; and from the same play we learn that some of the performers had only half a share. Others probably had still less.

It appears from a deed executed by Thomas Killigrew and others, that in the year 1666, the whole profit arising from acting plays, masques, &c. at the king's theatre, was divided into *twelve shares and three quarters*, of which Mr. Killigrew, the manager, had two shares and three quarters; and if we may trust to the statement in another very curious paper, (which however was probably exaggerated,) each share produced, at the lowest calculation, about 250l. per ann. *net*; and the total clear profits consequently were about 3187l. 10s. 0d.

These shares were then distributed among the proprietors of the theatre, who at that time were not actors, the performers, and the dramatick poets, who were retained in the service of the theatre, and received a part of the annual produce as a compensation for the pieces which they produced.

In a paper delivered by Sir Henry Herbert to Lord Clarendon and the Lord Chamberlain, July 11, 1662, he states the emolument which Mr. Thomas Killigrew then derived (from his two shares and three quarters,) at 19l. 6s. 0d. *per* week; according to which statement each share in the king's company produced but two hundred and ten pounds ten shillings a year. In Sir William D'Avenant's company, from the time their new theatre was opened in Portugal Row, near Lincoln's Inn Fields, (April 1662,) the total receipt (after deducting the nightly charges of " men hirelings and other customary expences,") was divided into fifteen shares, of which it was agreed by articles previously entered into, that ten should belong to D'Avenant: viz. two " towards the house-rent, buildings, scaffolding, and making of frames for scenes; one for a provision of habits, properties, and scenes, for a supplement of the said theatre; and seven to maintain all the women that are to perform or represent women's parts, in tragedies, comedies, &c. and in consideration of erecting and establishing his actors to be a company, and his pains and expences for that purpose for many years." The other five shares were divided in various proportions among the rest of the troop.

In the paper above referred to it is stated by Sir Henry Herbert, that D'Avenant " drew from these ten shares two hundreds pounds a week;" and if that statement was correct, each share in his playhouse then produced annually six hundred pounds, supposing the acting season to have then lasted for thirty weeks.

Such were the emoluments of the theatre soon after the Restoration; which I have stated here, from authentick documents, because they may assist us in our conjectures concerning the profits derived from stage-exhibitions at a more remote and darker period.

From the prices of admission into our ancient theatres in the time of Shakspeare, which have been already noticed, I formerly conjectured that about twenty pounds was a considerable receipt at the Blackfriars and Globe theatre, on any one day; and my conjecture is now confirmed by indisputable evidence. In Sir Henry Herbert's Office-book I find the following curious notices on this subject, under the year 1628:

" The kinges company with a generall consent and alacritye have given mee the benefitt of two dayes in the yeare, the one in summer, thother in winter, to bee taken out of the second daye of a revived playe, att my owne choyse. The housekeepers have likewyse given their shares, their dayly charge only deducted, which comes to some 2l. 5s. this 25 May, 1628.

" The benefitt of the first day, being a very unseasonable one in respect of the weather, comes but unto £4. 15. 0."

This agreement subsisted for five years and a half, during which time Sir Henry Herbert had ten benefits, the most profitable of which produced seventeen pounds, and ten shillings, *net*, on the 22d of Nov. 1628, when Fletcher's *Custom of the Country* was performed at Blackfriars; and the least emolument which he received was on the representation of a play which is not named, at the Globe, in the summer of the year 1632, which produced only the sum of one pound and five shillings, after deducting from the total receipt in each instance the nightly charge above mentioned. It also appears that his clear profit at an average on each of his nights, was £8. 19. 4. and the total nightly receipt was at an average—£11. 4. 4.

On the 30th of October, 1633, the managers of the king's company agreed to pay him the fixed sum of ten pounds every Christmas, and the same sum at Midsummer, in lieu of his two benefits, which sums they regularly paid him from that time till the breaking out of the civil wars.

From the receipts on these benefits I am led to believe that the prices were lower at the Globe theatre, and that therefore, though it was much larger than the winter theatre at Blackfriars, it did not produce a greater sum of money on any representation. If we suppose twenty pounds, clear of the nightly charges already mentioned, to have been a very considerable receipt at either of these houses, and that this sum was in our poet's time divided into forty shares, of which fifteen were appropriated to the housekeepers or proprietors, three to the purchase of copies of new plays, stagehabits, &c. and twenty-two to the actors, then the performer who had two shares on the representation of each play, received, when the theatre was thus successful, twenty shillings. But supposing the *average* nightly receipt (after deducting the nightly expences) to be about nine pounds, which we have seen to be the case, then his nightly dividend would be but nine shillings, and his weekly profit, if they played five times a week, two pounds five shillings. The acting season, I believe, at that time lasted forty weeks. In each of the companies then subsisting there were about twenty persons, six of whom probably were principal, and the others subordinate; so that we may suppose *two shares* to have been the reward of a principal actor; six of the second class perhaps enjoyed a whole share each; and each of the remaining eight half a share. On all these *data*, I think it may be safely concluded, that the performers of the first class did not derive from their profession more than ninety pounds a year at the utmost. Shakspeare, Heminge, Condell, Burbadge, Lowin, and Taylor had without doubt other shares as proprietors or leaseholders; but what the different proportions were which each of them possessed in that right, it is now impossible to ascertain. According to the supposition already stated, that fifteen shares out of forty were appropriated to the proprietors, then was there on this account a sum of six hundred and seventy-five pounds annually to be divided among them. Our poet, as author, actor, and proprietor, probably received from the theatre about two hundred pounds a year.—Having after a very long search lately discovered the will of Mr. Heminge, I hoped to have derived from it some information on this subject; but I was disappointed. He indeed more than once mentions his several parts or *shares held by lease in the Globe and Blackfriars playhouses*; but uses no expression by which the value of each of those shares can be ascertained. His books of account, which he appears to have regularly kept, and which, he says, will show that his shares yielded him "*a good yearly profit*," will probably, if they shall ever be found, throw much light on our early stage history.

Thus scanty and meagre were the apparatus and accommodations of our ancient theatres, on which those dramas were first exhibited, that have since engaged the attention of so many learned men, and delighted so many thousand spectators. Yet even then, we are told by a writer of that age,[4] "dramatick poesy was so lively expressed and represented on the publick stages and theatres of this city, as Rome in the *auge* of her pomp and glory, never saw it better performed; in respect of the action and art, not of the cost and and sumptuousness."

THE history of the stage as far as it relates to Shakspeare, naturally divides itself into three periods: the period which preceded his appearance as an actor or dramatick writer; that during which he flourished; and the time which has elapsed since his death. Having now gone through the two former of these periods, I shall take a transient view of the stage from the death of our great poet to the year 1741, still with a view to Shakspeare, and his works.

Soon after his death, four of the principal companies then subsisting, made a union, and were afterwards called *The United Companies*; but I know not precisely in what this union consisted. I suspect it arose from a penury of actors, and that the managers contracted to permit the performers in each house occasionally to assist their brethren in the other theatres in the representation of plays.

After the death of Shakspeare, the plays of Fletcher appear for several years to have been more admired, or at least to have been more frequently acted, than those of our poet.

---

[4] Sir George Buc. This writer, as I have already observed, wrote an express treatise concerning the English stage, which was never printed, and, I fear, is now irrecoverably lost.

During the latter part of the reign of James the First, Fletcher's pieces had the advantage of novelty to recommend them. I believe, between the time of Beaumont's death in 1615 and his own in 1625, this poet produced at least twenty-five plays. Sir Aston Cokain has informed us, in his poems, that of the thirty-five pieces improperly ascribed to Beaumont and Fletcher in the folio edition of 1647, much the greater part were written after Beaumont's death; and his account is partly confirmed by Sir Henry Herbert's Manuscript, from which it appears that Fletcher produced eleven new plays in the last four years of his life. If we were possessed of the Register kept by Sir George Buck, we should there, I make no doubt, find near twenty dramas written by the same author in the interval between 1615 and 1622.

Sir William D'Avenant, about sixteen months after the death of Ben Jonson, obtained from his Majesty (Dec. 13, 1638,) a grant of an annuity of one hundred pounds *per ann.* which he enjoyed as poet laureat till his death. In the following year (March 26, 1639,) a patent passed the great seal authorizing him to erect a playhouse, which was then intended to have been built behind *The Three Kings Ordinary* in Fleet-street: but this scheme was not carried into execution. I find from a Manuscript in the Lord Chamberlain's Office, that after the death of Christopher Beeston, Sir W. D'Avenant was appointed by the Lord Chamberlain, (June 27, 1639,) " Governor of the King and Queens company acting at the Cockpit in Drury Lane, during the lease which Mrs. Elizabeth Beeston, *alias* Hutcheson, hath or doth hold in the said house :" and I suppose he appointed her son Mr. William Beeston, his deputy, for from Sir Henry Herbert's office-book, he appears for a short time to have had the management of that theatre.

In the latter end of the year 1659, some months before the Restoration of K. Charles II. the theatres, which had been suppressed during the usurpation, began to revive, and several plays were performed at the Red Bull in St. John's Street, in that and the following year, before the return of the king. In June, 1660, three companies seem to have been formed; that already mentioned, one under Mr. William Beeston in Salisbury Court, and one at the Cockpit in Drury Lane under Mr. Rhodes, who had been wardrobe-keeper at the theatre in Blackfriars before the breaking out of the Civil Wars. Sir Henry Herbert, who still retained his office of Master of the Revels, endeavoured to obtain from these companies the same emoluments which he had formerly derived from the exhibition of plays; but after a long struggle, and after having brought several actions at law against Sir William D' Avenant, Mr. Betterton, Mr. Mohun, and others, he was obliged to relinquish his claims, and his office ceased to be attended with either authority or profit. It received its death wound from a grant from King Charles II. under the privy signet, August 21, 1660, authorizing Mr. Thomas Killigrew, one of the grooms of his majesty's bedchamber, and Sir William D'Avenant, to erect two new playhouses and two new companies, of which they were to have the regulation; and prohibiting any other theatrical representation in London, Westminster, or the suburbs, but those exhibited by the said two companies.

Mr. THOMAS BETTERTON having been a great admirer of Shakspeare, and having taken the trouble in the beginning of this century, when he was above seventy years of age, of travelling to Stratford-upon-Avon to collect materials for Mr. Rowe's life of our author, is entitled to particular notice from an editor of his works. Very inaccurate accounts of this actor have been given in the *Biographia Britannica* and several other books. It is observable, that biographical writers often give the world long dissertations concerning facts and dates, when the fact contested might at once be ascertained by visiting a neighbouring parish church: and this has been particularly the case of Mr. Betterton. He was the son of Matthew Betterton (under-cook to King Charles the First) and was baptized, as I learn from the register of St. Margaret's parish, August 11, 1635. He could not have appeared on the stage in 1656, as has been asserted, no theatre being then allowed. His first appearance was at the Cockpit, in Drury Lane, in Mr. Rhodes's company, who played there by a license in the year 1659, when Betterton was twenty-four years of age. He married Mrs. Mary Saunderson, an actress, who had been bred by Sir William D'Avenant, some time in the year 1663, as appears by the *Dramatis Personæ* of *The Slighted Maid*, printed in that year. From a paper now before me, which Sir Henry Herbert has entitled a *Breviat* of matters to be proved on the trial of an action brought by him against Mr. Betterton in 1662, I find that he continued to act at the Cockpit till November, 1660, when he and several other performers entered into articles with Sir William D'Avenant; in consequence

G 2

of which they began in that month to play at the theatre in
Salisbury Court, from whence after some time, I believe, they
returned to the Cockpit, and afterwards removed to a new
theatre in Portugal Row near Lincoln's Inn Fields.

On the 15th of Nov. 1660, Sir William D'Avenant's
company began to act under these articles at the theatre in
Salisbury-court, at which house or at the Cockpit they con-
tinued to play till March or April, 1662. In October 1660,
Sir Henry Herbert had brought an action on the case against
Mr. Mohun and several others of Killigrew's company,
which was tried in December, 1661, for representing plays
without being licensed by him, and obtained a verdict against
them. Encouraged by his success in that suit, soon after
D'Avenant's company opened their new theatre in Portugal
Row, he brought a similar action (May 6, 1662,) against
Mr. Betterton, of which I know not the event. In the declaration, now before me, it is stated that D'Avenant's company, between the 15th of November 1660, and the 6th of
May 1662, produced ten new plays, and 100 revived plays;
but the latter number being the usual style of declarations at
law, may have been inserted without a strict regard to the
fact.

Sir Henry Herbert likewise brought two actions on the
same ground against Sir William D'Avenant, in one of
which he failed, and in the other was successful. To put an
end to the contest, Sir William in June 1662 besought the
king to interfere.

The actors who had performed at the Red Bull, acted under the direction of Mr. Killigrew during the years 1660,
1661, 1662, and part of the year 1663, in Gibbon's tennis-
court in Vere Street, near Clare-market; during which time
a new theatre was built for them in Drury Lane, to which
they removed in April, 1663. In the list of their stock-plays,
there are but three of Shakspeare.

Downes the prompter has given a list of what he calls the
principal old stock plays acted by the king's servants, (which
title the performers under Mr. Killigrew acquired,) between
the time of the Restoration and the junction of the two companies in 1682; from which it appears that the only plays of
Shakspeare performed by them in that period, were *King
Henry IV*. P. I. *The Merry Wives of Windsor, Othello*, and
*Julius Cæsar*. Mr. Hart represented Othello, Brutus, and
Hotspur; Major Mohun, Iago, and Cassius; and Mr. Cartwright, Falstaff. Such was the lamentable taste of those times

that the plays of Fletcher, Jonson, and Shirley were much oftener exhibited than those of our author.

Sir William D'Avenant's Company, after having played for some time at the Cockpit in Drury Lane, and at Salisbury Court, removed in March or April 1662, to a new theatre in Portugal Row, near Lincoln's Inn Fields. Mr. Betterton, his principal actor, we are told by Downes, was admired in the part of Pericles, which he frequently performed before the opening of the new theatre; and while this company continued to act in Portugal Row, they represented the following plays of Shakspeare, and it should seem those only : *Macbeth* and *The Tempest*, altered by D'Avenant ; *King Lear, Hamlet, King Henry the Eighth, Romeo and Juliet*, and *Twelfth-night.* In *Hamlet*, the Prince of Denmark was represented by Mr. Betterton ; the Ghost by Mr. Richards ; Horatio by Mr. Harris : the Queen by Mrs. Davenport ; and Ophelia by Mrs. Saunderson. In *Romeo and Juliet*, Romeo was represented by Mr. Harris ; Mercutio by Mr. Betterton, and Juliet by Mrs. Saunderson. Mr. Betterton in *Twelfth Night* performed Sir Toby Belch, and in *Henry the Eighth*, the King. He was without doubt also the performer of King Lear. Mrs. Saunderson represented Catharine in *King Henry the Eighth*, and it may be presumed, Cordelia, and Miranda. She also performed Lady Macbeth, and Mr. Betterton Macbeth.

The theatre which had been erected in Portugal Row, being found too small, Sir William D'Avenant laid the foundation of a new playhouse in Dorset Garden, near Dorset Stairs, which however he did not live to see completed ; for he died in May, 1668, and it was not opened till 1671.

On the 9th of November, 1671, D'Avenant's company removed to their new theatre in Dorset Gardens, which was opened, not with one of Shakspeare's plays, but with Dryden's comedy called *Sir Martin Marall.*

Between the year 1671 and 1682, when the King's and the Duke of York's servants united, (about which time Charles Hart, the principal support of the former company, died,) *King Lear, Timon of Athens, Macbeth,* and *The Tempest*, were the only plays of our author that were exhibited at the theatre in Dorset Gardens ; and the three latter were not represented in their original state, but as altered by D'Avenant and Shadwell. Between 1682 and 1695, when Mr. Congreve, Mr. Betterton, Mrs. Barry, and Mrs. Bracegirdle, obtained a licence to open a new theatre in Lincoln's

Inn Fields, *Othello*, *A Midsummer-Night's Dream*, and
*The Taming of the Shrew*, are the only plays of Shakspeare
which Downes the prompter mentions, as having been per-
formed by the united companies : *A Midsummer-Night's
Dream* was transformed into an opera, and *The Taming of
the Shrew* was exhibited as altered by Lacy.    Dryden's
*Troilus and Cressida*, however, the two parts of *King
Henry IV*. *Twelfth Night*, *Macbeth*, *King Henry VIII.
Julius Cæsar*, and *Hamlet*, were without doubt sometimes
represented in the same period ;  and Tate and Durfey furnished the scene with miserable alterations of *Coriolanus,
King Richard II. King Lear*, and *Cymbeline*.[5]    Otway's
*Caius Marius*, which was produced in 1680, usurped the
place of our poet's *Romeo and Juliet* for near seventy years,
and Lord Lansdown's *Jew of Venice* kept possession of the
stage from the time of its first exhibition in 1701, to the
year 1741.    Dryden's *All for Love*, from 1678 to 1759,
was performed instead of our author's *Antony and Cleopatra*;
and D'Avenant's alteration of *Macbeth* in like manner was
preferred to our author's tragedy, from its first exhibition in
1663, for near eighty years.

In the year 1700 Cibber produced his alteration of *King
Richard III*.    I do not find that this play, which was so
popular in Shakspeare's time, was performed from the time of
the Restoration to the end of the seventeenth century.    The
play with Cibber's alterations was once performed at Drury
Lane in 1703, and lay dormant from that time to the 28th of
Jan. 1710, when it was revived at the Opera House in the
Haymarket; since which time it has been represented, I believe, more frequently than any of our author's dramas, except *Hamlet*.

On April 23, 1704, *The Merry Wives of Windsor*, by
command of the Queen, was performed at St. James's, by
the actors of both houses, and afterwards publickly represented at the theatre in Lincoln's Inn Field's, May 18, in
the same year, by Mr. Betterton's company; but although
the whole force of his company was exerted in the representation, the piece had so little success, that it was not re-

[5] *King Richard II.* and *King Lear* were produced by Tate in
1681, before the union of the two companies ; and *Coriolanus*,
under the title of *The Ingratitude of a Commonwealth*, in 1682.
In the same year appeared Durfey's alteration of *Cymbeline*,
under the title of *The Injured Princess.*

peated till Nov. 3, 1720, when it was again revived at the same theatre, and afterwards frequently performed.

From 1709, when Mr. Rowe published his edition of Shakspeare, the exhibition of his plays became much more frequent than before. Between that time and 1740, our poet's *Hamlet, Julius Cæsar, King Henry VIII. Othello, King Richard III. King Lear,* and the two parts of *King Henry IV.* were very frequently exhibited. Still, however, such was the wretched taste of the audiences of those days, that in many instances the contemptible alterations of his pieces were preferred to the originals. Durfey's *Injured Princess,* which had not been acted from 1697, was again revived at Drury Lane, October 5, 1717, and afterwards often represented. Even Ravenscroft's *Titus Andronicus,* in which all the faults of the original are greatly aggravated, took its turn on the scene, and after an intermission of fifteen years was revived at Drury Lane in August, 1717, and afterwards frequently performed both at that theatre and the theatre in Lincoln's Inn Fields, where it was exhibited for the first time, Dec. 21, 1720. *Coriolanus,* which had not been acted for twenty years, was revived at the theatre in Lincoln's Inn Fields, Dec. 13, 1718; and in Dec. 1719, *King Richard II.* was revived at the same theatre : but probably neither of these plays was then represented as originally written by Shakspeare.[6] *Measure for Measure,* which had not been acted, I imagine, from the time of the suppression of the theatres in 1642, was revived at the same theatre, Dec. 8, 1720, for the purpose of producing Mr. Quin in the character of the Duke, which he frequently performed with success in that and the following years. *Much Ado about Nothing,* which had not been acted for thirty years, was revived at Lincoln's Inn Fields, Feb. 9, 1721 ; but after two representations, on that and the following evening, was laid aside. In Dec. 1723, *King Henry V.* was announced for representation, " on Shakspeare's foundation," and performed at Drury Lane six times in that month ; after which we hear of it no more : and on Feb. 26, 1737, *King John* was revived at Covent Garden. Neither of these plays, I believe, had been exhibited from the time of the downfall of the stage.—At the same theatre our poet's second part of

---

[6] In the theatrical advertisement, Feb. 6, 1738, *King Richard II.* (which was then produced at Covent Garden,) was said not to have been acted for *forty* years.

*King Henry IV.* which had for fifty years been driven from the scene by the play which Mr. Betterton substituted in its place, resumed its station, being produced at Covent Garden, Feb. 16, 1738; and on the 23d of the same month Shakspeare's *King Henry V.* was performed there as originally written, after an interval, if the theatrical advertisement be correct, of forty years. In the following March the same company once exhibited *The First Part of King Henry VI.* for the first time, as they asserted, for fifty years.[7] *As you like it* was announced for representation at Drury Lane, December 20, 1740, as not having been acted for forty years, and represented twenty-six times in that season. At Goodman's Fields, Jan. 15, 1741, *The Winter's Tale* was announced, as not having been acted for one hundred years; but was not equally successful, being only performed nine times. At Drury Lane, Feb. 14, 1741, *The Merchant of Venice,* which, I believe, had not been acted for one hundred years, was once more restored to the scene by Mr. Macklin, who on that night first represented Shylock; a part which for near fifty years he performed with unrivalled success. In the following month the company at Goodman's Fields endeavoured to make a stand against him by producing *All's well that ends well,* which, they asserted, " had not been acted since Shakspeare's time." But the great theatrical event of this year was the appearance of Mr. Garrick at the theatre in Goodman's Fields, Oct. 9, 1741; whose good taste led him to study the plays of Shakspeare with more assiduity than any of his predecessors. Since that time, in consequence of Mr. Garrick's admirable performance of many of his principal characters, the frequent representation of his plays in nearly their original state, and above all, the various researches which have been made for the purpose of explaining and illustrating his works, our poet's reputation has been yearly increasing, and is now fixed upon a basis, which neither the lapse of time nor the fluctuation of opinion will ever be able to shake. Here therefore I conclude this imperfect account of the origin and progress of the English Stage.

[7] *King Henry VI.* altered from Shakspeare by Theophilus Cibber, was performed by a summer company at Drury Lane, July 5, 1723; but it met with no success, being represented only once.

# MR. POPE'S

# PREFACE.

IT is not my design to enter into a criticism upon this author; though to do it effectually, and not superficially, would be the best occasion that any just writer could take, to form the judgment and taste of our nation. For of all English poets Shakspeare must be confessed to be the fairest and fullest subject for criticism, and to afford the most numerous, as well as most conspicuous instances, both of beauties and faults of all sorts. But this far exceeds the bounds of a preface, the business of which is only to give an account of the fate of his works, and the disadvantages under which they have been transmitted to us. We shall hereby extenuate many faults which are his, and clear him from the imputation of many which are not : a design, which, though it can be no guide to future criticks to do him justice in one way, will at least be sufficient to prevent their doing him an injustice in the other.

I cannot however but mention some of his principal and characteristick excellencies, for which (notwithstanding his defects) he is justly and universally elevated above all other dramatick writers. Not that this is the proper place of praising him, but because I would not omit any occasion of doing it.

If ever any author deserved the name of an *original*, it was Shakspeare. Homer himself drew not his art so immediately from the fountains of nature; it proceeded through Ægyptian strainers and channels, and came to him not without some tincture of the learning, or some cast of the models, of those before him. The poetry of Shakspeare was inspiration indeed : he is not so much an imitator, as an instrument of nature; and it is not so just to say that he speaks from her, as that she speaks through him.

His *characters* are so much nature herself, that it is a sort of injury to call them by so distant a name as copies of her. Those of other poets have a constant resemblance, which shows that they received them from one another, and were but multipliers of the same image; each picture, like a mock-rainbow, is but the reflection of a reflection. But every single character in Shakspeare is as much an individual, as those in life itself: it is as impossible to find any two alike; and such as from their relation or affinity in any respect appear most to be twins, will, upon comparison, be found remarkably distinct. To this life and variety of character, we must add the wonderful preservation of it; which is such throughout his plays, that had all the speeches been printed without the very names of the persons, I believe one might have applied them with certainty to every speaker.[1]

The *power* over our *passions* was never possessed in a more eminent degree, or displayed in so different instances. Yet all along, there is seen no labour, no pains to raise them; no preparation to guide or guess to the effect, or be perceived to lead toward it: but the heart swells, and the tears burst out, just at the proper places: we are surprised the moment we weep; and yet upon reflection find the passion so just, that we should be surprised if we had not wept, and wept at that very moment.

How astonishing is it again, that the passions directly opposite to these, laughter and spleen, are no less at his command! that he is not more a master of the *great* than of the *ridiculous* in human nature; of our noblest tenderness, than of our vainest foibles; of our strongest emotions, than of our idlest sensations!

Nor does he only excel in the passions: in the coolness of reflection and reasoning he is full as admirable. His *sentiments* are not only in general the most pertinent and judicious upon every subject; but by a talent very peculiar, something between penetration and felicity, he hits upon that particular point on which the bent of each argument turns, or the force of each motive depends. This is perfectly amazing,

---

[1] Addison, in the 273d *Spectator*, has delivered a similar opinion respecting Homer: " There is scarce a speech or action in the *Iliad*, which the reader may not ascribe to the person who speaks or acts, without seeing his name at the head of it." STEEVENS,

from a man of no education or experience in those great and publick scenes of life which are usually the subject of his thoughts : so that he seems to have known the world by intuition, to have looked through human nature at one glance, and to be the only author that gives ground for a very new opinion, that the philosopher, and even the man of the world, may be *born*, as well as the poet.

It must be owned, that with all these great excellencies, he has almost as great defects; and that as he has certainly written better, so he has perhaps written worse, than any other. But I think I can in some measure account for these defects, from several causes and accidents; without which it is hard to imagine that so large and so enlightened a mind could ever have been susceptible of them. That all these contingencies should unite to his disadvantage seems to me almost as singularly unlucky, as that so many various (nay contrary) talents should meet in one man, was happy and extraordinary.

It must be allowed that stage-poetry, of all other, is more particularly levelled to please the *populace*, and its success more immediately depending upon the *common suffrage*. One cannot therefore wonder, if Shakspeare, having at his first appearance no other aim in his writings than to procure a subsistence, directed his endeavours solely to hit the taste and humour that then prevailed. The audience was generally composed of the meaner sort of people ; and therefore the images of life were to be drawn from those of their own rank : accordingly we find, that not our author's only, but almost all the old comedies have their scene among *tradesmen* and *mechanicks :* and even their historical plays strictly follow the common *old stories* or *vulgar traditions* of that kind of people. In tragedy, nothing was so sure to *surprize* and cause *admiration*, as the most strange, unexpected, and consequently most unnatural, events and incidents ; the most exaggerated thoughts ; the most verbose and bombast expression ; the most pompous rhymes, and thundering versification. In comedy, nothing was so sure to *please*, as mean buffoonery, vile ribaldry, and unmannerly jests of fools and clowns. Yet even in these our author's wit buoys up, and is borne above his subject : his genius in those low parts is like some prince of a romance in the disguise of a shepherd or peasant ; a certain greatness and spirit now and then break out, which manifest his higher extraction and qualities.

It may be added, that not only the common audience had
9

no notion of the rules of writing, but few even of the better
sort piqued themselves upon any great degree of knowledge
or nicety that way: till Ben Jonson getting possession of the
stage, brought critical learning into vogue: and that this was
not done without difficulty, may appear from those frequent
lessons (and indeed almost declamations) which he was
forced to prefix to his first plays, and put into the mouths of
his actors, the *grex*, *chorus*, &c. to remove the prejudices,
and inform the judgment of his hearers.   Till then, our authors had no thoughts of writing on the model of the ancients: their tragedies were only histories in dialogue; and
their comedies followed the thread of any novel as they found
it, no less implicitly than if it had been true history.

To judge therefore of Shakspeare by Aristotle's rules, is
like trying a man by the laws of one country, who acted
under those of another.   He writ to the *people*; and writ at
first without patronage from the better sort, and therefore
without aims of pleasing them : without assistance or advice
from the learned, as without the advantage of education or
acquaintance among them ; without that knowledge of the
best models, the ancients, to inspire him with an emulation
of them; in a word, without any views of reputation, and of
what poets are pleased to call immortality : some or all of
which have encouraged the vanity, or animated the ambition,
of other writers.

Yet it must be observed, that when his performances had
merited the protection of his prince, and when the encouragement of the court had succeeded to that of the town;
the works of his riper years are manifestly raised above those
of his former.   The dates of his plays sufficiently evidence
that his productions improved in proportion to the respect
he had for his auditors.   And I make no doubt this observation will be found true in every instance, were but editions
extant from which we might learn the exact time when every
piece was composed, and whether writ for the town, or the
court.

Another cause (and no less strong than the former) may
be deduced from our poet's being a *player*, and forming himself first upon the judgments of that body of men whereof he
was a member.   They have ever had a standard to themselves, upon other principles than those of Aristotle.   As
they live by the majority, they know no rule but that of
pleasing the present humour, and complying with the wit in
fashion; a consideration which brings all their judgment to a

short point.   Players are just such judges of what is *right* as the tailors are of what is *graceful*.   And in this view it will be but fair to allow, that most of our author's faults are less to be ascribed to his wrong judgment as a poet, than to his right judgment as a player.

By these men it would be thought a praise to Shakspeare, that he scarce ever *blotted a line*.   This they industriously propagated, as appears from what we are told by Ben Jonson in his *Discoveries*, and from the preface of *Heminge* and *Condell* to the first folio edition.   But in reality (however it has prevailed) there never was a more groundless report, or to the contrary of which there are more undeniable evidences. As, the comedy of *The Merry Wives of Windsor*, which he entirely new writ; *The History of Henry the Sixth*, which was first published under the title of *The Contention of York and Lancaster*; and that of *Henry the Fifth*, extremely improved; that of *Hamlet* enlarged to almost as much again as at first, and many others.   I believe the common opinion of his want of learning proceeded from no better ground.   This too might be thought a praise by some, and to this his errors have as injudiciously been ascribed by others.   For 'tis certain, were it true, it would concern but a small part of them; the most are such as are not properly defects, but superfoetations: and arise not from want of learning or reading, but from want of thinking or judging: or rather (to be more just to our author) from a compliance to those wants in others. As to a wrong choice of the subject, a wrong conduct of the incidents, false thoughts, forced expressions, &c. if these are not to be ascribed to the foresaid accidental reasons, they must be charged upon the poet himself, and there is no help for it.   But I think the two disadvantages which I have mentioned (to be obliged to please the lowest of the people, and to keep the worst of company) if the consideration be extended as far as it reasonably may, will appear sufficient to mislead and depress the greatest genius upon earth.   Nay, the more modesty with which such a one is endued, the more he is in danger of submitting and conforming to others, against his own better judgment.

But as to his *want of learning*, it may be necessary to say something more: there is certainly a vast difference between *learning* and *languages*.   How far he was ignorant of the latter, I cannot determine; but it is plain he had much reading at least, if they will not call it learning.   Nor is it any great matter, if a man has knowledge, whether he has

I 2

it from one language or from another. Nothing is more
evident than that he had a taste of natural philosophy, mechanicks, ancient and modern history, poetical learning, and
mythology : we find him very knowing in the customs, rites,
and manners of antiquity. In *Coriolanus* and *Julius Cæsar*,
not only the spirit, but manners, of the Romans are exactly
drawn ; and still a nicer distinction is shown between the
manners of Romans in the time of the former, and of
the latter. His reading in the ancient historians is no less
conspicuous, in many references to particular passages : and
the speeches copied from Plutarch in *Coriolanus* [a] may, I
think, as well be made an instance of his learning, as those
copied from Cicero in *Catiline* of Ben Jonson's. The manners of other nations in general, the Egyptians, Venetians,
French, &c. are drawn with equal propriety. Whatever
object of nature, or branch of science, he either speaks of
or describes, it is always with competent, if not extensive
knowledge : his descriptions are still exact ; all his metaphors
appropriated, and remarkably drawn from the true nature and
inherent qualities of each subject. When he treats of
ethick or politick, we may constantly observe a wonderful
justness of distinction, as well as extent of comprehension.
No one is more a master of the political story, or has more
frequent allusions to the various parts of it : Mr. Waller
(who has been celebrated for this last particular) has not
shown more learning this way than Shakspeare. We have
translations from *Ovid* published in his name,[b] among those
poems which pass for his, and for some of which we have
undoubted authority (being published by himself, and dedicated to his noble patron the Earl of Southampton :) he
appears also to have been conversant in *Plautus*, from whom
he has taken the plot of one of his plays : he follows the
Greek authors, and particularly Dares Phrygius, in another,
(although I will not pretend to say in what language he read
them.) The modern Italian writers of *novels* he was manifestly acquainted with ; and we may conclude him to be no
less conversant with the ancients of his own country, from
the use he has made of Chaucer in *Troilus and Cressida*, and
in *The Two Noble Kinsmen*, if that play be his, as there goes

---

[a] These, as the reader will find in the notes on that play, Shakspeare drew from Sir Thomas North's translation, 1579.
                                                    MALONE.

[b] They were written by Thomas Heywood.

a tradition it was (and indeed it has little resemblance of Fletcher, and more of our author than some of those which have been received as genuine.)

I am inclined to think this opinion proceeded originally from the zeal of the partizans of our author and Ben Jonson; as they endeavoured to exalt the one at the expence of the other. It is ever the nature of parties to be in extremes; and nothing is so probable, as that because Ben Jonson had much the more learning, it was said on the one hand that Shakspeare had none at all; and because Shakspeare had much the most wit and fancy, it was retorted on the other, that Jonson wanted both. Because Shakspeare borrowed nothing, it was said that Ben Jonson borrowed every thing. Because Jonson did not write extempore, he was reproached with being a year about every piece; and because Shakspeare wrote with ease and rapidity, they cried, he never once made a blot. Nay, the spirit of opposition ran so high, that whatever those of the one side objected to the other, was taken at the rebound, and turned into praises; as injudiciously, as their antagonist before had made them objections.

Poets are always afraid of envy; but sure they have as much reason to be afraid of admiration. They are the Scylla and Charybdis of authors; those who escape one, often fall by the other. *Pessimum genus inimicorum laudantes,* says Tacitus; and Virgil desires to wear a charm against those who praise a poet without rule or reason:

> " —— si ultra placitum laudârit, baccare frontem
> " Cingite, ne vati noceat ——."

But however this contention might be carried on by the partizans on either side, I cannot help thinking these two great poets were good friends, and lived on amicable terms, and in offices of society with each other. It is an acknowledged fact, that Ben Jonson was introduced upon the stage, and his first works encouraged, by Shakspeare. And after his death, that author writes, *To the memory of his beloved William Shakspeare,* which shows as if the friendship had continued through life. I cannot for my own part find any thing *invidious* or *sparing* in those verses, but wonder Mr. Dryden was of that opinion. He exalts him not only above all his contemporaries, but above Chaucer and Spenser, whom he will not allow to be great enough to be ranked with him; and challenges the names of Sophocles, Euripides, and Æschylus, nay, all Greece and Rome at once to equal him: and (which is very particular) expressly vindicates him from the imputation of wanting *art*, not enduring that all his excellencies should be attributed to *nature*. It is remarkable too, that the praise he gives him in his *Discoveries* seems to proceed from a *personal kindness*: he tells us, that he loved the man, as well as honoured his memory; celebrates the honesty, openness, and frankness of his temper; and only distinguishes, as he reasonably ought, between the real merit of the author, and the silly and derogatory applauses of the players. Ben Jonson might indeed be sparing in his commendations (though certainly he is not so in this instance) partly from his own nature, and partly from judgment. For men of judgment think they do any man more service in praising him justly, than lavishly. I say, I would fain believe they were friends, though the violence and ill-breeding of their followers and flatterers were enough to give rise to the contrary report. I hope that it may be with *parties*, both in wit and state, as with those monsters described by the poets; and that their *heads* at least may have something human, though their *bodies* and *tails* are wild beasts and serpents.

As I believe that what I have mentioned gave rise to the opinion of Shakspeare's want of learning; so what has continued it down to us may have been the many blunders and illiteracies of the first publishers of his works. In these editions their ignorance shines in almost every page; nothing is more common than *Actus tertia. Exit omnes. Enter three Witches solus.*[4] Their French is as bad as their Latin, both in construction and spelling: their very Welsh is false. Nothing is more likely than that those palpable blunders of Hector's quoting Aristotle, with others of that gross kind, sprung from the same root: it not being at all credible that these could be the errors of any man who had the least tincture of a school, or the least conversation with such as had. Ben Jonson (whom they will not think partial to him) allows him at least to have had *some* Latin; which is utterly inconsistent with mistakes like these. Nay, the constant blunders in proper names of persons and places, are such as

[4] *Enter three Witches solus.*] This blunder appears to be of Mr. Pope's own invention. It is not to be found in any one of the four folio copies of *Macbeth*, and there is no quarto edition of it extant. STEEVENS.

must have proceeded from a man, who had not so much as read any history in any language; so could not be Shakspeare's.

I shall now lay before the reader some of those almost innumerable errors, which have risen from one source, the ignorance of the players, both as his actors, and as his editors. When the nature and kinds of these are enumerated and considered, I dare to say that not Shakspeare only, but Aristotle or Cicero, had their works undergone the same fate, might have appeared to want sense as well as learning.

It is not certain that any one of his plays was published by himself. During the time of his employment in the theatre, several of his pieces were printed separately in quarto. What makes me think that most of these were not published by him, is the excessive carelessness of the press: every page is so scandalously false spelled, and almost all the learned and unusual words so intolerably mangled, that it is plain there either was no corrector to the press at all, or one totally illiterate. If any were supervised by himself, I should fancy *The Two Parts of Henry the Fourth*, and *Midsummer-Night's Dream*, might have been so: because I find no other printed with any exactness: and (contrary to the rest) there is very little variation in all the subsequent editions of them. There are extant two prefaces to the first quarto edition of *Troilus and Cressida* in 1609, and to that of *Othello*; by which it appears, that the first was published without his knowledge or consent, and even before it was acted, so late as seven or eight years before he died : and that the latter was not printed till after his death. The whole number of genuine plays, which we have been able to find printed in his life-time, amounts but to eleven. And of some of these, we meet with two or more editions by different printers, each of which has whole heaps of trash different from the other: which I should fancy was occasioned by their being taken from different copies belonging to different playhouses.

The folio edition (in which all the plays we now receive as his were first collected) was published by two players, Heminge and Condell, in 1623, seven years after his decease. They declare, that all the other editions were stolen and surreptitious, and affirm theirs to be purged from the errors of the former. This is true as to the literal errors, and no other; for in all respects else it is far worse than the quartos.

First, because the additions of trifling and bombast passages are in this edition far more numerous. For whatever had been added, since those quartos, by the actors, or had stolen from their mouths into the written parts, were from thence conveyed into the printed text, and all stand charged upon the author. He himself complained of this usage in *Hamlet*, where he wishes that *those who play the clowns would speak no more than is set down for them*. (Act III. sc. ii.) But as a proof that he could not escape it, in the old editions of *Romeo and Juliet* there is no hint of a great number of the mean conceits and ribaldries now to be found there. In others, the low scenes of mobs, plebeians, and clowns, are vastly shorter than at present: and I have seen one in particular (which seems to have belonged to the play-house, by having the parts divided with lines, and the actors names in the margin) where several of those very passages were added in a written hand, which are since to be found in the folio.

In the next place, a number of beautiful passages, which are extant in the first single editions, are omitted in this: as it seems, without any other reason, than their willingness to shorten some scenes: these men (as it was said of Procrustes) either lopping, or stretching an author, to make him just fit for their stage.

This edition is said to be printed from the *original copies*; I believe they meant those which had lain ever since the author's days in the play-house, and had from time to time been cut, or added to, arbitrarily. It appears that this edition, as well as the quartos, was printed (at least partly) from no better copies than the *prompter's-book*, or *piece-meal parts* written out for the use of the actors: for in some places their very⁵ names are through carelessness set down instead of the *Personæ Dramatis*; and in others the notes of direction to the *property-men* for their *moveables*, and to the *players* for their *entries*, are inserted into the text⁶ through the ignorance of the transcribers.

---

⁵ *Much Ado about Nothing*, Act II: " *Enter Prince Leonato, Claudio, and Jack Wilson*," instead of *Balthasar*. And in Act IV. *Cowley* and *Kemp* constantly through a whole scene,

Edit. fol. of 1623, and 1632.   POPE.

⁶ Such as

" My queen is murder'd! *Ring the little bell*."

" — His nose grew as sharp as a pen, *and a table of green fields* ;" which last words are not in the quarto.   POPE.

The plays not having been before so much as distinguished by *Acts* and *Scenes*, they are in this edition divided according as they played them; often when there is no pause in the action, or where they thought fit to make a breach in it, for the sake of musick, masques, or monsters.

Sometimes the scenes are transposed and shuffled backward and forward; a thing which could no otherwise happen, but by their being taken from separate and piece-meal written parts.

Many verses are omitted entirely, and others transposed; from whence invincible obscurities have arisen, past the guess of any commentator to clear up, but just where the accidental glimpse of an old edition enlightens us.

Some characters were confounded and mixed, or two put into one, for want of a competent number of actors. Thus in the quarto edition of *Midsummer-Night's Dream*, Act V. Shakspeare introduces a kind of master of the revels called *Philostrate*; all whose part is given to another character (that of *Egeus*) in the subsequent editions : so also in *Hamlet* and *King Lear*. This too makes it probable that the prompter's books were what they called the original copies.

From liberties of this kind, many speeches also were put into the mouths of wrong persons, where the author now seems chargeable with making them speak out of character: or sometimes perhaps for no better reason, than that a governing player, to have the mouthing of some favourite speech himself, would snatch it from the unworthy lips of an underling.

Prose from verse they did not know, and they accordingly printed one for the other throughout the volume.

Having been forced to say so much of the players, I think I ought in justice to remark, that the judgment, as well as condition of that class of people was then far inferior to what it is in our days. As then the best play-houses were inns and taverns, (the Globe, the Hope, the Red Bull, the Fortune, &c.) so the top of the profession were then mere players, not gentlemen of the stage : they were led into the buttery by the steward ;⁷ not placed at the lord's table, or lady's toilette: and consequently were entirely de-

There is no such line in any play of Shakspeare, as that quoted above by Mr. Pope. MALONE.

⁷ Mr. Pope probably recollected the following lines in *The*

prived of those advantages they now enjoy in the familiar conversation of our nobility, and an intimacy (not to say dearness) with people of the first condition.

From what has been said, there can be no question but had Shakspeare published his works himself (especially in his latter time, and after his retreat from the stage) we should not only be certain which are genuine, but should find in those that are, the errors lessened by some thousands. If I may judge from all the distinguishing marks of his style, and his manner of thinking and writing, I make no doubt to declare that those wretched plays, *Pericles, Locrine, Sir John Oldcastle, Yorkshire Tragedy, Lord Cromwell, The Puritan, London Prodigal,* and a thing called *The Double Falshood,*[7] cannot be admitted as his. And I should conjecture of some of the others, (particularly *Love's Labour's Lost, The Winter's Tale, Comedy of Errors,* and *Titus Andronicus,*) that only some characters, single scenes, or perhaps a few particular passages, were of his hand. It is very probable what occasioned some plays to be supposed Shakspeare's, was only this; that they were pieces produced by unknown authors, or fitted up for the theatre while it was under his administration; and no owner claiming them, they were adjudged to him, as they give strays to the lord of the manor: a mistake which (one may also observe) it was not for the interest of the house to remove. Yet the players themselves, Heminge and Condell, afterwards did Shakspeare the justice to reject those eight plays in their edition; though they were then printed in his name,[8] in every body's hands, and acted with some applause (as we learned from what Ben Jonson says of *Pericles* in his ode on the *New Inn*). That *Titus Andronicus* is one of this class I am the rather induced to believe, by finding the same author

*Taming of the Shrew,* spoken by a Lord, who is giving directions to his servant concerning some players :

" Go, sirrah, take them to the *buttery,*
" And give them friendly welcome, every one."

But he seems not to have observed that the players here introduced were *strollers ;* and there is no reason to suppose that our author, Heminge, Burbage, Lowin, &c. who were licensed by King James, were treated in this manner.   MALONE.

[7] *The Double Falshood,* or *The Distressed Lovers,* a play, acted at Drury Lane, 8vo. 1727. This piece was produced by Mr. Theobald as a performance of Shakspeare's.

[8] His name was affixed only to four of them.   MALONE.

9

openly express his contempt of it in the *Induction* to *Bartholomew Fair*, in the year 1614, when Shakspeare was yet living.    And there is no better authority for these latter sort, than for the former, which were equally published in his life-time.

If we give into this opinion, how many low and vicious parts and passages might no longer reflect upon this great genius, but appear unworthily charged upon him?    And even in those which are really his, how many faults may have been unjustly laid to his account from arbitrary additions, expunctions, transpositions of scenes and lines, confusion of characters and persons, wrong application of speeches, corruptions of innumerable passages by the ignorance, and wrong corrections of them again by the impertinence of his first editors?    From one or other of these considerations, I am verily persuaded, that the greatest and the grossest part of what are thought his errors would vanish, and leave his character in a light very different from that disadvantageous one, in which it now appears to us.

This is the state in which Shakspeare's writings lie at present; for since the above-mentioned folio edition, all the rest have implicitly followed it, without having recourse to any of the former, or ever making the comparison between them.    It is impossible to repair the injuries already done him; too much time has elapsed, and the materials are too few.    In what I have done I have rather given a proof of my willingness and desire, than of my ability, to do him justice.    I have discharged the dull duty of an editor, to my best judgment, with more labour than I expect thanks, with a religious abhorrence of all innovation, and without any indulgence to my private sense or conjecture.    The method taken in this edition will show itself.    The various readings are fairly put in the margin, so that every one may compare them; and those I have preferred into the text are constantly *ex fide codicum*, upon authority.    The alterations or additions, which Shakspeare himself made, are taken notice of as they occur.    Some suspected passages, which are excessively bad (and which seem interpolations by being so inserted that one can entirely omit them without any chasm, or deficience in the context) are degraded to the bottom of the page; with an asterisk referring to the places of their insertion.    The scenes are marked so distinctly, that every removal of place is specified; which is more necessary in this author than any other, since he shifts them more frequently; and sometimes, without attending to this particular, the reader would have met with obscurities. The more obsolete or unusual words are explained. Some of the most shining passages are distinguished by commas in the margin; and where the beauty lay not in particulars, but in the whole, a star is prefixed to the scene. This seems to me a shorter and less ostentatious method of performing the better half of criticism (namely, the pointing out an author's excellencies) than to fill a whole paper with citations of fine passages, with *general applauses*, or *empty exclamations* at the tail of them. There is also subjoined a catalogue of those first editions, by which the greater part of the various readings and of the corrected passages are authorized; most of which are such as carry their own evidence along with them. These editions now hold the place of originals, and are the only materials left to repair the deficiencies or restore the corrupted sense of the author: I can only wish that a greater number of them (if a greater were ever published) may yet be found, by a search more successful than mine, for the better accomplishment of this end.

I will conclude by saying of Shakspeare, that with all his faults, and with all the irregularity of his *drama*, one may look upon his works, in comparison of those that are more finished and regular, as upon an ancient majestick piece of *Gothick* architecture, compared with a neat modern building: the latter is more elegant and glaring, but the former is more strong and more solemn. It must be allowed that in one of these there are materials enough to make many of the other. It has much the greater variety, and much the nobler apartments; though we are often conducted to them by dark, odd, and uncouth passages. Nor does the whole fail to strike us with greater reverence, though many of the parts are childish, ill-placed, and unequal to its grandeur.[9]

---

[9] The following passage by Mr. Pope stands as a preface to the *various readings* at the end of the 8th volume of his edition of Shakspeare, 1728. For the notice of it I am indebted to Mr. Chalmers's *Supplemental Apology*, p. 261. REED.

"Since the publication of our first edition, there having been some attempts upon Shakspeare published by Lewis Theobald, (which he would not communicate during the time wherein that edition was preparing for the press, when we, by publick advertisements, did request the assistance of all lovers of this author,)

12

we have inserted, in this impression, as many of 'em as are judg'd of any the least advantage to the poet; the whole amounting to about *twenty-five* words.

"But to the end every reader may judge for himself, we have annexed a *compleat list* of the rest; which if he shall think *trivial*, or *erroneous*, either in part, or in whole; at worst it can spoil but a half sheet of paper, that chances to be left vacant here. And we purpose for the future, to do the same with respect to any other persons, who either thro' *candor* or *vanity*, shall communicate or publish, the least things tending to the illustration of our author. *We* have here omitted nothing but *pointings* and meer errors of the press, which I hope the corrector of it has rectify'd; if not, I cou'd wish as accurate an one as Mr. Th. [if he] had been at that trouble, which I desired Mr. Tonson to solicit him to undertake. A; P,"

# TEMPEST.*

B

* TEMPEST.] *The Tempest,* and *The Midsummer Night's Dream* are the noblest efforts of that sublime and amazing imagination peculiar to Shakspeare, which soars above the bounds of nature, without forsaking sense; or, more properly, carries nature along with him beyond her established limits. Fletcher seems particularly to have admired these two plays, and hath wrote two in imitation of them, *The Sea Voyage,* and *The Faithful Shepherdess.* But when he presumes to break a lance with Shakspeare, and write in emulation of him, as he does in *The False One,* which is the rival of *Antony and Cleopatra,* he is not so successful. After him, Sir John Suckling and Milton catched the brightest fire of their imagination from these two plays; which shines fantastically indeed in *The Goblins,* but much more nobly and serenely in *The Mask at Ludlow Castle.* WARBURTON.

No one has hitherto been lucky enough to discover the romance on which Shakspeare may be supposed to have founded this play, the beauties of which could not secure it from the criticism of Ben Jonson, whose malignity appears to have been more than equal to his wit. In the introduction to *Bartholomew Fair,* he says: " If there be never a *servant monster* in the fair, who can help it, he says, nor a nest of *antiques?* He is loth to make nature afraid in his plays, like those that beget *Tales, Tempests,* and such like drolleries." STEEVENS.

I was informed by the late Mr. Collins of Chichester, that Shakspeare's *Tempest,* for which no origin is yet assigned, was formed on a romance called *Aurelio and Isabella,* printed in Italian, Spanish, French, and English, in 1588. But though this information has not proved true on examination, an useful conclusion may be drawn from it, that Shakspeare's story is somewhere to be found in an Italian novel, at least that the story preceded Shakspeare. Mr. Collins had searched this subject with no less fidelity than judgment and industry; but his memory failing in his last calamitous indisposition, he probably gave me the name of one novel for another. I remember he added a circumstance which may lead to a discovery,—that the principal character of the romance, answering to Shakspeare's Prospero, was a chemical necromancer, who had bound a spirit like Ariel to obey his call, and perform his services. Taken at large, the magical part of the *Tempest* is founded on that sort of philosophy which was practised by John Dee and his associates, and has been called the Rosicrucian. The name Ariel came from the Talmudistick mysteries with which the learned Jews had infected this science. T. WARTON.

It was one of our author's last works. In 1598, he played a part in the original *Every Man in his Humour.* Two of the characters are *Prospero* and *Stephano.* Here Ben Jonson taught him the pronunciation of the latter word, which is always *right* in *The Tempest :*

" Is not this *Stephàno,* my drunken butler ?"

9

And always *wrong* in his earlier play, *The Merchant of Venice,*
which had been on the stage at least two or three years before
its publication in 1600 :

       " My friend *Stephāno,* signify I pray you," &c.
—So little did Mr. Capell know of his author, when he idly supposed his *school literature* might perhaps have been lost by the
*dissipation of youth,* or the *busy scene* of public life! FARMER.

    This play must have been written before 1614, when Jonson
sneers at it in his *Bartholomew Fair.* In the latter plays of
Shakspeare, he has less of pun and quibble than in his early ones.
In *The Merchant of Venice,* he expressly declares against them.
This perhaps might be one criterion to discover the dates of his
plays. BLACKSTONE.

    It was not printed till 1623, when it was published with the
rest of our author's plays in folio. Mr. Malone is of opinion it
was written about the year 1612.

# PERSONS REPRESENTED.*

Alonso, *king of* Naples.
Sebastian, *his brother.*
Prospero, *the rightful Duke of* Milan.
Antonio, *his brother, the usurping Duke of* Milan.
Ferdinand, *son to the king of* Naples.
Gonzalo, *an honest old counsellor of* Naples.
Adrian, } *lords.*
Francisco, } *lords.*
Caliban, *a savage and deformed slave.*
Trinculo, *a jester.*
Stephano, *a drunken butler.*
*Master of a ship, Boatswain, and Mariners.*

Miranda, *daughter to* Prospero.

Ariel, *an airy spirit.*
Iris,
Ceres,
Juno, } *spirits.*
Nymphs,
Reapers,

Other spirits attending on Prospero.

SCENE, *the sea, with a ship ; afterwards an uninhabited island.*

* This enumeration of persons is taken from the folio 1623.

STEEVENS.

# TEMPEST.

## ACT I.

### SCENE I. *On a Ship at Sea.*

*A Storm with Thunder and Lightning.*

*Enter a* Ship-master *and a* Boatswain.

*Master.* Boatswain,—
*Boats.* Here, master: What cheer?
*Mast.* Good: speak to the mariners: fall to't yarely,[1] or we run ourselves aground: bestir, bestir.
[*Exit.*

*Enter* Mariners.

*Boats.* Heigh, my hearts; cheerly, cheerly, my hearts; yare, yare: take in the top-sail; Tend to the master's whistle.——Blow till thou burst thy wind, if room enough!

*Enter* ALONSO, SEBASTIAN, ANTONIO, FERDI-NAND, GONZALO, *and others.*

*Alon.* Good Boatswain, have care. Where's the master? Play the men.[2]
*Boats.* I pray now, keep below.
*Ant.* Where is the master, Boatswain?
*Boats.* Do you not hear him? You mar our labour; Keep your cabins: you do assist the storm.

---

[1] —*fall to't* yarely,] i. e. Readily, nimbly. Our author is frequent in his use of this word.
[2] *Play the men.*] i. e. act with spirit, behave like men.

*Gon.* Nay, good, be patient.

*Boats.* When the sea is.   Hence! What care these roarers for the name of king? To cabin: silence: trouble us not.

*Gon.* Good; yet remember whom thou hast aboard.

*Boats.* None that I more love than myself.   You are a counsellor; if you can command these elements to silence, and work the peace of the present,[3] we will not hand a rope more; use your authority. If you cannot, give thanks you have lived so long, and make yourself ready in your cabin for the mischance of the hour, if it so hap.—Cheerly, good hearts—Out of our way, I say.                [*Exit.*

*Gon.*[4] I have great comfort from this fellow: methinks he hath no drowning mark upon him; his complexion is perfect gallows.   Stand fast, good fate, to his hanging! make the rope of his destiny our cable, for our own doth little advantage!  If he be not born to be hanged, our case is miserable.

                                             [*Exeunt.*

*Re-enter* Boatswain.

*Boats.* Down with the topmast; yare; lower, lower; bring her to try with main-course.[5] [*A cry within.*]   A plague upon this howling! they are louder than the weather, or our office.—

*Re-enter* SEBASTIAN, ANTONIO, *and* GONZALO.

Yet again? what do you here?  Shall we give o'er, and drown? Have you a mind to sink?

<hr>

[3] — *of the present,*] i. e. *of* the present *instant.*

[4] *Gonzalo.*] It may be observed of Gonzalo, that, being the only good man that appears with the king, he is the only man that preserves his cheerfulness in the wreck, and his hope on the island.                                   JOHNSON.

[5] — *bring her to* try with main-course.] This phrase occurs in Smith's *Sea Grammar,* 1627, 4to. under the article *How to handle*

*Seb.* A pox o' your throat! you bawling, blasphemous, incharitable dog!

*Boats.* Work you, then.

*Ant.* Hang, cur, hang! you whoreson, insolent noise-maker, we are less afraid to be drowned than thou art.

*Gon.* I'll warrant him from drowning; though the ship were no stronger than a nut-shell, and as leaky as an unstanched wench.[6]

*Boats.* Lay her a-hold, a-hold:[7] set her two courses; off to sea again,[8] lay her off.

*Enter* Mariners *wet.*

*Mar.* All lost! to prayers, to prayers! all lost!
*[Exeunt.*

*Boats.* What, must our mouths be cold?

*Gon.* The king and prince at prayers! let us assist them,
For our case is as theirs.

*Seb.* I am out of patience.

*Ant.* We are merely[9] cheated of our lives by drunkards.—
This wide-chapped rascal;—'Would, thou might'st lie drowning,
The washing of ten tides!

*Gon.* He'll be hanged yet;
Though every drop of water swear against it,
And gape at wid'st to glut him.[1]

a *Ship in a Storme:* "Let us lie at *Trie with our main course;* that is, to hale the tacke aboord, the sheat close aft, the boling set up, and the helme tied close aboord." STEEVENS.

[6] — *an unstanched wench.*] *Unstanched,* perhaps incontinent.

[7] *Lay her a-hold, a-hold:*] i. e. bring her to lie as near the wind as she can, in order to keep clear of the land, and get her out to sea.

[8] — *Set her two courses; off to sea again,*] The courses are the main-sail and fore-sail.

[9] —*merely*—] In this place, signifies *absolutely.* STEEVENS.

[1] — *to glut him.*] Shakspeare probably wrote, *t'englut him,* to

# TEMPEST.

[*A confused noise within.*] Mercy on us! We split,
we split!—Farewell, my wife and children! Farewell, brother![2] We split, we split, we split!—

   *Ant.* Let's all sink with the king.      [*Exit.*
   *Seb.* Let's take leave of him.      [*Exit.*
   *Gon.* Now would I give a thousand furlongs of
sea for an acre of barren ground; long heath, brown
furze,[3] any thing: The wills above be done! but I
would fain die a dry death.      [*Exit.*

## SCENE II.

*The island: before the cell of* Prospero.

*Enter* PROSPERO *and* MIRANDA.

   *Mira.* If by your art, my dearest father, you have
Put the wild waters in this roar, allay them:
The sky, it seems, would pour down stinking pitch,
But that the sea, mounting to the welkin's cheek,
Dashes the fire out. O, I have suffer'd
With those that I saw suffer! a brave vessel
Who had no doubt some noble creatures in her,[4]
Dash'd all to pieces. O, the cry did knock
Against my very heart! Poor souls! they perish'd.
Had I been any god of power, I would
Have sunk the sea within the earth, or e'er[5]

swallow him. In this signification *englut* from *engloutir*, Fr. occurs frequently. Yet Milton writes *glutted offal* for *swallowed*, and therefore perhaps the present text may stand.

  [2] *Mercy on us! &c.————Farewell, brother! &c.*] It is probable, that the lines succeeding the *confused noise within* should be considered as spoken by no determinate characters.

  [3] ———— *an acre of barren ground; long heath,* brown *furze, &c.*] Sir T. Hanmer reads—*ling,* heath, *broom,* furze.—Perhaps rightly, though he has been charged with tautology.

  [4] ———— *creatures in her,*] The old copy reads—*creature*; but the preceding as well as subsequent words of Miranda seem to demand the emendation suggested first by Theobald.

  [5] ———— *or e'er—*] i. e. *before.*

It should the good ship so have swallowed, and
The freighting souls within her.
  *Pro.*       Be collected;
No more amazement : tell your piteous heart,
There's no harm done.
  *Mir.*      O, woe the day!
  *Pro.*         No harm.[6]
I have done nothing but in care of thee,
(Of thee, my dear one.! thee, my daughter!) who
Art ignorant of what thou art, nought knowing
Of whence I am ; nor that I am more better[7]
Than Prospero, master of a full poor cell,[8]
And thy no greater father.
  *Mira.*      More to know
Did never meddle with my thoughts.[9]
  *Pro.*        'Tis time
I should inform thee further. Lend thy hand,
And pluck my magic garment from me.——So ;
       [*Lays down his mantle.*
Lie there my art.——Wipe thou thine eyes ; have
   comfort.
The direful spectacle of the wreck, which touch'd
The very virtue of compassion[1] in thee,
I have with such provision in mine art
So safely order'd, that there is no soul——[2]

---

 [6] *Pro. No harm.*]  Perhaps Shakspeare wrote,
   *O, woe the day ! no harm ?*
To which Prospero properly answers :
   *I have done nothing but in care of thee.*  JOHNSON.
 [7] —— *more better*—]  This ungrammatical expression is very
frequent among our oldest writers.
 [8] —— *full poor cell,*]  i. e. a cell in a great degree of poverty.
 [9] *Did never* meddle *with my thoughts.*]  i. e. *mix* with them.
  To meddle, means, also, *to interfere, to trouble, to busy itself.*
 [1] —— virtue *of compassion*—]  Virtue ; the most efficacious
part, as *The virtue of a plant is in the extract.*
 [2] —— *no soul*—]  Such interruptions are not uncommon to
Shakspeare.  He sometimes begins a sentence, and, before he
concludes it, entirely changes its construction, because another;

No, not so much perdition as an hair,
Betid to any creature in the vessel
Which thou heard'st cry, which thou saw'st sink.
　　　　　Sit down ;
For thou must now know further.
　　*Mira.*　　　　　　　　　　　You have often
Begun to tell me what I am ; but stopp'd
And left me to a bootless inquisition ;
Concluding, *Stay, not yet.*—
　　*Pro.*　　　　　　　　The hour's now come ;
The very minute bids thee ope thine ear ;
Obey, and be attentive.　Can'st thou remember
A time before we came unto this cell ?
I do not think thou can'st ; for then thou wast not
Out three years old.[3]
　　*Mira.*　　　　　　Certainly, sir, I can.
　　*Pro.* By what ? by any other house, or person ?
Of any thing the image tell me, that
Hath kept with thy remembrance.
　　*Mira.*　　　　　　　　'Tis far off,
And rather like a dream than an assurance
That my remembrance warrants : Had I not
Four or five women once, that tended me ?
　　*Pro.* Thou hadst, and more, Miranda : But how
　　　　　is it,
That this lives in thy mind ? What see'st thou else
In the dark backward and abysm of time ?[4]
If thou remember'st ought, ere thou cam'st here,
How thou cam'st here, thou may'st.
　　*Mira.*　　　　　　　But that I do not.

---

more forcible, occurs.　As this change frequently happens in conversation, it may be suffered to pass uncensured in the language
of the stage.　STEEVENS.
　　[3] Out *three years old.*] i. e. Quite three years old.
　　[4] ―― abysm *of time* ?] i. e. Abyss.　This method of spelling
the word is common to other antient writers.　They took it from
the French *abysme*, now written *abîme.*

*Pro.* Twelve years since, Miranda, twelve years
　　　since,[5]
Thy father was the duke of Milan, and
A prince of power.
　　*Mira.*　　　　　　Sir, are not you my father?
　　*Pro.* Thy mother was a piece of virtue, and
She said—thou wast my daughter; and thy father
Was duke of Milan; and his only heir
A princess; no worse issued.[6]
　　*Mira.*　　　　　　　　O, the heavens!
What foul play had we, that we came from thence?
Or blessed was't, we did?
　　*Pro.*　　　　　　Both, both, my girl;
By foul play, as thou say'st, were we heav'd thence;
But blessedly holp hither.
　　*Mira.*　　　　　　　O, my heart bleeds
To think o' the teen[7] that I have turn'd you to,
Which is from my remembrance! Please you fur-
　　　ther.
　　*Pro.* My brother, and thy uncle, call'd An-
　　　tonio,—
I pray thee, mark me,—that a brother should
Be so perfidious!—he whom, next thyself,
Of all the world I lov'd, and to him put
The manage of my state; as, at that time,
Through all the signiories it was the first,
And Prospero the prime duke; being so reputed
In dignity, and, for the liberal arts,
Without a parallel: those being all my study,
The government I cast upon my brother,

[5] *Twelve* years *since, Miranda, twelve* years *since,*] *Years,* in
the first instance, is used as a dissyllable, in the second as a mo-
nosyllable; a licence not peculiar to the prosody of Shakspeare.
[6] *A princess ;—no worse* issued.] The old copy reads—" And
princess." For the trivial change in the text I am answerable.
*Issued* is descended. STEEVENS.
[7] —— *teen* —] is sorrow, grief, trouble.

And to my state grew stranger, being transported,
And rapt in secret studies. Thy false uncle——
Dost thou attend me?

    *Mira.*                Sir, most heedfully.

    *Pro.* Being once perfected how to grant suits,
How to deny them; whom to advance, and whom
To trash for over-topping;[8] new created
The creatures that were mine; I say, or chang'd
        them,
Or else new form'd them; having both the key[9]
Of officer and office, set all hearts
To what tune pleas'd his ear; that now he was
The ivy, which had hid my princely trunk,
And suck'd my verdure out on't.——Thou attend'st
        not:
I pray thee, mark me.[1]

    *Mira.*            O good sir, I do.

    *Pro.* I thus neglecting worldly ends, all dedicate
To closeness, and the bettering of my mind
With that, which, but by being so retired,
O'er-priz'd all popular rate, in my false brother
Awak'd an evil nature: and my trust,
Like a good parent,[2] did beget of him

---

  [8] *To trash for over-topping;*] *To trash,* in old books of gardening, is to cut away the superfluities. It is used, also, by sportsmen in the North, when they correct a dog for misbehaviour in pursuing the game. A *trash,* among hunters, denotes a piece of leather, couples, or any other weight fastened round the neck of a dog, when his speed is superior to the rest of the pack; i. e. when he *over-tops* them, when he *hunts too quick.*
  See *Othello,* Act. II. sc. i.

  [9] —— *both the* key——] This is meant of a key for tuning the harpsichord, spinnet, or virginal; called now a tuning hammer.

  [1] *I pray thee, mark me.*] In the old copy, these words are the beginning of Prospero's next speech; but, for the restoration of metre, I have changed their place. STEEVENS.

  [2] *Like a good* parent, &c.] Alluding to the observation, that a father above the common rate of men has commonly a son below it. *Heroum filii noxæ.* JOHNSON.

A falsehood, in its contrary as great
As my trust was; which had, indeed, no limit,
A confidence sans bound.   He being thus lorded,
Not only with what my revenue yielded,
But what my power might else exact,—like one,
Who having, unto truth, by telling of it,
Made such a sinner of his memory,
To credit his own lie,'—he did believe
He was the duke; out of the substitution,⁴
And executing the outward face of royalty,
With all prerogative:—Hence his ambition
Growing,—Dost hear?
    *Mira.*          Your tale, sir, would cure deafness,
    *Pro.* To have no screen between this part he
         play'd,
And him he play'd it for, he needs will be
Absolute Milan: Me, poor man!—my library
Was dukedom large enough; of temporal royalties
He thinks me now incapable: confederates
(So dry he was for sway⁵) with the king of Naples,
To give him annual tribute, do him homage;
Subject his coronet to his crown, and bend
The dukedom, yet unbow'd, (alas, poor Milan!)
To most ignoble stooping.
    *Mira.*          O the heavens!
    *Pro.* Mark his condition, and the event; then
         tell me,
If this might be a brother.

---

³ ————————— *like one,*
*Who having, unto truth, by telling of it,*
*Made such a sinner of his memory,*
*To credit his own lie,*] There is, perhaps, no correlative, to which the word *it* can with grammatical propriety belong. *Lie,* however, seems, to have been the correlative to which the poet meant to refer, however ungrammatically.

⁴ *He was the duke; out of the substitution,*] The reader should place his emphasis on—was. STEEVENS.

⁵ *(So dry he was for sway)*] i. e. So *thirsty.*

*Mira.*　　　　　　　　　　　I should sin
To think but nobly[6] of my grandmother:
Good wombs have borne bad sons.

*Pro.*　　　　　　　　　　Now the condition.
This king of Naples, being an enemy
To me inveterate, hearkens my brother's suit;
Which was, that he in lieu o' the premises,—[7]
Of homage, and I know not how much tribute,—
Should presently extirpate me and mine
Out of the dukedom; and confer fair Milan,
With all the honours, on my brother: Whereon,
A treacherous army levied, one midnight
Fated to the purpose, did Antonio open
The gates of Milan; and, i' the dead of darkness,
The ministers for the purpose hurried thence
Me, and thy crying self.

*Mira.*　　　　　　　　　Alack, for pity!
I, not rememb'ring how I cry'd out then,
Will cry it o'er again: it is a hint,[8]
That wrings mine eyes.[9]

*Pro.*　　　　　　　　　Hear a little further,
And then I'll bring thee to the present business
Which now's upon us; without the which, this
　　　　story
Were most impertinent.

*Mira.*　　　　　　　　Wherefore did they not
That hour destroy us?

*Pro.*　　　　　　　　Well demanded, wench;
My tale provokes that question. Dear, they durst
　　　　not;
(So dear the love my people bore me) nor set
A mark so bloody on the business; but

---

[6] *To think* but *nobly*—] *But,* i. e. in this place *otherwise than.*
[7] ——in lieu o' *the premises,* &c.] In *lieu of,* means here, in consideration of; an unusual acceptation of the word.
[8] ——*a* hint,] *Hint* is *suggestion.*
[9] *That* wrings *mine eyes.*] i. e. squeezes the water out of them.

With colours fairer painted their foul ends.
In few, they hurried us aboard a bark;
Bore us some leagues to sea; where they prepared
A rotten carcase of a boat, not rigg'd,
Nor tackle, sail, nor mast; the very rats
Instinctively had quit it: there they hoist us,
To cry to the sea that roar'd to us; to sigh
To the winds, whose pity, sighing back again,
Did us but loving wrong.

  *Mira.*       Alack! what trouble
Was I then to you!

  *Pro.*       O! a cherubim
Thou wast, that did preserve me! Thou didst smile,
Infused with a fortitude from heaven,
When I have deck'd the sea[1] with drops full salt;
Under my burden groan'd; which rais'd in me
An undergoing stomach,[2] to bear up
Against what should ensue.

  *Mira.*       How came we ashore?

  *Pro.* By Providence divine.
Some food we had, and some fresh water, that
A noble Neapolitan, Gonzalo,
Out of his charity (who being then appointed
Master of this design,) did give us;[3] with

---

[1] —— deck'd *the sea*—] *To deck the sea,* if explained to honour, adorn, or dignify, is indeed ridiculous, but the original import of the verb *deck,* is *to cover;* so, in some parts, they yet say *deck the table.* This sense may be borne, but perhaps the poet wrote *fleck'd,* which I think is still used in rustic language of drops falling upon water. Dr. Warburton reads *mock'd;* the Oxford edition *brack'd.* JOHNSON.

To *deck* signifies in the North to *sprinkle;* and *degg'd,* which means the same, is in daily use in the North of England. When clothes that have been washed are too much dried, it is necessary to moisten them before they can be ironed, which is always done by *sprinkling;* this operation the maidens universally call *degging.*

[2] *An undergoing stomach,*] *Stomach* is *stubborn resolution.*

[3] *Some food we had, and some fresh water, that*
 *A noble Neapolitan, Gonzalo,*

Rich garments, linens, stuffs, and necessaries,
Which since have steaded much; so, of his gentle-
      ness,
Knowing I lov'd my books, he furnish'd me,
From my own library, with volumes that
I prize above my dukedom.
    *Mira.*            'Would I might
But ever see that man!
    *Pro.*          Now I arise :—⁴
Sit still, and hear the last of our sea-sorrow.
Here in this island we arrived; and here
Have I, thy school-master, made thee more profit
Than other princes can, that have more time
For vainer hours, and tutors not so careful.
    *Mira.* Heavens thank you for't! And now, I
      pray you, sir,

*Out of his charity, (who being then appointed*
   *Master of this design,) did give us ;*] Mr. Steevens has suggested, that we might better read—*he being then appointed ;*
and so we should certainly now write : but the reading of the
old copy is the true one, that mode of phraseology being the
idiom of Shakspeare's time.  MALONE.

    I have left the passage in question as I found it, though with
slender reliance on its integrity.

    What Mr. Malone has styled " the idiom of Shakspeare's
time," can scarce deserve so creditable a distinction.

    The genuine idiom of our language, at its different periods, can
only be ascertained by reference to contemporary writers whose
works were skilfully revised as they passed through the press, and
are therefore unsuspected of corruption.  A sufficient number of
such books are before us.  If they supply examples of phraseology resembling that which Mr. Malone would establish, there
is an end of controversy between us.  STEEVENS.

  ⁴ *Now I arise :*]  Perhaps these words belong to Miranda,
and we should read :
      Mir. *'Would I might*
   *But ever see that man !—Now I arise.*
      Pro. *Sit still, and hear the last of our sea-sorrow.*
  As the words—" now I arise "—may signify, " now I *rise* in
my narration,"—" now my story *heightens* in its consequence,"
I have left the passage in question undisturbed.  We still say,
that the interest of a drama *rises* or declines.  STEEVENS.

*Miranda sleeps.*

Pro. { *Come away, servant, come; I am ready now*
*approach my Ariel: come.*

Published by F. C. Rivington London Jan. 1805.

(For still 'tis beating in my mind,) your reason
For raising this sea-storm?
  *Pro.*        Know thus far forth.—
By accident most strange, bountiful fortune,
Now my dear lady,[b] hath mine enemies
Brought to this shore: and by my prescience
I find my zenith doth depend upon
A most auspicious star; whose influence
If now I court not, but omit, my fortunes
Will ever after droop.—Here cease more questions;
Thou art inclin'd to sleep; 'tis a good dulness,[c]
And give it way;—I know thou can'st not
   choose.—    [MIRANDA *sleeps.*
Come away, servant, come: I am ready now;
Approach, my Ariel; come.

### *Enter* ARIEL.

 *Ari.* All hail, great master! grave sir, hail! I
  come
To answer thy best pleasure; be't to fly,
To swim, to dive into the fire, to ride
On the curl'd clouds;[7] to thy strong bidding, task
Ariel, and all his quality.[8]
  *Pro.*       Hast thou, spirit,
Perform'd to point[9] the tempest that I bade thee?
 *Ari.* To every article.

---

 [5] *Now my dear lady,*] i. e. *now my auspicious mistress.*
 [6] ——*'tis a good dulness,*] Dr. Warburton rightly observes,
that this sleepiness, which Prospero by his art had brought upon
Miranda, and of which he knew not how soon the effect would
begin, makes him question her so often whether she is attentive
to his story. JOHNSON.
 [7] *On the curl'd clouds;*] So, in *Timon—Crisp* heaven.
 [8] —— *and all his quality.*] i. e. all his confederates.
 [9] *Perform'd to point —*] i. e. to the minutest article; a literal
translation of the French phrase—*a point.*

I boarded the king's ship, now on the beak,[1]
Now in the waist,[2] the deck, in every cabin,
I flam'd amazement: Sometimes, I'd divide,
And burn in many places;[3] on the top-mast
The yards and bowsprit, would I flame distinctly,
Then meet, and join: Jove's lightnings, the pre-
    cursors
O' the dreadful thunder-claps, more momentary
And sight-out-running were not: The fire, and
    cracks
Of sulphurous roaring, the most mighty Neptune
Seem'd to besiege, and make his bold waves tremble,
Yea, his dread trident shake.[4]
   *Pro.*            My brave spirit!
Who was so firm, so constant, that this coil
Would not infect his reason?
   *Ari.*           Not a soul
But felt a fever of the mad, and play'd
Some tricks of desperation: All, but mariners,
Plung'd in the foaming brine, and quit the vessel,[5]
Then all a-fire with me: the king's son, Ferdinand,
With hair up-starting (then like reeds, not hair,)
Was the first man that leap'd; cried, *Hell is empty,*
*And all the devils are here.*

---

[1] — *now on the* beak,] The beak was a strong pointed body
at the head of the ancient gallies; it is used here for the forecastle, or the boltsprit. JOHNSON.
[2] *Now in the* waist,] The part between the quarter-deck and
the forecastle. JOHNSON.
[3] —— *Sometimes I'd divide,*
    *And burn in many places;*] Burton says, that the Spirits of
*fire,* in form of fire-drakes and blazing stars, "oftentimes sit on
ship-masts," &c. *Melanch.* P. I. § 2. p. 30. edit. 1632. WARTON.
[4] *Yea, his dread trident shake.*] Lest the metre should appear
defective, it is necessary to apprize the reader, that in Warwickshire, and other midland counties, *shake* is still pronounced by
the common people as if it was written *shaake,* a dissyllable.
                           FARMER.
[5] —— *and* quit *the vessel,*] *Quit* for *quitted.*

*Pro.* Why, that's my spirit!
But was not this nigh shore?
   *Ari.* Close by, my master.
   *Pro.* But are they, Ariel, safe?
   *Ari.* Not a hair perish'd;
On their sustaining[6] garments not a blemish,
But fresher than before: and, as thou bad'st me,
In troops I have dispers'd them 'bout the isle:
The king's son have I landed by himself;
Whom I left cooling of the air with sighs,
In an odd angle of the isle, and sitting,
His arms in this sad knot.
   *Pro.* Of the king's ship,
The mariners, say, how thou hast dispos'd,
And all the rest o' the fleet?
   *Ari.* Safely in harbour
Is the king's ship; in the deep nook, where once
Thou call'dst me up at midnight to fetch dew
From the still-vex'd Bermoothes,[7] there she's hid:
The mariners all under hatches stowed;
Whom, with a charm join'd to their suffer'd labour,
I have left asleep: and for the rest o' the fleet,
Which I dispers'd, they all have met again;
And are upon the Mediterranean flote,[8]
Bound sadly home for Naples;
Supposing that they saw the king's ship wreck'd,
And his great person perish.

---

[6] —— *sustaining*—] i. e. their garments that bore them up and supported them; or their garments which *bore*, without being injured, the drenching of the sea.

[7] The epithet here applied to the Bermudas, will be best understood by those who have seen the chafing of the sea over the rugged rocks by which they are surrounded, and which render access to them so dangerous. It was in our poet's time the current opinion, that Bermudas was inhabited by *monsters*, and *devils.*—*Setebos*, the god of Caliban's dam, was an American devil, worshipped by the giants of Patagonia. HENLEY.

[8] —— *the Mediterranean* flote,] *Flote* is *wave*.

*Pro.*                              Ariel, thy charge
Exactly is perform'd; but there's more work:
What is the time o' the day?

*Ari.*                              Past the mid season.

*Pro.* At least two glasses: The time 'twixt six
      and now,
Must by us both be spent most preciously.

*Ari.* Is there more toil? Since thou dost give
      me pains,
Let me remember thee what thou hast promis'd,
Which is not yet perform'd me.

*Pro.*                              How now? moody?
What is't thou can'st demand?

*Ari.*                              My liberty.

*Pro.* Before the tiine be out? no more.

*Ari.*                              I pray thee
Remember, I have done thee worthy service;
Told thee no lies, made no mistakings, serv'd
Without or grudge, or grumblings: thou didst
      promise
To bate me a full year.

*Pro.*                              Dost thou forget[9]

9 *Dost thou forget*—] That the character and conduct of Prospero may be understood, something must be known of the system
of enchantment, which supplied all the marvellous found in the
romances of the middle ages. This system seems to be founded on
the opinion that the fallen spirits, having different degrees of guilt,
had different habitations allotted them at their expulsion, some being confined in hell, *some* (as Hooker, who delivers the opinion of
our poet's age, expresses it,) *dispersed in air, some on earth, some
in water, others in caves, dens, or minerals under the earth.* Of
these, some were more malignant and mischievous than others.
The earthy spirits seem to have been thought the most depraved,
and the aerial the less vitiated. Thus Prospero observes of Ariel:
     *Thou wast a spirit too delicate*
    *To act her earthy and abhorr'd commands.*
Over these spirits a power might be obtained by certain rites performed or charms learned. This power was called *The black Art,*
or *Knowledge of Enchantment.* The enchanter being, (as king
James observes in his *Demonology*) one who *commands the devil,*

From what a torment I did free thee?

*Ari-*      No.

*Pro.* Thou dost; and think'st
It much to tread the ooze of the salt deep;
To run upon the sharp wind of the north;
To do me business in the veins o' the earth,
When it is bak'd with frost.

*Ari.*      I do not, sir.

*Pro.* Thou liest, malignant thing! Hast thou
     forgot
The foul witch Sycorax, who, with age, and envy,
Was grown into a hoop? hast thou forgot her?

*Ari.* No, sir.

*Pro.*      Thou hast: Where was she born?
     speak; tell me.

*Ari.* Sir, in Argier.[1]

*Pro.*      O, was she so? I must,
Once in a month, recount what thou has been,
Which thou forget'st. This damn'd witch, Sycorax,
For mischiefs manifold, and sorceries terrible
To enter human hearing, from Argier,
Thou know'st was banish'd; for one thing she did,
They would not take her life: Is not this true?

*Ari.* Ay, sir.

*Pro.* This blue-ey'd hag was hither brought with
     child,

---

*whereas the witch serves him.* The art was held by all, though not equally criminal, yet unlawful, and therefore Casaubon, speaking of one who had commerce with spirits, blames him, though he imagines him *one of the best kind, who dealt with them by way of command.* Thus Prospero repents of his art in the last scene. The spirits were always considered as in some measure enslaved to the enchanter, at least for a time, and as serving with unwillingness; therefore Ariel so often begs for liberty; and Caliban observes, that the spirits serve Prospero with no good will, but *hate him rootedly.* JOHNSON.

[1] ——*in* Argier.] *Argier* is the ancient English name for *Algiers.*

And here was left by the sailors : Thou, my slave,
As thou report'st thyself, wast then her servant :
And, for thou wast a spirit too delicate
To act her earthy and abhorr'd commands,
Refusing her grand hests, she did confine thee,
By help of her more potent ministers,
And in her most unmitigable rage,
Into a cloven pine ; within which rift
Imprison'd, thou did'st painfully remain
A dozen years ; within which space she died,
And left thee there ; where thou did'st vent thy groans,
As fast as mill-wheels strike : Then was this island,
(Save for the son that she did litter here,
A freckled whelp, hag-born,) not honour'd with
A human shape.

  *Ari.*    Yes ; Caliban her son,
  *Pro.* Dull thing, I say so ; he, that Caliban,
Whom now I keep in service. Thou best know'st
What torment I did find thee in : thy groans
Did make wolves howl, and penetrate the breasts
Of ever-angry bears ; it was a torment
To lay upon the damn'd, which Sycorax
Could not again undo ; it was mine art,
When I arriv'd, and heard thee, that made gape
The pine, and let thee out.

  *Ari.*    I thank thee, master.
  *Pro.* If thou more murmur'st, I will rend an oak,
And peg thee in his knotty entrails, till
Thou hast howl'd away twelve winters.

  *Ari.*    Pardon, master :
I will be correspondent to command,
And do my spiriting gently.

  *Pro.*    Do so ; and after two days
I will discharge thee.

  *Ari.*    That's my noble master !
What shall I do ? say what ? what shall I do ?

*Pro.* Go make thyself like to a nymph o' the sea;[1]
Be subject to no sight but mine; invisible
To every eye-ball else.   Go, take this shape,
And hither come in't: hence, with diligence.

*[Exit* ARIEL.

Awake, dear heart, awake! thou  hast slept well;
Awake!

*Mira.* The strangeness[2] of your story put
Heaviness in me.

*Pro.*                    Shake it off: Come on;
We'll visit Caliban, my slave, who never        -
Yields us kind answer.

*Mira.*                    'Tis a villain, sir,
I do not love to look on.

*Pro.*                    But, as 'tis,
We cannot miss him:[4] he does make our fire,
Fetch in our wood; and serves in offices
That profit us.   What ho! slave! Caliban!
Thou earth, thou! speak.

*Cal.* [*Within.*] There's wood enough within.

*Pro.* Come forth, I say; there's other business
              for thee:
Come forth, thou tortoise! when?

[1] *= to a nymph o' the sea;*] There does not appear to be sufficient cause why *Ariel* should assume this new shape, as he was
to be invisible to all eyes but those of Prospero.   STEEVENS.

[2] *The strangeness—*] Why should a wonderful story produce
sleep? I believe experience will prove, that any violent agitation
of the mind easily subsides in slumber, especially when, as in
Prospero's relation, the last images are pleasing.   JOHNSON.

The poet seems to have been apprehensive that the audience,
as well as Miranda, would sleep over this long but necessary
tale, and therefore strives to break it.   First, by making Prospero
divest himself of his magic robe and wand: then by waking her
attention no less than six times by verbal interruption: then by
varying the action when he rises and bids her continue sitting:
and lastly, by carrying on the business of the fable while Miranda sleeps, by which she is continued on the stage till the poet
has occasion for her again.   WARNER.

[4] *We cannot miss him:*] That is, we cannot do without him.

*Re-enter* ARIEL, *like a water-nymph.*

Fine apparition! My quaint Ariel,
Hark in thine ear.

*Ari.*                My lord, it shall be done. [*Exit.*

*Pro.* Thou poisonous slave, got by the devil
  himself

Upon thy wicked dam, come forth!

*Enter* CALIBAN.

*Cal.* As wicked dew[5] as e'er my mother brush'd
With raven's feather from unwholesome fen,
Drop on you both! a south-west blow on ye,
And blister you all o'er.

*Pro.* For this, be sure, to-night thou shalt have
  cramps,

Side-stitches that shall pen thy breath up; urchins[6]
Shall, for that vast of night that they may work,[7]
All exercise on thee: thou shalt be pinch'd
As thick as honey-combs, each pinch more stinging
Than bees that made them.

*Cal.*                I must eat my dinner.

This island's mine, by Sycorax my mother,

---

[5] Cal. *As wicked dew—*] Wicked, having baneful qualities.

[6] ——*urchins—*] i. e. hedgehogs; or perhaps, here, fairies.

[7] ——*for that* vast of night *that they may work,*] The *vast of night* means the night which is naturally empty and deserted, without action; or when all things lying in sleep and silence, makes the world appear one great uninhabited *waste.*

*Vastum* is likewise the ancient law term for waste, uncultivated land.

It should be remembered, that, in the pneumatology of former ages, these particulars were settled with the most minute exactness, and the different kinds of visionary beings had different allotments of time suitable to the variety or consequence of their employments. During these spaces, they were at liberty to act, but were always obliged to leave off at a certain hour, that they might not interfere in that portion of night which belonged to others.

Which thou tak'st from me. When thou camest
      first,
Thou strok'dst me, and mad'st much of me; would'st
      give me
Water with berries in't; and teach me how
To name the bigger light, and how the less,
That burn by day and night: and then I lov'd thee,
And shew'd thee all the qualities o' the isle,
The fresh springs, brine pits, barren place, and fer-
      tile;
Cursed be I that did so!——All the charms
Of Sycorax, toads, beetles, bats, light on you!
For I am all the subjects that you have,
Which first was mine own king; and here you sty me
In this hard rock, whiles you do keep from me
The rest of the island.
    *Pro.*               Thou most lying slave,
Whom stripes may move, not kindness: I have us'd
      thee,
Filth as thou art, with human care; and lodg'd thee
In mine own cell, till thou did'st seek to violate
The honour of my child.
    *Cal.* O ho, O ho![8]——'would it had been done!
Thou did'st prevent me; I had peopled else
This isle with Calibans.
    *Pro.*               Abhorred slave;
Which any print of goodness will not take,
Being capable of all ill! I pitied thee,
Took pains to make thee speak, taught thee each
      hour
One thing or other: when thou did'st not, savage,
Know thine own meaning,[9] but would'st gabble like

---

[8] *O ho! O ho!*] This savage exclamation was originally and
constantly appropriated by the writers of our ancient Mysteries
and Moralities, to the Devil; and has, in this instance, been
transferred to his descendant Caliban. STEEVENS.
[9] —— *when thou didst not, savage,*

A thing most brutish, I endow'd thy purposes
With words that made them known: But thy vile
    race,'
Though thou did'st learn, had that in't which good
    natures
Could not abide to be with; therefore wast thou
Deservedly confin'd into this rock,
Who had'st deserv'd more than a prison.
   *Cal.* You taught me language; and my profit
    on't
Is, I know how to curse: the red plague rid you, *
For learning me your language!
   *Pro.*             Hag-seed, hence!
Fetch us in fuel; and be quick, thou wert best,
To answer other business. Shrug'st thou, malice?
If thou neglect'st, or dost unwillingly
What I command, I'll rack thee with old cramps;
Fill all thy bones with aches; make thee roar
That beasts shall tremble at thy din.
   *Cal.*          No, pray thee!—
I must obey: his art is of such power,   [*Aside.*
It would control my dam's god, Setebos,³
And make a vassal of him.
   *Pro.*       So, slave; hence!
              [*Exit* CALIBAN.

---

*Know thine own meaning,*] By this expression, however defective, the poet seems to have meant—*When thou didst utter sounds, to which thou hadst no determinate meaning.*

¹ —— *But thy* vile race,] *Race*, in this place, seems to signify original disposition, inborn qualities.

² ——*the* red *plague* rid *you,*] The *erysipelas* was anciently called the *red plague.* The word *rid*, means to *destroy.*

³ —— *my dam's god,* Setebos,] Mr. Warner has observed, on the authority of *John Barbot*, that " the *Patagons* are reported to dread a great horned devil called *Setebos.*" We learn from Magellan's voyage, that *Setebos* was the supreme god of the Patagons, and Cheleule was an inferior one. *Setebos* is also mentioned in Hackluyt's *Voyages*, 1598.

*Re-enter* ARIEL *invisible,[4] playing and singing ;*
    FERDINAND *following him.*

### ARIEL'S Song.

*Come unto these yellow sands,*
    *And then take hands :*
*Court'sied when you have, and kiss'd,[5]*
    *(The wild waves whist,)*
*Foot it featly here and there ;*
*And, sweet sprites, the burden bear.*
    *Hark, hark !*
*Bur.* Bowgh, wowgh.         [*dispersedly.*
    *The watch-dogs bark :*
*Bur.* Bowgh, wowgh.         [*dispersedly.*
    *Hark, hark ! I hear*
*The strain of strutting chanticlere*
*Cry, Cock-a-doodle-doo.*

*Fer.* Where should this musick be ? i' the air, or
    the earth ?
It sounds no more :——and sure it waits upon
Some god of the island. Sitting on a bank
Weeping again the king my father's wreck,[6]

---

[4] *Re-enter Ariel* invisible,] In the wardrobe of the Lord Admiral's men (i. e. company of comedians,) 1598, was——" a robe for to goo *invisebell.*"
[5] *Court'sied when you have, and* kiss'd,] As was anciently at the beginning of some dances.
[6] *Weeping* again *the king my father's wreck,*] Thus the old copy : but in the books of Shakspeare's age *again* is sometimes printed instead of *against,* [i. e. opposite to,] which I am persuaded was our author's word. The placing Ferdinand in such a situation that he could still gaze upon the wrecked vessel, is one of Shakspeare's touches of nature. *Again* is inadmissible : for this would import that Ferdinand's tears had ceased for a time ; whereas he himself tells us, afterwards, that from the hour of his father's wreck they had *never* ceased to flow :
    "——Myself am Naples,

This musick crept by me upon the waters;
Allaying both their fury, and my passion,
With its sweet air: thence I have follow'd it,
Or it hath drawn me rather:—But 'tis gone.
No, it begins again.

ARIEL sings.

*Full fathom five thy father lies;*[7]
   *Of his bones are coral made;*
*Those are pearls that were his eyes:*
   *Nothing of him that doth fade,*[8]
*But doth suffer a sea-change*[9]
*Into something rich and strange.*
*Sea-nymphs hourly ring his knell:*
*Hark! now I hear them,—ding-dong, bell.*

                    [*Burden*, ding-dong.[1]

*Fer.* The ditty does remember my drown'd fa-
     ther:—

    " Who with mine eyes, *ne'er since at ebb*, beheld
    " The king my father wreck'd."   MALONE.
  By the word—*again*, I suppose the prince means only to describe the *repetition* of his sorrows. Besides, it appears from
Miranda's description of the storm, that the ship had been *swallowed* by the waves, and, consequently, could no longer be an
object of sight.  STEEVENS.
  [7] *Full fathom five thy father lies;* &c.] The songs in this play,
Dr. Wilson, who reset and published two of them, tells us, in
his *Court Ayres*, or *Ballads*, published at Oxford, 1660, that
" *Full fathom five*," and " *Where the bee sucks*," had been first
set by Robert Johnson, a composer contemporary with Shakspeare.  BURNEY.
  [8] *Nothing of him that doth fade,*
    *But doth suffer a sea-change* —] Every thing about him,
that is liable to alteration, is changed.
  [9] *But doth* suffer *a sea*-change —] So, in Milton's *Masque* :
    " And *underwent* a quick immortal *change*."
                           STEEVENS.
  [1] The same burden to a song occurs in *The Merchant of Venice*. It should here be—
      Ding-dong, *ding-dong, ding-dong,* bell.

9

This is no mortal business, nor no sound
That the earth owes:⁹—I hear it now above me.

   *Pro.* The fringed curtains⁰ of thine eye advance
And say, what thou seest yond'.

   *Mira.*                 What is't? a spirit?
Lord, how it looks about! Believe me, sir,
It carries a brave form:—But 'tis a spirit.

   *Pro.* No, wench; it eats and sleeps, and hath
       such senses
As we have, such: This gallant, which thou seest,
Was in the wreck; and but he's something stain'd
With grief, that's beauty's canker, thou might'st
       call him
A goodly person: he hath lost his fellows,
And strays about to find them.

   *Mira.*              I might call him
A thing divine; for nothing natural
I ever saw so noble.

   *Pro.*         It goes on,      [*Aside.*
As my soul prompts it:—Spirit, fine spirit? I'll
       free thee
Within two days for this.

   *Fer.*         Most sure, the goddess
On whom these airs attend!—Vouchsafe, my prayer
May know, if you remain upon this island;
And that you will some good instruction give,
How I may bear me here: My prime request,
Which I do last pronounce, is, O you wonder!
If you be made or no?⁴

   ² *That the earth owes:*] *To owe,* in this place, as well as many others, signifies *to own.*
   ³ *The fringed curtains, &c.*] The same expression occurs in *Pericles, Prince of Tyre,* 1609:
     " ———— her eyelids
     " Begin to part their *fringes* of bright gold."
   ⁴ *If you be made, or no?*] Some copies read *maid,* and the critics are not fully agreed in their opinions. Mr. M. Mason says, " The question is, whether our readers will adopt a natural and

*Mira.*                              No wonder, sir;
But, certainly a maid.
    *Fer.*                              My language! heavens!——
I am the best of them that speak this speech,
Were I but where 'tis spoken.
    *Pro.*                              How! the best?
What wert thou, if the king of Naples heard thee?
    *Fer.* A single thing, as I am now, that wonders
To hear thee speak of Naples: He does hear me;
And, that he does, I weep: myself am Naples;
Who with mine eyes, ne'er since at ebb, beheld
The king my father wreck'd.
    *Mira.*                              Alack, for mercy!
    *Fer.* Yes, faith, and all his Lords; the duke of
        Milan,
And his brave son, being twain.[5]
    *Pro.*                              The duke of Milan,
And his more braver daughter, could control thee,[6]
If now 'twere fit to do't:——At the first sight
                               [*Aside.*
They have chang'd eyes:——Delicate Ariel,
I'll set thee free for this!——A word, good sir;
I fear you have done yourself some wrong:[7] a
    word.
    *Mira.* Why speaks my father so ungently? This
Is the third man that e'er I saw; the first
That e'er I sigh'd for: pity move my father
To be inclin'd my way!
    *Fer.*                              O, if a virgin,

simple expression, which requires no comment, or one which the
ingenuity of many commentators has but imperfectly supported."
   [5] *And his brave son, being twain.*] This is a slight forgetfulness.
Nobody was lost in the wreck, yet we find no such character as
the son of the duke of Milan. THEOBALD.
   [6] —— *control thee,*] Confute, or unanswerably contradict thee.
   [7] —— *I fear you have done yourself some wrong :*] i. e. I fear
that, in asserting yourself to be *King of Naples,* you have uttered

And your affection not gone forth, I'll make you
The queen of Naples.
    *Pro.*                  Soft, sir; one word more.——
They are both in either's powers; but this swift
        business
I must uneasy make, lest too light winning [*Aside.*
Make the prize light.——One word more; I charge
        thee,
That thou attend me : thou dost here usurp
The name thou ow'st not; and hast put thyself
Upon this island, as a spy, to win it
From me, the lord on't.
    *Fer.*              No, as I am a man.
    *Mira.* There's nothing ill can dwell in such a
        temple :
If the ill spirit have so fair an house,
Good things will strive to dwell with't.
    *Pro.*                  Follow me.——
                               [*To* FERD.
Speak not you for him; he's a traitor.——Come.
I'll manacle thy neck and feet together :
Sea-water shalt thou drink, thy food shall be
The fresh-brook muscles, wither'd roots, and husks
Wherein the acorn cradled : Follow.
    *Fer.*                    No;
I will resist such entertainment, till
Mine enemy has more power.       [*He draws.*
    *Mira.*            O dear father,
Make not too rash a trial of him, for
He's gentle, and not fearful.[6]
    *Pro.*              What, I say,
My foot my tutor! Put thy sword up, traitor;

a falsehood, which is below your character, and, consequently,
injurious to your honour. STEEVENS.
  [6] *He's gentle, and not* fearful.] *Fearful* signifies both terrible
and *timorous.* In this place it may mean *timorous;* or it may
signify *formidable,* as in *K. Hen. IV :*

Who mak'st a shew, but dar'st not strike, thy con-
          science
Is so possess'd with guilt: come from thy ward;[9]
For I can here disarm thee with this stick,
And make thy weapon drop.

    *Mira.*                      Beseech you, father!

    *Pro.* Hence; hang not on my garments.

    *Mira.*                      Sir, have pity;
I'll be his surety.

    *Pro.*               Silence! one word more
Shall make me chide thee, if not hate thee. What!
An advocate for an imposter? hush!
Thou think'st there are no more such shapes as he,
Having seen but him and Caliban: Foolish wench!
To the most of men this is a Caliban,
And they to him are angels.

    *Mira.*                   My affections
Are then most humble; I have no ambition
To see a goodlier man.

    *Pro.*             Come on; obey: [*To* FERD.
Thy nerves are in their infancy again,
And have no vigour in them.

    *Fer.*                So they are:
My spirits, as in a dream, are all bound up.[1]
My father's loss, the weakness which I feel,
The wreck of all my friends, or this man's threats,

---

" A mighty and a *fearful* head they are."
and then the meaning of the passage is obvious. One of the original meanings, if not the sole meaning, of the word *gentle* is
noble, *high-minded:* and to this day a Scotch woman in the situation of the young lady in *The Tempest,* would express herself
nearly in the same terms.—Don't provoke him; for being gentle,
that is, *high-spirited,* he won't tamely bear an insult.

   [9] —— *come from thy* ward;] Desist from any hope of awing
me by that posture of defence.   JOHNSON.

   [1] —— *My spirits, as in a dream, are all bound up.*] Alluding
to a common sensation in dreams; when we struggle, but cannot
run, strike, &c.   WARBURTON.

To whom I am subdued, are but light to me,[2]
Might I but through my prison once a day
Behold this maid : all corners else o' the earth
Let liberty make use of ; space enough
Have I in such a prison.

    *Pro.* It works :—Come on.—
Thou hast done well, fine Ariel !—Follow me.—
                              [*To* FERD. *and* MIR.
Hark, what thou else shalt do me.        [*To* ARIEL.
    *Mira.*                         Be of comfort ;
My father's of a better nature, sir,
Than he appears by speech ; this is unwonted,
Which now came from him.
    *Pro.*                  Thou shalt be as free
As mountain winds : but then exactly do
All points of my command.
    *Ari.*              To the syllable.
    *Pro.* Come, follow : speak not for him. [*Exeunt.*

## ACT II.

### SCENE I. *Another part of the Island.*

*Enter* ALONSO, SEBASTIAN, ANTONIO, GONZALO,
ADRIAN, FRANCISCO, *and others.*

    *Gon.* 'Beseech you, sir, be merry : you have cause
(So have we all) of joy ; for our escape
Is much beyond our loss : Our hint of woe[3]

---

    [2] —— are *but light to me,*] This passage, as it stands at present,
with all allowance for poetical licence, cannot be reconciled to
grammar. I suspect that our author wrote—" *were* but light to
me," in the sense of—*would be.*—In the preceding line the old
copy reads—*nor* this man's threats. The emendation was made
by Mr. Steevens. MALONE.
    [3] —— *Our* hint *of* woe —] *Hint* is that which recalls to the
memory ; or here it may mean circumstance.

Is common ; every day, some sailor's wife,
The masters of some merchant,[4] and the merchant,
Have just our theme of woe : but for the miracle,[5]
I mean our preservation, few in millions
Can speak like us : then wisely, good sir, weigh
Our sorrow with our comfort.

 *Alon.*        Pr'ythee, peace.

 *Seb.* He receives comfort like cold porridge.

 *Ant.* The visitor[6] will not give him o'er so.

 *Seb.* Look, he's winding up the watch of his wit ;
By and by it will strike.

 *Gon.* Sir,—

 *Seb.* One :—Tell.

 *Gon.* When every grief is entertain'd, that's offer'd,
Comes to the entertainer—

 *Seb.* A dollar.

 *Gon.* Dolour comes to him, indeed ; you have
spoken truer than you proposed.

 *Seb.* You have taken it wiselier than I meant you
should.

 *Gon.* Therefore, my lord,—

---

 [4] *The* masters *of some merchant*, &c.] Thus the old copy. If the
passage be not corrupt (as I suspect it is) we must suppose that
by *masters* our author means the *owners* of a merchant ship, or the
*officers* to whom the navigation of it had been trusted. I suppose,
however, that our author wrote—
   " The *mistress* of some merchant," &c.
*Mistress* was anciently spelt—*maistresse* or *maistres.* Hence, perhaps, arose the present typographical error. See *Merchant of Venice,* Act IV. sc. i. STEEVENS.

 [5] *Have just our theme* of woe : *but for the miracle,*] The words
—*of woe,* appear to me as an idle interpolation. Three lines before we have " our hint *of woe*—." STEEVENS.

 [6] *The* visitor —] Why Dr. Warburton should change *visitor* to
*'viser,* for *adviser,* I cannot discover. Gonzalo gives not only advice but comfort, and is therefore properly called *The visitor,* like
others who visit the sick or distressed to give them consolation. In
some of the Protestant churches there is a kind of officers termed consolators for the sick. JOHNSON.

*Ant.* Fye, what a spendthrift is he of his tongue!

*Alon.* I pr'ythee spare.

*Gon.* Well, I have done: But yet——

*Seb.* He will be talking.

*Ant.* Which of them, he, or Adrian, for a good wager, first begins to crow?

*Seb.* The old cock.

*Ant.* The cockrel.

*Seb.* Done: the wager?

*Ant.* A laughter.

*Seb.* A match.

*Adr.* Though this island seem to be desert,——

*Seb.* Ha, ha, ha!

*Ant.* So, you've pay'd.⁷

*Adr.* Uninhabitable, and almost inaccessible,——

*Seb.* Yet,

*Adr.* Yet——

*Ant.* He could not miss it.

*Adr.* It must needs be of subtle, tender, and delicate temperance.⁸

*Ant.* Temperance was a delicate wench.⁹

*Seb.* Ay, and a subtle; as he most learnedly delivered.

*Adr.* The air breathes upon us here most sweetly.

*Seb.* As if it had lungs, and rotten ones.

*Ant.* Or, as 'twere perfumed by a fen.

*Gon.* Here is every thing advantageous to life.

*Ant.* True; save means to live.

---

⁷ —— you've *pay'd.*] This passage scarcely deserves explanation; but the meaning is this: Antonio lays a wager with Sebastian, that Adrian would crow before Gonzalo, and the wager was a laughter. Adrian speaks first, so Antonio is the winner. Sebastian laughs at what Adrian had said, and Antonio immediately acknowledges that by his laughing he has paid the bet.

⁸ —— *and delicate* temperance.] or *temperature.*

⁹ Temperance *was a delicate wench.*] In the puritanical times it was usual to christen children from the titles of religious and moral virtues.

D 2

*Seb.* Of that there's none, or little.

*Gon.* How lush[1] and lusty the grass looks ? how green ?

*Ant.* The ground, indeed, is tawny.

*Seb.* With an eye of green in't.[2]

*Ant.* He misses not much.

*Seb.* No; he doth but mistake the truth totally.

*Gon.* But the rarity of it is (which is indeed almost beyond credit)——

*Seb.* As many vouch'd rarities are.

*Gon.* That our garments, being, as they were, drenched in the sea, hold, notwithstanding, their freshness, and glosses ; being rather new dy'd, than stain'd with salt water.

*Ant.* If but one of his pockets could speak, would it not say, he lies ?

*Seb.* Ay, or very falsely pocket up his report.

*Gon.* Methinks, our garments are now as fresh as when we put them on first in Africk, at the marriage of the king's fair daughter Claribel,[3] to the king of Tunis.

*Seb.* 'Twas a sweet marriage, and we prosper well in our return.

*Adr.* Tunis was never graced before with such a paragon to their queen.

*Gon.* Not since widow Dido's time.

*Ant.* Widow ? a pox o'that ! How came that widow in ? Widow Dido![4]

[1] *How* lush, &c.] *Lush* here signifies *rauk ;* but it appears to have sometimes signified *juicy, succulent.* Spenser in his *Shepheard's Calender,* (Feb.) applies the epithet *lusty* to green.

[2] *With an eye of green in't.*] An *eye* is a small shade of colour.

[3] —— *Claribel* ——] This name is probably taken from the bl. l. *History of George Lord Faukonbridge.* CLARIBEL is there the concubine of king Richard I. and the mother of Lord Falconbridge.

[4] —— *Widow Dido !*] The name of a widow brings to their minds their own shipwreck, which they consider as having made many widows in Naples. JOHNSON.

*Seb.* What if he had said, widower Æneas too? good lord, how you take it!

*Adr.* Widow Dido, said you? you make me study of that: She was of Carthage, not of Tunis.

*Gon.* This Tunis, sir, was Carthage.

*Adr.* Carthage?

*Gon.* I assure you, Carthage.

*Ant.* His word is more than the miraculous harp.[5]

*Seb.* He hath rais'd the wall, and houses too.

*Ant.* What impossible matter will he make easy next?

*Seb.* I think he will carry this island home in his pocket, and give it his son for an apple.

*Ant.* And, sowing the kernels of it in the sea, bring forth more islands.

*Gon.* Ay?

*Ant.* Why, in good time.

*Gon.* Sir, we were talking, that our garments seem now as fresh, as when we were at Tunis at the marriage of your daughter, who is now queen.

*Ant.* And the rarest that e'er came there.

*Seb.* 'Bate, I beseech you, widow Dido.

*Ant.* O, widow Dido; ay, widow Dido.

*Gon.* Is not, sir, my doublet as fresh as the first day I wore it? I mean, in a sort.

*Ant.* That sort was well fish'd for.

*Gon.* When I wore it at your daughter's marriage?

*Alon.* You cram these words into mine ears,
against
The stomach of my sense:[6] 'Would I had never
Married my daughter there! for, coming thence,

---

[5] —— *the miraculous harp.*] Alluding to the wonders of Am-
phion's music. STEEVENS.

[6] *The stomach of my* sense:] By *sense*, is meant both *reason
and natural affection.* Mr. M. Mason, however, supposes,
" *sense*, in this place, means *feeling.*" STEEVENS.

My son is lost; and, in my rate, she too?
Who is so far from Italy remov'd,
I ne'er again shall see her. O thou mine heir
Of Naples and of Milan, what strange fish
Hath made his meal on thee!

 *Fran.*        Sir, he may live;
I saw him beat the surges under him,
And ride upon their backs; he trod the water,
Whose enmity he flung aside, and breasted
The surge most swoln that met him; his bold head
'Bove the contentious waves he kept, and oar'd
Himself with his good arms in lusty stroke
To the shore, that o'er his wave-worn basis bow'd,
As stooping to relieve him; I not doubt,
He came alive to land.

 *Alon.*       No, no, he's gone.

 *Seb.* Sir, you may thank yourself for this great loss;
That would not bless our Europe with your
     daughter,
But rather lose her to an African;
Where she, at least, is banish'd from your eye,
Who hath cause to wet the grief on't.

 *Alon.*         Pr'ythee, peace.

 *Seb.* You were kneel'd to, and importun'd other-
     wise
By all of us; and the fair soul herself
Weigh'd[7] between lothness and obedience, at
Which end o' the beam she'd bow. We have lost
     your son,
I fear, for ever: Milan and Naples have
More widows in them of this business' making,
Than we bring men to comfort them:[8] the fault's
Your own.

---

[7] *Weigh'd,*]  *Weigh'd* means *deliberated.*
[8] *Than we bring men to comfort them:*] It does not clearly
appear whether the king and these lords thought the ship lost.
This passage seems to imply, that they were themselves confident

*Alon.* So is the dearest of the loss.
*Gon.*                                   My lord Sebastian,
The truth you speak doth lack some gentleness,
And time to speak it in ; you rub the sore,
When you should bring the plaster.
*Seb.*                                        Very well.
*Ant.* And most chirurgeonly.
*Gon.* It is foul weather in us all, good sir,
When you are cloudy.
*Seb.*                          Foul weather ?
*Ant.*                                       Very foul.
*Gon.* Had I plantation of this isle, my lord,—
*Ant.* He'd sow it with nettle-seed.
- *Seb.*                             Or docks, or mallows.
*Gon.* And were the king of it, What would I do?
*Seb.* 'Scape being drunk for want of wine.
*Gon.* I' the commonwealth I would by con-
        traries
Execute all things : for no kind of traffick
Would I admit ; no name of magistrate ;
Letters should not be known ; no use of service,
Of riches or of poverty ; no contracts,
Successions ; bound of land, tilth, vineyard, none :
No use of metal, corn, or wine, or oil :
No occupation ; all men idle, all ;
And women too ; but innocent and pure :
No sovereignty :—
*Seb.*                    And yet he would be king on't.
*Ant.* The latter end of his commonwealth for-
        gets the beginning.[9]

of returning, but imagined part of the fleet destroyed. Why,
indeed, should Sebastian plot against his brother in the following
scene, unless he knew how to find the kingdom which he was to
inherit ?  JOHNSON.

[9] *The latter end of his commonwealth forgets the beginning.*]
All this dialogue is a fine satire on the Utopian treatises of government, and the impracticable inconsistent schemes therein recommended. WARBURTON.

*Gon.* All things in common nature should pro-
      duce
Without sweat or endeavour : treason, felony,
Sword, pike, knife, gun, or need of any engine,'
Would I not have ; but nature should bring forth,
Of its own kind, all foizon,² all abundance,
To feed my innocent people.

*Seb.* No marrying 'mong his subjects ?

*Ant.* None, man ; all idle ; whores, and knaves.

*Gon.* I would with such perfection govern, sir,
To excel the golden age.

*Seb.*                 'Save his majesty !

*Ant.* Long live Gonzalo !

*Gon.*              And, do you mark me, sir ?——

*Alon.* Pr'ythee, no more : thou dost talk nothing
      to me.

*Gon.* I do well believe your highness ; and did
it to minister occasion to these gentlemen, who are
of such sensible and nimble lungs, that they always
use to laugh at nothing.

*Ant.* 'Twas you we laugh'd at.

*Gon.* Who, in this kind of merry fooling, am
nothing to you : so you may continue, and laugh at
nothing still.

*Ant.* What a blow was there given ?

*Seb.* An it had not fallen flat-long.

*Gon.* You are gentlemen of brave mettle ; you
would lift the moon out of her sphere, if she would
continue in it five weeks without changing.

---

There is something so strikingly applicable to modern times in
this text and note, that the Editor could not persuade himself to
omit the latter, although unnecessary in other respects.    C.

¹ —— *any* engine,)   An *engine* is the *rack*, or here it may
mean any instrument of war, or military machine.

² —— *all* foizon,]   *Foison*, or *foison*, signifies plenty, *ubertas ;*
and sometimes moisture, or juice of grass.

*Enter* ARIEL *invisible, playing solemn musick.*[1]

*Seb.* We would so, and then go a bat-fowling.
*Ant.* Nay, good my lord, be not angry.
*Gon.* No, I warrant you; I will not adventure
my discretion so weakly. Will you laugh me asleep,
for I am very heavy?
*Ant.* Go sleep, and hear us.
　　　　　[*All sleep but* ALON. SEB. *and* ANT.
*Alon.* What, all so soon asleep! I wish mine eyes
Would, with themselves, shut up my thoughts: I
　　　find,
They are inclin'd to do so.
*Seb.* 　　　　　　　Please you, sir,
Do not omit the heavy offer of it:
It seldom visits sorrow; when it doth,
It is a comforter.
*Ant.* 　　　　　We two, my lord,
Will guard your person, while you take your rest,
And watch your safety.
*Alon.* 　　　　　Thank you: wondrous heavy.—
　　　　　[ALONSO *sleeps. Exit* ARIEL.
*Seb.* What a strange drowsiness possesses them?
*Ant.* It is the quality o' the climate.
*Seb.* 　　　　　　　　　　Why
Doth it not then our eye-lids sink? I find not
Myself dispos'd to sleep.
*Ant.* 　　　　　Nor I; my spirits are nimble.
They fell together all, as by consent;
They dropp'd as by a thunder-stroke. What
　　　might,
Worthy Sebastian?—O, what might?—No more:—
And yet, methinks, I see it in thy face,

---

[1] Enter Ariel, &c. *playing solemn musick.*] This stage-direction
does not mean to tell us that Ariel himself was the *fidicen;* but
that solemn musick attended his appearance, or was an accompaniment to his entry. STEEVENS.

What thou should'st be : the occasion speaks thee;
  and
My strong imagination sees a crown
Dropping upon thy head.
  *Seb.*      What, art thou waking?
  *Ant.* Do you not hear me speak?
  *Seb.*      I do; and, surely,
It is a sleepy language; and thou speak'st
Out of thy sleep: What is it thou did'st say?
This is a strange repose, to be asleep
With eyes wide open; standing, speaking, moving,
And yet so fast asleep.
  *Ant.*     Noble Sebastian,
Thou let'st thy fortune sleep—die rather; wink'st
Whiles thou art waking.
  *Seb.*    Thou dost snore distinctly;
There's meaning in thy snores.
  *Ant.* I am more serious than my custom: you
Must be so too, if heed me; which to do
Trebles thee o'er.[4]
  *Seb.*    Well; I am standing water.
  *Ant.* I'll teach you how to flow.
  *Seb.*      Do so: to ebb,
Hereditary sloth instructs me.
  *Ant.*      O,
If you but knew, how you the purpose cherish,
Whiles thus you mock it! how, in stripping it,
You more invest it![5] Ebbing men, indeed,

---

[4] *I am more serious than my custom: you*
 *Must be so too, if heed me; which to do,*
 Trebles thee o'er.] The meaning of this passage seems to
be—You must put on more than your usual seriousness, if you are
disposed to pay a proper attention to my proposal; which attention if you bestow, it will in the end make you *thrice what you
are.* Sebastian is already brother to the throne; but, being made
a king by Antonio's contrivance, (would be, according to our
author's idea of greatness) *thrice* the man he was before. In this
sense he would be *trebled* o'er. MALONE.

Most often do so near the bottom run,
By their own fear or sloth.
   *Seb.*                    Pr'ythee say on :
The setting of thine eye, and cheek, proclaim
A matter from thee ; and a birth, indeed,
Which throes thee much to yield.
   *Ant.*                      Thus, sir :
Although this lord of weak remembrance,[6] this
(Who shall be of as little memory,
When he is earth'd), hath here almost persuaded
(For he's a spirit of persuasion only,)
The king, his son's alive : 'tis as impossible
That he's undrown'd, as he that sleeps here, swims.[7]

[5] *If you but knew, how you the purpose cherish,*
*Whiles thus you mock it ! how, in stripping it,*
*You more invest it !*] A judicious critic, in *The Edinburgh Magazine*, for Nov. 1786, offers the following illustration of this obscure passage. " Sebastian introduces the simile of water. It is taken up by Antonio, who says he will teach his stagnant water to flow. ' —It has already learned to ebb,' says Sebastian. To which Antonio replies, ' *O, if you but knew how much even that metaphor, which you use in jest, encourages to the design which I hint at ; how, in stripping the words of their common meaning, and using them figuratively, you adapt them to your own situation !*". STEEVENS.

[6] —— *this lord of weak remembrance.*] This lord, who, being now in his dotage, has outlived his faculty of remembering ; and who, once laid in the ground, shall be as little remembered himself, as he can now remember other things. JOHNSON.

[7] —— *hath here almost persuaded,*
*(For he's a spirit of persuasion, only*
*Professes to persuade) the king his son's alive ;*
*'Tis as impossible that he's undrown'd,*
*As he, that sleeps here, swims.*] Of this entangled sentence I can draw no sense from the present reading, and therefore imagine that the author gave it thus :
      *For he, a spirit of persuasion, only*
      *Professes to persuade the king, his son's alive ;*
Of which the meaning may be either, that *he alone, who is a spirit of persuasion, professes to persuade the king ;* or that, He *only professes to persuade,* that is, *without being so persuaded himself he makes a show of persuading the king.* JOHNSON.

*Seb.* I have no hope
That he's undrown'd.

    *Ant.*            O, out of that no hope,
What great hope have you! no hope, that way, is
Another way so high an hope, that even
Ambition cannot pierce a wink beyond,[8]
But doubts discovery there.    Will you grant, with
       me,
That Ferdinand is drown'd?

    *Seb.*            He's gone.

    *Ant.*            Then, tell me,
Who's the next heir of Naples?

    *Seb.*            Claribel.

    *Ant.* She that is queen of Tunis: she that dwells
Ten leagues beyond man's life;[9] she that from
       Naples
Can have no note,[1] unless the sun were post,
(The man i' the moon's too slow,) till new-born
       chins
Be rough and razorable; she, from whom[2]
We were all sea-swallow'd, though some cast again;[8]

---

The meaning may be—He is a mere rhetorician, one who professes the art of persuasion, and nothing else; i. e. he professes to persuade another to believe that of which he himself is not convinced; he is content to be plausible, and has no further aim. So (as Mr. Malone observes,) in *Troilus and Cressida :*—"why, he'll answer nobody, he *professes* not answering." STEEVENS.

[8] —— *a wink beyond,*] That this is the utmost extent of the prospect of ambition, the point where the eye can pass no farther, and where objects lose their distinctness, so that what is there discovered, is faint, obscure, and doubtful. JOHNSON.

[9] —— *beyond man's life;*] i. e. at a greater distance than the life of man is long enough to reach. STEEVENS.

[1] —— *she that from Naples*
*Can have no* note, &c.] *Note* is *notice,* or *information.*
Shakspeare's great ignorance of geography is not more conspicuous in any instance than in this, where he supposes Tunis and Naples to have been at such an immeasurable distance from each other.

[2] —— *she, from whom* —] i. e. in coming from whom.

And, by that, destin'd[4] to perform an act,
Whereof what's past is prologue ; what to come,
In yours and my discharge.[5]
    *Seb.*              What stuff is this ?——How say you ?
'Tis true, my brother's daughter's queen of Tunis :
So is she heir of Naples ; 'twixt which regions
There is some space.
    *Ant.*            A space whose every cubit
Seems to cry out, *How shall that Claribel*
*Measure us back to Naples?*——Keep in Tunis,
And let Sebastian wake !——Say, this were death
That now hath seiz'd them ; why, they were no worse
Than now they are : There be, that can rule Naples,
As well as he that sleeps ; lords, that can prate
As amply and unnecessarily,
As this Gonzalo ; I myself could make
A chough[6] of as deep chat. O, that you bore
The mind that I do ! what a sleep were this
For your advancement ! Do you understand me ?
    *Seb.* Methinks, I do.
    *Ant.*            And how does your content
Tender your own good fortune ?
    *Seb.*                 I remember,
You did supplant your brother Prospero.
    *Ant.*                 True :
And, look, how well my garments sit upon me ;
Much feater than before : My brother's servants
Were then my fellows, now they are my men.
    *Seb.* But, for your conscience——

---

    [3] ——*though some* cast *again ;*] *Cast* is here used in the same sense as in *Macbeth*, Act II. sc. iii : "——though he took my legs from me, I made a shift to *cast* him." STEEVENS.
    [4] *And, by that,* destin'd—] It is a common plea of wickedness to call temptation destiny. JOHNSON.
    [5] *In yours and my discharge.*] i. e. depends on what you and I are to perform.
    [6] *A chough* —] Is a bird of the jack-daw kind.

*Ant.* Ay, sir ; where lies that ; if it were a kybe,
'Twould put me to my slipper : But I feel not
This deity in my bosom ; twenty consciences,
That stand 'twixt me and Milan, candied be they,
And melt, ere they molest !⁷ Here lies your brother,
No better than the earth he lies upon,
If he were that which now he's like : whom I,
With this obedient steel, three inches of it,
Can lay to bed for ever : whiles you, doing thus,
To the perpetual wink for aye⁸ might put
This ancient morsel,⁹ this sir Prudence, who
Should not upbraid our course.    For all the rest,
They'll take suggestion, as a cat laps milk ;¹
They'll tell the clock to any business that
We say befits the hour.

    *Seb.*            Thy case, dear friend,
Shall be my precedent ; as thou got'st Milan,
I'll come by Naples.    Draw thy sword : one stroke
Shall free thee from  the tribute which thou pay'st ;
And I the king shall love thee.

    *Ant.*                Draw together :

---

⁷ And *melt, ere they molest !*] I had rather read—
       Would *melt, ere they molest.*

i. e. *Twenty consciences, such as stand between me and my hopes, though they were congealed, would melt before they could molest me,* or prevent the execution of my purposes.   JOHNSON.

Let twenty consciences be first congealed, and then dissolved, ere they molest me, or prevent me from executing my purposes.
                                    MALONE.

I would read  " Candy'd be they, *or* melt ;" and the expression then has spirit and propriety.  *Had I twenty consciences,* says Antonio, *they might be hot or cold for me ; they should not give me the smallest trouble.*—*Edinburgh Magazine,* Nov. 1786.
                                     STEEVENS.

⁸——*for* aye—] i. e. for ever.
⁹ *This ancient* morsel,]   For morsel, Dr. Warburton reads— *ancient moral,* very elegantly and judiciously ; yet I know not whether the author might not write *morsel,* as we say a *piece of a man.*   JOHNSON.
¹ —— *take* suggestion,] i. e. Receive any hint of villainy.

And when I rear my hand, do thou the like,
To fall it on Gonzalo.

  *Seb.*          O, but one word.

                   [*They converse apart.*

     *Musick.*    *Re-enter* ARIEL, *invisible.*

  *Ari.* My master through his art foresees the
          danger
That these, his friends, are in ; and sends me forth,
(For else his project dies,) to keep them living.[2]

                [*Sings in* GONZALO's *ear.*

> *While you here do snoring lie*
> *Open-ey'd conspiracy*
>    *His time doth take :*
> *If of life you keep a care,*
> *Shake off slumber, and beware :*
>    *Awake ! Awake !*

[2] ——— *to keep* them *living.*] By *them*, as the text now stands,
Gonzalo and Alonso must be understood. Dr. Johnson objects
very justly to this passage. " As it stands, says he, at present,
the sense is this. He sees *your* danger, and will therefore save
*them.*" He therefore would read—" That *these* his friends are
in." The confusion has, I think, arisen from the omission of a
single letter. Our author, I believe, wrote—
     " ————— and sends me forth,
     " For else his project dies, to keep them living."
I. e. he has sent me forth, to keep his projects alive, which else
would be destroyed by the murder of his friend Gonzalo.
                            MALONE.
     I have received Dr. Johnson's amendment. Ariel, finding that
Prospero was equally solicitous for the preservation of Alonso and
Gonzalo, very naturally styles them both his *friends*, without adverting to the guilt of the former. Toward the success of Prospero's design, their lives were alike necessary. Mr. Henley says that,
" By *them* are meant *Sebastian* and *Antonio.* The project of Prospero, which depended upon Ariel's *keeping them alive*, may be
seen, Act III. The song of Ariel, however, sufficiently points out
which were the immediate objects of his protection. He cannot

*Ant.* Then let us both be sudden.

*Gon.* Now good angels preserve the king!

[*They awake.*

*Alon.* Why, how now, ho! awake! Why are
    you drawn?[3]
Wherefore this ghastly looking?

*Gon.*                          What's the matter?

*Seb.* Whiles we stood here securing your repose,
Even now, we heard a hollow burst of bellowing
Like bulls, or rather lions; did it not wake you?
It struck mine ear most terribly.

*Alon.*                              I heard nothing.

*Ant.* O, 'twas a din to fright a monster's ear;
To make an earthquake! sure it was the roar
Of a whole herd of lions.

*Alon.*                          Heard you this, Gonzalo?

*Gon.* Upon mine honour, sir, I heard a humming,
And that a strange one too, which did awake me:
I shak'd you, sir, and cry'd; as mine eyes open'd,
I saw their weapons drawn:——there was a noise,
That's verity: 'Best stand upon our guard;
Or that we quit this place: let's draw our weapons.

*Alon.* Lead off this ground; and let's make
    further search
For my poor son.

*Gon.*          Heavens keep him from these beasts!
For he is, sure, i' the island.

*Alon.*                          Lead away.

*Ari.* Prospero my lord shall know what I have
    done:                                  [*Aside.*
So, king, go safely on to seek thy son.      [*Exeunt.*

---

be supposed to have any reference to what happens in the last
scene of the next act.  STEEVENS.

[3] ——*drawn?*] Having your swords drawn.

## SCENE II.

*Another part of the Island.*

*Enter* CALIBAN, *with a burden of wood.*

*A noise of thunder heard.*

*Cal.* All the infections that the sun sucks up
From bogs, fens, flats, on Prosper fall, and make him
By inch-meal a disease! His spirits hear me,
And yet I needs must curse. But they'll nor pinch,
Fright me with urchin shows, pitch me i' the mire,
Nor lead me, like a fire-brand, in the dark
Out of my way, unless he bid them; but
For every trifle are they set upon me:
Sometimes like apes, that moe[4] and chatter at me,
And after, bite me; then like hedge-hogs, which
Lie tumbling in my bare-foot way, and mount
Their pricks[5] at my foot-fall; sometime am I
All wound with adders,[6] who, with cloven tongues,
Do hiss me into madness:—Lo! now! lo!

*Enter* TRINCULO.

Here comes a spirit of his; and to torment me,
For bringing wood in slowly: I'll fall flat;
Perchance, he will not mind me.

*Trin.* Here's neither bush nor shrub, to bear off
any weather at all, and another storm brewing; I
hear it sing i' the wind: yond' same black cloud,
yond' huge one, looks like a foul bumbard[7] that

---

4 —— *that* moe, &c.] i. e. make mouths.
5 *Their* pricks —] i. e. prickles.
6 —— wound *with adders*,] *wound*, or twisted about.
7 —— *looks like a foul* bumbard —] This word means a large
vessel for holding drink, as well as the piece of ordnance so called.

would shed his liquor. If it should thunder, as it
did before, I know not where to hide my head:
yond' same cloud cannot chuse but fall by pailfuls.——
What have we here? a man or a fish? Dead or
alive? A fish: he smells like a fish; a very ancient
and fish-like smell; a kind of, not of the newest,
Poor-John. A strange fish! Were I in England
now, (as once I was,) and had but this fish painted,[8]
not a holiday fool there but would give a piece of silver: there would this monster make a man;[9] any
strange beast there makes a man: when they will
not give a doit to relieve a lame beggar, they will
lay out ten to see a dead Indian. Legg'd like a man!
and his fins like arms! Warm, o' my troth! I do
now let loose my opinion, hold it no longer; this is
no fish, but an islander, that hath lately suffered by
a thunder-bolt. [*Thunder.*] Alas! the storm is
come again: my best way is to creep under his gaberdine;[1] there is no other shelter hereabout:
Misery acquaints a man with strange bedfellows. I
will here shroud, till the dregs of the storm be past.

*Enter* STEPHANO, *singing; a bottle in his hand.*

STE. *I shall no more to sea, to sea,*
   *Here shall I dye a-shore;——*

This is a very scurvy tune to sing at a man's funeral:
Well, here's my comfort.     [*Drinks.*

*The master, the swabber, the boatswain, and I,*
  *The gunner, and his mate,*

---

[8] —— *this fish painted,*] To exhibit fishes, either real or ima-
ginary, was very common about the time of our author.
                STEEVENS.

[9] —— make *a man;*] That is, make a man's fortune.

[1] —— *his* gaberdine:] A *gaberdine* is properly the coarse frock
or outward garment of a peasant. Spanish *Gaberdina.*
 It here, however, means a loose felt cloak. MALONE.

*Lov'd Mall, Meg, and Marian, and Margery,*
*But none of us car'd for Kate:*
*For she had a tongue with a tang,*
*Would cry to a sailor, Go, hang:*
*She lov'd not the savour of tar nor of pitch,*
*Yet a tailor might scratch her where-e'er she did itch:*
*Then to sea, boys, and let her go hang.*

This is a scurvy tune too: But here's my comfort.

[*Drinks.*

*Cal.* Do not torment me: O!

*Ste.* What's the matter? Have we devils here? Do you put tricks upon us with savages,[2] and men of Inde? Ha! I have not 'scap'd drowning, to be afeard now of your four legs; for it hath been said, As proper a man as ever went on four legs, cannot make him give ground: and it shall be said so again, while Stephano breathes at nostrils.

*Cal.* The spirit torments me: O!

*Ste.* This is some monster of the isle, with four legs; who hath got, as I take it, an ague: Where the devil should he learn our language? I will give him some relief, if it be but for that: If I can recover him, and keep him tame, and get to Naples with him, he's a present for any emperor that ever trod on neat's-leather.

*Cal.* Do not torment me, pr'ythee; I'll bring my wood home faster.

*Ste.* He's in his fit now; and does not talk after the wisest. He shall taste of my bottle: if he have never drunk wine afore, it will go near to remove his fit: if I can recover him, and keep him tame, I will not take too much[3] for him: he shall pay for him that hath him, and that soundly.

---

[2] —— *savages*,] The folio reads—*salvages*, and rightly. It was the spelling and pronunciation of the time.

[3] —— too much —] *Too much* means, *any sum, ever so much.*

*Cal.* Thou dost me yet but little hurt; thou wilt
Anon, I know it by thy trembling;[4]
Now Prosper works upon thee.

*Ste.* Come on your ways; open your mouth:
here is that which will give language to you, cat;[5]
open your mouth: this will shake your shaking, I
can tell you, and that soundly: you cannot tell who's
your friend: open your chaps again.

*Trin.* I should know that voice: It should be—
But he is drowned; and these are devils: O! defend me!—

*Ste.* Four legs, and two voices; a most delicate
monster! His forward voice[6] now is to speak well of
his friend; his backward voice is to utter foul
speeches, and to detract. If all the wine in my bottle will recover him, I will help his ague: Come,
—Amen![7] I will pour some in thy other mouth.

*Trin.* Stephano,—

*Ste.* Doth thy other mouth call me? Mercy!
mercy! This is a devil, and no monster: I will
leave him; I have no long spoon.[8]

*Trin.* Stephano!—if thou beest Stephano, touch

It has, however, been observed to me, that when the vulgar mean
to ask an extravagant price for any thing, they say, with a laugh,
I won't make him pay twice for it. This sense sufficiently accom-
modates itself to Trinculo's expression. Mr. M. Mason explains
the passage differently.—" I will not take for him even more than
he is worth." STEEVENS.

I think the meaning is, Let me take what sum I will, however
great, *I shall not take too much for him:* it is impossible for me to
sell him too dear. MALONE.

[4] —— *I know it by thy* trembling;] This *tremor* is always represented as the effect of being possessed by the devil.

[5] —— cat;] *Good liquor will make a cat speak.*

[6] *His forward voice, &c.*] The person of Fame was anciently
described in this manner.

[7] —— *Amen!*] Means, stop your draught.

[8] *I have no long spoon.*] Alluding to the proverb, *A long
spoon to eat with the devil.*

me, and speak to me; for I am Trinculo;—be not
afeard,—thy good friend Trinculo.

*Ste.* If thou beest Trinculo, come forth; I'll pull
thee by the lesser legs: if any be Trinculo's legs,
these are they. Thou art very Trinculo, indeed:
How cam'st thou to be the siege of this moon-calf? [9]
Can he vent Trinculos?

*Trin.* I took him to be killed with a thunder-
stroke:—But art thou not drowned, Stephano? I
hope now, thou art not drowned. Is the storm
over=blown? I hid me under the dead moon-calf's
gaberdine, for fear of the storm: And art thou living, Stephano? O Stephano, two Neapolitans
'scap'd!

*Ste.* Pr'ythee, do not turn me about; my stomach is not constant.

*Cal.* These be fine things, and if they be not
sprites.
That's a brave god, and bears celestial liquor:
I will kneel to him.

*Ste.* How did'st thou 'scape? how cam'st thou
hither? swear by this bottle, how thou cam'st hither. I escaped upon a butt of sack, which the sailors heaved over-board, by this bottle! which I
made of the bark of a tree, with mine own hands,
since I was cast a-shore.

*Cal.* I'll swear, upon that bottle, to be thy
True subject; for the liquor is not earthly.

*Ste.* Here; swear then how thou escap'dst.'

---

[9] —— *to be the* siege *of this* moon-calf? ] *Siege* signifies *stool*
in every sense of the word, and is here used in the dirtiest. A
*moon-calf* is an inanimate shapeless mass, supposed by Pliny to be
engendered of woman only.

' Ste. *Here; swear then how thou escap'dst.*] Mr. Ritson proposes to alter this line thus:

Ste. [*to Cal.*] Here, swear then. [*to Trin.*] How escap'dst
thou?

*Trin.* Swam a-shore, man, like a duck; I can swim like a duck, I'll be sworn.

*Ste.* Here, kiss the book: Though thou canst swim like a duck, thou art made like a goose.

*Trin.* O Stephano, hast any more of this?

*Ste.* The whole butt, man; my cellar is in a rock by the sea-side, where my wine is hid. How now, moon-calf? how does thine ague?

*Cal.* Hast thou not dropped from heaven?[2]

*Ste.* Out o' the moon, I do assure thee: I was the man in the moon, when time was.

*Cal.* I have seen thee in her, and I do adore thee;
My mistress shewed me thee, thy dog, and bush.

*Ste.* Come, swear to that; kiss the book: I will furnish it anon with new contents: swear.

*Trin.* By this good light, this is a very shallow monster:—I afeard of him? a very weak monster:[3] —The man i' the moon?—a most poor credulous monster: Well drawn, monster, in good sooth.

*Cal.* I'll shew thee every fertile inch o' the island;
And kiss thy foot: I pr'ythee, be my god.

*Trin.* By this light, a most perfidious and drunken monster; when his god's asleep, he'll rob his bottle.

*Cal.* I'll kiss thy foot: I'll swear myself thy subject.

*Ste.* Come on then; down and swear.

*Trin.* I shall laugh myself to death at this puppy-

---

[2] *Hast thou not dropped from heaven?*] The new-discovered Indians of the island of St. Salvador, asked, whether Columbus and his companions were *not come down from heaven?*

[3] *I* afeard of him?—*a very weak monster :* &c.] It is to be observed, that Trinculo, the speaker, is not charged with being afraid; but it was his consciousness that he was so that drew this brag from him. This is nature. WARBURTON.

headed monster: a most scurvy monster! I could
find in my heart to beat him,—

*Ste.* Come, kiss.

*Trin.* —but that the poor monster's in drink:
An abominable monster!

*Cal.* I'll shew thee the best springs; I'll pluck
    thee berries;
I'll fish for thee, and get thee wood enough.
A plague upon the tyrant that I serve!
I'll bear him no more sticks, but follow thee,
Thou wond'rous man.

*Trin.* A most ridiculous monster; to make a wonder of a poor drunkard.

*Cal.* I pr'ythee, let me bring thee where crabs grow;
And I with my long nails will dig thee pig-nuts;
Shew thee a jay's nest, and instruct thee how
To snare the nimble marmozet; I'll bring thee
To clust'ring filberds, and sometimes I'll get thee
Young sea-mells⁴ from the rock: Wilt thou go with
    me?

---

⁴ —— *sea-mells*—] This word has puzzled the commentators: Dr. Warburton reads *shamois*; Mr. Holt, who wrote notes upon this play, observes, that limpets are in some places called *scams*, and therefore I had once suffered *scamels* to stand. Theobald had very reasonably proposed to read *sea-malls* or *sea-mells*. I have no doubt but Theobald's proposed amendment ought to be received. Sir Joseph Banks informs me, that in Willoughby's, or rather John Ray's *Ornithology*, p. 34, No. 3, is mentioned the common sea-mall, *Larus cinereus minor*; and that young sea gulls have been esteemed a delicate food in this country, we learn from Plott, who, in his *History of Staffordshire*, p. 231, gives an account of the mode of taking a species of gulls called in that country pewits, with a plate annexed, at the end of which he writes, " they being accounted a good dish at the most plentiful tables." To this it may be added, that Sir Robert Sibbald, in his *Ancient State of the Shire of Fife*, mentions, amongst fowls which frequent a neighbouring island, several sorts of *sea-malls*, and one in particular, the *katiewake*, a fowl of the *Larus* or *mall kind*, of the bigness of an ordinary pigeon, which some hold, says he, to be as savoury and as good meat as a partridge is. REED.

*Ste.* I pr'ythee now, lead the way, without any more talking.—Trinculo, the king and all our company else being drowned, we will inherit here.— Here; bear my bottle. Fellow Trinculo, we'll fill him by and by again.

*Cal. Farewell master: farewell, farewell.*

[*Sings drunkenly.*

*Trin.* A howling monster; a drunken monster.

*Cal. No more dams I'll make for fish;*
    *Nor fetch in firing*
    *At requiring,*
  *Nor scrape trenchering, nor wash dish;*
    *'Ban 'Ban, Ca—Caliban,*
    *Has a new master—Get a new man.*[5]

Freedom, hey-day! hey-day, freedom! freedom, hey-day, freedom!

*Ste.* O brave monster! lead the way. [*Exeunt.*

# ACT III.

## SCENE I. *Before* Prospero's *Cell.*

### Enter FERDINAND, *bearing a log.*

*Fer.* There be some sports are painful; but their labour
Delight in them sets off: some kinds of baseness
Are nobly undergone; and most poor matters
Point to rich ends. This my mean task would be
As heavy to me, as 'tis odious; but
The mistress, which I serve, quickens what's dead,
And makes my labours pleasures: O, she is
Ten times more gentle than her father's crabbed;

---

[5] ——— *Get a new man.*] When Caliban sings this last part of his ditty, he must be supposed to turn his head scornfully toward the cell of Prospero, whose service he had deserted.

And he's compos'd of harshness.   I must remove
Some thousands of these logs, and pile them up,
Upon a sore injunction : My sweet mistress
Weeps when she sees me work; and says such
            baseness
Had ne'er like éxecutor.   I forget :[6]
But these sweet thoughts do even refresh my labours ;
Most busy-less, when I do it.

*Enter* MIRANDA, *and* PROSPERO *at a distance.*

*Mira.*                          Alas, now ! pray you,
Work not so hard ;  I would the lightning had
Burnt up those logs, that you are enjoin'd to pile !
Pray, set it down, and rest you : when this burns,
'Twill weep for having wearied you : My father
Is hard at study ; pray now, rest yourself ;
He's safe for these three hours.
    *Fer.*                          O most dear mistress,
The sun will set, before I shall discharge
What I must strive to do.
    *Mira.*                          If you'll sit down,
I'll bear your logs the while : Pray, give me that ;
I'll carry it to the pile.
    *Fer.*                  No, precious creature :
I had rather crack my sinews, break my back,
Than you should such dishonour undergo,
While I sit lazy by.
    *Mira.*                  It would become me
As well as it does you : and.I should do it
With much more ease ; for my good will is to it,
And yours against.

---

[6] —— *I forget :*] Perhaps Ferdinand means to say—I forget
*my task ;* but *that is not surprizing, for I am thinking on Miranda, and* these sweet thoughts, &c.   He may, however, mean,
that he *forgets or thinks little of the baseness of his employment.*
Whichsoever be the sense, *And,* or *For,* should seem more proper in the next line, than *But.*   MALONE.

*Pro.*                    Poor worm! thou art infected;
This visitation shews it.

*Mira.*                    You look wearily.

*Fer.* No, noble mistress: 'tis fresh morning with
        me,
When you are by at night.   I do beseech you,
(Chiefly, that I might set it in my prayers),
What is your name?

*Mira.*                    Miranda:—O my father
I have broke your hest[7] to say so!

*Fer.*                    Admir'd Miranda
Indeed, the top of admiration; worth
What's dearest to the world! Full many a lady
I have ey'd with best regard; and many a time
The harmony of their tongues hath into bondage
Brought my too diligent ear: for several virtues
Have I lik'd several women; never any
With so full soul, but some defect in her
Did quarrel with the noblest grace she ow'd,
And put it to the foil: But you, O you,
So perfect, and so peerless, are created
Of every creature's best.

*Mira.*                    I do not know
One of my sex; no woman's face remember,
Save from my glass, mine own; nor have I seen
More that I may call men, than you, good friend,
And my dear father: how features are abroad,
I am skill-less of; but, by my modesty,
(The jewel in my dower,) I would not wish
Any companion in the world but you;
Nor can imagination form a shape,
Besides yourself, to like of: But I prattle
Something too wildly, and my father's precepts
Therein forget.

*Fer.*                    I am, in my condition,

_____

7 —— *hest* —] For *behest*; i. e. command.

A prince, Miranda; I do think a king;
(I would, not so!) and would no more endure
This wooden slavery, than I would suffer
The flesh-fly blow my mouth.⁸——Hear my soul
        speak ;——
The very instant that I saw you, did
My heart fly to your service; there resides,
To make me slave to it; and for your sake,
Am I this patient log-man.

    *Mira.*              Do you love me?

    *Fer.*  O heaven, O earth, bear witness to this
        sound,
And crown what I profess with kind event,
If I speak true; if hollowly, invert
What best is boded me, to mischief! I,
Beyond all limit of what else i' the world,⁹
Do love, prize, honour you.

    *Mira.*              I am a fool,
To weep at what I am glad of.¹

    *Pro.*              Fair encounter
Of two most rare affections! Heavens rain grace
On that which breeds between them!

    *Fer.*            Wherefore weep you?

    *Mira.* At mine unworthiness, that dare not offer
What I desire to give; and much less take,

---

⁸ *The flesh-fly* blow *my mouth.*] Mr. Malone observes, that to *blow,* in this instance, signifies to " swell and inflame." But I believe he is mistaken. To *blow,* as it stands in the text, means *the act of a fly, by which she lodges eggs in flesh.* STEEVENS.

⁹ —— *of* what else i' *the world,*] i. e. of *aught* else, of whatsoever else there is in the world.

¹ *I am a fool,*
    *To weep at what I am glad of.*] This is one of those touches of nature that distinguish Shakspeare from all other writers. It was necessary, in support of the character of Miranda, to make her appear unconscious that excess of sorrow and excess of joy find alike their relief from tears; and as this is the first time that consummate pleasure had made any near approaches to her heart, she calls such a seeming contradictory expression of it, *folly.* STEEVENS.

What I shall die to want: But this is trifling;
And all the more it seeks to hide itself,
The bigger bulk it shews. Hence, bashful cunning!
And prompt me, plain and holy innocence!
I am your wife, if you will marry me;
If not I'll die your maid: to be your fellow²
You may deny me; but I'll be your servant,
Whether you will or no.

    *Fer.*              My mistress, dearest,
And I thus humble ever.

    *Mira.*              My husband then?

    *Fer.* Ay, with a heart as willing
As bondage e'er of freedom: here's my hand.

    *Mira.* And mine, with my heart in't:³ And now
            farewell,
Till half an hour hence.

    *Fer.*            A thousand! thousand!
               [*Exeunt* FER. *and* MIR.

    *Pro.* So glad of this as they, I cannot be,
Who are surpriz'd with all;⁴ but my rejoicing
At nothing can be more. I'll to my book;
For yet ere supper time, must I perform
Much business appertaining.          [*Exit.*

---

² —— *your* fellow —] i. e. companion.
³ —— *here's my hand.*
    Mira. *And mine, with my heart in't :*] It is still customary in the west of England, when the conditions of a bargain are agreed upon, for the parties to ratify it by joining their hands, and at the same time for the purchaser to give an earnest. HENLEY.

⁴ *So glad of this as they, I cannot be,*
*Who are surpriz'd* with all;] The sense might be clearer, were we to make a slight transposition:
        " So glad of this as they, who are surpriz'd
        " With all, I cannot be—"
Perhaps, however, more consonantly with ancient language, we should join two of the words together, and read—
        " Who are surpriz'd *withal.* STEEVENS.

## SCENE II.

*Another part of the Island.*

*Enter* STEPHANO *and* TRINCULO; CALIBAN *following with a bottle.*

*Ste.* Tell not me;——when the butt is out, we will drink water; not a drop before: therefore bear up, and board 'em:⁵ Servant-monster, drink to me.

*Trin.* Servant-monster? the folly of this island! They say, there's but five upon this isle: we are three of them; if the other two be brained like us, the state totters.

*Ste.* Drink, servant-monster, when I bid thee; thy eyes are almost set in thy head.

*Trin.* Where should they be set else? he were a brave monster indeed, if they were set in his tail.

*Ste.* My man-monster hath drowned his tongue in sack: for my part, the sea cannot drown me: I swam, ere I could recover the shore, five-and-thirty leagues, off and on, by this light.——Thou shalt be my lieutenant, monster, or my standard.

*Trin.* Your lieutenant, if you list; he's no standard.⁶

*Ste.* We'll not run, monsieur monster.

*Trin.* Nor go neither: but you'll lie, like dogs; and yet say nothing neither.

---

⁵ —— *bear up, and board 'em:*] A metaphor alluding to a chace at sea.

⁶ —————— *or my standard.*

*Trin. Your lieutenant, if you list; he's no* standard.] Meaning, he is so much intoxicated, as not to be able to stand. The quibble between *standard*, an ensign, and *standard*, a fruit-tree that grows without support, is evident. STEEVENS.

*Ste.* Moon-calf, speak once in thy life, if thou
beest a good moon-calf.

*Cal.* How does thy honour? Let me lick thy
          shoe :
I'll not serve him, he is not valiant.

*Trin.* Thou liest, most ignorant monster; I am
in case to justle a constable : why, thou deboshed
fish thou,[7] was there ever a man a coward, that hath
drunk so much sack as I to-day? Wilt thou tell
a monstrous lie, being but half a fish, and half a
monster?

*Cal.* Lo, how he mocks me! wilt thou let him,
my lord?

*Trin.* Lord, quoth he!—that a monster should
be such a natural!

*Cal.* Lo, lo, again! bite him to death, I pr'ythee.

*Ste.* Trinculo, keep a good tongue in your head;
if you prove a mutineer, the next tree—The poor
monster's my subject, and he shall not suffer indignity.

*Cal.* I thank my noble lord. Wilt thou be
          pleased
To hearken once again the suit I made thee?

*Ste.* Marry will I : kneel and repeat it; I will
stand, and so shall Trinculo.

*Enter* ARIEL, *invisible.*

*Cal.* As I told thee
Before, I am subject to a tyrant;[8]
A sorcerer, that by his cunning hath
Cheated me of this island.

*Ari.*                          Thou liest.

*Cal.* Thou liest, thou jesting monkey, thou;

[7] —— *thou* deboshed *fish thou,*] the same as *debauched.*
[8] —— *a* tyrant ;] *Tyrant* is here employed as a trisyllable.

I would, my valiant master would destroy thee :
I do not lie.

*Ste.* Trinculo, if you trouble him any more in
his tale, by this hand, I will supplant some of your
teeth.

*Trin.* Why, I said nothing.

*Ste.* Mum then, and no more.—[*To* CALIBAN.]
Proceed.

*Cal.* I say, by sorcery he got this isle ;
From me he got it. If thy greatness will
Revenge it on him—for, I know, thou dar'st ;
But this thing dare not.

*Ste.* That's most certain.

*Cal.* Thou shalt be lord of it, and I'll serve thee.

*Ste.* How now shall this be compassed ? Canst
thou bring me to the party ?

*Cal.* Yea, yea, my lord ; I'll yield him thee asleep,
Where thou may'st knock a nail into his head.

*Ari.* Thou liest, thou canst not.

*Cal.* What a pied ninny's this ?[9] Thou scurvy
            patch !—
I do beseech thy greatness, give him blows,
And take his bottle from him : when that's gone,
He shall drink nought but brine ; for I'll not shew
            him
Where the quick freshes are.

*Ste.* Trinculo, run into no further danger : interrupt the monster one word further, and, by this

[9] *What a pied ninny's this ?*] It should be remembered that
*Trinculo* is no *sailor*, but a *jester* ; and is so called in the ancient
*dramatis personæ.* He therefore wears the party-coloured dress
of one of these characters. STEEVENS.

Dr. Johnson observes, that Caliban could have no knowledge
of the striped coat usually worn by fools ; and would therefore
transfer this speech to Stephano. But though *Caliban* might not
know this circumstance, Shakspeare did. Surely he who has
given to all countries and all ages the manners of his own, might
forget himself here, as well as in other places. MALONE.

hand, I'll turn my mercy out of doors, and make a stock-fish of thee.

*Trin.* Why, what did I? I did nothing; I'll go further off.

*Ste.* Didst thou not say, he lied?

*Ari.* Thou liest.

*Ste.* Do I so? take thou that. [*Strikes him.*] As you like this, give me the lie another time.

*Trin.* I did not give the lie:——Out o' your wits, and hearing too?——A pox o' your bottle! this can sack, and drinking do.——A murrain on your monster, and the devil take your fingers!

*Cal.* Ha, ha, ha!

*Ste.* Now, forward with your tale. Pr'ythee stand further off.

*Cal.* Beat him enough: after a little time, I'll beat him too.

*Ste.* Stand further.——Come, proceed.

*Cal.* Why, as I told thee, 'tis a custom with him
I' the afternoon to sleep: there thou may'st brain
        him,
Having first seiz'd his books; or with a log
Batter his skull, or paunch him with a stake,
Or cut his wezand with thy knife: Remember,
First to possess his books; for without them
He's but a sot, as I am,' nor hath not
One spirit to command: They all do hate him,
As rootedly as I: Burn but his books;
He has brave utensils, (for so he calls them,)

Which, when he has a house, he'll deck withal.
And that most deeply to consider, is
The beauty of his daughter ; he himself
Calls her a non-pareil : I ne'er saw woman,
But only Sycorax my dam, and she ;
But she as far surpasseth Sycorax,
As greatest does least.

*Ste.* Is it so brave a lass ?

*Cal.* Ay, lord ; she will become thy bed, I warrant,
And bring thee forth brave brood.

*Ste.* Monster, I will kill this man : his daughter
and I will be king and queen ; (save our graces !)
and Trinculo and thyself shall be viceroys :—Dost
thou like the plot, Trinculo ?

*Trin.* Excellent.

*Ste.* Give me thy hand ; I am sorry I beat thee :
but, while thou livest, keep a good tongue in thy
head.

*Cal.* Within this half hour will he be asleep ;
Wilt thou destroy him then ?

*Ste.*                                         Ay, on mine honour.

*Ari.* This will I tell my master.

*Cal.* Thou mak'st me merry : I am full of plea-
            sure ;
Let us be jocund : Will you troll the catch[a]
You taught me but while-ere ?

*Ste.* At thy request, monster, I will do reason,
any reason : Come on, Trinculo, let us sing. [*Sings.*
        *Flout 'em, and skout 'em ; and skout 'em, and*
            *flout 'em ;*
        *Thought is free.*

*Cal.* That's not the tune.

        [ARIEL *plays the tune on a tabor and pipe.*

*Ste.* What is this same ?

---

[a] *Will you* troll *the catch* —] To troll *a catch, is to dismiss it trippingly from the tongue.*

*Trin.* This is the tune of our catch, played by the picture of No-body.[3]

*Ste.* If thou beest a man, shew thyself in thy likeness : if thou beest a devil, take't as thou list.

*Trin.* O, forgive me my sins !

*Ste.* He that dies, pays all debts : I defy thee :—
Mercy upon us !

*Cal.* Art thou afeard ?[4]

*Ste.* No, monster, not I.

*Cal.* Be not afeard ; the isle is full of noises,
Sounds, and sweet airs, that give delight, and hurt
     not.
Sometimes a thousand twangling instruments
Will hum about mine ears ; and sometime voices,
That, if I then had wak'd after long sleep,
Will make me sleep again : and then, in dreaming,
The clouds, methought, would open, and shew
     riches
Ready to drop upon me ; that, when I wak'd,
I cry'd to dream again.

*Ste.* This will prove a brave kingdom to me, where
I shall have my musick for nothing.

*Cal.* When Prospero is destroyed.

*Ste.* That shall be by and by : I remember the
story.

*Trin.* The sound is going away : let's follow it,
and after, do our work.

---

[3] *This is the tune of our catch, played by the picture of* No-body.]
A ridiculous figure, sometimes represented on signs. *Westward for Smelts,* a book which our author appears to have read, was printed for John Trundel in Barbican, at the *sign* of the *No-body.*
                                   MALONE.

The allusion is here to the print of *No-body,* as prefixed to the anonymous comedy of " *No-body* and *Some-body* ;" without date, but printed before the year 1600.  REED.

[4] —— *afeard ?* ] Thus the old copy.—*To affear* is an obsolete verb, with the same meaning as to *affray.*  Between *aferde* and *afraide* in the time of Chaucer, there might have been some nice distinction, which is at present lost.  STEEVENS.

*Ste.* Lead, monster; we'll follow.—I would, I
could see this taborer : he lays it on.

*Trin.* Wilt come ? I'll follow, Stephano.[5]

[*Exeunt.*

## SCENE III.

*Another part of the Island.*

*Enter* ALONSO, SEBASTIAN, ANTONIO, GONZALO,
ADRIAN, FRANCISCO, *and others.*

*Gon.* By'r lakin,[6] I can go no further, sir ;
My old bones ache : here's a maze trod, indeed,
Through forth-rights and meanders ! by your pa-
tience,
I needs must rest me.

*Alon.*                      Old lord, I cannot blame thee,
Who am myself attach'd with weariness,
To the dulling of my spirits : sit down, and rest.
Even here I will put off my hope, and keep it
No longer for my flatterer : he is drown'd,
Whom thus we stray to find ; and the sea mocks
Our frustrate search[7] on land : Well, let him go.

*Ant.* I am right glad that he's so out of hope.

[*Aside to* SEBASTIAN.

Do not, for one repulse, forego the purpose
That you resolv'd to effect.

---

[5] *Wilt come ? I'll follow, Stephano.*] The first words are addressed to Caliban, who, vexed at the folly of his new companions
idly running after the musick, while they ought only to have attended to the main point, the dispatching Prospero, seems, for
some little time, to have staid behind. HEATH.

The words—*Wilt come ?* should be added to Stephano's speech.
*I'll follow,* is Trinculo's answer. RITSON.

[6] *By'r lakin,*] i. e. The diminutive only of our lady, i. e. lady-
kin. STEEVENS.

[7] Our *frustrate* search —] *Frustrate* for frustrated.

F 2

*Seb.*                               The next advantage
Will we take thoroughly.
    *Ant.*                          Let it be to-night;
For, now they are oppress'd with travel, they
Will not, nor cannot, use such vigilance,
As when they are fresh.
    *Seb.*          .           I say, to-night: no more.

*Solemn and strange musick; and* Prospero *above,*
   *invisible. Enter several strange Shapes, bringing*
   *in a banquet ; they dance about it with gentle ac-*
   *tions of salutation ; and, inviting the King, &c.*
   *to eat, they depart.*

    *Alon.* What harmony is this? my good friends,
       hark!
    *Gon.* Marvellous sweet musick!
    *Alon.* Give us kind keepers, heavens! What
      were these?
    *Seb.* A living drollery:[8] Now I will believe,
That there are unicorns; that, in Arabia
There is one tree, the phœnix' throne;[9] one phœnix
At this hour reigning there.
    *Ant.*                         I'll believe both;
And what does else want credit, come to me,
And I'll be sworn 'tis true: Travellers ne'er did lie,
Though fools at home condemn them.

---

   [8] *A living* drollery:] Shows, called *drolleries*, were in Shakspeare's time performed by puppets only. From these our modern *drolls*, exhibited at fairs, &c. took their name. *A living
drollery*, i. e. a drollery not represented by wooden machines,
but by personages who are alive.
   [9] —— *one tree, the* phœnix' *throne ;*] Our poet had probably
Lyly's *Euphues, and his England,* particularly in his thoughts:
signat. Q 3.—" As there is but one phœnix in the world, so is
there but *one tree* in Arabia wherein she buildeth." See also,
Florio's Italian Dictionary, 1598: " *Rasin,* a tree in Arabia,
whereof there is but *one* found, and upon it the phœnix sits."
                                 MALONE.

*Gon.*                                          If in Naples
I should report this now, would they believe me?
If I should say, I saw such islanders,
(For, certes,¹ these are people of the island,)
Who, though they are of monstrous shape, yet, note,
Their manners are more gentle-kind,² than of
Our human generation you shall find
Many, nay, almost any.
 *Pro.*                          Honest lord,
Thou hast said well; for some of you there present,
Are worse than devils.                    [*Aside.*
 *Alon.*                     I cannot too much muse,³
Such shapes, such gesture, and such sound, expres-
   sing
(Although they want the use of tongue,) a kind
Of excellent dumb discourse.
 *Pro.*                     Praise in departing.⁴
          [*Aside.*

 *Fran.* They vanish'd strangely.
 *Seb.*                          No matter, since
They have left their viands behind; for we have
   stomachs.—
Will't please you taste of what is here!
 *Alon.*                               Not I.

---

¹ *For, certes, &c.*] *Certes* is an obsolete word, signifying *certainly.*
² *Their manners are more* gentle-kind,] The old copy has—
" gentle, kind—." I read (in conformity to a practice of our
author, who delights in such compound epithets, of which the
first adjective is to be considered as an adverb,) *gentle-kind.*
Thus, in *K. Richard III.* we have *childish-foolish, senseless-
obstinate,* and *mortal-staring.* STEEVENS.
³ —— *too much* muse,] To *muse,* in ancient language, is to
admire, to wonder.
⁴ *Praise in departing.*] i. e. Do not praise your entertainment
too soon, lest you should have reason to retract your commendation. It is a proverbial saying.

*Gon.* Faith, sir, you need not fear : When we
    were boys,
Who would believe that there were mountaineers,[5]
Dew-lapp'd like bulls, whose throats had hanging at
    them
Wallets of flesh ? or that there were such men,
Whose heads stood in their breasts ?[6] which now
    we find,
Each putter-out on five for one,[7] will bring us
Good warrant of.
    *Alon.*           I will stand to, and feed,
Although my last : no matter, since I feel,
The best is past :[8]—Brother, my lord the duke,
Stand to, and do as we.

---

[5] —— *that there were* mountaineers, &c.] Whoever is curious
to know the particulars relative to these *mountaineers,* may consult *Maundeville's Travels,* printed in 1503, by Wynken de
Worde ; but it is yet a known truth that the inhabitants of the
Alps have been long accustomed to such excrescences or tumours.
    *Quis tumidum guttur miratur in Alpibus?* STEEVENS.
    [6] —— *men,*
*Whose heads stood in their breasts ?*] Our author might have
had this intelligence likewise from the translation of Pliny, B. V.
chap. 8 : " The Blemmyi, by report, have no heads, but mouth
and eyes both in their breasts." STEEVENS.
    [7] *Each putter-out,* &c.] The ancient custom here alluded to
was this. In this age of travelling, it was a practice with those
who engaged in long and hazardous expeditions, to place out a
sum of money on condition of receiving great interest for it at
their return home.
    " —— *on* five for one" means *on the terms of five for one.*
The old copy has :
    " ———— *of* five for one."
    The words are only transposed, and the author probably wrote :
    " Each putter-out of *one for five.*"
    [8] *I will stand to and feed,*
    *Although my last : no matter, since I feel*
    *The best is past.*] This passage was probably intended to be
in a rhyme, thus :
    " *I will stand to and feed ; although my last,*
    " *No matter, since I feel the best is past.*"

*Thunder and lightning. Enter* ARIEL *like a harpy; claps his wings upon the table, and, with a quaint device, the banquet vanishes.*[9]

*Ari.* You are three men of sin, whom destiny
(That hath to instrument this lower world,'
And what is in't,) the never-surfeited sea
Hath caused to belch up ; and on this island
Where man doth not inhabit ; you 'mongst men
Being most unfit to live.   I have made you mad ;
   [*Seeing* ALON. SEB. &c. *draw their swords.*
And  even with  such  like  valour,  men  hang  and
        drown
Their  proper selves.   You fools ! I and my fellows
Are ministers of fate ;  the elements,
Of  whom your swords are temper'd, may as well
Wound the loud winds, or with bemock'd-at stabs
Kill the still-closing waters, as diminish
One dowle that's in my plume ;[2] my fellow-ministers
Are like invulnerable : if you could hurt,
Your swords are now too massy for your strengths,

---

[9] —— *and, with a quaint device, the banquet vanishes.*] Though
I will not undertake to prove that all the culinary pantomimes exhibited in France and Italy were known and imitated in this kingdom, I may observe that flying, rising, and descending services
were to be  found at entertainments given by the  Duke of Burgundy, &c. in 1453, and by the Grand Duke of Tuscany in 1600,
&c.    See M. Le Grand d'Aussi's *Histoire de la vie privée des
François*, Vol. III. p. 294, &c. Examples, therefore, of machinery
similar to that of Shakspeare in the present instance, were to be
met with, and perhaps had been adopted on the stage, as well as
at publick festivals here in England.   STEEVENS.
   [1] *that hath to* instrument *this lower world, &c.*] i. e. that
makes use of this world, and every thing in it, as its *instruments*
to bring about its ends.
   [2] *One* dowle *that's in my* plume ;] Bailey, in his Dictionary,
says, that *dowle* is a feather, or rather the single particles of the
down.   Cole, in his Latin Dictionary, 1679, interprets " young
*dowle*," by *lanugo.*

And will not be uplifted : But, remember,
(For that's my business to you,) that you three
From Milan did supplant good Prospero ;
Expos'd unto the sea, which hath requit it,
Him, and his innocent child : for which foul deed
The powers, delaying, not forgetting, have
Incens'd the seas and shores, yea, all the creatures,
Against your peace : Thee, of thy son, Alonso,
They have bereft ; and do pronounce by me,
Ling'ring perdition (worse than any death
Can be at once,) shall step by step attend
You, and your ways ; whose wraths to guard you
        from
(Which here, in this most desolate isle ; else falls
Upon your heads,) is nothing, but heart's sorrow,
And a clear life³ ensuing.⁴

*He vanishes in thunder : then, to soft musick, enter
   the Shapes again, and dance with mops and
   mowes,⁵ and carry out the table.*

  *Pro.* [*Aside.*] Bravely the figure of this harpy
        hast thou
Perform'd, my Ariel ; a grace it had, devouring :
Of my instruction hast thou nothing 'bated,
In what thou hadst to say : so, with good life,⁶

  ³ —— clear *life*,——] Pure, blameless, innocent.
  ⁴ —— *is nothing, but heart's sorrow,*
     *And a clear life ensuing.*] That is—*a miserable fate, which
nothing but contrition and amendment of life can avert.* MALONE.
  ⁵ —— *with* mops *and* mowes——] The old copy, by a manifest
error of the press, reads—with *mocks.* But to *mock* and to *mowe,*
seem to have had a meaning somewhat similar : i. e. to insult, by
making mouths, or wry faces. MALONE and STEEVENS.
  ⁶ —— *with* good life,] *With good life* may mean, with *exact
presentation of their several characters, with observation strange*
of their particular and distinct parts. So we say, he acted to the
*life.* JOHNSON.
  *Good life,* however, in *Twelfth Night,* seems to be used for in-

And observation strange, my meaner ministers
Their several kinds have done:[7] my high charms
       work,
And these, mine enemies, are all knit up
In their distractions : they now are in my power ;
And in these fits I leave them, whilst I visit
Young Ferdinand, (whom they suppose is drown'd,)
And his and my loved darling.
                  [*Exit* PROSPERO *from above.*
  *Gon.* I' the name of something holy, sir, why
       stand you
In this strange stare ?
  *Alon.*            O, it is monstrous ! monstrous !
Methought, the billows spoke, and told me of it ;
The winds did sing it to me ; and the thunder,
That deep and dreadful organ-pipe, pronounc'd
The name of Prosper ; it did bass my trespass.[8]
Therefore my son i' the ooze is bedded ; and
I'll seek him deeper than e'er plummet sounded,
And with him there lie mudded.[9]        [*Exit.*
  *Seb.*            But one fiend at a time,
I'll fight their legions o'er.

---

nocent *jollity*, as we now say a *bon vivant :* " Would you, (says
the *Clown*) have a love song, or a song of *good life ?"* It may,
therefore, in the present instance, mean, *honest alacrity, or
cheerfulness.* STEEVENS.
  To do any thing with *good life*, is still a provincial expression in
the West of England, and signifies, to do it *with the full bent
and energy of mind :*—" And *observation strange,"* is with *such
minute attention to the orders given, as to excite admiration.*
                                  HENLEY.
  [7] *Their several* kinds have done :] i. e. have discharged the
several functions allotted to their different natures.
  [8] —— bass *my trespass.*] The deep pipe told it me in a rough
bass sound. JOHNSON.
  [9] *And* with him *there lie mudded.*
  But *one fiend*—] *with him*, and *but*, are probably playhouse
interpolations.
  *The Tempest* was evidently one of the last works of Shakspeare ;

*Ant.*　　　　　　　　　I'll be thy second.
　　　　　　　　　[*Exeunt* SEB. *and* ANT.
*Gon.* All three of them are desperate; their great
　　　guilt,
Like poison given¹ to work a great time after,
Now 'gins to bite the spirits :——I do beseech you
That are of suppler joints, follow them swiftly,
And hinder them from what this ecstacy²
May now provoke them to:
*Adr.*　　　　　　　　Follow, I pray you.
　　　　　　　　　　　　[*Exeunt.*

## ACT. IV.

### SCENE I. *Before* Prospero's *Cell.*

*Enter* PROSPERO, FERDINAND, *and* MIRANDA.

*Pro.* If I have too austerely punish'd you,
Your compensation makes amends; for I
Have given you here a thread of mine own life.³
Or that for which I live; whom once again
I tender to thy hand : all thy vexations

and it is therefore natural to suppose the metre of it must have
been exact and regular. Dr. Farmer concurs with me in this
supposition. STEEVENS.
　¹ *Like* poison *given, &c.*] The natives of Africa have been
supposed to be possessed of the secret how to temper poisons
with such art as not to operate till several years after they were
administered. Their drugs were then as certain in their effect, as
subtle in their preparation.
　² —— *this* ecstacy——] *Ecstacy* meant not anciently, as at present, *rapturous pleasure*, but alienation of mind. Mr. Locke has
not inelegantly styled it *dreaming with our eyes open.*
　³ —— a thread *of mine own life*,] The old copy reads—*third.*
The word *thread* was formerly so spelt. HAWKINS.
　" A *third* of mine own life" is a *fibre* or a *part* of my own life.
*Prospero* considers himself as the *stock* or *parent-tree*, and his
daughter as a *fibre* or *portion* of himself, and for whose benefit
he himself lives. TOLLET.

Were but my trials of thy love, and thou
Hast strangely stood the test :⁴ here, afore Heaven,
I ratify this my rich gift.    O Ferdinand,
Do not smile at me, that I boast her off,
For thou shalt find she will outstrip all praise,
And make it halt behind her.
   *Fer.*                               I do believe it,
Against an oracle.
   *Pro.* Then, as my gift, and thine own acquisition
Worthily purchas'd, take my daughter : But
If thou dost break her virgin knot before
All sanctimonious ceremonies⁵ may
With full and holy rite be minister'd,
No sweet aspersion⁶ shall the heavens let fall
To make this contract grow : but barren hate,
Sour-ey'd disdain, and discord, shall bestrew
The union of your bed with weeds so loathly,
That you shall hate it both : therefore, take heed,
As Hymen's lamps shall light you.
   *Fer.*                               As I hope
For quiet days, fair issue, and long life,
With such love as 'tis now ; the murkiest den,
The most opportune place, the strong'st suggestion
Our worser Genius can, shall never melt
Mine honour into lust ; to take away
The edge of that day's celebration,
When I shall think, or Phœbus' steeds are founder'd,
Or night kept chain'd below.

⁴ —— strangely *stood the test :*] Strangely is used by way of commendation, *merveilleusement, to a wonder.*
⁵ *If thou dost break her* virgin knot *before*
*All sanctimonious ceremonies,* &c.] This is a manifest allusion to the zones of the ancients which were worn as guardians of chastity by marriageable young women.    HENLEY.
⁶ *No sweet* aspersion —] *Aspersion* is here used in its primitive sense of *sprinkling.*    At present it is expressive only of calumny and detraction.    STEEVENS.

*Pro.*                                    Fairly spoke:[7]
Sit then, and talk with her, she is thine own.—
What, Ariel; my industrious servant Ariel!

*Enter* ARIEL.

*Ari.* What would my potent master? here I am.
*Pro.* Thou and thy meaner fellows your last service
Did worthily perform; and I must use you
In such another trick: go, bring the rabble,[8]
O'er whom I give thee power, here, to this place:
Incite them to quick motion; for I must
Bestow upon the eyes of this young couple
Some vanity of mine art;[9] it is my promise,
And they expect it from me.
    *Ari.*                              Presently?
    *Pro.* Aye, with a twink.
    *Ari.* Before you can say, *Come,* and *go,*
And breathe twice; and cry *so, so;*
Each one, tripping on his toe,
Will be here with mop and mowe:
Do you love me, master? no.
    *Pro.* Dearly, my delicate Ariel: Do not approach,
Till thou dost hear me call.
    *Ari.*                          Well I conceive.  [*Exit.*
    *Pro.* Look, thou be true; do not give dalliance
Too much the rein: the strongest oaths are straw
To the fire i' the blood: be more abstemious,
Or else, good night, your vow!
    *Fer.*                            I warrant you, sir.
The white cold virgin snow upon my heart
Abates the ardour of my liver.
    *Pro.*                            Well.—

---

[7] Fairly *spoke:*] *Fairly* is here used as a trisyllable.
[8] —— *the rabble,*] The crew of meaner spirits.
[9] *Some* vanity *of mine art;*] i. e. illusion of mine art.

Now come, my Ariel: bring a corollary,[1]
Rather than want a spirit: appear, and pertly.—
No tongue;[2] all eyes; be silent.     [*Soft musick.*

## *A Masque. Enter* IRIS.

*Iris.* Ceres, most bounteous lady, thy rich leas
Of wheat, rye, barley, vetches, oats, and pease;
Thy turfy mountains, where live nibbling sheep,
And flat meads thatch'd with stover,[3] them to keep;
Thy banks with peonied and lilied brims,[4]
Which spongy April at thy hest betrims,
To make cold nymphs chaste crowns; and thy broom
    groves,[5]

[1] —— *bring a* corollary,] i. e. bring more than are sufficient, rather than fail for want of numbers. *Corollary* means *surplus.*

[2] *No tongue*;] Those who are present at incantations are obliged to be strictly silent, " else," as we are afterwards told, the " spell is marred." JOHNSON.

[3] —— thatch'd *with* stover,] *Stover* (in Cambridgeshire and other counties) signifies hay made of coarse rank grass, such as even cows will not eat while it is green. *Stover* is likewise used as *thatch* for cart-lodges, and other buildings that deserve but rude and cheap coverings.

[4] *Thy banks with* peonied *and* lilied *brims,*] The old edition reads *pioned* and *twilled* brims, which gave rise to Mr. Holt's conjecture, that the poet originally wrote:
    " with pioned *and* tilled *brims.*"
*Peonied* is the emendation of Hanmer. Spenser, and the author of *Mulcasses the Turk*, a tragedy, 1610, use *pioning* for digging. Mr. Henley would read *pioned* and *twilled*; but Mr. Steevens adheres to the reading in the text, and adds, That it was enough for our author that *peonies* and *lilies* were well known flowers, and he placed them on any bank, and produced them in any of the genial months that particularly suited his purpose. He, who has confounded the customs of different ages and nations, might easily confound the produce of the seasons.

[5] —— *and thy* broom *groves,*] *Broom*, in this place, signifies the *Spartium scoparium*, of which brooms are frequently made. Near Gamlingay, in Cambridgeshire, it grows high enough to conceal the tallest cattle as they pass through it; and in places where it is cultivated, still higher.

Whose shadow the dismissed bachelor loves,
Being lass-lorn ;[6] thy pole-clipt vineyard ;[7]
And thy sea-marge, steril, and rocky-hard,
Where thou thyself dost air : The queen o' the sky,
Whose watery arch, and messenger, am I,
Bids thee leave these ; and with her sovereign grace,
Here on this grass-plot, in this very place,
To come and sport : her peacocks fly amain ;
Approach, rich Ceres, her to entertain.

### Enter CERES.

*Cer.* Hail many-colour'd messenger, that ne'er
Dost disobey the wife of Jupiter ;
Who, with thy saffron wings, upon my flowers
Diffusest honey-drops, refreshing showers ;
And with each end of thy blue bow dost crown
My bosky acres,[8] and my unshrubb'd down,
Rich scarf to my proud earth ; Why hath thy queen
Summon'd me hither, to this short-grass'd-green ?[9]

*Iris.* A contract of true love to celebrate ;
And some donation freely to estate
On the bless'd lovers.

*Cer.*                        Tell me, heavenly bow,
If Venus, or her son, as thou dost know,
Do now attend the queen ? since they did plot
The means, that dusky Dis my daughter got,
Her and her blind boy's scandal'd company
I have forsworn.

*Iris.*                  Of her society
Be not afraid ; I met her deity

[6] *Being* lass-lorn ;] *Lass-lorn* is forsaken of his mistress.
[7] —— *thy pole*-clipt vineyard ;] To *clip* is to *twine round or embrace.* The poles are *clipped* or embraced by the vines.
[8] *My* bosky *acres,* &c.] *Bosky* is woody. Bosky acres are fields divided from each other by hedge-rows. *Boscus* is middle Latin for *wood.*
[9] —— *to this* short-grass'd green ?] The old copy reads short-grass'd green. *Short graz'd green* means *grazed so as to be short.*

Cutting the clouds towards Paphos; and her son
Dove-drawn with her: here thought they to have
   done
Some wanton charm upon this man and maid,
Whose vows are, that no bed-rite shall be paid
Till Hymen's torch be lighted: but in vain;
Mars's hot minion is return'd again;
Her waspish-headed son has broke his arrows,
Swears he will shoot no more, but play with spar-
   rows,
And be a boy right out.
 *Cer.*      Highest queen of state,
Great Juno comes: I know her by her gait.

## *Enter* JUNO.

*Jun.* How does my bounteous sister? Go with me,
To bless this twain, that they may prosperous be,
And honour'd in their issue.

## SONG.

Jun. *Honour, riches, marriage-blessing,*
   *Long continuance, and increasing,*
   *Hourly joys be still upon you!*
   *Juno sings her blessings on you.*
Cer. *Earth's increase, and foison plenty,*[1]
   *Barns, and garners never empty;*
   *Vines, with clust'ring bunches growing;*
   *Plants, with goodly burden bowing;*
   *Spring come to you, at the farthest,*
   *In the very end of harvest!*
   *Scarcity, and want, shall shun you;*
   *Ceres' blessing so is on you.*

[1] **Earth's increase, *and foison plenty,* &c.**] Earth's *increase,*
is **the** *produce* of the earth.——foison *plenty,* i. e. plenty to the
utmost abundance; *foison* signifying plenty.

*Fer.* This is a most majestic vision, and
Harmonious charmingly: May I be bold
To think these spirits?
    *Pro.*              Spirits, which by mine art
I have from their confines call'd to enact
My present fancies.
    *Fer.*           Let me live here ever;
So rare a wonder'd father,[2] and a wife,
Make this place Paradise.
              [Juno *and* Ceres *whisper, and send* Iris
                    *on employment.*

    *Pro.*              Sweet now, silence;
Juno and Ceres whisper seriously;
There's something else to do: hush and be mute,
Or else our spell is marr'd.
    *Iris.* You nymphs, call'd Naiads, of the wan-
            d'ring brooks,[3]
With your sedg'd crowns, and ever-harmless looks,
Leave your crisp channels,[4] and on this green land
Answer your summons: Juno does command:
Come, temperate nymphs, and help to celebrate
A contract of true love; be not too late.

### Enter certain Nymphs.

You sun-burn'd sickle-men, of August weary,
Come hither from the furrow, and be merry;
Make holy-day: your rye=straw hats put on,
And these fresh nymphs encounter every one
In country footing.

---

  [2] —— *a* wonder'd *father,*] i. e. able to perform wonders.
  [3] —— wand'ring *brooks,*] The modern editors read—*winding*
*brooks.* The old copy—*windring.* STEEVENS.
  [4] *Leave your* crisp channels;] *Crisp,* i. e. *curling, winding.*
*Crisp,* however, may allude to the little wave or *curl* (as it is
commonly called) that the gentlest wind occasions on the surface of waters. STEEVENS.

*Enter certain Reapers properly habited ; they join
with the Nymphs in a graceful dance ; towards
the end whereof* PROSPERO *starts suddenly, and
speaks ; after which, to a strange, hollow, and
confused noise, they heavily vanish.*

*Pro.* [*aside.*] I had forgot that foul conspiracy
Of the beast Caliban, and his confederates,
Against my life ; the minute of their plot
Is almost come.—[*To the Spirits.*] Well done ;—
      avoid ;—no more.
*Fer.* This is most strange :[3] your father's in some
      passion
That works him strongly.
*Mira.*              Never till this day,
Saw I him touch'd with anger so distemper'd.
*Pro.* You do look, my son, in a mov'd sort
As if you were dismay'd : be cheerful, sir :
Our revels now are ended : these our actors,
As I foretold you, were all spirits, and
Are melted into air, into thin air :
And, like the baseless fabrick of this vision,
The cloud-capp'd towers, the gorgeous palaces,
The solemn temples, the great globe itself,
Yea, all which it inherit,[4] shall dissolve ;
And, like this insubstantial pageant faded,[5]

[3] *This is* most *strange :*] I have introduced the word—*most*,
on account of the metre, which otherwise is defective.—In the
first line of Prospero's next speech there is likewise an omission,
but I have not ventured to supply it. STEEVENS.

[4] ——— *all which it* inherit,] i. e. all who possess, who dwell
upon it. MALONE.

[5] *And, like this insubstantial* pageant faded,] *Faded* means
here—having vanished ; from the Latin, *vado.* So, in *Hamlet :*
    " It *faded* on the crowing of the cock."
To feel the justice of this comparison, and the propriety of the
epithet, the nature of these exhibitions should be remembered.
The ancient English *pageants* were shows exhibited on the recep-

Leave not a rack behind : ⁶ We are such stuff
As dreams are made of, and our little life
Is rounded with a sleep.——Sir, I am vex'd ;
Bear with my weakness ; my old brain is troubled.
Be not disturb'd with my infirmity :
If you be pleas'd, retire into my cell,
And there repose ; a turn or two I'll walk,
To still my beating mind.

    *Fer. Mira.*               We wish your peace.

                                    [*Exeunt.*

    *Pro.* Come with a thought :——I thank you :——
        Ariel, come.

---

tion of a prince, or any other solemnity of a similar kind. They
were presented on occasional stages erected in the streets.
Originally they appear to have been nothing more than dumb
shows; but before the time of our author, they had been enlivened
by the introduction of speaking personages, who were characteristically habited. The speeches were sometimes in verse ; and
as the procession moved forward, the speakers, who constantly
bore some allusion to the ceremony, either conversed together in
the form of a dialogue, or addressed the noble person whose presence occasioned the celebrity. On these allegorical spectacles
very costly ornaments were bestowed.

  ⁶ *Leave not a* rack *behind* :] " The winds (says Lord Bacon)
which move the clouds above, which we call the *rack*, and are not
perceived below, pass without noise." Mr. Steevens would explain
the word *rack* somewhat differently, by calling it *the last fleeting vestige of the highest clouds, scarce perceptible on account of their distance and tenuity.* What was anciently called the *rack*, is now
termed by sailors—the *scud.* The word is common to many authors
contemporary with Shakspeare. But Sir Thomas Hanmer reads
*tract,* for which there are some authorities; and Mr. Malone *wrack,*
a misspelling for *wreck ;* and after producing authorities, says, it
has been urged, that " objects which have only a visionary and
insubstantial existence, can, when the vision is faded, leave nothing
*real,* and consequently no *wreck* behind them." But the objection is founded on misapprehension. The words—" Leave not a
rack (or wreck) behind," relate not to " the baseless fabrick of
this vision," but to the final destruction of the world, of which
the towers, temples, and palaces, shall (*like* a vision, or a pageant,)
be dissolved, and leave no vestige behind.

*Enter* ARIEL.

*Ari.* Thy thoughts I cleave to:[7] What's thy
    pleasure?

*Pro.*                Spirit,
We must prepare to meet with Caliban.[8]

*Ari.* Ay, my commander; when I presented Ceres,
I thought to have told thee of it; but I fear'd,
Lest I might anger thee.

    *Pro.* Say again, where didst thou leave these var-
    lets?

    *Ari.* I told you, sir, they were red-hot with
    drinking:
So full of valour, that they smote the air
For breathing in their faces; beat the ground
For kissing of their feet; yet always bending
Towards their project: Then I beat my tabor,
At which, like unback'd colts, they prick'd their
    ears,
Advanc'd their eye-lids, lifted up their noses,
As they smelt musick; so I charm'd their ears,
That, calf-like, they my lowing follow'd, through
Tooth'd briers, sharp furzes, pricking goss,[9] and
    thorns,
Which enter'd their frail shins: at last I left them
I' the filthy mantled pool beyond your cell,
There dancing up to the chins, that the foul lake
O'erstunk their feet.

---

[7] *Thy thoughts I cleave to:*] To *cleave to,* is to *unite with
closely.*

[8] —— *to meet with Caliban.*] *To meet with* is to *counteract;*
to play stratagem against stratagem.

[9] —— *pricking goss,*] I know not how Shakspeare distinguished *goss* from *furze;* for what he calls *furze* is called *goss*
or *gorse* in the midland counties. STEEVENS.

    By the latter, Shakspeare means the low sort of *gorse* that only
grows upon wet ground, and which is well described by the name
of *whins* in Markham's *Farewell to Husbandry.* It has prickles
like those of a rose-tree or a gooseberry. TOLLET.

G 2

*Pro.*                 This was well done, my bird ;
Thy shape invisible retain thou still :
The trumpery in my house, go, bring it hither,
For stale to catch these thieves.[1]
    *Ari.*                  I go, I go. [*Exit.*
    *Pro.* A devil, a born devil, on whose nature
Nurture can never stick ;[2] on whom my pains,
Humanely taken, all, all lost,[3] quite lost :
And as, with age, his body uglier grows,
So his mind cankers :[4] I will plague them all,

*Re-enter* ARIEL *loaden with glistering apparel, &c.*

Even to roaring :——Come, hang them on this line.

PROSPERO *and* ARIEL *remain invisible.*    *Enter* CA-
    LIBAN, STEPHANO, *and* TRINCULO, *all wet.*

    *Cal.* Pray you, tread softly, that the blind mole
            may not
Hear a foot fall :[5] we now are near his cell.

---

[1] *For stale to catch these thieves.*] *Stale* is a word in *fowling*, and is used to mean a *bate* or *decoy* to catch birds. STEEVENS.
[2] *Nurture can never stick ;*] *Nurture* is *education.*
[3] —— *all, all lost,*] The first of these words was probably introduced by the carelessness of the transcriber or compositor. We might safely read—*are* all lost. MALONE.
[4] *And as, with age, his body uglier grows,*
    *So his mind cankers :*] Shakspeare, when he wrote this description, perhaps recollected what his patron's most intimate friend, the great Lord Essex, in an hour of discontent, said of Queen Elizabeth :—" *that she grew old, and cankered, and that her mind was become as crooked as her carcase :* "—a speech, which, according to Sir Walter Raleigh, cost him his head, and which, we may therefore suppose, was at that time much talked of. This play being written in the time of King James, these obnoxious words might be safely repeated. MALONE.
[5] —— *the blind mole may not*
    *Hear a foot fall :*] This quality of hearing, which the mole is supposed to possess in so high a degree, is mentioned in *Euphues*, 4to. 1581, p. 64 : " Doth not the lion for strength, the turtle for

*Ste.* Monster, your fairy, which, you say, is a harmless fairy, has done little better than played the Jack with us.[6]

*Trin.* Monster, I do smell all horse-piss; at which my nose is in great indignation.

*Ste.* So is mine. Do you hear, monster? If I should take a displeasure against you; look you,—

*Trin.* Thou wert but a lost monster.

*Cal.* Good my lord, give me thy favour still:
Be patient, for the prize I'll bring thee to
Shall hood-wink this mischance: therefore, speak softly,
All's hush'd as midnight yet.

*Trin.* Ay, but to lose our bottles in the pool,—

*Ste.* There is not only disgrace and dishonour in that, monster, but an infinite loss.

*Trin.* That's more to me than my wetting: yet this is your harmless fairy, monster.

*Ste.* I will fetch off my bottle, though I be o'er ears for my labour.

*Cal.* Pr'ythee, my king, be quiet: Seest thou here,
This is the mouth o' the cell: no noise, and enter.
Do that good mischief, which may make this island
Thine own for ever, and I, thy Caliban,
For aye thy foot-licker.

*Ste.* Give me thy hand: I do begin to have bloody thoughts.

*Trin.* O king Stephano! O peer! O worthy Stephano! look, what a wardrobe here is for thee![7]

---

love, the ant for labour, excel man? Doth not the eagle see clearer, the vulture smell better, *the moale heare lightlyer?*"
REED.

[6] —— *has done little better than played the* Jack *with us.*] i. e. He has played *Jack with a lantern;* has led us about like an *ignis fatuus,* by which travellers are decoyed into the mire.

[7] Trin. *O king Stephano! O peer! O worthy Stephano! look*

*Cal.* Let it alone, thou fool; it is but trash.

*Trin.* O, ho, monster; we know what belongs to a frippery:[8]—O king Stephano!

*Ste.* Put off that gown, Trinculo; by this hand, I'll have that gown.

*Trin.* Thy grace shall have it.

*Cal.* The dropsy drown this fool! what do you mean,
To doat thus on such luggage? Let's along,
And do the murder first: if he awake,
From toe to crown he'll fill our skins with pinches;
Make us strange stuff.

*Ste.* Be you quiet, monster.——Mistress line, is not this my jerkin? Now is the jerkin under the line:[9] now, jerkin, you are like to lose your hair, and prove a bald jerkin.

*Trin.* Do, do: We steal by line and level, an't like your grace.

*Ste.* I thank thee for that jest: here's a garment for't: wit shall not go unrewarded, while I am king of this country: *Steal by line and level*, is an excellent pass of pate; there's another garment for't.

*what a wardrobe here is for thee!*] An allusion to an old celebrated ballad, which begins thus: *King Stephen was a worthy peer* —and celebrates that king's parsimony with regard to his *wardrobe.*

[8] —— *we know what belongs to a* frippery:] A *frippery* was a shop where old clothes were sold. *Fripperie*, Fr. The person who kept one of these shops was called a *fripper.* Strype, in his life of Stowe, says, that these *frippers* lived in Birchin-lane and Cornhill.

[9] —— *under the line:*] An allusion to what often happens to people who pass the line. The violent fevers which they contract in that hot climate, make them lose their hair. Perhaps the allusion is to a more indelicate disease than any peculiar to the equinoxial. Shakspeare seems to design an equivoque between the equinoxial and the girdle of a woman. It may be necessary, however, to observe, as a further elucidation of this miserable jest, that the lines on which clothes are hung, are usually made of twisted horse-*hair.*

*Trin.* Monster, come, put some lime¹ upon your
fingers, and away with the rest.

*Cal.* I will have none on't: we shall lose our
time,
And all be turn'd to barnacles, or to apes²
With foreheads villainous low.³

*Ste.* Monster, lay-to your fingers; help to bear
this away, where my hogshead of wine is, or I'll
turn you out of my kingdom: go to, carry this.

*Trin.* And this.

*Ste.* Ay, and this.

*A noise of hunters heard.⁴   Enter divers Spirits,
in shape of hounds, and hunt them about.  PROS-
PERO and ARIEL, setting them on.*

*Pro.* Hey, Mountain, hey!

*Ari.* Silver! there it goes, Silver!

*Pro.* Fury, Fury! there, Tyrant, there! hark,
hark!

                   [CAL. STE. *and* TRIN. *are driven out.*
Go, charge my goblins that they grind their joints
With dry convulsions; shorten up their sinews
With aged cramps; and more pinch-spotted make
them,
Than pard, or cat o' mountain.

*Ari.*                   Hark, they roar.

---

¹ —— *put some* lime, &c.] That is, *bird-lime.*

² —— *to* barnacles, *or to apes* —] Skinner says *barnacle* is
*Anser Scoticus.* The *barnacle* is a kind of shell-fish growing on
the bottoms of ships, and which was anciently supposed, when
broken off, to become one of these geese. This vulgar error deserves no serious confutation.

³ *With* foreheads *villainous* low.] *Low foreheads* were anciently
reckoned among deformities.

⁴ *A noise of hunters heard.*] Shakspeare might have had in
view " *Arthur's Chace,* which many believe to be in France, and
think that it is a kennel of black dogs followed by unknown
huntsmen with an exceeding great sound of horns, as if it was a
very hunting of some wild beast."

*Pro.* Let them be hunted soundly :  At this hour
Lie at my mercy all mine enemies :
Shortly shall all my labours end, and thou
Shalt have the air at freedom :  for a little,
Follow, and do me service.                          [*Exeunt.*


## ACT V.

*SCENE I.   Before the Cell of* Prospero.

*Enter* PROSPERO *in his magick robes ;   and* ARIEL.

*Pro.* Now does my project gather to a head :
My charms crack not ;  my spirits obey ;  and time
Goes upright with his carriage.[5]    How's the day ?
*Ari.* On the sixth hour ;  at which time, my lord,
You said our work should cease.
*Pro.*                                  I did say so,
When first I rais'd the tempest.    Say, my spirit,
How fares the king and his ?
*Ari.*                                   Confin'd together
In the same fashion as you gave in charge ;
Just as you left them, sir ;  all prisoners
In the lime-grove which weather-fends your cell ;
They cannot budge, till your release.[6]    The king,
His brother, and yours, abide all three distracted ;
And the remainder mourning over them,
Brim-full of sorrow and dismay ;  but chiefly
Him you term'd, sir, *The good old lord, Gonzalo ;*
His tears run down his beard, like winter's drops

[5] —— *and time*
*Goes upright with his carriage.*] Alluding to one carrying a
burthen. This critical period of my life proceeds as I could wish.
Time brings forward all the expected events, without faultering
under his burthen.  STEEVENS.
[6] —— *till your release.*] i. e. till you release them.  MALONE.

From caves of reeds : your charm so strongly works
       them,
That if you now beheld them, your affections
Would become tender.
    *Pro.*              Dost thou think so, spirit ?
    *Ari.* Mine would, sir, were I human.
    *Pro.*              And mine shall.
Hast thou, which art but air, a touch, a feeling[7]
Of their afflictions ? and shall not myself,
One of their kind, that relish all as sharply,
Passion as they,[8] be kindlier mov'd than thou art ?
Though with their high wrongs I am struck to the
       quick,
Yet, with my nobler reason 'gainst my fury
Do I take part : the rarer action is
In virtue than in vengeance : they being penitent,
The sole drift of my purpose doth extend
Not a frown further : Go, release them, Ariel ;
My charms I'll break, their senses I'll restore,
And they shall be themselves.
    *Ari.*            I'll fetch them, sir. [*Exit.*
    *Pro.* Ye elves of hills, brooks, standing lakes,
       and groves ;[9]
And ye, that on the sands with printless foot

[7] —— a touch, a feeling ——] A *touch* is a *sensation.*
[8] —— that relish all as sharply,
  *Passion as they,*] I feel every thing with the same quick sensibility, and am moved by the same passions as they are.
[9] *Ye elves of hills, brooks, standing lakes, and groves ;*] This speech Dr. Warburton rightly observes to be borrowed from Medea's in Ovid : and, " it proves, says Mr. Holt, beyond contradiction, that Shakspeare was perfectly acquainted with the sentiments of the ancients on the subject of inchantments." The original lines are these :
  " Auræque, & venti, montesque, amnesque, lacusque,
  " Diique omnes nemorum, diique omnes noctis, adeste."
The translation of which, by Golding, is by no means literal, and Shakspeare hath closely followed it. FARMER.
  *Ye elves of hills, &c.*] *Fairies* and *elves* are frequently, in the poets, mentioned together, without any distinction of character.

Do chase the ebbing Neptune, and do fly him,
When he comes back ; you demy-puppets, that
By moon-shine do the green-sour ringlets make,
Whereof the ewe not bites ; and you, whose pas-
      time
Is to make midnight mushrooms ; that rejoice
To hear the solemn curfew ; by whose aid
(Weak masters though ye be,)[1] I have be-dimm'd
The noon-tide sun, call'd forth the mutinous winds,
And 'twixt the green sea and the azur'd vault
Set roaring war : to the  dread rattling thunder
Have I given fire, and rifted Jove's stout oak
With his own bolt : the strong-bas'd promontory
Have I made shake ; and by the spurs pluck'd up
The pine and cedar : graves, at my command,
Have waked their sleepers ; oped, and let them forth
By my so potent art : But this rough magick[2]
I here abjure : and, when I have requir'd
Some heavenly musick, (which even now I do,)
To work mine end upon their senses, that
This airy charm is for, I'll break my staff,
Bury it certain fathoms in the earth,
And, deeper than did ever plummet sound,
I'll drown my book.                    [*Solemn musick.*

[1] (*Weak* masters *though ye be,*)] The meaning of this passage
may be, *Though you are but inferior masters of these supernatural
powers—though you possess them but in a low degree.* STEEVENS.
        ———by whose aid,
  (*Weak* masters *though ye be,*)] That is : ye are powerful auxi-
liaries, but weak if left to yourselves ;—your employment is then
to make green ringlets, and midnight mushrooms, and to play the
idle pranks mentioned by Ariel in his next song ; yet by your aid
I have been enabled to invert the course of nature.   We say pro-
verbially, " Fire is a good *servant*, but a bad *master*."
                                              BLACKSTONE.
[2] ——— But *this rough magick*, &c.] This speech of Prospero
sets out with a long and distinct invocation to the various ministers
of his art : yet to what purpose they were invoked does not very
distinctly appear. Had our author written—" *All this,*" &c. instead
  11

*Re-enter* ARIEL: *after him,* ALONSO, *with a fran-
tick gesture, attended by* GONZALO; SEBASTIAN
*and* ANTONIO *in like manner, attended by* ADRIAN
*and* FRANCISCO: *they all enter the circle which*
PROSPERO *had made, and there stand charmed;
which* PROSPERO *observing, speaks.*

A solemn air, and the best comforter
To an unsettled fancy, cure thy brains,[3]
Now useless, boil'd within thy skull![4] There stand,
For you are spell-stopp'd.——
Holy Gonzalo, honourable man,
Mine eyes, even sociable to the shew of thine,
Fall fellowly drops.[5]——The charm dissolves apace;
And as the morning steals upon the night,

of—" *But* this," &c. the conclusion of the address would have
been more pertinent to its beginning. STEEVENS.
  [3] *A solemn air, and the best comforter*
    *To an unsettled* fancy, cure thy brains, &c.] Prospero does
not desire *them* to cure *their brains.* His expression is optative,
not imperative; and means—*May* musick cure thy brains! i. e.
settle them. Mr. Malone reads:
    " To an unsettled fancy's cure! Thy brains,
    " Now useless, *boil* within thy scull:"—— STEEVENS.
  The old copy reads—*fancy.* For this emendation I am answerable. Prospero begins by observing, that the air which had been
played was admirably adapted to compose unsettled minds. He
then addresses Gonzalo and the rest, who had just before gone
into the circle: " Thy brains, now useless boil within thy scull,"
&c. [the soothing strain not having yet begun to operate.] Afterwards, perceiving that the musick begins to have the effect intended, he adds, " The charm dissolves apace." Mr. Pope and
the subsequent editors read—*boil'd.* MALONE.
  [4] —— *boil'd within thy skull!*] So, in *A Midsummer Night's
Dream,* " seething brains," &c. occur: and in *The Winter's Tale,*
we have " *boil'd brains.*"
  [5] ——*fellowly drops.*] I would read, *fellow* drops. The additional syllable only injures the metre, without enforcing the
sense. *Fellowly,* however, is an adjective used by Tusser.
                                                STEEVENS.

Melting the darkness, so their rising senses
Begin to chase the ignorant fumes[5] that mantle
Their clearer reason.—O my good Gonzalo,
My true preserver, and a loyal sir
To him thou follow'st; I will pay thy graces
Home, both in word and deed.—Most cruelly
Didst thou, Alonso, use me and my daughter:
Thy brother was a furtherer in the act;—
Thou'rt pinch'd for't now, Sebastian.—Flesh and
       blood,[6]
You brother mine, that entertain'd ambition,
Expell'd remorse and nature;[7] who, with Sebastian,
(Whose inward pinches therefore are most strong,)
Would here have kill'd your king; I do forgive
       thee,
Unnatural though thou art!—Their understanding
Begins to swell; and the approaching tide
Will shortly fill the reasonable shores,
That now lie foul and muddy. Not one of them,
That yet looks on me, or would know me:—Ariel,
Fetch me the hat and rapier in my cell;
                      [*Exit* ARIEL.
I will dis-case me, and myself present,
As I was sometime Milan:—quickly, spirit;
Thou shalt ere long be free.

ARIEL *re-enters, singing, and helps to attire*
              PROSPERO.

ARI. *Where the bee sucks, there suck I;*
      *In a cowslip's bell I lie:*[8]

---

[5] —— *the ignorant fumes*—] i. e. the fumes of ignorance.
[6] *Thou'rt pinch'd for't now, Sebastian. — Flesh and blood,*] Thus the old copy: Theobald points the passage in a different manner, and perhaps rightly:
     " Thou'rt pinch'd for't now, Sebastian, flesh and blood."
[7] — remorse *and* nature;] *Remorse* is by our author and the contemporary writers generally used for *pity,* or *tenderness of heart. Nature* is natural affection. MALONE.

> *There I couch when owls do cry.*[*]
> *On the bat's back I do fly,*
> *After summer, merrily:*[1]

[*] *In a* cowslip's *bell I lie :*]   So, in Drayton's *Nymphidia :*
  " At midnight, the appointed hour;
  " And for the queen a fitting *bower,*
  " Quoth he, is that fair *cowslip* flower
  " On Hipcut hill that bloweth."
The date of this poem not being ascertained, we know not whether our author was indebted to it, or was himself copied by Drayton.   I believe, the latter was the imitator.   *Nymphidia* was not written, I imagine, till after the English Don Quixote had appeared in 1612.   MALONE.

[?] —— *when owls do cry.*] i. e. at night.   As this passage is now printed, Ariel says that he reposes in a cowslip's bell during the night.   Perhaps, however, a full point ought to be placed after the word *couch,* and a comma at the end of the line.   If the passage should be thus regulated, Ariel will then take his departure by night, the proper season for the bat to set out upon the expedition.   MALONE.

[1] *After summer, merrily :*]   This is the reading of all the editions.   Yet Mr. Theobald has substituted *sun-set,* because Ariel talks of riding on the bat in this expedition.   An idle fancy.   That circumstance is given only to design the *time of night* in which fairies travel.   One would think the consideration of the circumstances should have set him right.   Ariel was a spirit of great delicacy, bound by the charms of Prospero to a constant attendance on his occasions.   So that he was confined to the island winter and summer.   But the roughness of winter is represented by Shakspeare as disagreeable to fairies, and such like delicate spirits, who, on this account, constantly follow *summer.*
WARBURTON.
To this Mr. Steevens objects that the bat is no bird of passage, and the expression is therefore probably used to signify, *not that he pursues summer,* but that, *after summer is past,* he rides upon the warm down of a bat's back; which suits not improperly with the delicacy of his airy being.   But Mr. Malone thinks that though the bat is " no bird of passage," Shakspeare probably meant to express what Dr. Warburton supposes.   When Shakspeare had determined to send Ariel in pursuit of summer, wherever it could be found, as most congenial to such an airy being, is it then surprising that he should have made the *bat,* rather than " the wind, his post-horse;" an animal thus delighting in that season, and reduced by winter to a state of lifeless inactivity?

*Merrily, merrily, shall I live* now,
*Under the blossom that hangs on the bough.*[2]

*Pro.* Why, that's my dainty Ariel: I shall miss
    thee ;
But yet thou shalt have freedom : so, so, so.——
To the king's ship, invisible as thou art :
There shalt thou find the mariners asleep
Under the hatches ; the master, and the boatswain,
Being awake, enforce them to this place ;
And presently, I pr'ythee.
   *Ari.* I drink the air[3] before me, and return
Or e'er your pulse twice beat.      [*Exit* ARIEL.
   *Gon.* All torment, trouble, wonder, and amaze-
    ment
Inhabits here : Some heavenly power guide us
Out of this fearful country!
   *Pro.*              Behold, sir king,
The wronged duke of Milan, Prospero :
For more assurance that a living prince
Does now speak to thee, I embrace thy body ;
And to thee, and thy company, I bid
A hearty welcome.
   *Alon.*          Whe'r thou beest he, or no,[4]
Or some enchanted trifle to abuse me,
As late I have been, I not know : thy pulse
Beats, as of flesh and blood ; and, since I saw thee,

---

   [2] —— *shall I live now,*
   *Under the blossom that hangs on the bough.*] This thought
is not thrown out at random. It composed a part of the magical
system of these days. The idea was probably first suggested by
the description of the venerable elm which Virgil planted at the
entrance of the infernal shades.
   [3] *I drink the air* ——] To drink the air —— is an expression of
swiftness of the same kind as *to devour the way* in *K. Henry IV.*
   [4] Whe'r *thou beest he, or no,*] *Whe'r* for *whether*, is an abbre-
viation frequently used both by Shakspeare and Jonson.

The affliction of my mind amends, with which,
I fear, a madness held me: this must crave
(An if this be at all,) a most strange story.
Thy dukedom I resign;⁵ and do entreat
Thou pardon me my wrongs:—But how should Prospero
Be living, and be here?

  *Pro.*      First, noble friend,
Let me embrace thine age; whose honour cannot
Be measur'd, or confin'd.

  *Gon.*      Whether this be,
Or be not, I'll not swear.

  *Pro.*      You do yet taste
Some subtilties o' the isle,⁶ that will not let you
Believe things certain:—Welcome, my friends all:—
But you, my brace of lords, were I so minded,
          [*Aside to* SEB. *and* ANT.
I here could pluck his highness' frown upon you,
And justify you traitors; at this time
I'll tell no tales.

  *Seb.* The devil speaks in him.     [*Aside.*

  *Pro.*      No:——
For you, most wicked sir, whom to call brother
Would even infect my mouth, I do forgive
Thy rankest fault; all of them; and require
My dukedom of thee, which, perforce, I know,
Thou must restore.

  *Alon.*      If thou beest Prospero,

---

⁵ *Thy dukedom I resign,*] The duchy of Milan being through the treachery of Antonio made feudatory to the crown of Naples, Alonso promises to resign his claim of sovereignty for the future.
⁶ *You do yet taste*
  *Some* subtilties o' *the isle,*] This is a phrase adopted from ancient cookery and confectionary. When a dish was so contrived as to appear unlike what it really was, they called it a subtilty. Dragons, castles, trees, &c. made out of sugar, had the like denomination.

Give us particulars of thy preservation:
How thou hast met us here, who three hours since[7]
Were wreck'd upon this shore; where I have lost,
How sharp the point of this remembrance is!
My dear son Ferdinand.

   *Pro.*                  I am woe for't, sir.[8]

   *Alon.* Irreparable is the loss; and patience
Says, it is past her cure.

   *Pro.*                  I rather think,
You have not sought her help; of whose soft grace
For the like loss, I have her sovereign aid,
And rest myself content.

   *Alon.*              You the like loss?

   *Pro.* As great to me, as late;[9] and, portable
To make the dear loss, have I means much weaker
Than you may call to comfort you; for I
Have lost my daughter.

   *Alon.*             A daughter?
O heavens! that they were living both in Naples,
The king and queen there! that they were, I wish

---

   [7] —— *who* three hours *since* ——] The unity of time is most
rigidly observed in this piece. The fable scarcely takes up a
greater number of hours than are employed in the representation; and from the very particular care which our author takes
to point out this circumstance in so many other passages, as well
as here, it should seem as if it were not accidental, but purposely
designed to shew the admirers of Ben Jonson's art, and the ca-
villers of the time, that he too could write a play within all the
strictest laws of regularity, when he chose to load himself with
the critick's fetters. The *Boatswain* marks the progress of the
day again—*which but three glasses since,* &c. and at the beginning
of this act the duration of the time employed on the stage is particularly ascertained; and it refers to a passage in the first act,
of the same tendency. The storm was raised *at least* two glasses
after mid day, and Ariel was promised that *the work should cease*
at the *sixth hour.* STEEVENS.

   [8] *I am woe for't, sir.*] i. e. *I am sorry for it.* To be woe, is
often used by old writers to signify, *to be sorry.*

   [9] *As great to me, as late;*] My loss is as great as yours, and
has as lately happened to me. JOHNSON.

Myself were mudded in that oozy bed
Where my son lies. When did you lose your daugh-
    ter ?
*Pro.* In this last tempest. I perceive, these lords
At this encounter do so much admire,
That they devour their reason ; and scarce think
Their eyes do offices of truth, their words
Are natural breath :[1] but, howsoe'er you have
Been justled from your senses, know for certain,
That I am Prospero, and that very duke
Which was thrust forth of Milan; who most
    strangely
Upon this shore, where you were wreck'd, was
    landed,
To be the lord on't. No more yet of this ;
For 'tis a chronicle of day by day,
Not a relation for a breakfast, nor
Befitting this first meeting. Welcome, sir ;
This cell's my court : here have I few attendants,
And subjects none abroad : pray you, look in.
My dukedom since you have given me again,
I will requite you with as good a thing ;
At least, bring forth a wonder, to content ye,
As much as me my dukedom.

---

[1] ———— their *words*
    *Are natural breath :*] An anonymous correspondent thinks
that *their* is a corruption, and that we should read—*these* words.
His conjecture appears not improbable. The lords had no doubt
concerning *themselves.* Their doubts related only to *Prospero,*
whom they at first apprehended to be some " inchanted trifle to
abuse them." They doubt, says he, whether what they see and
hear is a mere illusion; whether the person they behold is a
living mortal, whether the words they hear are spoken by a
human creature. MALONE.

*The entrance of the Cell opens, and discovers* FER-
DINAND *and* MIRANDA *playing at chess.*

*Mira.* Sweet lord, you play me false.
   *Fer.*             No, my dearest love,
I would not for the world.
   *Mira.* Yes, for a score of kingdoms,¹ you should
          wrangle,
And I would call it fair play.
   *Alon.*            If this prove
A vision of the island, one dear son
Shall I twice lose.
   *Seb.*        A most high miracle !
   *Fer.* Though the seas threaten they are merci-
        ful :
I have curs'd them without cause.
                  [FERD. *kneels to* ALON.
   *Alon.*           Now all the blessings
Of a glad father compass thee about !
Arise, and say how thou cam'st here.
   *Mira.*           O ! wonder !
How many goodly creatures are there here !
How beauteous mankind is ! O brave new world,
That has such people in't !
   *Pro.*         'Tis new to thee.

---

¹ *Yes, for a score of* kingdoms, &c.] I take the sense to be
only this : Ferdinand would not, he says, play her false for the
*world* : yea, answers she, I would allow you to do it for something less than the world, for *twenty kingdoms*, and I wish you
well enough to allow you, after a little *wrangle*, that your play
was fair. So, likewise, Dr. Grey. JOHNSON.
   I would recommend another punctuation, and then the sense
would be as follows :
      *Yes, for a score of kingdoms you should wrangle,*
      *And I would call it fair play :*
because such a contest would be worthy of you. STEEVENS.

*Alon.* What is this maid, with whom thou wast
 at play?
Your eld'st acquaintance cannot be three hours:
Is she the goddess that hath sever'd us,
And brought us thus together?
    *Fer.*                      Sir, she's mortal;
But, by immortal providence, she's mine;
I chose her, when I could not ask my father
For his advice; nor thought I had one: she
Is daughter to this famous duke of Milan,
Of whom so often I have heard renown,
But never saw before; of whom I have
Received a second life, and second father
This lady makes him to me.
    *Alon.*                 I am hers:
But O, how oddly will it sound, that I
Must ask my child forgiveness!
    *Pro.*                There, sir, stop;
Let us not burden our remembrances
With a heaviness that's gone.
    *Gon.*              I have inly wept,
Or should have spoke ere this. Look down, you
 gods,
And on this couple drop a blessed crown;
For it is you, that have chalk'd forth the way
Which brought us hither!
    *Alon.*          I say, Amen, Gonzalo!
    *Gon.* Was Milan thrust from Milan, that his
 issue
Should become kings of Naples? O, rejoice
Beyond a common joy; and set it down
With gold on lasting pillars: In one voyage
Did Claribel her husband find at Tunis;
And Ferdinand, her brother, found a wife,
Where he himself was lost; Prospero his dukedom,
In a poor isle; and all of us, ourselves,
When no man was his own.

*Alon.*                              Give me your hands :
                                     [*To* FER. *and* MIR.
Let grief and sorrow still embrace his heart,
That doth not wish you joy !
     *Gon.*                          Be't so ! Amen !

*Re-enter* ARIEL, *with the Master and* Boatswain
           *amazedly following.*

O look, sir, look, sir; here are more of us !
I prophesied, if a gallows were on land,
This fellow could not drown : Now, blasphemy,
That    swear'st    grace    o'erboard,    not    an    oath    on
          shore ?
Hast thou no mouth by land ? What is the news ?
     *Boats.* The  best  news  is,  that  we  have  safely
          found
Our king, and company : the next our ship,—
Which, but three glasses since, we gave out split,—
Is tight, and yare, and bravely rigg'd, as when
We first put out to sea.
     *Ari.*                      Sir, all this service ⎞
Have I done since I went.                          ⎬*Aside.*
     *Pro.*          .          My tricksy spirit!³ ⎠
     *Alon.* These  are  not  natural  events;  they
          strengthen,
From  strange  to  stranger:—Say,  how  came  you
          hither ?
     *Boats.* If I did think, sir, I were well awake,
I'd strive to tell you.  We were dead of sleep,⁴
And (how, we know not,) all clapp'd under hatches,

---

    ³ *My* tricksy *spirit* ]  Is, my clever, adroit spirit.  Shakspeare
uses the same word in *The Merchant of Venice.*
    ⁴ ——*dead* of *sleep,*]  Thus the old copy.  Modern editors
—asleep.
    Mr. Malone says, " *On* sleep" was the ancient English phrase-
ology.

Where, but even now, with strange and several
　　　noises
Of roaring, shrieking, howling, gingling chains,
And more diversity of sounds, all horrible,
We were awak'd; straitway, at liberty:
Where we, in all her trim, freshly beheld
Our royal, good, and gallant ship; our master
Capering to eye her: On a trice, so please you,
Even in a dream, were we divided from them,
And were brought moping hither.

　　*Ari.* 　　　　　　　　Was't well done?⎫
　　*Pro.* Bravely, my diligence. Thou shalt ⎬*Aside.*
　　　be free. 　　　　　　　　　　　　　⎭

　　*Alon.* This is as strange a maze as e'er men trod:
And there is in this business more than nature
Was ever conduct of:⁵ some oracle
Must rectify our knowledge.
　　*Pro.* 　　　　　　　　　Sir, my liege,
Do not infest your mind with beating on
The strangeness of this business:⁶ at pick'd leisure,
Which shall be shortly, single I'll resolve you
(Which to you shall seem probable,)⁷ of every
These happen'd accidents: till when, be cheerful,
And think of each thing well.—— Come hither,
　　　spirit; 　　　　　　　　　　　　[*Aside.*
Set Caliban and his companions free:
Untie the spell. [*Exit* ARIEL.] How fares my gra-
　　　cious sir?

⁵ —— conduct of:] *Conduct* for *conductor.*
　*Conduct* is yet used in the same sense: the person at Cambridge who reads prayers in King's and in Trinity College Cha-
pels, is still so styled. HENLEY.
　⁷ —— *with* beating *on*
　*The strangeness, &c.*] *Beating* may mean *hammering*, work-
ing in the mind, dwelling long upon.
　⁷ (*Which to you* shall seem probable,)] I will inform you how
all these wonderful accidents have happened; which, though they
now appear to you strange, will then seem probable. MALONE.

There are yet missing of your company
Some few odd lads, that you remember not.


*Re-enter* ARIEL, *driving in* CALIBAN, STEPHANO,
*and* TRINCULO, *in their stolen Apparel.*

*Ste.* Every man shift for all the rest, and let no
man take care for himself; for all is but fortune :—
Coragio, bully-monster, Coragio!⁸

*Trin.* If these be true spies which I wear in my
head, here's a goodly sight.

*Cal.* O Setebos, these be brave spirits, indeed!
How fine my master is! I am afraid
He will chastise me.

*Seb.* Ha, ha;
What things are these, my lord Antonio!
Will money buy them?

*Ant.* Very like ; one of them
Is a plain fish,⁹ and, no doubt, marketable.

*Pro.* Mark but the badges of these men, my lords,
Then say, if they be true :¹—This mis-shapen
              knave,——
His mother was a witch; and one so strong
That could control the moon,² make flows and ebbs,

---

⁷ —— Coragio!] An exclamation of encouragement.

⁹ *Is a* plain fish,] That is, plainly, evidently a fish. So, in
Fletcher's *Scornful Lady,* " that *visible* beast, the butler," means
the butler who is *visibly* a beast. M. MASON.

It is not easy to determine the shape which our author designed
to bestow on his monster. That he has hands, legs, &c. we gather from the remarks of Trinculo, and other circumstances in
the play. How then is he *plainly a fish?* Perhaps Shakspeare
himself had no settled ideas concerning the form of *Caliban.*

STEEVENS.

¹ —— *true :*] That is, *honest.* A *true man* is, in the language
of that time, opposed to a *thief.*

² *His mother was a witch; and one so* strong
  *That could control the moon,* &c.] This was the phraseology of
the times. After the statute against *witches,* revenge or ignorance

9

And deal in her command, without her power :[3]
These three have robb'd me : and this demi-devil
(For he's a bastard one,) had plotted with them
To take my life : two of these fellows you
Must know, and own ; this thing of darkness I
Acknowledge mine.

 *Cal.*      I shall be pinch'd to death.

 *Alon.* Is not this Stephano, my drunken butler ?

 *Seb.* He is drunk now : where had he wine ?

 *Alon.* And Trinculo is reeling ripe : Where
   should they

Find this grand liquor that hath gilded them ?[4]——
How cam'st thou in this pickle ?

 *Trin.* I have been in such a pickle, since I saw

frequently induced people to charge those against whom they harboured resentment, or entertained prejudices, with the crime of witchcraft, which had just then been declared a capital offence. In our ancient reporters are several cases where persons charged in this manner sought redress in the courts of law. And it is remarkable in all of them, to the scandalous imputation of being *witches*, the term——a *strong* one, is constantly added. In Michaelmas Term, 9 Car. I. the point was settled that no action could be supported on so general a charge, and that the epithet *strong* did not inforce the other words. In this instance, I believe, the opinion of the people at large was not in unison with the sages in Westminster Hall. Several of these cases are collected together in I. Viner. 422. REED.

[3] *And deal in her command, without her power :*] I suppose Prospero means, that Sycorax, with less general power than the moon, could produce the same effects on the sea. STEEVENS.

[4] *And Trinculo is reeling ripe : where should they*
 *Find this* grand LIQUOR *that hath* gilded *them ?*] Shakspeare, to be sure, wrote—grand 'LIXIR, alluding to the *grand* Elixir of the alchymists, which they pretend would restore youth and confer immortality. This, as they said, being a preparation of gold, they called *Aurum potabile ;* which Shakspeare alluded to in the word *gilded.* But the joke here is to insinuate that, notwithstanding all the boasts of the chemists, sack was the only restorer of youth and bestower of immortality. WARBURTON.

 As the alchymist's *Elixir* was supposed to be a liquor, the old reading may stand, and the allusion holds good without any alteration. STEEVENS.

you last, that, I fear me, will never out of my
bones : I shall not fear fly=blowing.[5]

*Seb.* Why, how now, Stephano?

*Ste.* O, touch me not; I am not Stephano, but
a cramp.[6]

*Pro.* You'd be king of the isle, sirrah?

*Ste.* I should have been a sore one then.[7]

*Alon.* This is as strange a thing as e'er I look'd
on.　　　　　　　　　*[Pointing to* CALIBAN.

*Pro.* He is as disproportion'd in his manners,
As in his shape :——Go, sirrah, to my cell;
Take with you your companions; as you look
To have my pardon, trim it handsomely.

*Cal.* Ay, that I will; and I'll be wise hereafter,
And seek for grace : What a thrice-double ass
Was I, to take this drunkard for a god,
And worship this dull fool?

*Pro.*　　　　　　　　　　Go to; away!

*Alon.* Hence, and bestow your luggage where
you found it.

*Seb.* Or stole it, rather.

　　　　　　　*[Exeunt* CAL. STE. *and* TRIN.

*Pro.* Sir, I invite your highness, and your train,
To my poor cell : where you shall take your rest
For this one night; which (part of it,) I'll waste
With such discourse, as, I not doubt, shall make it
Go quick away : the story of my life,
And the particular accidents, gone by,

---

[5] —— fly-blowing.] This pickle alludes to their plunge into
the stinking pool : and *pickling* preserves meat from *fly-blowing.*

[6] —— *but a* cramp,] i. e. I am all over a *cramp.* Prospero
had ordered Ariel to *shorten up their sinews with aged cramps.*
*Touch me not* alludes to the *soreness* occasioned by them.

[7] *I should have been a* sore *one then.*] The same quibble occurs
afterwards in the *Second Part of King Henry VI :* " Mass, 'twill
be *sore* law then, for he was thrust in the mouth with a spear,
and 'tis not whole yet." Stephano also alludes to the *sores*
about him. STEEVENS.

Since I came to this isle : And in the morn,
I'll bring you to your ship, and so to Naples,
Where I have hope to see the nuptial
Of these our dear-beloved solemniz'd ;
And thence retire me to my Milan, where
Every third thought shall be my grave.

*Alon.*                                        I long
To hear the story of your life, which must
Take the ear strangely.

*Pro.*                          I'll deliver all ;
And promise you calm seas, auspicious gales,
And sail so expeditious, that shall catch
Your royal fleet far off.——My Ariel ;——chick,——
That is thy charge ; then to the elements
Be free, and fare thou well !——[*aside.*]   Please you,
          draw near.                          [*Exeunt.*

# EPILOGUE.

## SPOKEN BY PROSPERO.

*NOW my charms are all o'erthrown,*
*And what strength I have's mine own;*
*Which is most faint: now 'tis true,*
*I must be here confin'd by you,*
*Or sent to Naples: Let me not,*
*Since I have my dukedom got,*
*And pardon'd the deceiver, dwell*
*In this bare island, by your spell;*
*But release me from my bands,*
*With the help of your good hands.*[8]
*Gentle breath of yours my sails*
*Must fill, or else my project fails,*
*Which was to please: Now I want*
*Spirits to enforce, art to enchant;*
*And my ending is despair,*
*Unless I be reliev'd by prayer;*[9]
*Which pierces so, that it assaults*
*Mercy itself, and frees all faults.*

---

[8] *With the help of your good hands.*] By your applause, by clapping hands. JOHNSON.
Noise was supposed to dissolve a spell. STEEVENS.
[9] *And my ending is despair,*
  *Unless I be reliev'd by pray'r;*] This alludes to the old stories told of the despair of necromancers in their last moments, and of the efficacy of the prayers of their friends for them.
WARBURTON.

*As you from crimes would pardon'd be,*
*Let your indulgence set me free.*[1]

[1] It is observed of *The Tempest*, that its plan is regular; this the author of *The Revisal* thinks, what I think too, an accidental effect of the story, not intended or regarded by our author. But, whatever might be Shakspeare's intention in forming or adopting the plot, he has made it instrumental to the production of many characters, diversified with boundless invention, and preserved with profound skill in nature, extensive knowledge of opinions, and accurate observation of life. In a single drama are here exhibited princes, courtiers, and sailors, all speaking in their real characters. There is the agency of airy spirits, and of an earthly goblin. The operations of magick, the tumults of a storm, the adventures of a desert island, the native effusion of untaught affection, the punishment of guilt, and the final happiness of the pair for whom our passions and reason are equally interested.

JOHNSON.

# TWO GENTLEMEN

## OF

# VERONA.*

\* Two Gentlemen of Verona.] Some of the incidents in this play may be supposed to have been taken from *The Arcadia*, Book I. chap. vi. where Pyrocles consents to head the Helots. (The *Arcadia* was entered on the books of the Stationers' Company, Aug. 23d, 1588.) The love adventure of Julia resembles that of Viola in *Twelfth Night*, and is, indeed, common to many of the ancient novels. STEEVENS.

Mrs. Lenox observes, and I think not improbably, that the story of *Proteus* and *Julia* might be taken from a similar one in the *Diana* of George of *Montemayor*.—" This pastoral romance," says she, " was translated from the Spanish in Shakspeare's time." I have seen no earlier translation than that of Bartholomew Yong, who dates his dedication in November, 1598; and Meres, in his *Wit's Treasury*, printed the same year, expressly mentions the *Two Gentlemen of Verona*. Indeed *Montemayor* was translated two or three years before, by one Thomas Wilson; but this work, I am persuaded, was never published *entirely*; perhaps some parts of it were, or the tale might have been translated by others. However, Mr. Steevens says, very truly, that this kind of love-adventure is frequent in the old *novelists*. FARMER.

There is no earlier translation of the *Diana* entered on the books of the Stationers' Company, than that of B. Younge, Sept. 1598. Many translations, however, after they were licensed, were capriciously suppressed. Among others, " The Decameron of Mr. John Boccace, Florentine," was " recalled by my lord of Canterbury's commands." STEEVENS.

It is observable (I know not for what cause) that the style of this comedy is less figurative, and more natural and unaffected, than the greater part of this author's, though supposed to be one of the first he wrote. POPE.

It may very well be doubted whether Shakspeare had any other hand in this play than the enlivening it with some speeches and lines thrown in here and there, which are easily distinguished, as being of a different stamp from the rest. HANMER.

To this observation of Mr. Pope, which is very just, Mr. Theobald has added, that this is one of Shakspeare's *worst plays*, and *is less corrupted than any other*. Mr. Upton peremptorily determines, *that if any proof can be drawn from manner and style, this play must be sent packing, and seek for its parent elsewhere. How otherwise*, says he, *do painters distinguish copies from originals? and have not authors their peculiar style and manner, from which a true critic can form as unerring judgment as a painter?* I am afraid this illustration of a critic's science will not prove what is desired. A painter knows a copy from an original by rules somewhat resembling those by which critics know a translation, which, if it be literal, and literal it must be to resemble the copy of a picture, will be easily distinguished. Copies are known from originals, even when the painter copies his own picture; so, if an author should literally translate his work, he would lose the manner of an original.

Mr. Upton confounds the copy of a picture with the imitation of a painter's manner. Copies are easily known; but good imitations are not detected with equal certainty, and are, by the best judges, often mistaken. Nor is it true that the writer has always peculiarities equally distinguishable with those of the painter. The peculiar manner of each arises from the desire, natural to every performer, of facilitating his subsequent work by recurrence to his former ideas; this recurrence produces that repetition which is called habit. The painter, whose work is partly intellectual and partly manual, has habits of the mind, the eye, and the hand; the writer has only habits of the mind. Yet, some painters have differed as much from themselves as from any other; and I have been told, that there is little resemblance between the first works of Raphael and the last. The same variation may be expected in writers; and if it be true, as it seems, that they are less subject to habit, the difference between their works may be yet greater.

But by the internal marks of a composition we may discover the author with probability, though seldom with certainty. When I read this play I cannot but think that I find, both in the serious and ludicrous scenes, the language and sentiments of Shakspeare. It is not, indeed, one of his most powerful effusions; it has neither many diversities of character, nor striking delineations of life; but it abounds in γνωμαι beyond most of his plays, and few have more lines or passages, which, singly considered, are eminently beautiful. I am yet inclined to believe that it was not very successful, and suspect that it has escaped corruption, only because being seldom played, it was less exposed to the hazards of transcription. JOHNSON.

This comedy, I believe, was written in 1595. MALONE.

# PERSONS REPRESENTED.

Duke of Milan, *father to* Silvia.
Valentine, } *Gentlemen of* Verona.
Proteus,
Antonio, *father to* Proteus.
Thurio, *a foolish rival to* Valentine.
Eglamore, *agent for* Silvia, *in her escape.*
Speed, *a clownish servant to* Valentine.
Launce, *servant to* Proteus.
Panthino, *servant to* Antonio.
Host, *where* Julia *lodges in* Milan.
Out-laws.

Julia, *a lady of* Verona, *beloved by* Proteus.
Silvia, *the duke's daughter, beloved by* Valentine.
Lucetta, *waiting-woman to* Julia.

*Servants, musicians.*

SCENE, *sometimes in* Verona ; *sometimes in* Milan;
*and on the frontiers of* Mantua.

Of these characters the old copy has—Pro*th*eus ; but this is
merely the antiquated mode of spelling *Proteus.* Shakspeare's
character was so called, from his disposition to change ; and *Panthino,* in the enumeration of characters in the old copy, is called
*Panthion,* but in the play, always *Panthino.*

# TWO GENTLEMEN

OF

# VERONA.

## ACT I.

### SCENE I. *An open place in* Verona.

*Enter* VALENTINE *and* PROTEUS.

*Val.* Cease to persuade, my loving Proteus ;
Home-keeping youth have ever homely wits ;
Wer't not, affection chains thy tender days
To the sweet glances of thy honour'd love,
I rather would entreat thy company,
To see the wonders of the world abroad,
Than living dully sluggardiz'd at home,
Wear out thy youth with shapeless idleness.[1]
But, since thou lov'st, love still, and thrive therein,
Even as I would, when I to love begin.
   *Pro.* Wilt thou be gone ? Sweet Valentine, adieu!
Think on thy Proteus, when thou, haply, seest
Some rare note-worthy object in thy travel :
Wish me partaker in thy happiness,
When thou dost meet good hap ; and, in thy
       danger,
If ever danger do environ thee,

---

[1] —— *shapeless* idleness.] The expression is fine, as implying
that *idleness* prevents the giving any form or character to the
manners. WARBURTON.

Commend thy grievance to my holy prayers,
For I will be thy bead's-man, Valentine.
    *Val.* And on a love-book pray for my success.
    *Pro.* Upon some book I love, I'll pray for thee.
    *Val.* That's on some shallow story of deep love,
How young Leander cross'd the Hellespont.[2]
    *Pro.* That's a deep story of a deeper love ;
For he was more than over shoes in love.
    *Val.* 'Tis true ; for you are over boots in love,
And yet you never swam the Hellespont.
    *Pro.* Over the boots ? nay, give me not the
        boots.[3]
    *Val.* No, I'll not, for it boots thee not.
    *Pro.*                                What ?
    *Val.*                               To be
In love, where scorn is bought with groans ; coy
        looks,
With heart-sore sighs ; one fading moment's mirth,
With twenty watchful, weary, tedious nights ;
If haply won, perhaps, a hapless gain ;
If lost, why then a grievous labour won ;
However, but a folly[4] bought with wit,

---

   [2] ——— *some shallow story of deep love,*
     *How young Leander cross'd the Hellespont.*]    The poem of
*Musæus,* entitled HERO AND LEANDER, is meant. Marlow's
translation of this piece was extremely popular, and deservedly so,
many of Marlow's lines being as smooth as those of Dryden.
   [3] ——— *nay, give me not* the boots.]    A proverbial expression,
though now disused, signifying, don't make a laughing stock of
me ; don't play with me.
   Perhaps this expression took its origin from a sport the country
people in Warwickshire use at their harvest-home, where one sits
as judge to try misdemeanors committed in harvest, and the punishment for the men, is to be laid on a bench, and slapped on the
breech with a pair of *boots.* This they call *giving them the boots.*
The *boots,* however, were an ancient engine of torture in Scotland.
   [4] *However, but a folly,* &c.]    This love will end in a *foolish
action,* to produce which you are long to spend your *wit,* or it will
end in the loss of your *wit,* which will be overpowered by the
folly of love. JOHNSON.

Or else a wit by folly vanquished.

*Pro.* So, by your circumstance, you call me fool.

*Val.* So, by your circumstance, I fear, you'll prove.

*Pro.* 'Tis love you cavil at; I am not love.

*Val.* Love is your master, for he masters you:
And he that is so yoked by a fool,
Methinks should not be chronicled for wise.

*Pro.* Yet writers say, As in the sweetest bud
The eating canker dwells, so eating love
Inhabits in the finest wits of all.

*Val.* And writers say, As the most forward bud
Is eaten by the canker ere it blow,
Even so by love the young and tender wit
Is turn'd to folly; blasting in the bud,
Losing his verdure even in the prime,
And all the fair effects of future hopes.
But wherefore waste I time to counsel thee,
That art a votary to fond desire?
Once more adieu: my father at the road
Expects my coming, there to see me shipp'd.

*Pro.* And thither will I bring thee, Valentine.

*Val.* Sweet Proteus, no; now let us take our leave.
At Milan,⁵ let me hear from thee by letters,
Of thy success in love, and what news else
Betideth here in absence of thy friend;
And I likewise will visit thee with mine.

*Pro.* All happiness bechance to thee in Milan!

*Val.* As much to you at home! and so, farewell.
                              [*Exit* VALENTINE.

*Pro.* He after honour hunts, I after love:

---

⁵ At *Milan*,] The old copy has—*To* Milan, and may be right.
" *To Milan* "—may here be intended as an imperfect sentence.
I am now bound for Milan; or let me hear from thee by letters
addressed to me at Milan.   MALONE.

He leaves his friends, to dignify them more ;
I leave myself, my friends, and all for love.
Thou, Julia, thou hast metamorphos'd me ;
Made me neglect my studies, lose my time,
War with good counsel, set the world at nought ;
Made wit with musing weak, heart sick with
    thought.

*Enter* SPEED.[6]

*Speed.* Sir Proteus, save you : Saw you my mas-
    ter ?

*Pro.* But now he parted hence, to embark for
    Milan.

*Speed.* Twenty to one then, he is shipp'd already ;
And I have play'd the sheep, in losing him.

*Pro.* Indeed a sheep doth very often stray,
An if the shepherd be awhile away.

*Speed.* You conclude that my master is a shep-
    herd then, and I a sheep ?

*Pro.* I do.

*Speed.* Why then my horns are his horns, whether
    I wake or sleep.

*Pro.* A silly answer, and fitting well a sheep.

*Speed.* This proves me still a sheep.

*Pro.* True ; and thy master a shepherd.

*Speed.* Nay, that I can deny by a circumstance.

*Pro.* It shall go hard, but I'll prove it by an-
    other.

*Speed.* The shepherd seeks the sheep, and not the
sheep the shepherd ; but I seek my master, and my
master seeks not me : therefore, I am no sheep.

*Pro.* The sheep for fodder follow the shepherd,

---

6 Mr. Pope's opinion that this scene was interpolated by the
players seems advanced without any proof, only to give a greater
licence to criticism.  JOHNSON.

the shepherd for food follows not the sheep ; thou
for wages followest thy master, thy master for wages
follows not thee : therefore, thou art a sheep.

*Speed.* Such another proof will make me cry baa.

*Pro.* But dost thou hear ? gav'st thou my letter
to Julia ?

*Speed.* Ay, sir : I, a lost mutton, gave your letter
to her, a laced mutton ;[7] and she, a laced mutton,
gave me, a lost mutton, nothing for my labour !

*Pro.* Here's too small a pasture for such a store
of muttons.

*Speed.* If the ground be overcharged, you were
best stick her.

*Pro.* Nay, in that you are astray ; 'twere best
pound you.

*Speed.* Nay, sir, less than a pound shall serve me
for carrying your letter.

*Pro.* You mistake ; I mean the pound, a pinfold.

*Speed.* From a pound to a pin ? fold it over and
over,
'Tis threefold too little for carrying a letter to your
lover.

*Pro.* But what said she ? did she nod ?
[SPEED *nods.*

*Speed.* I.

*Pro.* Nod, I ; why, that's noddy.[8]

*Speed.* You mistook, sir ; I say, she did nod : and
you ask me, if she did nod ; and I say, I.

*Pro.* And that set together, is—noddy.

---

[7] *a* laced mutton ;] A *laced mutton* was in our author's time so
established a term for a courtezan, that a street in Clerkenwell,
which was much frequented by women of the town, was then
called *Mutton-lane.*

[8] —— *why that's* noddy.] Mr. Steevens says noddy *was a
game at cards,* but this play upon syllables is hardly worth explaining. The speakers intend to fix the name of *noddy,* that is,
*fool,* on each other.

*Speed.* Now you have taken the pains to set it together, take it for your pains.

*Pro.* No, no, you shall have it for bearing the letter.

*Speed.* Well, I perceive, I must be fain to bear with you.

*Pro.* Why, sir, how do you bear with me?

*Speed.* Marry, sir, the letter very orderly; having nothing but the word, noddy, for my pains.

*Pro.* Beshrew me, but you have a quick wit.

*Speed.* And yet it cannot overtake your slow purse.

*Pro.* Come, come, open the matter in brief: What said she?

*Speed.* Open your purse, that the money, and the matter, may be both at once delivered.

*Pro.* Well, sir, here is for your pains: What said she?

*Speed.* Truly, sir, I think you'll hardly win her.

*Pro.* Why? Could'st thou perceive so much from her?

*Speed.* Sir, I could perceive nothing at all from her; no, not so much as a ducat for delivering your letter: And being so hard to me that brought your mind, I fear, she'll prove as hard to you in telling her mind.⁹ Give her no token but stones; for she's as hard as steel.

*Pro.* What, said she nothing?

*Speed.* No, not so much as—*take this for thy pains.* To testify your bounty, I thank you, you

---

⁹ —— *in telling* her *mind.*] The old copy has " —in telling *your* mind"—which Mr. Malone thinks is right. The meaning is—*She being so hard to me who was the bearer of your mind, I fear she will prove no less so to you, when you address her in person.* The opposition is between *brought* and *telling.*

have testern'd me;[1] in requital whereof, henceforth carry your letters yourself: and so, sir, I'll commend you to my master.

*Pro.* Go, go, be gone, to save your ship from
       wreck;
Which cannot perish, having thee aboard,
Being destined to a drier death on shore:——
I must go send some better messenger;
I fear, my Julia would not deign my lines,
Receiving them from such a worthless post.
                  [*Exeunt.*

## SCENE II.

*The same.   Garden of* Julia's *house.*

*Enter* JULIA *and* LUCETTA.

*Jul.* But say, Lucetta, now we are alone,
Would'st thou then counsel me to fall in love?
   *Luc.* Ay, madam; so you stumble not unheed-
      fully.
   *Jul.* Of all the fair resort of gentlemen,
That every day with parle encounter me,
In thy opinion, which is worthiest love?
   *Luc.* Please you, repeat their names, I'll shew
      my mind
According to my shallow simple skill.
   *Jul.* What think'st thou of the fair Sir Egla-
      mour?[2]

[1] —— *you have* testern'd *me;*] You have gratified me with a *tester, testern,* or *testen,* that is, with a sixpence. JOHNSON.

[2] *What think'st thou of the fair* Sir Eglamour?] This *Sir Eglamour* must not be confounded with the *persona dramatis* of the same name. The latter lived at Milan, and had vowed " pure chastity" upon the death of his " true love." Perhaps *Sir Eglamour* was once the common cant term for an insignificant inamorato.

*Luc.* As of a knight well-spoken, neat and fine;
But, were I you, he never should be mine.

*Jul.* What think'st thou of the rich Mercatio?

*Luc.* Well of his wealth; but of himself, so, so.

*Jul.* What think'st thou of the gentle Proteus?

*Luc.* Lord, lord! to see what folly reigns in us!

*Jul.* How now! what means this passion at his name?

*Luc.* Pardon, dear madam; 'tis a passing shame,
That I, unworthy body as I am,
Should censure thus on lovely gentlemen.[3]

*Jul.* Why not on Proteus, as of all the rest?

*Luc.* Then thus,——of many good I think him best.

*Jul.* Your reason?

*Luc.* I have no other but a woman's reason;
I think him so, because I think him so.

*Jul.* And would'st thou have me cast my love on him?

*Luc.* Ay, if you thought your love not cast away.

*Jul.* Why, he of all the rest hath never mov'd me.

*Luc.* Yet he of all the rest, I think, best loves ye.

*Jul.* His little speaking shows his love but small.

*Luc.* Fire, that is closest kept, burns most of all.

*Jul.* They do not love, that do not show their love.

*Luc.* O, they love least, that let men know their love.

*Jul.* I would, I knew his mind.

*Luc.* Peruse this paper, madam.

Jul. *To Julia,*—Say, from whom?

*Luc.* That the contents will shew.

*Jul.* Say, say; who gave it thee?

[3] *Should* censure *thus, &c.*] To *censure*, in our author's time, generally signified to give one's judgment.

9

*Luc.* Sir Valentine's page; and sent, I think,
    from Proteus:
He would have given it you, but I, being in the way,
Did in your name receive it; pardon the fault, I pray.
*Jul.* Now, by my modesty, a goodly broker![4]
Dare you presume to harbour wanton lines?
To whisper and conspire against my youth?
Now, trust me, 'tis an office of great worth,
And you an officer fit for the place.
There, take the paper, see it be return'd;
Or else return no more into my sight.
*Luc.* To plead for love deserves more fee than
    hate.
*Jul.* Will you be gone?
*Luc.*          That you may ruminate. [*Exit.*
*Jul.* And yet, I would, I had o'erlook'd the letter.
It were a shame to call her back again,
And pray her to a fault for which I chid her.
What fool is she, that knows I am a maid,
And would not force the letter to my view?
Since maids, in modesty, say *No*, to that[5]
Which they would have the profferer construe, *Ay.*
Fie, fie! how wayward is this foolish love,
That, like a testy babe, will scratch the nurse,
And presently, all humbled, kiss the rod!
How churlishly I chid Lucetta hence,
When willingly I would have had her here!
How angrily I taught my brow to frown,
When inward joy enforc'd my heart to smile!
My penance is, to call Lucetta back,
And ask remission for my folly past:—
What ho! Lucetta!

<hr>

[4] —— *a goodly* broker!] A *broker* was used for matchmaker, sometimes for a procuress. JOHNSON.
[5] —— *say No, to that,* &c.] A paraphrase on the old proverb "Maids say *nay*, and take it."

*Re-enter* LUCETTA.

*Luc.*                    What would your ladyship?
*Jul.* Is it near dinner time?
*Luc.*                    I would it were;
That you might kill your stomach on your meat,[1]
And not upon your maid.
*Jul.*                    What is't you took up
So gingerly?
*Luc.*        Nothing.
*Jul.*                    Why didst thou stoop then?
*Luc.* To take a paper up that I let fall.
*Jul.* And is that paper nothing.
*Luc.*                    Nothing concerning me.
*Jul.* Then let it lie for those that it concerns.
*Luc.* Madam, it will not lie where it concerns,
Unless it have a false interpreter.
*Jul.* Some love of yours hath writ to you in
        rhyme.
*Luc.* That I might sing it, madam, to a tune:
Give me a note: your ladyship can set.
*Jul.* As little by such toys as may be possible:
Best sing it to the tune of *Light o' love.*
*Luc.* It is too heavy for so light a tune.
*Jul.* Heavy? belike, it hath some burden then.
*Luc.* Ay; and melodious were it, would you sing
        it.
*Jul.* And why not you?
*Luc.*                    I cannot reach so high.
*Jul.* Let's see your song;—How now, minion?
*Luc.* Keep tune there still, so you will sing it out:
And yet, methinks, I do not like this tune.
*Jul.* You do not?

---

[1] —— stomach *on your meat*,] *Stomach* was used for *passion*
or *obstinacy.* JOHNSON.

Fuseli del.        Bromley sculp.

Julia. *Go, get you gone; and let the papers lie.*

Published by F & C Rivington London Jan. 8. 1803.

*Luc.* No, madam; it is too sharp.

*Jul.* You, minion, are too saucy.

*Luc.* Nay, now you are too flat,
And mar the concord with too harsh a descant:[6]
There wanteth but a mean[7] to fill your song.

*Jul.* The mean is drown'd with your unruly base.

*Luc.* Indeed, I bid the base for Proteus.[8]

*Jul.* This babble shall not henceforth trouble me.
Here is a coil with protestation!——

[*Tears the letter.*

Go, get you gone; and let the papers lie:
You would be fingering them, to anger me.

*Luc.* She makes it strange; but she would be best
    pleas'd
To be so anger'd with another letter.     [*Exit.*

*Jul.* Nay, would I were so anger'd with the same!
O hateful hands, to tear such loving words!
Injurious wasps! to feed on such sweet honey,
And kill the bees, that yield it, with your stings!
I'll kiss each several paper for amends.
And, here is writ—*kind Julia;*—unkind Julia!
As in revenge of thy ingratitude,
I throw thy name against the bruising stones,
Trampling contemptuously on thy disdain.
Look, here is writ—*love-wounded Proteus:*——
Poor wounded name! my bosom, as a bed,
Shall lodge thee, till thy wound be throughly heal'd;
And thus I search it with a sovereign kiss.
But twice, or thrice, was Proteus written down?
Be calm, good wind, blow not a word away,
Till I have found each letter in the letter,

---

[6] ———*too harsh a descant:*] *Descant* is a term in music, signifying in general that kind of harmony in which one part is broken, and formed into a kind of paraphrase on the other.

[7] ——— *but a mean, &c.*] The *mean* is the *tenor* in music.

[8] To *bid the base* means here, I believe, *to challenge to a contest.*
                                              MALONE.

11

Except mine own name; that some whirlwind bear
Unto a ragged, fearful, hanging rock,
And throw it thence into the raging sea!
Lo, here in one line is his name twice writ,—
*Poor forlorn Proteus, passionate Proteus,*
*To the sweet Julia;* that I'll tear away;
And yet I will not, sith so prettily
He couples it to his complaining names;
Thus will I fold them one upon another;
Now kiss, embrace, contend, do what you will.

*Re-enter* LUCETTA.

*Luc.* Madam, dinner's ready, and your father
    stays.
*Jul.* Well, let us go.
*Luc.* What, shall these papers lie like tell-tales
    here?
*Jul.* If you respect them, best to take them up.
*Luc.* Nay, I was taken up for laying them down:
Yet here they shall not lie, for catching cold.[9]
*Jul.* I see you have a month's mind to them.[1]
*Luc.* Ay, madam, you may say what sights you
    see;
I see things too, although you judge I wink.
*Jul.* Come, come, wilt please you go?
                          [*Exeunt.*

---

[9] *Yet here they shall not lie,* for catching cold.] i. e. *lest they should catch cold.* This mode of expression is not frequent in Shakspeare, but occurs in every play of Beaumont and Fletcher.

[1] *I see, you have a* month's mind *to them.*] A *month's mind* was an *anniversary* in times of popery. There was also *a year's mind,* and *week's mind.* But *a month's mind,* in the ritual sense, signifies not desire or inclination, but remembrance.

## SCENE III.

*The same. A room in* Antonio's *House.*

*Enter* ANTONIO *and* PANTHINO.

*Ant.* Tell me, Panthino, what sad talk[2] was that,
Wherewith my brother held you in the cloister ?
*Pan.* 'Twas of his nephew Proteus, your son.
*Ant.* Why, what of him ?
*Pan.*                      He wonder'd, that your lordship
Would suffer him to spend his youth at home ;
While other men, of slender reputation,[3]
Put forth their sons to seek preferment out :
Some, to the wars, to try their fortune there ;
Some, to discover islands far away ;[4]
Some, to the studious universities.
For any, or for all these exercises,
He said, that Proteus, your son, was meet :
And did request me, to impórtune you,
To let him spend his time no more at home,
Which would be great inpeachment to his age,[5]
In having known no travel in his youth.
- *Ant.* Nor need'st thou much impórtune me to that
Whereon this month I have been hammering.
I have consider'd well his loss of time ;
And how he cannot be a perfect man,
Not being try'd, and tutor'd in the world :

---

[2] —— *what sad talk* — ] *Sad* is the same as *grave* or *serious*.
[3] —— *of* slender reputation,] i. e. who are thought slightly of.
[4] *Some to discover islands far away ;*] In Shakspeare's time, voyages for the discovery of the islands of America were much in vogue. And the sons of the best families in England, went very frequently on these adventures. WARBURTON.
[5] —— *great* impeachment *to his age,*] *Impeachment,* i. e. reproach or *imputation.*

Experience is by industry atchiev'd,
And perfected by the swift course of time :
Then, tell me, whither were I best to send him ?

   *Pan.* I think, your lordship is not ignorant,
How his companion, youthful Valentine,
Attends the emperor in his royal court.[6]

   *Ant.* I know it well.

   *Pan.* 'Twere good, I think, your lordship sent
       him thither :
There shall he practise tilts and tournaments,
Hear sweet discourse, converse with noblemen ;
And be in eye of every exercise,
Worthy his youth and nobleness of birth.

   *Ant.* I like thy counsel ; well hast thou advis'd :
And, that thou may'st perceive how well I like it,
The execution of it shall make known ;
Even with the speediest execution
I will dispatch him to the emperor's court.

   *Pan.* To-morrow, may it please you, Don Al-
       phonso,
With other gentlemen of good esteem,
Are journeying to salute the emperor,
And to commend their service to his will.

---

[6] *Attends the emperor in his royal court.*] Shakspeare has been
guilty of no mistake in placing the emperor's court at Milan in this
play.   Several of the first German emperor's held their courts
there occasionally, it being, at that time, their immediate property,
and the chief town of their Italian dominions.   Some of them
were crowned kings of Italy at Milan, before they received the
imperial crown at Rome.  Nor has the poet fallen into any contradiction by giving a duke to Milan at the same time that the emperor held his court there.   The first dukes of that, and all the
other great cities in Italy, were not sovereign princes, as they afterwards became ; but were merely governors, or viceroys, under the emperors, and removeable at their pleasure.  Such was
the *Duke of Milan* mentioned in this play.  Mr. M. Mason adds,
that ".during the wars in Italy between Francis I. and Charles
V. the latter frequently resided at Milan."  STEEVENS.

*Ant.* Good company ; with them shall Proteus go:
And, in good time,[7]—now will we break with him.[8]

*Enter* PROTEUS.

*Pro.* Sweet love ! sweet lines ! sweet life !
Here is her hand, the agent of her heart ;
Here is her oath for love, her honour's pawn :
O, that our fathers would applaud our loves,
To seal our happiness with their consents !
O heavenly Julia !
    *Ant.* How now ? what letter are you reading there?
    *Pro.* May't please your Lordship, 'tis a word or
        two
Of commendation sent from Valentine,
Deliver'd by a friend that came from him.
    *Ant.* Lend me the letter ; let me see what news.
    *Pro.* There is no news, my lord ; but that he writes
How happily he lives, how well-belov'd,
And daily graced by the emperor ;
Wishing me with him, partner of his fortune.
    *Ant.* And how stand you affected to his wish ?
    *Pro.* As one relying on your lordship's will,
And not depending on his friendly wish.
    *Ant.* My will is something sorted with his wish :
Muse not that I thus suddenly proceed ;
For what I will, I will, and there an end.
I am resolv'd that thou shalt spend some time
With Valentinus in the emperor's court ;
What maintenance he from his friends receives,
Like exhibition[9] shalt thou have from me.
To-morrow be in readiness to go :

---

[7] —— in good time,] *In good time* was the old expression
when something happened that suited the thing in hand.
  [8] —— *now will we* break *with him.*] That is, *break* the matter
to him.
  [9] *Like* exhibition ——] i. e. allowance.

L 2

Excuse it not, for I am peremptory.

*Pro.* My lord, I cannot be so soon provided ;
Please you, deliberate a day or two.

*Ant.* Look, what thou want'st, shall be sent after
        thee :
No more of stay ; to-morrow thou must go.——
Come on, Panthino ; you shall be employ'd
To hasten on his expedition.

                   [*Exeunt* ANT. *and* PAN.

*Pro.* Thus have I shunn'd the fire, for fear of
        burning ;
And drench'd me in the sea, where I am drown'd :
I fear'd to shew my father Julia's letter,
Lest he should take exceptions to my love ;
And with the vantage of mine own excuse
Hath he excepted most against my love.
O, how this spring of love resembleth[1]
   The uncertain glory of an April day ;
Which now shows all the beauty of the sun,
    And by and by a cloud takes all away !

*Re-enter* PANTHINO.

*Pan.* Sir Proteus, your father calls for you ;
He is in haste, therefore, I pray you, go.

*Pro.* Why, this it is ! my heart accords thereto ;
And yet a thousand times it answers, no.   [*Exeunt.*

---

[1] *Resembleth* is here used as a quadrisyllable, as if it was written *resembeleth.* Shakspeare takes the same liberty with many other words, in which *l,* or *r,* is subjoined to another consonant.

# ACT II.

*SCENE I.* Milan. *An Apartment in the* Duke's
Palace.

*Enter* VALENTINE *and* SPEED.

*Speed.* Sir, your glove.

*Val.* Not mine ; my gloves are on.

*Speed.* Why then this may be yours, for this is
but one.[a]

*Val.* Ha! let me see: ay, give it me, it's mine :—
Sweet ornament that decks a thing divine!
Ah Silvia! Silvia!

*Speed.* Madam Silvia! madam Silvia!

*Val.* How now, sirrah?

*Speed.* She is not within hearing, sir.

*Val.* Why, sir, who bade you call her?

*Speed.* Your worship, sir ; or else I mistook.

*Val.* Well, you'll still be too forward.

*Speed.* And yet I was last chidden for being too
slow.

*Val.* Go to, sir ; tell me, do you know madam
Silvia?

*Speed.* She that your worship loves?

*Val.* Why, how know you that I am in love?

*Speed.* Marry, by these special marks : First,
you have learned, like sir Proteus, to wreath your
arms like a male-content ; to relish a love-song, like
a Robin-red-breast ; to walk alone, like one that
had the pestilence ; to sigh, like a school-boy that
had lost his A. B. C ; to weep, like a young wench

---

[a] Val. *Not mine ; my gloves are* on.
Speed. *Why then this may be yours, for this is but* one.] It
should seem from this passage, that the word *one* was anciently
pronounced as if it were written *on*.

that had buried her grandam : to fast, like one that takes diet ; [3] to watch, like one that fears robbing; to speak puling, like a beggar at Hallowmas.[4]     You were wont, when you laughed, to crow like a cock; when you walked, to walk like one of the lions ; when you fasted, it was presently after dinner ; when you looked sadly, it was for want of money : and now you are metamorphosed with a mistress, that, when I look on you, I can hardly think you my master.

*Val.* Are all these things perceived in me ?

*Speed.* They are all perceived without you.

*Val.* Without me ? they cannot.

*Speed.* Without you ? nay, that's certain, for, without you were so simple, none else would : [5] but you are so without these follies, that these follies are within you, and shine through you like the water in an urinal ; that not an eye, that sees you, but is a physician to comment on your malady.

*Val.* But tell me, dost thou know my lady Silvia ?

*Speed.* She, that you gaze on so, as she sits at supper ?

*Val.* Hast thou observed that ? even she I mean.

*Speed.* Why, sir, I know her not.

*Val.* Dost thou know her by my gazing on her, and yet knowest her not ?

*Speed.* Is she not hard favoured, sir ?

*Val.* Not so fair, boy, as well favoured.

*Speed.* Sir, I know that well enough.

*Val.* What dost thou know ?

---

[3] —— *takes* diet :] is under a regimen.

[4] —— *Hallowmas.*] This is about the feast of All-Saints, when the poor people in *Staffordshire*, and perhaps in other country places, go from parish to parish *a souling* as they call it ; i. e. begging and *puling* (or singing small, as Bailey's *Dict.* explains *puling*,) for *soul-cakes*, or any good thing to make them merry.

[5] —— *none else would :*] None else would *be so simple.*

*Speed.* That she is not so fair, as (of you) well favoured.

*Val.* I mean, that her beauty is exquisite, but her favour infinite.

*Speed.* That's because the one is painted, and the other out of all count.

*Val.* How painted! and how out of count?

*Speed.* Marry, sir, so painted, to make her fair, that no man counts of her beauty.

*Val.* How esteemest thou me? I account of her beauty.

*Speed.* You never saw her since she was deformed.

*Val.* How long hath she been deformed?

*Speed.* Ever since you loved her.

*Val.* I have loved her ever since I saw her; and still I see her beautiful.

*Speed.* If you love her, you cannot see her.

*Val.* Why?

*Speed.* Because love is blind. O, that you had mine eyes; or your own had the lights they were wont to have, when you chid at sir Proteus for going ungartered![6]

*Val.* What should I see then?

*Speed.* Your own present folly, and her passing deformity: for he, being in love, could not see to garter his hose; and you, being in love, cannot see to put on your hose.

*Val.* Belike, boy, then you are in love; for last morning you could not see to wipe my shoes.

*Speed.* True, sir; I was in love with my bed: I thank you, you swinged me for my love, which makes me the bolder to chide you for yours.

---

[6] ——*for going* ungartered!] This is enumerated by Rosalind in *As you like it,* Act III. sc. ii. as one of the undoubted marks of love: " Then your hose should be *ungartered,* your bonnet unbanded," &c. MALONE.

*Val.* In conclusion, I stand affected to her.

*Speed.* I would you were set ;[7] so, your affection would cease.

*Val.* Last night she enjoined me to write some lines to one she loves.

*Speed.* And have you ?

*Val.* I have.

*Speed.* Are they not lamely writ ?

*Val.* No, boy, but as well as I can do them ;— Peace, here she comes.

*Enter* SILVIA,

*Speed.* O excellent motion! O exceeding puppet! now will he interpret to her.[8]

*Val.* Madam and mistress, a thousand good-morrows.

*Speed.* O, 'give you good even! here's a million of manners. [*Aside.*

*Sil.* Sir Valentine and servant,[9] to you two thousand.

*Speed.* He should give her interest, and she gives it him.

*Val.* As you enjoin'd me, I have writ your letter
Unto the secret nameless friend of yours ;
Which I was much unwilling to proceed in,
But for my duty to your ladyship.

*Sil.* I thank you, gentle servant : 'tis very clerkly done.

---

[7] *I would you were set ;*] *set* for *seated*, in opposition to *stand.*

[8] *O excellent* motion! &c.] *Motion*, in Shakspeare's time, signified *puppet*, or rather perhaps a *puppet-show ;* the master whereof may properly be said to be an interpreter, as being the explainer of the inarticulate language of the actors.

[9] *Sir Valentine and* servant,] Here Silvia calls her lover *servant*, and again below, her *gentle servant.* This was the language of ladies to their lovers at the time when Shakspeare wrote.

[1] —— *'tis very* clerkly *done.*] i. e. like a scholar.

11

*Val.* Now trust me, madam, it came hardly off;
For, being ignorant to whom it goes,
I writ at random, very doubtfully.

*Sil.* Perchance you think too much of so much
pains?

*Val.* No, madam; so it stead you, I will write,
Please you command, a thousand times as much:
And yet,—

*Sil.* A pretty period! Well, I guess the sequel;
And yet I will not name it:—and yet I care not;—
And yet take this again;—and yet I thank you;
Meaning henceforth to trouble you no more.

*Speed.* And yet you will; and yet another yet.
[*Aside.*

*Val.* What means your ladyship? do you not
like it?

*Sil.* Yes, yes; the lines are very quaintly writ:
But since unwillingly, take them again;
Nay, take them.

*Val.* Madam, they are for you.

*Sil.* Ay, ay, you writ them, sir, at my request;
But I will none of them; they are for you:
I would have had them writ more movingly.

*Val.* Please you, I'll write your ladyship another.

*Sil.* And, when it's writ, for my sake read it
over:
And, if it please you, so: if not, why, so.

*Val.* If it please me, madam! what then?

*Sil.* Why, if it please you, take it for your labour,
And so good morrow, servant. [*Exit* Silvia.

*Speed.* O jest unseen, inscrutable, invisible,
As a nose on a man's face, or a weathercock on a
steeple!
My master sues to her; and she hath taught her
suitor,
He being her pupil, to become her tutor.

O excellent device! was there ever heard a better?
That my master, being scribe, to himself should
      write the letter?

*Val.* How now, sir? what are you reasoning with
yourself?

*Speed.* Nay, I was rhyming; 'tis you that have
the reason.

*Val.* To do what?

*Speed.* To be a spokesman from madam Silvia.

*Val.* To whom?

*Speed.* To yourself; why, she wooes you by a figure.

*Val.* What figure?

*Speed.* By a letter, I should say.

*Val.* Why, she hath not writ to me?

*Speed.* What needs she, when she hath made you
write to yourself? Why, do you not perceive the jest?

*Val.* No, believe me.

*Speed.* No believing you indeed, sir: But did you
perceive her earnest?

*Val.* She gave me none, except an angry word.

*Speed.* Why, she hath given you a letter.

*Val.* That's the letter I writ to her friend.

*Speed.* And that letter hath she deliver'd, and
there an end.[2]

*Val.* I would, it were no worse.

*Speed.* I'll warrant you, 'tis as well:
*For often you have writ to her; and she, in modesty,
Or else for want of idle time, could not again reply;
Or fearing else some messenger, that might her mind
      discover,
Herself hath taught her love himself to write unto
      her lover.——*
All this I speak in print;[3] for in print I found it.——
Why muse you, sir? 'tis dinner time.

---

[2] ——*and there an end.*] I. e. there's the conclusion of the matter.
[3] *All this I speak* in print;] *In print* means *with exactness.*

*Val.* I have dined.

*Speed.* Ay, but hearken, sir; though the cameleon Love can feed on the air, I am one that am nourished by my victuals, and would fain have meat; O, be not like your mistress; be moved, be moved. [*Exeunt.*

## SCENE II.

Verona. *A room in Julia's House.*

*Enter* PROTEUS *and* JULIA.

*Pro.* Have patience, gentle Julia.

*Jul.* I must, where is no remedy.

*Pro.* When possibly I can; I will return.

*Jul.* If you turn not, you will return the sooner:
Keep this remembrance for thy Julia's sake.
[*Giving a ring.*

*Pro.* Why then we'll make exchange; here, take you this.

*Jul.* And seal the bargain with a holy kiss.

*Pro.* Here is my hand for my true constancy;
And when that hour o'er-slips me in the day,
Wherein I sigh not, Julia, for thy sake,
The next ensuing hour some foul mischance
Torment me for my love's forgetfulness!
My father stays my coming; answer not;
The tide is now: nay, not the tide of tears;
That tide will stay me longer than I should:
[*Exit* JULIA.

Julia, farewell.—What! gone without a word?
Ay, so true love should do: it cannot speak;
For truth hath better deeds, than words, to grace it.

*Enter* PANTHINO.

*Pan.* Sir Proteus, you are staid for.

*Pro.* Go; I come, I come:—
Alas! this parting strikes poor lovers dumb.
[*Exeunt.*

## SCENE III.

*The same.   A Street.*

*Enter* LAUNCE, *leading a dog.*

*Laun.* Nay, 'twill be this hour ere I have done weeping; all the kind of the Launces have this very fault: I have received my proportion, like the prodigious son, and am going with sir Proteus to the Imperial's court. I think, Crab my dog be the sourest-natured dog that lives: my mother weeping, my father wailing, my sister crying, our maid howling, our cat wringing her hands, and all our house in a great perplexity, yet did not this cruel-hearted cur shed one tear; he is a stone, a very pebble-stone, and has no more pity in him than a dog: a Jew would have wept to have seen our parting; why, my grandam having no eyes, look you, wept herself blind at my parting. Nay, I'll show you the manner of it: This shoe is my father;—no, this left shoe is my father;—no, no, this left shoe is my mother;—nay, that cannot be so neither:—yes, it is so, it is so; it hath the worser sole; This shoe, with the hole in it, is my mother, and this my father; A vengeance on't! there 'tis: now, sir, this staff is my sister; for, look you, she is as white as a lily, and as small as a wand: this hat is Nan, our maid; I am the dog:—no, the dog is himself, and I am the dog,[4]—O, the dog is me, and I am myself; ay, so, so. Now come I to my father; *Father, your blessing;* now should not the shoe

---

[4] —— *I am the dog,* &c.] Sir T. Hanmer reads: *I am the dog, no, the dog is himself and I am* me, *the dog is* the dog, *and I am myself.* This certainly is more reasonable, but I know not how much reason the author intended to bestow on Launce's soliloquy.
                                                        JOHNSON.

speak a word for weeping; now should I kiss my father; well, he weeps on :—now come I to my mother, (O, that she could speak now!) like a wood woman ;'—well, I kiss her ;—why, there 'tis ; here's my mother's breath up and down ; now come I to my sister ; mark the moan she makes : now the dog all this while sheds not a tear, nor speaks a word ; but see how I lay the dust with my tears.

### *Enter* PANTHINO.

*Pan.* Launce, away, away, aboard ; thy master is shipped, and thou art to post after with oars. What's the matter? why weep'st thou, man? Away, ass ; you will lose the tide, if you tarry any longer.

*Laun.* It is no matter if the ty'd were lost ; for it is the unkindest ty'd that ever man ty'd.

*Pan.* What's the unkindest tide?

*Laun.* Why, he that's ty'd here ; Crab, my dog.

*Pan.* Tut, man, I mean thou'lt lose the flood : and, in losing the flood, lose thy voyage ; and, in losing thy voyage, lose thy master ; and, in losing thy master, lose thy service ; and, in losing thy service,—Why dost thou stop my mouth?

*Laun.* For fear thou should'st lose thy tongue.

*Pan.* Where should I lose my tongue?

*Laun.* In thy tale.

*Pan.* In thy tail?

*Laun.* Lose the tide, and the voyage, and the master, and the service? The tide !—Why, man, if the river were dry, I am able to fill it with my tears ; if the wind were down, I could drive the boat with my sighs.

*Pan.* Come, come away, man ; I was sent to call thee.

---

' —— *like a* wood woman ;—] i. e. crazy, frantic with grief; or distracted, from any other cause.

*Laun.* Sir, call me what thou darest.
*Pan.* Wilt thou go?
*Laun.* Well, I will go.                    [*Exeunt.*

## SCENE IV.

Milan.     *An Apartment in the* Duke's *Palace.*

*Enter* VALENTINE, SILVIA, THURIO, *and* SPEED.

*Sil.* Servant—
*Val.* Mistress?
*Speed.* Master, sir Thurio frowns on you.
*Val.* Ay, boy, it's for love.
*Speed.* Not of you.
*Val.* Of my mistress then.
*Speed.* 'Twere good, you knocked him.
*Sil.* Servant, you are sad.
*Val.* Indeed, madam, I seem so.
*Thu.* Seem you that you are not?
*Val.* Haply, I do.
*Thu.* So do counterfeits.
*Val.* So do you.
*Thu.* What seem I, that I am not?
*Val.* Wise.
*Thu.* What instance of the contrary?
*Val.* Your folly.
*Thu.* And how quote you my folly?[6]
*Val.* I quote it in your jerkin.
*Thu.* My jerkin is a doublet.
*Val.* Well, then, I'll double your folly.
*Thu.* How?
*Sil.* What, angry, sir Thurio? do you change colour?

[6] —— *how quote you my folly?*] To *quote* is to observe. Valentine in his answer plays upon the word, which was pronounced as if written *coat.*

9

*Val.* Give him leave, madam; he is a kind of cameleon.

*Thu.* That hath more mind to feed on your blood, than live in your air.

*Val.* You have said, sir.

*Thu.* Ay, sir, and done too, for this time.

*Val.* I know it well, sir; you always end ere you begin.

*Sil.* A fine volley of words, gentlemen, and quickly shot off.

*Val.* 'Tis indeed, madam; we thank the giver.

*Sil.* Who is that, servant?

*Val.* Yourself, sweet lady; for you gave the fire: sir Thurio borrows his wit from your ladyship's looks, and spends what he borrows, kindly in your company.

*Thu.* Sir, if you spend word for word with me, I shall make your wit bankrupt.

*Val.* I know it well, sir: you have an exchequer of words, and, I think, no other treasure to give your followers; for it appears by their bare liveries, that they live by your bare words.

*Sil.* No more, gentlemen, no more; here comes my father.

### *Enter* DUKE.

*Duke.* Now, daughter Silvia, you are hard beset.
Sir Valentine, your father's in good health:
What say you to a letter from your friends
Of much good news?

*Val.*                     My lord, I will be thankful
To any happy messenger from thence.

*Duke.* Know you Don Antonio, your countryman?[7]

---

[7] *Know you* Don *Antonio, your countryman* ?] The word *Don* should be omitted; the characters are *Italians,* not *Spaniards.* Yet Don *Alphonso* occurs in a preceding scene.

*Val.* Ay, my good lord, I know the gentleman
To be of worth, and worthy estimation,
And not without desert[5] so well reputed.

*Duke.* Hath he not a son?

*Val.* Ay, my good lord; a son, that well deserves
The honour and regard of such a father.

*Duke.* You know him well?

*Val.* I knew him, as myself; for from our infancy
We have convers'd, and spent our hours together:
And though myself have been an idle truant,
Omitting the sweet benefit of time,
To clothe mine age with angel-like perfection;
Yet hath sir Proteus, for that's his name,
Made use and fair advantage of his days;
His years but young, but his experience old;
His head unmellow'd, but his judgement ripe;
And, in a word, (for far behind his worth
Come all the praises that I now bestow,)
He is complete in feature, and in mind,
With all good grace to grace a gentleman.

*Duke.* Beshrew me, sir, but, if he make this good,
He is as worthy for an empress' love,
As meet to be an emperor's counsellor.
Well, sir; this gentleman is come to me,
With commendation from great potentates;
And here he means to spend his time a-while:
I think, 'tis no unwelcome news to you.

*Val.* Should I have wish'd a thing, it had been he.

*Duke.* Welcome him then according to his worth;
Silvia, I speak to you: and you, sir Thurio:—
For Valentine, I need not 'cite him to it:[9]
I'll send him hither to you presently.   [*Exit* DUKE.

*Val.* This is the gentleman, I told your ladyship,

---

[5] —— *not without desert* ——] And not dignified with so much
reputation without proportionate merit.   JOHNSON.

[9] *I need not 'cite him to it:*] i. e. incite him to it.

Had come along with me, but that his mistress
Did hold his eyes lock'd in her crystal looks.
  *Sil.* Belike, that now she hath enfranchis'd them
Upon some other pawn for fealty.
  *Val.* Nay, sure, I think, she holds them prisoners
      still.
  *Sil.* Nay, then he should be blind; and, being
      blind,
How could he see his way to seek out you?
  *Val.* Why, lady, love hath twenty pair of eyes.
  *Thu.* They say, that love hath not an eye at all.
  *Val.* To see such lovers, Thurio, as yourself;
Upon a homely object love can wink.


*Enter* PROTEUS.


  *Sil.* Have done, have done; here comes the gen-
      tleman.
  *Val.* Welcome, dear Proteus!—Mistress, I be-
      seech you,
Confirm his welcome with some special favour.
  *Sil.* His worth is warrant for his welcome hither,
If this be he you oft have wish'd to hear from.
  *Val.* Mistress, it is: sweet lady, entertain him
To be my fellow-servant to your ladyship.
  *Sil.* Too low a mistress for so high a servant.
  *Pro.* Not so, sweet lady; but too mean a servant
To have a look of such a worthy mistress.
  *Val.* Leave off discourse of disability:—
Sweet lady, entertain him for your servant.
  *Pro.* My duty will I boast of, nothing else.
  *Sil.* And duty never yet did want his meed;
Servant, you are welcome to a worthless mistress.
  *Pro.* I'll die on him that says so, but yourself.
  *Sil.* That you are welcome?

VOL. I.           M

*Pro.*                    No; that you are worthless.'

*Enter* Servant.

*Ser.* Madam, my lord your father² would speak
    with you.
*Sil.* I'll wait upon his pleasure.    [*Exit* Servant.
    Come, sir Thurio,
Go with me :—Once more, new servant, welcome :
I'll leave you to confer of home-affairs ;
When you have done, we look to hear from you.
    *Pro.* We'll both attend upon your ladyship.
            [*Exeunt* SILVIA, THURIO, *and* SPEED.
*Val.* Now, tell me, how do all from whence you
    came ?
*Pro.* Your friends are well, and have them much
    commended.
*Val.* And how do yours ?
*Pro.*                        I left them all in health.
*Val.* How does your lady, and how thrives your
    love ?
*Pro.* My tales of love were wont to weary you ;
I know, you joy not in a love-discourse.
*Val.* Ay, Proteus, but that life is alter'd now :
I have done penance for contemning love ;
Whose high imperious³ thoughts have punish'd me
With bitter fasts, with penitential groans,

---

    ¹ No; *that you are* worthless.]    I have inserted the particle *no*,
to fill up the measure.    JOHNSON.
    ² Ser. *Madam, my lord your father* —]    This speech in all the
editions is assigned improperly to Thurio; but he has been all
along upon the stage, and could not know that the duke wanted
his daughter.    Besides, the first line and half of Silvia's answer
is evidently addressed to two persons.    A servant, therefore, must
come in and deliver the message ; and then Silvia goes out with
Thurio.    THEOBALD.
    ³ Whose *high imperious*—]    *Imperious* is an epithet very fre-
quently applied to *love* by Shakspeare and his contemporaries.

9

With nightly tears, and daily heart-sore sighs;
For, in revenge of my contempt of love,
Love hath chac'd sleep from my enthralled eyes,
And made them watchers of mine own heart's
       sorrow.
O, gentle Proteus, love's a mighty lord;
And hath so humbled me, as, I confess,
There is no woe to his correction,[4]
Nor, to his service, no such joy on earth!
Now, no discourse, except it be of love;
Now can I break my fast, dine, sup, and sleep,
Upon the very naked name of love.
   *Pro.* Enough; I read your fortune in your eye:
Was this the idol that you worship so?
   *Val.* Even she; and is she not a heavenly saint?
   *Pro.* No; but she is an earthly paragon.
   *Val.* Call her divine.
   *Pro.*                I will not flatter her.
   *Val.* O, flatter me; for love delights in praises.
   *Pro.* When I was sick, you gave me bitter pills;
And I must minister the like to you.
   *Val.* Then speak the truth by her; if not divine,
Yet let her be a principality,[5]
Sovereign to all the creatures on the earth.
   *Pro.* Except my mistress.
   *Val.*               Sweet, except not any;
Except thou wilt except against my love.
   *Pro.* Have I not reason to prefer mine own?
   *Val.* And I will help thee to prefer her too:
She shall be dignified with this high honour,——
To bear my lady's train; lest the base earth
Should from her vesture chance to steal a kiss,

---

[4] —— *no woe to his correction,*] No misery that *can be compared to* the punishment inflicted by love.
[5] —— *a* principality,] The first or *principal* of women. So
the old writers use *state.* " *She is a lady, a great* state."

And, of so great a favour growing proud,
Disdain to root the summer-swelling flower,[6]
And make rough winter everlastingly.

    *Pro.* Why, Valentine, what braggardism is this?
    *Val.* Pardon me, Proteus: all I can, is nothing
To her, whose worth makes other worthies nothing;
She is alone.[7]

    *Pro.* Then let her alone.
    *Val.* Not for the world: why, man, she is mine
          own;
And I as rich in having such a jewel,
As twenty seas, if all their sand were pearl,
The water nectar, and the rocks pure gold.
Forgive me, that I do not dream on thee,
Because thou seest me dote upon my love.
My foolish rival, that her father likes,
Only for his possessions are so huge,
Is gone with her along; and I must after,
For love, thou know'st, is full of jealousy.

    *Pro.* But she loves you?
    *Val.*                  Ay, we are betroth'd;
Nay, more, our marriage hour,
With all the cunning manner of our flight,
Determin'd of: how I must climb her window;
The ladder made of cords; and all the means
Plotted; and 'greed on, for my happiness.
Good Proteus, go with me to my chamber,
In these affairs to aid me with thy counsel.

    *Pro.* Go on before; I shall enquire you forth:
I must unto the road,[8] to disembark
Some necessaries that I needs must use;
And then I'll presently attend you.

---

    [6] —— summer-swelling *flower,*] i. e. the flower which swells in summer, till it expands itself into bloom.
    [7] *She is alone.*] She stands by herself; is incomparable.
    [8] —— *the* road,] The haven, where ships *ride* at anchor.

*Val.* Will you make haste?

*Pro.* I will.— [*Exit* VAL.

Even as one heat another heat expels,
Or as one nail by strength drives out another,
So the remembrance of my former love
Is by a newer object quite forgotten.
Is it mine eye, or Valentinus' praise,
Her true perfection, or my false transgression,
That makes me, reasonless, to reason thus?
She's fair; and so is Julia, that I love;—
That I did love, for now my love is thaw'd;
Which, like a waxen image 'gainst a fire,⁹
Bears no impression of the thing it was.
Methinks, my zeal to Valentine is cold;
And that I love him not, as I was wont:
O! but I love his lady too, too much;
And that's the reason I love him so little.
How shall I dote on her with more advice,¹
That thus without advice begin to love her?
'Tis but her picture² I have yet beheld,
And that hath dazzled my reason's light;
But when I look on her perfections,²
There is no reason but I shall be blind.
If I can check my erring love, I will;
If not, to compass her I'll use my skill. [*Exit.*

⁹ —— *a* waxen image *'gainst a fire,*] Alluding to the figures
made by witches, as representatives of those whom they designed
to torment or destroy.

¹ —— *with* more advice,] *With more advice, is on further
knowledge, on better consideration.* The word, as Mr. Malone
observes, is still current among mercantile people, whose constant
language is, " we are *advised* by letters from abroad," meaning
*informed.* So, in bills of exchange, the conclusion always is—
" Without further *advice.*"

² *'Tis but her picture*—] Proteus means, that, as yet, he had
seen only her outward form, without having known her long
enough to have any acquaintance with her mind.

³ *And that hath* dazzled *my reason's light;
But when I look,* &c.] Our author uses *dazzled* as a trisyllable.

## SCENE V.

*The same.   A street.*

*Enter* SPEED *and* LAUNCE.

*Speed.* Launce! by mine honesty, welcome to Milan.[4]

*Laun.* Forswear not thyself, sweet youth; for I am not welcome. I reckon this always——that a man is never undone, till he be hanged; nor never welcome to a place, till some certain shot be paid, and the hostess say, welcome.

*Speed.* Come on, you mad-cap, I'll to the ale-house with you presently; where, for one shot of five-pence, thou shalt have five thousand welcomes. But, sirrah, how did thy master part with madam Julia?

*Laun.* Marry, after they closed in earnest, they parted very fairly in jest.

*Speed.* But shall she marry him?

*Laun.* No.

*Speed.* How then? shall he marry her?

*Laun.* No, neither.

*Speed.* What, are they broken?

*Laun.* No, they are both as whole as a fish.

*Speed.* Why then, how stands the matter with them?

*Laun.* Marry, thus; when it stands well with him, it stands well with her.

*Speed.* What an ass art thou? I understand thee not.

*Laun.* What a block art thou, that thou can'st not? My staff understands me.

*Speed.* What thou say'st?

[4] —— to Milan.] It is *Padua* in the former editions.

*Laun.* Ay, and what I do, too : look thee, I'll but lean, and my staff understands me.

*Speed.* It stands under thee, indeed.

*Laun.* Why, stand under and understand is all one.

*Speed.* But tell me true, will't be a match?

*Laun.* Ask my dog : if he say, ay, it will ; if he say, no, it will ; if he shake his tail, and say nothing, it will.

*Speed.* The conclusion is then, that it will.

*Laun.* Thou shalt never get such a secret from me, but by a parable.

*Speed.* 'Tis well that I get it so. But, Launce, how say'st thou, that my master is become a notable lover ?[5]

*Laun.* I never knew him otherwise.

*Speed.* Than how?

*Laun.* A notable lover, as thou reportest him to be.

*Speed.* Why, thou whoreson ass, thou mistakest me.

*Laun.* Why, fool, I meant not thee ; I meant thy master.

*Speed.* I tell thee, my master is become a hot lover.

*Laun.* Why, I tell thee, I care not though he burn himself in love. If thou wilt go with me to the ale-house, so ; if not, thou art an Hebrew, a Jew, and not worth the name of a Christian.

*Speed.* Why?

*Laun.* Because thou hast not so much charity in thee, as to go to the ale[6] with a Christian : Wilt thou go?

*Speed.* At thy service.                    [*Exeunt.*

[5] —— *how say'st thou, that my master is become a notable lover ?*] i. e. What say'st thou to this circumstance,—namely, that my master is become a notable lover?

[6] —— *the* ale ——] *Ales* were merry meetings instituted in country places.

## SCENE VI.[7]

*The same.    An Apartment in the Palace.*

*Enter* PROTEUS.

*Pro.* To leave my Julia, shall I be forsworn;
To love fair Silvia, shall I be forsworn;
To wrong my friend, I shall be much forsworn;
And even that power, which gave me first my oath,
Provokes me to this threefold perjury.
Love bade me swear, and love bids me forswear:
O sweet-suggesting love,[8] if thou hast sinn'd,
Teach me, thy tempted subject, to excuse it.
At first I did adore a twinkling star,
And now I worship a celestial sun.
Unheedful vows may heedfully be broken;
And he wants wit, that wants resolved will
To learn his wit to exchange the bad for better.—
Fye, fye, unreverend tongue! to call her bad,
Whose sovereignty so oft thou hast preferr'd
With twenty thousand soul-confirming oaths.
I cannot leave to love, and yet I do;
But there I leave to love, where I should love.
Julia I lose, and Valentine I lose:

[7] It is to be observed, that, in the folio edition, there are no directions concerning the scenes; they have been added by the later editors, and may therefore be changed by any reader that can give more consistency or regularity to the drama by such alterations. I make this remark in this place, because I know not whether the following soliloquy of Proteus is so proper in the street.    JOHNSON.
The reader will perceive that the scenery has been changed, though Dr. Johnson's observation is continued.    STEEVENS.
[8] *O sweet-suggesting love,*]    To *suggest* is to *tempt,* in our author's language.

If I keep them, I needs must lose myself;
If I lose them, thus find I by their loss,
For Valentine, myself: for Julia, Silvia.
I to myself am dearer than a friend;
For love is still more precious in itself:
And Silvia, witness heaven, that made her fair!
Shews Julia but a swarthy Ethiope.
I will forget that Julia is alive,
Rememb'ring that my love to her is dead; ·
And Valentine I'll hold an enemy,
Aiming at Silvia as a sweeter friend.
I cannot now prove constant to myself,
Without some treachery used to Valentine :—
This night, he meaneth with a corded ladder
To climb celestial Silvia's chamber-window;
Myself in counsel, his competitor : [9]
Now presently I'll give her father notice
Of their disguising, and pretended flight; [1]
Who, all enrag'd, will banish Valentine;
For Thurio, he intends, shall wed his daughter:
But, Valentine being gone, I'll quickly cross,
By some sly trick, blunt Thurio's dull proceeding.
Love, lend me wings to make my purpose swift,
As thou hast lent me wit to plot this drift! [*Exit.*

## SCENE VII.

Verona. *A Room in* Julia's *House.*

*Enter* JULIA *and* LUCETTA.

*Jul.* Counsel, Lucetta! gentle girl, assist me!
And, even in kind love, I do conjure thee,—

[9] —— *in counsel, his* competitor :] *Competitor is confederate, assistant, partner.*

[1] —— pretended *flight ;*] *Pretended* flight is *proposed* or *intended* flight: the verb *pretendre* in French, has the same signification.

Who art the table wherein all my thoughts
Are visibly charácter'd and engrav'd,—
To lesson me; and tell me some good mean,
How, with my honour, I may undertake
A journey to my loving Proteus.
  *Luc.* Alas! the way is wearisome and long.
  *Jul.* A true-devoted pilgrim is not weary
To measure kingdoms with his feeble steps;
Much less shall she, that hath love's wings to fly;
And when the flight is made to one so dear,
Of such divine perfection, as sir Proteus.
  *Luc.* Better forbear, till Proteus make return.
  *Jul.* O, know'st thou not, his looks are my soul's
    food?
Pity the dearth that I have pined in,
By longing for that food so long a time.
Didst thou but know the inly touch of love,
Thou would'st as soon go kindle fire with snow,
As seek to quench the fire of love with words.
  *Luc.* I do not seek to quench your love's hot fire;
But qualify the fire's extreme rage,
Lest it should burn above the bounds of reason.
  *Jul.* The more thou dam'st it up, the more it
    burns;
The current, that with gentle murmur glides,
Thou know'st, being stopp'd, impatiently doth rage;
But, when his fair course is not hindered,
He makes sweet musick with the enamel'd stones,
Giving a gentle kiss to every sedge
He overtaketh in his pilgrimage;
And so by many winding nooks he strays,
With willing sport, to the wild ocean.
Then let me go, and hinder not my course:
I'll be as patient as a gentle stream,
And make a pastime of each weary step,
Till the last step have brought me to my love;
And there I'll rest, as, after much turmoil,

A blessed soul doth in Elysium.

*Luc.* But in what habit will you go along?

*Jul.* Not like a woman, for I would prevent
The loose encounters of lascivious men:
Gentle Lucetta, fit me with such weeds
As may beseem some well-reputed page.

*Luc.* Why then your ladyship must cut your hair.

*Jul.* No, girl; I'll knit it up in silken strings,
With twenty odd-conceited true-love knots:
To be fantastic may become a youth
Of greater time than I shall show to be.

*Luc.* What fashion, madam, shall I make your
breeches?

*Jul.* That fits as well, as—" tell me, good my
lord,
" What compass will you wear your farthingale?"
Why, even that fashion thou best lik'st, Lucetta.

*Luc.* You must needs have them with a cod-piece,
madam.

*Jul.* Out, out, Lucetta!² that will be ill-favour'd.

*Luc.* A round hose, madam, now's not worth a
pin,
Unless you have a cod-piece to stick pins on.

*Jul.* Lucetta, as thou lov'st me, let me have
What thou think'st meet, and is most mannerly:
But tell me, wench, how will the world repute me,
For undertaking so unstaid a journey?
I fear me, it will make me scandaliz'd.

*Luc.* If you think so, then stay at home, and go
not.

*Jul.* Nay, that I will not.

*Luc.* Then never dream on infamy, but go.
If Proteus like your journey, when you come,

---

² Out, out, *Lucetta !* &c.] Dr. Percy observes, that this inter-
jection is still used in the North. It seems to have the same
meaning as *apage,* Lat.

No matter who's displeas'd, when you are gone :
I fear me, he will scarce be pleas'd withal.
 *Jul.* That is the least, Lucetta, of my fear :
A thousand oaths, an ocean of his tears,
And instances as infinite of love,
Warrant me welcome to my Proteus.
 *Luc.* All these are servants to deceitful men.
 *Jul.* Base men, that use them to so base effect !
But truer stars did govern Proteus' birth :
His words are bonds, his oaths are oracles ;
His love sincere, his thoughts immaculate ;
His tears, pure messengers sent from his heart ;
His heart as far from fraud, as heaven from earth.
 *Luc.* Pray heaven, he prove so, when you come
   to him !
 *Jul.* Now, as thou lov'st me, do him not that
   wrong,
To bear a hard opinion of his truth :
Only deserve my love, by loving him ;
And presently go with me to my chamber,
To take a note of what I stand in need of,
To furnish me upon my longing journey,[1]
All that is mine I leave at thy dispose,
My goods, my lands, my reputation ;
Only, in lieu thereof, dispatch me hence :
Come, answer not, but to it presently ;
I am impatient of my tarriance.    [*Exeunt.*

---

[1] *my* longing *journey.*]  Dr. Grey observes, that *longing*
is a participle active, with a passive signification ; for *longed,*
wished, or desired.  But Julia may mean a journey which she
shall *pass in longing.*

## ACT III.

*SCENE I.* Milan.  *An Ante-room in the* Duke's Palace.

*Enter* DUKE, THURIO, *and* PROTEUS.

*Duke.* Sir Thurio, give us leave, I pray, awhile;
We have some secrets to confer about.——
                    [*Exit* THURIO.
Now, tell me, Proteus, what's your will with me?
   *Pro.* My gracious lord, that which I would
       discover,
The law of friendship bids me to conceal:
But, when I call to mind your gracious favours
Done to me, undeserving as I am,
My duty pricks me on to utter that
Which else no worldly good should draw from me.
Know, worthy prince, sir Valentine, my friend,
This night intends to steal away your daughter;
Myself am one made privy to the plot.
I know, you have determin'd to bestow her
On Thurio, whom your gentle daughter hates;
And should she thus be stolen away from you,
It would be much vexation to your age.
Thus, for my duty's sake, I rather chose
To cross my friend in his intended drift,
Than, by concealing it, heap on your head
A pack of sorrows, which would press you down,
Being unprevented, to your timeless grave.
   *Duke.* Proteus, I thank thee for thine honest
       care;
Which to requite, command me while I live.
This love of theirs myself have often seen,
Haply, when they have judged me fast asleep;
And oftentimes have purpos'd to forbid

Sir Valentine her company, and my court:
But, fearing lest my jealous aim[4] might err,
And so, unworthily, disgrace the man,
(A rashness that I ever yet have shunn'd,)
I gave him gentle looks; thereby to find
That which thyself hast now disclos'd to me.
And, that thou may'st perceive my fear of this,
Knowing that tender youth is soon suggested,
I nightly lodge her in an upper tower,
The key whereof myself have ever kept;
And thence she cannot be convey'd away.

   *Pro.* Know, noble lord, they have devis'd a mean
How he her chamber-window will ascend,
And with a corded ladder fetch her down;
For which the youthful lover now is gone,
And this way comes he with it presently;
Where, if it please you, you may intercept him,
But, good my lord, do it so cunningly,
That my discovery be not aimed at;[5]
For love of you, not hate unto my friend,
Hath made me publisher of this pretence.[6]

   *Duke.* Upon mine honour, he shall never know
That I had any light from thee of this.

   *Pro.* Adieu, my lord; sir Valentine is coming.
                               [*Exit.*

*Enter* VALENTINE.

   *Duke.* Sir Valentine, whither away so fast?
   *Val.* Please it your grace, there is a messenger
That stays to bear my letters to my friends,
And I am going to deliver them.
   *Duke.* Be they of much import?

---

4 —— *jealous* aim —]   *Aim* is *guess,* in this instance.
5 —— *be not* aimed *at ;*]   Be not *guessed.*
6 —— *of this* pretence.]   *Pretence* is *design.*

*Val.* The tenor of them doth but signify
My health, and happy being at your court.
  *Duke.* Nay, then no matter; stay with me a
        while;
I am to break with thee of some affairs,
That touch me near, wherein thou must be secret.
'Tis not unknown to thee, that I have sought
To match my friend, sir Thurio, to my daughter.
  *Val.* I know it well, my lord; and, sure, the
        match
Were rich and honourable; besides, the gentleman
Is full of virtue, bounty, worth, and qualities
Beseeming such a wife as your fair daughter:
Cannot your grace win her to fancy him?
  *Duke.* No, trust me; she is peevish, sullen, fro-
        ward,
Proud, disobedient, stubborn, lacking duty;
Neither regarding that she is my child,
Nor fearing me as if I were her father:
And, may I say to thee, this pride of hers,
Upon advice, hath drawn my love from her;
And, where[7] I thought the remnant of mine age
Should have been cherish'd by her child-like duty,
I now am full resolved to take a wife,
And turn her out to who will take her in:
Then let her beauty be her wedding-dower;
For me and my possessions she esteems not.
  *Val.* What would your grace have me to do in
        this?
  *Duke.* There is a lady, sir, in Milan, here,[8]
Whom I affect; but she is nice, and coy,
And nought esteems my aged eloquence:

---

[7] *And,* where —] *Where,* the same here as *whereas.*
[8] —— *sir, in* Milan, *here,*] It ought to be thus, instead of——
*in* Verona, *here*—— for the scene apparently is in Milan, as is clear
from several passages in the first act, and in the beginning of the
first scene of the fourth act.

Now, therefore, would I have thee to my tutor,
(For long agone I have forgot to court:
Besides, the fashion of the time⁹ is chang'd ;)
How, and which way, I may bestow myself,.
To be regarded in her sun-bright eye.
 *Val.* Win her with gifts, if she respect not words ;
Dumb jewels often, in their silent kind,
More than quick words, do move a woman's mind.
 *Duke.* But she did scorn a present that I sent her.
 *Val.* A woman sometimes scorns what best con-
  tents her :
Send her another ; never give her o'er ;
For scorn at first makes after-love the more.
If she do frown, 'tis not in hate of you,
But rather to beget more love in you :
If she do chide, 'tis not to have you gone ;
For why, the fools are mad, if left alone.
Take no repulse, whatever she doth say :
For, *get you gone*, she doth not mean, *away :*
Flatter, and praise, commend, extol their graces ;
Though ne'er so black, say, they have angels' faces.
That man that hath a tongue, I say, is no man,
If with his tongue he cannot win a woman.
 *Duke.* But she, I mean, is promis'd by her friends
Unto a youthful gentleman of worth ;
And kept severely from resort of men,
That no man hath access by day to her.
 *Val.* Why then I would resort to her by night.
 *Duke.* Ay, but the doors be lock'd, and keys
  kept safe,
That no man hath recourse to her by night.
 *Val.* What lets,¹ but one may enter at her win-
  dow ?

---

 ⁹ —— *the fashion of the time* —] The modes of courtship,
the acts by which men recommended themselves to ladies.
 ¹ *What lets,*] i. e. what hinders.

*Duke.* Her chamber is aloft, far from the ground ;
And built so shelving that one cannot climb it
Without apparent hazard of his life.

*Val.* Why then a ladder, quaintly made of cords,
To cast up with a pair of anchoring hooks,
Would serve to scale another Hero's tower,
So bold Leander would adventure it.

*Duke.* Now as thou art a gentleman of blood,
Advise me where I may have such a ladder.

*Val.* When would you use it ? pray, sir, tell me
that.

*Duke.* This very night ; for love is like a child,
That longs for every thing that he can come by.

*Val.* By seven o'clock I'll get you such a ladder.

*Duke.* But, hark thee ; I will go to her alone ;
How shall I best convey the ladder thither ?

*Val.* It will be light, my lord, that you may bear it
Under a cloak, that is of any length.

*Duke.* A cloak as long as thine will serve the
turn ?

*Val.* Ay, my good lord.

*Duke.* Then let me see thy cloak :
I'll get me one of such another length.

*Val.* Why, any cloak will serve the turn, my
lord.

*Duke.* How shall I fashion me to wear a cloak ?——
I pray thee, let me feel thy cloak upon me.——
What letter is this same ? What's here ?——*To Silvia ?*
And here an engine fit for my proceeding !
I'll be so bold to break the seal for once. [*Reads.*
*My thoughts do harbour with my Silvia nightly ;*
*And slaves they are to me, that send them flying :*
*O, could their master come and go as lightly,*
*Himself would lodge, where senseless they are lying.*
*My herald thoughts in thy pure bosom rest them ;*
*While I, their king, that thither them impórtune,*

*Do curse the grace that with such grace hath bless'd*
                *them,*
   *Because myself do want my servants' fortune:*
*I curse myself, for they are sent by me,*[1]
*That they should harbour where their lord should be.*
What's here?
*Silvia, this night I will enfranchise thee:*
'Tis so ; and here's the ladder for the purpose.—
Why, Phaëton, (for thou art Merops' son,)[2]
Wilt thou aspire to guide the heavenly car,
And with thy daring folly burn the world ?
Wilt thou reach stars, because they shine on thee ?
Go, base intruder ! over-weening slave !
Bestow thy fawning smiles on equal mates ;
And think, my patience, more than thy desert,
Is privilege for thy departure hence :
Thank me for this, more than for all the favours,
Which, all too much, I have bestow'd on thee.
But if thou linger in my territories,
Longer than swiftest expedition
Will give thee time to leave our royal court,
By heaven, my wrath shall far exceed the love
I ever bore my daughter, or thyself.
Be gone, I will not hear thy vain excuse,
But, as thou lov'st thy life, make speed from hence.
                                      [*Exit* DUKE.

   *Val.* And why not death, rather than living tor-
                ment ?
To die, is to be banish'd from myself ;
And Silvia is myself : banish'd from her,
Is self from self : a deadly banishment !

---

   [1] —— for *they are sent by me*,] *For* is the same as *for that,*
*since.*
   [2] ——*Merops' son*,] Thou art Phaëton in thy rashness, but
without his pretensions ; thou art not the son of a divinity, but a
*terræ filius*, a low-born wretch ; Merops is thy true father, with
whom Phaëton was falsely reproached.   JOHNSON.

What light is light, if Silvia be not seen?
What joy is joy, if Silvia be not by?
Unless it be to think that she is by,
And feed upon the shadow of perfection.
Except I be by Silvia in the night,
There is no musick in the nightingale;
Unless I look on Silvia in the day,
There is no day for me to look upon:
She is my essence; and I leave to be,
If I be not by her fair influence
Foster'd, illumin'd, cherish'd, kept alive.
I fly not death, to fly his deadly doom:[4]
Tarry I here, I but attend on death;
But, fly I hence, I fly away from life.

*Enter* PROTEUS *and* LAUNCE.

*Pro.* Run, boy, run, run, and seek him out.
*Laun.* So-ho! so-ho!
*Pro.* What seest thou?
*Laun.* Him we go to find: there's not a hair on's head, but 'tis a Valentine.
*Pro.* Valentine?
*Val.* No.
*Pro.* Who then? his spirit?
*Val.* Neither.
*Pro.* What then?
*Val.* Nothing.
*Laun.* Can nothing speak? master, shall I strike?
*Pro.* Whom would'st thou strike?
*Laun.* Nothing.
*Pro.* Villain, forbear.

---

[4] *I fly not death*, to fly his *deadly* doom:] *To fly his doom*, used for *by flying*, or *in flying*, is a Gallicism. The sense is, by avoiding the execution of his sentence I shall not escape death. If I stay here, I suffer myself to be destroyed; If I go away, I destroy myself. JOHNSON.

*Laun.* Why, sir, I'll strike nothing : I pray you,—

*Pro.* Sirrah, I say, forbear : Friend Valentine, a
    word.

*Val.* My ears are stopp'd, and cannot hear good
    news,
So much of bad already hath possess'd them.

*Pro.* Then in dumb silence will I bury mine,
For they are harsh, untuneable, and bad.

*Val.* Is Silvia dead ?

*Pro.* No, Valentine.

*Val.* No Valentine, indeed, for sacred Silvia !—
Hath she forsworn me ?

*Pro.* No, Valentine.

*Val.* No Valentine, if Silvia have forsworn me !—
What is your news ?

*Laun.* Sir, there's a proclamation that you are
    vanish'd.

*Pro.* That thou art banished, O, that's the news ;
From hence, from Silvia, and from me thy friend.

*Val.* O, I have fed upon this woe already,
And now excess of it will make me surfeit.
Doth Silvia know that I am banished ?

*Pro.* Ay, ay ; and she hath offer'd to the doom,
(Which, unrevers'd, stands in effectual force,)
A sea of melting pearl, which some call tears :
Those at her father's churlish feet she tender'd ;
With them, upon her knees, her humble self ;
Wringing her hands, whose whiteness so became
    them,
As if but now they waxed pale for woe :
But neither bended knees, pure hands held up,
Sad sighs, deep groans, nor silver-shedding tears,
Could penetrate her uncompassionate sire ;
But Valentine, if he be ta'en, must die.
Besides, her intercession chaf'd him so,
When she for thy repeal was suppliant,
That to close prison he commanded her,

With many bitter threats of 'biding there.

 *Val.* No more; unless the next word that thou
   speak'st,
Have some malignant power upon my life:
If so, I pray thee, breathe it in mine ear,
As ending anthem of my endless dolour.

 *Pro.* Cease to lament for that thou can'st not help,
And study help for that which thou lament'st.
Time is the nurse and breeder of all good.
Here if thou stay, thou canst not see thy love;
Besides, thy staying will abridge thy life.
Hope is a lover's staff; walk hence with that,
And manage it against despairing thoughts.
Thy letters may be here, though thou art hence:
Which, being writ to me, shall be deliver'd
Even in the milk-white bosom of thy love.[5]
The time now serves not to expostulate:
Come, I'll convey thee through the city gate,
And, ere I part with thee, confer at large
Of all that may concern thy love-affairs:
As thou lov'st Silvia, though not for thyself,
Regard thy danger, and along with me.

 *Val.* I pray thee, Launce, an if thou seest my boy,
Bid him make haste and meet me at the north-gate.

 *Pro.* Go, sirrah, find him out. Come, Valentine.

 *Val.* O my dear Silvia, hapless Valentine!
    [*Exeunt* VALENTINE *and* PROTEUS.

---

[5] *Even in the* milk-white bosom of thy love.] Trifling as the
remark may appear, before the meaning of this *address of letters
to the bosom of a mistress* can be understood, it should be known
that women anciently had a pocket in the fore part of their stays,
in which they not only carried love-letters and love-tokens, but
even their money and materials for needle-work. In many parts
of England the rustic damsels still observe the same practice;
and a very old lady informs me that she remembers, when it was
the fashion to wear prominent stays, it was no less the custom
for stratagem and gallantry to drop its literary favours within the
front of them. STEEVENS.

*Laun.* I am but a fool, look you; and yet I have the wit to think, my master is a kind of knave: but that's all one, if he be but one knave.[6] He lives not now, that knows me to be in love: yet I am in love; but a team of horse shall not pluck that from me; nor who 'tis I love, and yet 'tis a woman: but that woman I will not tell myself; and yet 'tis a milk-maid; yet 'tis not a maid, for she hath had gossips:[7] yet 'tis a maid, for she is her master's maid, and serves for wages. She hath more qualities than a water-spaniel,—which is much in a bare-christian.[8] Here is the cat-log [*Pulling out a paper*] of her conditions.[9] Imprimis, *She can fetch and carry.* Why, a horse can do no more; nay, a horse cannot fetch, but only carry; therefore is she better than a jade. Item, *She can milk;* look you, a sweet virtue in a maid with clean hands.

*Enter* SPEED.

*Speed.* How now, signior Launce? what news with your mastership?

*Laun.* With my master's ship? why it is at sea.

*Speed.* Well, your old vice still; mistake the word: What news then in your paper?

*Laun.* The blackest news that ever thou heard'st.

[6] Laun. *I am but a fool, look you; and yet I have the wit to think, my master is a kind of knave: but that's all one, if he be but one* KNAVE.] In Shakspeare's language, *one knave* may signify a *knave on only one occasion,* a *single knave.* We still use a *double* villain, for a villain beyond the common rate of guilt.
                             JOHNSON.

[7] —— *for she hath had* gossips:] *Gossips* not only signify those who answer for a child in baptism, but the tattling women who attend lyings-in.

[8] —— *a* bare *christian.*] Launce is quibbling on. *Bare* has two senses; *mere* and *naked.* This is used here in both.

[9] —— *her* conditions.] L e. qualities.

*Speed.* Why, man, how black?

*Laun.* Why, as black as ink.

*Speed.* Let me read them.

*Laun.* Fye on thee, jolt-head; thou canst not read.

*Speed.* Thou liest, I can.

*Laun.* I will try thee: Tell me this: Who begot thee?

*Speed.* Marry, the son of my grandfather.

*Laun.* O illiterate loiterer! it was the son of thy grandmother:[1] this proves, that thou canst not read.

*Speed.* Come, fool, come: try me in thy paper.

*Laun.* There; and saint Nicholas be thy speed![2]

*Speed.* Imprimis, *She can milk.*

*Laun.* Ay, that she can.

*Speed.* Item, *She brews good ale.*

*Laun.* And thereof comes the proverb,— Blessing of your heart, you brew good ale.

*Speed.* Item, *She can sew.*

*Laun.* That's as much as to say, can she so?

*Speed.* Item, *She can knit.*

*Laun.* What need a man care for a stock with a wench, when she can knit him a stock.[3]

*Speed.* Item, *She can wash and scour.*

*Laun.* A special virtue; for then she need not be washed and scoured.

[1] —— *the son of thy* grandmother:] It is undoubtedly true that the mother only knows the legitimacy of the child. I suppose *Launce* infers, that if he could read, he must have read this well-known observation. STEEVENS.

[2] —— saint Nicholas *be thy speed!*] St. Nicholas presided over scholars, who were therefore called *St. Nicholas's clerks.* That this saint presided over young scholars, may be gathered from Knight's *Life of Dean Colet,* p. 362, for by the statutes of Paul's school there inserted, the children are required to attend divine service at the cathedral on his anniversary. The legend of this saint makes him to have been a bishop, while he was a boy.

[3] —— *knit him a* stock.] i. e. *stocking.*

*Speed.* Item, *She can spin.*

*Laun.* Then may I set the world on wheels, when she can spin for her living.

*Speed.* Item, *She hath many nameless virtues.*

*Laun.* That's as much as to say, bastard virtues; that, indeed, know not their fathers, and therefore have no names.

Speed. *Here follow her vices.*

*Laun.* Close at the heels of her virtues.

*Speed.* Item, *She is not to be kissed fasting, in respect of her breath.*

*Laun.* Well, that fault may be mended with a breakfast : Read on.

*Speed.* Item, *She hath a sweet mouth.*

*Laun.* That makes amends for her sour breath.

*Speed.* Item, *She doth talk in her sleep.*

*Laun.* It's no matter for that, so she sleep not in her talk.

*Speed.* Item, *She is slow in words.*

*Laun.* O villain, that set this down among her vices! To be slow in words, is a woman's only virtue: I pray thee, out with't; and place it for her chief virtue.

*Speed.* Item, *She is proud.*

*Laun.* Out with that too; it was Eve's legacy, and cannot be ta'en from her.

*Speed.* Item, *She hath no teeth.*

*Laun.* I care not for that neither, because I love crusts.

*Speed.* Item, *She is curst.*

*Laun.* Well; the best is, she hath no teeth to bite.

*Speed.* *She will often praise her liquor.*[4]

*Laun.* If her liquor be good, she shall: if she will not, I will; for good things should be praised.

---

[4] ——*praise her liquor.*] i. e. often shew how well she likes it.

*Speed.* Item, *She is too liberal.*[5]

*Laun.* Of her tongue she cannot; for that's writ down she is slow of: of her purse she shall not; for that I'll keep shut: now of another thing she may; and that I cannot help. Well, proceed.

*Speed.* Item, *She hath more hair than wit, and more faults than hairs, and more wealth than faults.*

*Laun.* Stop there; I'll have her: she was mine, and not mine, twice or thrice in that last article: Rehearse that once more.

*Speed.* Item, *She hath more hair than wit,*[6]—

*Laun.* More hair than wit,—it may be; I'll prove it: The cover of the salt hides the salt, and therefore it is more than the salt; the hair that covers the wit, is more than the wit; for the greater hides the less. What's next?

*Speed.* —*And more faults than hairs,*—

*Laun.* That's monstrous: O, that that were out!

*Speed.* —*And more wealth than faults.*

*Laun.* Why, that word makes the faults gracious:[7] Well, I'll have her: And if it be a match, as nothing is impossible,—

*Speed.* What then?

*Laun.* Why, then I will tell thee,—that thy master stays for thee at the north gate.

*Speed.* For me?

*Laun.* For thee? ay: who art thou? he hath staid for a better man than thee.

*Speed.* And must I go to him?

*Laun.* Thou must run to him, for thou hast staid so long, that going will scarce serve the turn.

*Speed.* Why didst not tell me sooner? 'pox of your love-letters! [*Exit.*

[5] —— *She is too* liberal.] *Liberal,* is licentious and gross in language.

[6] —— *She hath* more hair than wit,] An old English proverb.

[7] —— *makes the faults* gracious:] *Gracious,* in old language, means *graceful.*

*Laun.* Now will he be swinged for reading my letter : An unmannerly slave, that will thrust himself into secrets !—I'll after, to rejoice in the boy's correction.                                                    [*Exit.*

## SCENE II.

*The same.    A Room in the* Duke's *Palace.*

*Enter* Duke *and* Thurio ; Proteus *behind.*

*Duke.* Sir Thurio, fear not, but that she will love
        you,
Now Valentine is banish'd from her sight.
    *Thu.* Since his exile she hath despis'd me most,
Forsworn my company, and rail'd at me,
That I am desperate of obtaining her.
    *Duke.* This weak impress of love is as a figure
Trenched in ice ;[8] which with an hour's heat
Dissolves to water, and doth lose his form.
A little time will melt her frozen thoughts,
And worthless Valentine shall be forgot.—
How now, sir Proteus ? Is your countryman,
According to our proclamation, gone ?
    *Pro.* Gone, my good lord.
    *Duke.* My daughter takes his going grievously.
    *Pro.* A little time, my lord, will kill that grief.
    *Duke.* So I believe ; but Thurio thinks not so.—
Proteus, the good conceit I hold of thee,
(For thou hast shown some sign of good desert,)
Makes me the better to confer with thee.
    *Pro.* Longer than I prove loyal to your grace,
Let me not live to look upon your grace.
    *Duke.* Thou know'st how willingly I would effect
The match between sir Thurio and my daughter.
    *Pro.* I do, my lord.

---

[8] Trenched *in ice ;*] Cut, carved in ice. From *Trancker,* to cut.

*Duke.* And also, I think, thou art not ignorant
How she opposes her against my will.

*Pro.* She did my lord, when Valentine was here.

*Duke.* Ay, and perversely she persévers so.
What might we do, to make the girl forget
The love of Valentine, and love sir Thurio?

*Pro.* The best way is to slander Valentine
With falshood, cowardice, and poor descent;
Three things that women highly hold in hate.

*Duke.* Ay, but she'll think, that it is spoke in
hate.

*Pro.* Ay, if his enemy deliver it:
Therefore it must with circumstance,[9] be spoken
By one, whom she esteemeth as his friend.

*Duke.* Then you must undertake to slander him.

*Pro.* And that, my lord, I shall be loth to do:
'Tis an ill office for a gentleman;
Especially, against his very friend.[1]

*Duke.* Where your good word cannot advantage
him,
Your slander never can endamage him;
Therefore the office is indifferent,
Being entreated to it by your friend,

*Pro.* You have prevail'd, my lord: if I can do it,
By aught that I can speak in his dispraise,
She shall not long continue love to him.
But say, this weed her love from Valentine,
It follows not that she will love sir Thurio.

*Thu.* Therefore, as you unwind her love[2] from
him,

---

[9] —— *with circumstance,*] With the addition of such incidental particulars as may induce belief. JOHNSON.

[1] —— *his* very *friend.*] *Very* is immediate.

[2] —— *as you unwind her love* ——] As you wind off her love from him, make me the *bottom* on which you wind it. The housewife's term for a ball of thread wound upon a central body, is a *bottom of thread.*

Lest it should ravel, and be good to none,
You must provide to bottom it on me:
Which must be done, by praising me as much
As you in worth dispraise sir Valentine.

*Duke.* And, Proteus, we dare trust you in this
          kind;
Because we know, on Valentine's report,
You are already love's firm votary,
And cannot soon revolt and change your mind.
Upon this warrant shall you have access,
Where you with Silvia may confer at large;
For she is lumpish, heavy, melancholy,
And, for your friend's sake, will be glad of you;
Where you may temper her,[3] by your persuasion,
To hate young Valentine, and love my friend.

*Pro.* As much as I can do, I will effect:—
But you, sir Thurio, are not sharp enough;
You must lay lime,[4] to tangle her desires,
By wailful sonnets, whose composed rhymes
Should be full fraught with serviceable vows.

*Duke.* Ay, much the force of heaven-bred poesy.

*Pro.* Say, that upon the altar of her beauty
You sacrifice your tears, your sighs, your heart:
Write till your ink be dry; and with your tears
Moist it again; and frame some feeling line,
That may discover such integrity:[5]
For Orpheus' lute was strung with poets' sinews;
Whose golden touch could soften steel and stones,
Make tigers tame, and huge leviathans

---

[3] —— *you may* temper *her*,] Mould her, like wax, to whatever shape you please.

[4] —— *lime*,] That is, *birdlime.*

[5] —— *such integrity:*] *Such integrity* may mean such ardour and sincerity as would be manifested by practising the directions given in the four preceding lines. STEEVENS.

I suspect that a line following this has been lost; the import of which perhaps was—
" As her obdurate heart may penetrate." MALONE.

9

Forsake unsounded deeps to dance on sands.
After your dire lamenting elegies,
Visit by night your lady's chamber-window,
With some sweet concert: to their instruments
Tune a deploring dump;[6] the night's dead silence
Will well become such sweet complaining grievance.
This, or else nothing, will inherit her.[7]

    *Duke.* This discipline shows thou hast been in
        love.

    *Thu.* And thy advice this night I'll put in practice:
Therefore, sweet Proteus, my direction-giver,
Let us into the city presently
To sort[8] some gentlemen well skill'd in musick:
I have a sonnet, that will serve the turn,
To give the onset to thy good advice.

    *Duke.* About it, gentlemen.

    *Pro.* We'll wait upon your grace till after supper:
And afterward determine our proceedings.

    *Duke.* Even now about it; I will pardon you.[9]

                            *[Exeunt.*

# ACT IV.

## SCENE I. *A Forest, near* Mantua.

### *Enter certain* Out-laws.

1 *Out.* Fellows, stand fast; I see a passenger.
2 *Out.* If there be ten, shrink not, but down
        with 'em.

---

[6] *Tune a deploring* dump;] A *dump* was the ancient term for
a *mournful elegy.*
  [7] —— *will* inherit *her.*] To *inherit,* is, by our author, sometimes used, as in this instance, for *to obtain possession* of, without
any idea of acquiring *by inheritance.*
  [8] *To sort* ——] i. e. to choose out.
  [9] —— *I will pardon you.*] I will excuse you from waiting.

*Enter* VALENTINE *and* SPEED.

3 *Out.* Stand, sir, and throw us that you have
    about you ;
If not, we'll make you sit, and rifle you.

*Speed.* Sir, we are undone ! these are the villains
That all the travellers do fear so much.

*Val.* My friends,——

1 *Out.* That's not so, sir ; we are your enemies.

2 *Out.* Peace ; we'll hear him.

3 *Out.* Ay, by my beard, will we ;   ·
For he's a proper man.'

*Val.* Then know, that I have little wealth to
    lose ;
A man I am, cross'd with adversity :
My riches are these poor habiliments,
Of which if you should here disfurnish me,
You take the sum and substance that I have.

2 *Out.* Whither travel you ?

*Val.* To Verona.

1 *Out.* Whence came you ?

*Val.* From Milan.

3 *Out.* Have you long sojourn'd there ?

*Val.* Some sixteen months ; and longer might
    have staid,
If crooked fortune had not thwarted me.

1 *Out.* What, were you banish'd thence ?

*Val.* I was.

2 *Out.* For what offence ?

*Val.* For that which now torments me to re-
    hearse :
I kill'd a man, whose death I much repent ;
But yet I slew him manfully in fight,

---

' —— *a* proper *man.*] i. e. a *well-looking* man ; he has the appearance of a gentleman.

Without false vantage, or base treachery.

*1 Out.* Why ne'er repent it, if it were done so :
But were you banish'd for so small a fault?

*Val:* I was, and held me glad of such a doom.

*1 Out.* Have you the tongues?

*Val.* My youthful travel therein made me happy ;
Or else I often had been miserable.

*3 Out.* By the bare scalp of Robin Hood's fat
      friar,[2]
This fellow were a king for our wild faction.

*1 Out.* We'll have him : sirs, a word.

*Speed.*               Master, be one of them ;
It is an honourable kind of thievery.

*Val.* Peace, villain !

*2 Out.* Tell us this : Have you any thing to take
      to?

*Val.* Nothing, but my fortune.

*3 Out.* Know then, that some of us are gentle-
      men,
Such as the fury of ungovern'd youth
Thrust from the company of awful men :[3]
Myself was from Verona banished,
For practising to steal away a lady,
An heir, and near allied unto the duke.

*2 Out.* And I from Mantua, for a gentleman,
Whom, in my mood,[4] I stabb'd unto the heart.

*1 Out.* And I, for such like petty crimes as these.

---

[2] —— Robin Hood's *fat friar*,] *Robin Hood* was captain of a
band of robbers, and was much inclined to rob churchmen. But
by Robin Hood's *fat friar*, Shakspeare means *Friar Tuck*, who
was confessor and companion to this noted out-law.

[3] —— awful *men :*] Reverend, worshipful, such as magistrates,
and other principal members of civil communities. JOHNSON.

Dr. Farmer would read— *lawful* men—i. e. *legales* homines.

*Awful men* means men *well governed, observant of law and authority ; full of, or subject to awe.* In the same kind of sense as
we use *fearful.* RITSON.

[4] *Whom, in my* mood,] *Mood* is anger or resentment.

But to the purpose,—(for we cite our faults,
That they may hold excus'd our lawless lives,)
And, partly, seeing you are beautified
With goodly shape ; and by your own report
A linguist ; and a man of such perfection,
As we do in our quality[5] much want ;—

   2 *Out.* Indeed, because you are a banish'd man,
Therefore, above the rest, we parley to you:
Are you content to be our general ?
To make a virtue of necessity,
And live, as we do, in this wilderness ?

   3 *Out.* What say'st thou ?  wilt thou be of our
          consórt ?[6]
Say, ay, and be the captain of us all :
We'll do thee homage, and be rul'd by thee,
Love thee as our commander, and our king.

   1 *Out.* But if thou scorn our courtesy, thou diest.

   2 *Out.* Thou shalt not live to brag what we have
          offer'd.

   *Val.* I take your offer, and will live with you ;
Provided that you do no outrages
On silly women, or poor passengers.

   3 *Out.* No, we detest such vile base practices.
Come, go with us, we'll bring thee to our crews,
And shew thee all the treasure we have got ;
Which, with ourselves, all rest at thy dispose.
                                        [*Exeunt.*

---

   [5] —— *in our* quality —] Our *quality* means our profession,
calling, or condition of life.
   [6] Our company.

## SCENE II.

*Milan.* *Court of the Palace.*

*Enter* PROTEUS.

*Pro.* Already have I been false to Valentine,
And now I must be as unjust to Thurio.
Under the colour of commending him,
I have access my own love to prefer ;
But Silvia is too fair, too true, too holy,
To be corrupted with my worthless gifts.
When I protest true loyalty to her,
She twits me with my falshood to my friend :
When to her beauty I commend my vows,
She bids me think, how I have been forsworn
In breaking faith with Julia whom I lov'd :
And, notwithstanding all her sudden quips,[7]
The least whereof would quell a lover's hope,
Yet, spaniel-like, the more she spurns my love,
The more it grows, and fawneth on her still.
But here comes Thurio : now must we to her window,
And give some evening musick to her ear.

*Enter* THURIO *and Musicians.*

*Thu.* How now, sir Proteus? are you crept be-
        fore us ?
*Pro.* Ay, gentle Thurio ; for, you know, that
        love
Will creep in service where it cannot go.[8]

---

[7] —— sudden *quips*,] That is, hasty passionate reproaches and
scoffs.
[8] —— *you know, that love*
    *Will* creep *in service where it cannot go.*] Kindness will
*creep* where *it* cannot *gang,* is a *Scottish proverb.*

*Thu.* Ay, but, I hope, sir, that you love not here.
*Pro.* Sir, but I do; or else I would be hence.
*Thu.* Whom? Silvia?
*Pro.* Ay, Silvia,—for your sake.
*Thu.* I thank you for your own. Now, gentlemen,
Let's tune, and to it lustily a while.

*Enter* Host, *at a distance; and* Julia *in boy's clothes.*

*Host.* Now, my young guest! methinks you're
allycholly; I pray you, why is it?
*Jul.* Marry, mine host, because I cannot be merry.
*Host.* Come, we'll have you merry: I'll bring you
where you shall hear musick, and see the gentleman
that you ask'd for.
*Jul.* But shall I hear him speak?
*Host.* Ay, that you shall.
*Jul.* That will be musick.     [*Musick plays.*
*Host.* Hark! hark!
*Jul.* Is he among these?
*Host.* Ay: but peace, let's hear 'em.

### SONG.

*Who is Silvia? what is she,*
   *That all our swains commend her?*
*Holy, fair, and wise is she;*
   *The heavens such grace did lend her,*
*That she might admired be.*

*Is she kind, as she is fair?*
   *For beauty lives with kindness:*
*Love doth to her eyes repair,*
   *To help him of his blindness;*
*And, being help'd, inhabits there.*

*Then to Silvia let us sing,*
 *That Silvia is excelling ;*
*She excels each mortal thing,*
 *Upon the dull earth dwelling :*
*To her let us garlands bring.*


*Host.* How now ? are you sadder than you were
 before ?
How do you, man ? the musick likes you not.
*Jul.* You mistake ; the musician likes me not.
*Host.* Why, my pretty youth ?
*Jul.* He plays false, father.
*Host.* How ? out of tune on the strings ?
*Jul.* Not so ; but yet so false that he grieves my
very heart-strings.
*Host.* You have a quick ear.
*Jul.* Ay, I would I were deaf ! it makes me have
a slow heart.
*Host.* I perceive, you delight not in musick.
*Jul.* Not a whit, when it jars so.
*Host.* Hark, what fine change is in the musick !
*Jul.* Ay ; that change is the spite.
*Host.* You would have them always play but one
thing ?
*Jul.* I would always have one play but one thing.
But, host, doth this sir Proteus, that we talk on,
often resort unto this gentlewoman ?
*Host.* I tell you what Launce, his man, told me,
he loved her out of all nick.[9]
*Jul.* Where is Launce ?
*Host.* Gone to seek his dog ; which, to-morrow,
by his master's command, he must carry for a pre-
sent to his lady.
*Jul.* Peace ! stand aside ! the company parts.


[9] —— *out of all* nick.] Beyond all reckoning or count.
Reckonings are kept upon nicked or notched sticks or tallies.

*Pro.* Sir Thurio, fear not you! I will so plead,
That you shall say, my cunning drift excels.
*Thu.* Where meet we?
*Pro.* At saint Gregory's well.
*Thu.* Farewell. [*Exeunt* THURIO *and Musicians.*


SILVIA *appears above, at her window.*


*Pro.* Madam, good even to your ladyship.
*Sil.* I thank you for your musick, gentlemen:
Who is that, that spake?
*Pro.* One, lady, if you knew his pure heart's truth,
You'd quickly learn to know him by his voice.
*Sil.* Sir Proteus, as I take it.
*Pro.* Sir Proteus, gentle lady, and your servant.
*Sil.* What is your will?
*Pro.*                        That I may compass yours.
*Sil.* You have your wish; my will is even this,—
That presently you hie you home to bed.
Thou subtle, perjur'd, false, disloyal man!
Think'st thou, I am so shallow, so conceitless,
To be seduced by thy flattery,
That hast deceiv'd so many with thy vows?
Return, return, and make thy love amends.
For me,—by this pale queen of night I swear,
I am so far from granting thy request,
That I despise thee for thy wrongful suit;
And by and by intend to chide myself,
Even for this time I spend in talking to thee.
*Pro.* I grant, sweet love, that I did love a lady;
But she is dead.
*Jul.* 'Twere false, if I should speak it;
For, I am sure, she is not buried.    [*Aside.*
*Sil.* Say, that she be; yet Valentine, thy friend,
Survives; to whom, thyself art witness,
I am betroth'd: And art thou not asham'd

To wrong him with thy importúnacy.

*Pro.* I likewise hear, that Valentine is dead.

*Sil.* And so, suppose, am I; for in his grave
Assure thyself, my love is buried.

*Pro.* Sweet lady, let me rake it from the earth.'

*Sil.* Go to thy lady's grave, and call her's thence;
Or, at the least, in her's sepulchre thine.

*Jul.* He heard not that.      [*Aside.*

*Pro.* Madam, if your heart be so obdúrate,
Vouchsafe me yet your picture for my love,
The picture that is hanging in your chamber;
To that I'll speak, to that I'll sigh and weep:
For, since the substance of your perfect self
Is else devoted, I am but a shadow;
And to your shadow I will make true love.

*Jul.* If 'twere a substance, you would, sure, de-
    ceive it,
And make it but a shadow, as I am.   [*Aside.*

*Sil.* I am very loth to be your idol, sir;
But, since your falshood shall become you well '
To worship shadows, and adore false shapes,
Send to me in the morning, and I'll send it:
And so, good rest.

*Pro.*      As wretches have o'er-night,
That wait for execution in the morn.

   [*Exeunt* PROTEUS; *and* SILVIA, *from above.*

---

' *But, since* your falshood *shall become you well* —] This is
hardly sense. We may read, with very little alteration:
  " But since *you're false,* it shall become you well."
             JOHNSON.

  I believe the text is right, and that our author means, however
licentious the expression,—But, since your falshood well becomes,
or is well suited to, the worshipping of shadows, and the adoring
of false shapes, send to me in the morning for my picture, &c.
Or, in other words, But, since the worshipping of shadows and the
adoring of false shapes shall well become *you, false as you are,*
send, &c. *To worship shadows,* &c. I consider as the objective
case, as well as *you.* *Since* is, I think, here an adverb, not a
preposition. MALONE.

*Jul.* Host, will you go?

*Host.* By my hallidom, I was fast asleep.

*Jul.* Pray you, where lies sir Proteus?

*Host.* Marry, at my house: Trust me, I think, 'tis almost day.

*Jul.* Not so; but it hath been the longest night That e'er I watch'd, and the most heaviest.[2]

[*Exeunt.*

## SCENE III.

### *The same.*

#### *Enter* EGLAMOUR.

*Egl.* This is the hour that madam Silvia Entreated me to call, and know her mind; There's some great matter she'd employ me in.—— Madam, madam!

*SILVIA appears above, at her window.*

*Sil.*          Who calls?

*Egl.*               Your servant, and your friend; One that attends your ladyship's command.

*Sil.* Sir Eglamour, a thousand times good-morrow.

*Egl.* As many, worthy lady, to yourself. According to your ladyship's impose,[3] I am thus early come, to know what service It is your pleasure to command me in.

*Sil.* O Eglamour, thou art a gentleman, (Think not, I flatter, for, I swear, I do not,) Valiant, wise, remorseful,[4] well accomplish'd.

---

[2] —— *most heaviest.*] This use of the double superlative is frequent in our author.

[3] —— *your ladyship's* impose,] *Impose* is *injunction, command.* A task set at college, in consequence of a fault, is still called an *imposition.* A tax likewise is said to be *imposed.*

[4] —— remorseful,] *Remorseful* is pitiful.

Thou art not ignorant, what dear good will
I bear unto the banish'd Valentine ;
Nor how my father would enforce me marry
Vain Thurio, whom my very soul abhorr'd.
Thyself hast loved ;  and I have heard thee say,
No grief did ever come so near thy heart,
As when thy lady and thy true love died,
Upon whose grave thou vow'dst pure chastity.[5]
Sir Eglamour, I would to Valentine,
To Mantua, where, I hear, he makes abode;
And, for the ways are dangerous to pass,
I do desire thy worthy company,
Upon whose faith and honour I repose.
Urge not my father's anger, Eglamour,
But think upon my grief, a lady's grief;
And on the justice of my flying hence,
To keep me from a most unholy match,
Which heaven and fortune still reward with plagues.
I do desire thee, even from a heart
As full of sorrows as the sea of sands,
To bear me company, and go with me :
If not, to hide what I have said to thee,
That I may venture to depart alone.
   *Egl.* Madam, I pity much your grievances ;[6]
Which since I know they virtuously are plac'd,
I give consent to go along with you ;

[5] —— *Upon whose grave thou vow'dst pure* chastity.] It was
common in former ages for widowers and widows to make vows
of chastity in honour of their deceased wives or husbands. In
Dugdale's *Antiquities of Warwickshire*, page 1013, there is the
form of a commission by the bishop of the diocese for taking a
vow of chastity made by a widow. It seems, that, besides observing the vow, the widow was, for life, to wear a veil and a mourning habit.  Some such distinction we may suppose to have been
made in respect of male votarists; and therefore this circumstance
might inform the players how sir Eglamour should be drest ; and
will account for Silvia's having chosen him as a person in whom she
could confide without injury to her own character.  STEEVENS.
   [6] —— *grievances ;*]  Sorrows, sorrowful affections.

Recking as little⁷ what betideth me
As much I wish all good befortune you.
When will you go?
  *Sil.*     This evening coming.
 *Egl.* Where shall I meet you?
  *Sil.*      At friar Patrick's cell,
Where I intend holy confession.
 *Egl.* I will not fail your ladyship:
Good-morrow, gentle lady.
 *Sil.* Good-morrow, kind sir Eglamour. [*Exeunt.*


### SCENE IV.

*The same.*

*Enter* LAUNCE, *with his dog.*

When a man's servant shall play the cur with him,
look you, it goes hard : one that I brought up of a
puppy ; one that I saved from drowning, when three
or four of his blind brothers and sisters went to it! I
have taught him—even as one would say precisely,
Thus I would teach a dog. I was sent to deliver
him, as a present to mistress Silvia, from my master;
and I came no sooner into the dining-chamber, but
he steps me to her trencher, and steals her capon's
leg. O, 'tis a foul thing when a cur cannot keep
himself⁸ in all companies! I would have, as one
should say, one that takes upon him to be a dog indeed, to be, as it were, a dog at all things. If I had
not had more wit than he, to take a fault upon me
that he did, I think verily he had been hanged
for't; sure as I live he had suffered for't: you shall

---

⁷ Recking *as little* —] To *reck* is to care for. Chaucer and
Spenser use this word with the same signification.
⁸ —— keep *himself* —] i. e. restrain himself.

judge.. He thrusts me himself into the company of three or four gentleman-like dogs, under the duke's table : he had not been there (bless the mark) a pissing while ;° but all the chamber smelt him. *Out with the dog*, says one ; *What cur is that ?* says another ; *Whip him out*, says a third ; *Hang him up*, says the duke. I, having been acquainted with the smell before, knew it was Crab ; and goes me to the fellow that whips the dogs: [1] *Friend,* quoth I, *you mean to whip the dog ? Ay, marry, do I*, quoth he. *You do him the more wrong*, quoth I ; *'twas I did the thing you wot of.* He makes me no more ado, but whips me out of the chamber. How many masters would do this for their servant? Nay, I'll be sworn, I have sat in the stocks for puddings he hath stolen, otherwise he had been executed : I have stood on the pillory for geese he hath killed, otherwise he had suffered for't : thou think'st not of this now!—Nay, I remember the trick you served me, when I took my leave of madam Silvia ; did not I bid thee still mark me, and do as I do? When did'st thou see me heave up my leg, and make water against a gentlewoman's farthingale? didst thou ever see me do such a trick ?

*Enter* PROTEUS *and* JULIA.

*Pro.* Sebastian is thy name ? I like thee well, And will employ thee in some service presently.
*Jul.* In what you please ;—I will do what I can.
*Pro.* I hope, thou wilt.—How now, you whoreson peasant ?                    [*To* LAUNCE.
Where have you been these two days loitering ?

---

° *a pissing while ;*] A proverbial expression.
[1] *The fellow that* whips *the dogs :*] This appears to have been part of the office of an *usher of the table.*

*Laun.* Marry, sir, I carried mistress Silvia the dog you bade me.

*Pro.* And what says she, to my little jewel?

*Laun.* Marry, she says, your dog was a cur; and tells you, currish thanks is good enough for such a present.

*Pro.* But she received my dog?

*Laun.* No, indeed, she did not: here have I brought him back again.

*Pro.* What, didst thou offer her this from me?

*Laun.* Ay, sir; the other squirrel [a] was stolen from me by the 'hangman's boys in the market-place: and then I offered her mine own; who is a dog as big as ten of yours, and therefore the gift the greater.

*Pro.* Go, get thee hence, and find my dog again,
Or ne'er return again into my sight.
Away, I say: Stay'st thou to vex me here?
A slave, that, still an end, [b] turns me to shame.

                  *[Exit* LAUNCE.

Sebastian, I have entertained thee,
Partly, that I have need of such a youth,
That can with some discretion do my business,
For 'tis no trusting to yon foolish lowt;
But, chiefly, for thy face, and thy behaviour;
Which (if my augury deceive me not)
Witness good bringing up, fortune, and truth:
Therefore know thou, for this I entertain thee.
Go presently, and take this ring with thee,
Deliver it to madam Silvia:

---

[a] —— *the other* squirrel, &c.] Launce speaks of his master's present as a diminutive animal, more resembling a *squirrel* in size, than a dog.

[b] —— an end.] i. e. *in the end*, at the conclusion of every business he undertakes. STEEVENS.

*Still an end*, and *most an end*, are vulgar expressions, and mean commonly, generally.

She loved me well, deliver'd it to me.[4]

   *Jul.* It seems, you loved her not, to leave her
        token :[5]

She's dead, belike.

   *Pro.*           Not so; I think, she lives.

   *Jul.* Alas!

   *Pro.* Why dost thou cry, alas!

   *Jul.* I cannot choose but pity her.

   *Pro.* Wherefore should'st thou pity her?

   *Jul.* Because, methinks, that she loved you as well
As you do love your lady Silvia:
She dreams on him that has forgot her love;
You dote on her, that cares not for your love.
'Tis pity, love should be so contrary;
And thinking on it makes me cry, alas!

   *Pro.* Well, give her that ring, and therewithal
This letter;—that's her chamber.—Tell my lady,
I claim the promise for her heavenly picture.
Your message done, hie home unto my chamber,
Where thou shalt find me sad and solitary.

                        [*Exit* PROTEUS.

   *Jul.* How many women would do such a message?
Alas, poor Proteus! thou hast entertain'd
A fox, to be the shepherd of thy lambs:
Alas, poor fool! why do I pity him
That with his very heart despiseth me?
Because he loves her, he despiseth me;
Because I love him, I must pity him.
This ring I gave him, when he parted from me,
To bind him to remember my good will:
And now am I (unhappy messenger)

---

   [4] *She loved me well, deliver'd it to me.*] i. e. She *who* delivered it
to me, loved me well.  MALONE.
   [5] *It seems, you loved her not, to leave her token :*] Johnson, not
recollecting the force of the word *leave,* proposes an amendment
of this passage, which is unnecessary; for, in the language of
the time, to *leave* means to *part with,* or *give away.*

         11

To plead for that, which I would not obtain;
To carry that which I would have refus'd;
To praise his faith, which I would have disprais'd.[6]
I am my master's true confirmed love;
But cannot be true servant to my master,
Unless I prove false traitor to myself.
Yet I will woo for him; but yet so coldly,
As, heaven, it knows, I would not have him speed,

*Enter* SILVIA, *attended.*

Gentlewoman, good day! I pray you, be my mean
To bring me where to speak with madam Silvia.
   *Sil.* What would you with her, if that I be she?
   *Jul.* If you be she, I do entreat your patience
To hear me speak the message I am sent on.
   *Sil.* From whom?
   *Jul.* From my master, sir Proteus, madam.
   *Sil.* O!—he sends you for a picture?
   *Jul.* Ay, madam.
   *Sil.* Ursula, bring my picture there.
                             *[Picture brought.*
Go, give your master this: tell him from me,
One Julia, that his changing thoughts forget,
Would better fit his chamber, than this shadow.
   *Jul.* Madam, please you peruse this letter.——
Pardon me, madam; I have unadvis'd
Delivered you a paper that I should not;
This is the letter to your ladyship.
   *Sil.* I pray thee, let me look on that again.
   *Jul.* It may not be; good madam, pardon me.
   *Sil.* There, hold.
I will not look upon your master's lines:
I know, they are stuff'd with protestations,

   [6] *To carry that, which I would have refus'd; &c.*] The sense is, to go and present that which I wish not to be accepted, to praise him whom I wish to be dispraised. JOHNSON.

And full of new-found oaths ; which he will break,
As easily as I do tear his paper.

*Jul.* Madam, he sends your ladyship this ring.

*Sil.* The more shame for him that he sends it me;
For, I have heard him say a thousand times,
His Julia gave it him at his departure :
Though his false finger hath profan'd the ring,
Mine shall not do his Julia so much wrong.

*Jul.* She thanks you.

*Sil.* What say'st thou ?

*Jul.* I thank you, madam, that you tender her :
Poor gentlewoman ! my master wrongs her much.

*Sil.* Dost thou know her ?

*Jul.* Almost as well as I do know myself
To think upon her woes, I do protest,
That I have wept an hundred several times.

*Sil.* Belike, she thinks that Proteus hath forsook
her.

*Jul.* I think she doth, and that's her cause of
sorrow.

*Sil.* Is she not passing fair ?

*Jul.* She hath been fairer, madam, than she is :
When she did think my master lov'd her well,
She, in my judgement, was as fair as you ;
But since she did neglect her looking-glass,
And threw her sun-expelling mask away,
The air hath starv'd the roses in her cheeks,
And pinch'd the lily-tincture of her face,
That now she is become as black as I.

*Sil.* How tall was she ?[7]

*Jul.* About my stature : for, at Pentecost,
When all our pageants of delight were play'd,
Our youth got me to play the woman's part,
And I was trimm'd in madam Julia's gown ;
Which served me as fit, by all men's judgement,

<hr>

[7] *How tall was she ?*] We should read—" How tall *is* she?"

10

As if the garment had been made for me :
Therefore, I know she is about my height.
And, at that time, I made her weep a-good,⁸
For I did play a lamentable part ;
Madam, 'twas Ariadne, passioning⁹
For Theseus' perjury, and unjust flight ;
Which I so lively acted with my tears,
That my poor mistress, moved therewithal,
Wept bitterly ; and, would I might be dead,
If I in thought felt not her very sorrow !

   *Sil.* She is beholden to thee, gentle youth !—
Alas, poor lady ! desolate and left !—
I weep myself, to think upon thy words.
Here, youth, there is my purse ; I give thee this
For thy sweet mistress' sake, because thou lov'st her.
Farewell.                              [*Exit* SILVIA.

   *Jul.* And she shall thank you for't, if e'er you
           know her.
A virtuous gentlewoman, mild, and beautiful.
I hope my master's suit will be but cold,
Since she respects my mistress' love so much.¹
Alas, how love can trifle with itself !
Here is her picture : Let me see ; I think,
If I had such a tire, this face of mine
Were full as lovely as is this of hers :
And yet the painter flatter'd her a little,
Unless I flatter with myself too much.

⁸ —— *weep* a-good,] i. e. in good earnest.  *Tout de bon.* Fr.
⁹ —— '*twas Ariadne,* passioning.]    *To passion* is used as a
verb, by writers contemporary with Shakspeare.
   —— '*twas Ariadne,* passioning —] On her being deserted by
Theseus in the night, and left on the island of Naxos.
¹ —— my mistress' *love so much.*]    She had in her preceding
speech called Julia *her mistress ;* but it is odd enough that she
should thus describe herself, when she is *alone.* Sir T. Hanmer
reads—" *his* mistress ;" but without necessity.  Our author knew
that his audience considered the disguised Julia in the present
scene as a page to Proteus, and this, I believe, and the love of
antithesis, produced the expression.  MALONE.

Her hair is auburn, mine is perfect yellow:
If that be all the difference in his love,
I'll get me such a colour'd periwig.[2]
Her eyes are grey as glass;[3] and so are mine:
Ay, but her forehead's low,[4] and mine's as high.
What should it be, that he respects in her,
But I can make respective[5] in myself,
If this fond love were not a blinded god?
Come, shadow, come, and take this shadow up,
For 'tis thy rival. O thou senseless form,
Thou shalt be worshipp'd, kiss'd, lov'd, and ador'd;
And, were there sense in his idolatry,
My substance should be statue in thy stead.[6]
I'll use thee kindly for thy mistress' sake,
That us'd me so; or else, by Jove I vow,
I should have scratch'd out your unseeing eyes,
To make my master out of love with thee. [*Exit.*

[2] *I'll get me such a colour'd* periwig.] It should be remembered, that false hair was worn by the ladies, long before *wigs* were in fashion. These false coverings, however, were called *periwigs.*

[3] *Her eyes are grey as glass;*] So Chaucer, in the character of his Prioress:

"Ful semely hire wimple y-pinched was;
"Hire nose tretis; hire *eyen grey as glas.*" THEOBALD.

[4] —— *her forehead's low,*] A high forehead was in our author's time accounted a feature eminently beautiful.

[5] —— respective —] i. e. *respectable.*

[6] *My substance should be* statue *in thy stead.*] It appears from hence, and a passage in Massinger, that the word *statue* was formerly used to express a *portrait.* *Statue* here, should be written *statua,* and pronounced as it generally, if not always, was in our author's time, a word of three syllables. Alterations have been often improperly made in the text of Shakspeare, by supposing *statue* to be intended by him for a dissyllable.

# ACT. V.

## SCENE I. *The same. An Abbey.*

### *Enter* EGLAMOUR.

*Egl.* The sun begins to gild the western sky ;
And now, it is about the very hour
That Silvia, at Patrick's cell, should meet me.
She will not fail ; for lovers break not hours,
Unless it be to come before their time ;
So much they spur their expedition.

### *Enter* SILVIA.

See, where she comes : Lady, a happy evening !
   *Sil.* Amen, amen ! go on, good Eglamour !
Out at the postern by the abbey-wall ;
I fear, I am attended by some spies.
   *Egl.* Fear not : the forest is not three leagues off :
If we recover that, we are sure enough.[7]   [*Exeunt.*

# SCENE II.

*The same. An Apartment in the* Duke's *Palace.*

### *Enter* THURIO, PROTEUS, *and* JULIA.

   *Thu.* Sir Proteus, what says Silvia to my suit ?
   *Pro.* O, sir, I find her milder than she was ;
And yet she takes exceptions at your person.
   *Thu.* What, that my leg is too long ?
   *Pro.* No ; that it is too little.
   *Thu.* I'll wear a boot, to make it somewhat
      rounder.

---

[7] —— sure *enough.*] *Sure* is safe, out of danger.

*Pro.* But love will not be spurr'd to what it loaths.

*Thu.* What says she to my face?

*Pro.* She says, it is a fair one.

*Thu.* Nay, then the wanton lies; my face is black.

*Pro.* But pearls are fair; and the old saying is,
Black men are pearls in beauteous ladies' eyes.[8]

*Jul.* 'Tis true, such pearls as put out ladies' eyes;
For I had rather wink than look on them. [*Aside.*

*Thu.* How likes she my discourse?

*Pro.* Ill, when you talk of war.

*Thu.* But well, when I discourse of love, and
    peace?

*Jul.* But better, indeed, when you hold your
    peace. [*Aside.*

*Thu.* What says she to my valour?

*Pro.* O, sir, she makes no doubt of that.

*Jul.* She needs not, when she knows it cowardice.
    [*Aside.*

*Thu.* What says she to my birth?

*Pro.* That you are well deriv'd.

*Jul.* True; from a gentleman to a fool. [*Aside.*

*Thu.* Considers she my possessions?

*Pro.* O, ay; and pities them.

*Thu.* Wherefore?

*Jul.* That such an ass should owe them. [*Aside.*

*Pro.* That they are out by lease.[9]

*Jul.* Here comes the duke.

---

8 *Black men are pearls, &c.*] " A black man is a jewel in a
fair woman's eye," is one of Ray's proverbial sentences.

9 *That they are out by lease.*] Because Thurio's folly has let
them on disadvantageous terms; or, because they are let to others,
and are not in his own dear hands; or, by Thurio's *possessions*,
he himself understands his lands and estate. But Proteus chooses
to take the word likewise in a figurative sense, as signifying his
*mental endowments:* and when he says they are *out by lease*, he
means they are no longer enjoyed by their master, (who is a
fool,) but are leased out to another.

*Enter* DUKE.

*Duke.* How now, sir Proteus? how now, Thurio?
Which of you saw sir Eglamour of late?
*Thu.* Not I.
*Pro.*          Nor I.
*Duke.*          .          Saw you my daughter?
*Pro.*                    Neither.
*Duke.* Why, then she's fled unto that peasant
          Valentine;
And Eglamour is in her company.
'Tis true; for friar Laurence met them both,
As he in penance wander'd through the forest:
Him he knew well, and guess'd that it was she;
But, being mask'd, he was not sure of it:
Besides, she did intend confession
At Patrick's cell this even; and there she was not:
These likelihoods confirm her flight from hence.
Therefore, I pray you, stand not to discourse,
But mount you presently; and meet with me
Upon the rising of the mountain-foot
That leads towards Mantua, whither they are fled.
Dispatch, sweet gentlemen, and follow me. [*Exit.*
     *Thu.* Why, this it is to be a peevish girl,[1]
That flies her fortune when it follows her:
I'll after; more to be reveng'd on Eglamour,
Than for the love of reckless Silvia.[2]          [*Exit.*
     *Pro.* And I will follow, more for Silvia's love,
Than hate of Eglamour that goes with her. [*Exit.*
     *Jul.* And I will follow, more to cross that love,
Than hate for Silvia, that is gone for love.          [*Exit.*

---

[1] ——— *a* peevish *girl*,] i. e. in ancient language, *foolish.*
[2] ——— reckless *Silvia.*] i. e. careless, heedless.

## SCENE III.

*Frontiers of* Mantua. *The Forest.*

*Enter* SILVIA, *and* Out-laws.

*Out.* Come, come ;
Be patient, we must bring you to our captain.
*Sil.* A thousand more mischances than this one
Have learn'd me how to brook this patiently.
2 *Out.* Come, bring her away.
1 *Out.* Where is the gentleman that was with her ?
3 *Out.* Being nimble-footed, he hath out-run us,
But Moyses, and Valerius, follow him.
Go thou with her to the west end of the wood,
There is our captain : we'll follow him that's fled ;
The thicket is beset, he cannot 'scape.
1 *Out.* Come, I must bring you to our captain's
    cave ;
Fear not ; he bears an honourable mind,
And will not use a woman lawlessly.
*Sil.* O Valentine, this I endure for thee. [*Exeunt,*

## SCENE IV.

*Another part of the Forest.*

*Enter* VALENTINE.

*Val.* How use doth breed a habit in a man !
This shadowy desert, unfrequented woods,
I better brook than flourishing peopled towns :
Here can I sit alone, unseen of any,
And to the nightingale's complaining notes,
Tune my distresses, and record my woes.[3]

---

[3] —— record *my woes.*] To *record* anciently signified to *sing*.
To *record* is a term still used by bird-fanciers, to express the
first essays of a bird in singing.

F 2

O thou that dost inhabit in my breast,
Leave not the mansion so long tenantless ;
Lest, growing ruinous, the building fall,
And leave no memory of what it was ![4]
Repair me with thy presence, Silvia ;
Thou gentle nymph, cherish thy forlorn swain !—
What halloing, and what stir, is this to-day ?
These are my mates, that make their wills their law,
Have some unhappy passenger in chase :
They love me well ; yet I have much to do,
To keep them from uncivil outrages.
Withdraw thee, Valentine ; who's this comes here ?
                                        [*Steps aside.*

*Enter* PROTEUS, SILVIA, *and* JULIA.

*Pro.* Madam, this service I have done for you,
(Though you respect not aught your servant doth,)
To hazard life, and rescue you from him
That wou'd have forc'd your honour and your love.
Vouchsafe me, for my meed,[5] but one fair look ;
A smaller boon than this I cannot beg,
And less than this, I am sure, you cannot give.
    *Val.* How like a dream is this I see and hear !
Love, lend me patience to forbear a while.  [*Aside.*
    *Sil.* O miserable, unhappy that I am !
    *Pro.* Unhappy, were you, madam, ere I came ;
But, by my coming, I have made you happy.
    *Sil.* By thy approach thou mak'st me most un-
            happy.
    *Jul.* And me, when he approacheth to your pre-
            sence.                              [*Aside.*
    *Sil.* Had I been seized by a hungry lion,

---

[4] *O thou that dost,* &c.—]  It is hardly possible to point out
four lines in any of the plays of Shakspeare, more remarkable for
ease and elegance.  STEEVENS.
   [5] —— *my* meed,] i. e. reward.

I would have been a breakfast to the beast,
Rather than have false Proteus rescue me.
O, heaven be judge, how I love Valentine,
Whose life's as tender to me as my soul;
And full as much, (for more there cannot be,)
I do detest false perjur'd Proteus:
Therefore be gone, solicit me no more.
   *Pro.* What dangerous action, stood it next to
       death,
Would I not undergo for one calm look?
O, 'tis the curse in love, and still approv'd,[6]
When women cannot love where they're belov'd.
   *Sil.* When Proteus cannot love where he's belov'd.
Read over Julia's heart, thy first best love,
For whose dear sake thou didst then rend thy faith
Into a thousand oaths; and all those oaths
Descended into perjury, to love me.
Thou hast no faith left now, unless thou hadst two,
And that's far worse than none; better have none
Than plural faith, which is too much by one:
Thou counterfeit to thy true friend!
   *Pro.*                In love,
Who respects friend?
   *Sil.*           All men but Proteus.
   *Pro.* Nay, if the gentle spirit of moving words
Can no way change you to a milder form,
I'll woo you like a soldier, at arms' end;
And love you 'gainst the nature of love, force you.
   *Sil.* O heaven!
   *Pro.*          I'll force thee yield to my desire.
   *Val.* Ruffian, let go that rude uncivil touch;
Thou friend of an ill fashion!
   *Pro.*             Valentine?
   *Val.* Thou common friend, that's without faith
       or love;

---

[6] —— *and still* approv'd,] *Approv'd is felt, experienced.*

(For such is a friend now,) treacherous man!
Thou hast beguil'd my hopes; nought but mine eye
Could have persuaded me: Now I dare not say
I have one friend alive; thou would'st disprove me.
Who should be trusted now, when one's right hand
Is perjur'd to the bosom? Proteus,
I am sorry, I must never trust thee more,
But count the world a stranger for thy sake.
The private wound is deepest:⁷ O time, most curst!
'Mongst all foes, that a friend should be the worst!

 *Pro.* My shame and guilt confound me.——
Forgive me, Valentine: if hearty sorrow
Be a sufficient ransom for offence,
I tender it here; I do as truly suffer,
As e'er I did commit.

 *Val.*       Then I am paid;
And once again I do receive thee honest:——
Who by repentance is not satisfied,
Is nor of heaven, nor earth; for these are pleas'd:
By penitence the Eternal's wrath's appeas'd:——
And, that my love may appear plain and free,
All that was mine in Silvia, I give thee.⁸

---

 ⁷ *The private wound, &c.*] *Deepest, highest,* and other similar words, were sometimes used by the poets of Shakspeare's age as monosyllables.

 ⁸ *All that was mine in* Silvia, *I give thee.*] This passage either hath been much sophisticated, or is one great proof that the main parts of this play did not proceed from Shakspeare; for it is impossible he could make Valentine act and speak so much out of character, or give to Silvia so unnatural a behaviour, as to take no notice of this strange concession, if it had been made. HANMER.

 Valentine from seeing *Silvia* in the company of Proteus, might conceive she had escaped with him from her father's court, for purposes of love, though she could not foresee the violence which his villainy might offer, after he had seduced her under the pretence of an honest passion. If Valentine, however, be supposed to hear all that passeth between them in this scene, I am afraid I have only to subscribe to the opinions of my predecessors.

                 STEEVENS.

 ——— *I give thee,*] Transfer these two lines to the end of Thu-

# MERRY WIVES

## OF

## WINDSOR.*

* MERRY WIVES OF WINDSOR.] A few of the incidents in this comedy might have been taken from an old translation of *Il Pecorone* by Giovanni Fiorentino. I have lately met with the same story in a very contemptible performance, intitled, *The fortunate, the deceived, and the unfortunate Lovers.* Of this book, as I am told, there are several impressions; but that in which I read it was published in 1632, quarto. A somewhat similar story occurs in *Piaccvoli Notti di Straparola,* Nott. 4ᵃ. Fav. 4ᵃ.

This comedy was first entered at Stationers' Hall, Jan. 18, 1601, by John Busby. STEEVENS.

This play should be read between *K. Henry IV.* and *K. Henry V.* in Johnson's opinion. But Mr. Malone says, it ought rather to be read between *The First* and *The Second Part of King Henry IV.* in the latter of which young Henry becomes king. In the last act, Falstaff says:

" Herne the hunter, quoth you ? am I a ghost ?
" 'Sblood, the fairies hath made a ghost of me.
" What, hunting at this time of night !
" I'le lay my life the mad *prince of Wales*
" Is stealing his father's deare."

and in this play, as it now appears, Mr. Page discountenances the addresses of Fenton to his daughter, because " he keeps company with the wild *prince,* and with Poins."

*The Fishwife's Tale of Brainford* in WESTWARD FOR SMELTS, a book which Shakspeare seems to have read, (having borrowed from it a part of the fable of *Cymbeline,*) probably led him to lay the scene of Falstaff's love adventures at *Windsor.* It begins thus : " In *Windsor* not long agoe dwelt a sumpterman, who had to wife a very faire but wanton creature, over whom, not without cause, he was something *jealous ;* yet had he never any proof of her inconstancy." MALONE.

The adventures of *Falstaff* in this play seem to have been taken from the story of *The Lovers of Pisa,* in an old piece, called *Tarleton's Newes out of Purgatorie.* Mr. *Warton* observes, in a note to the last *Oxford* edition, that the play was probably not written as we now have it, before 1607, at the earliest. I agree with my very ingenious friend in this supposition, but yet the argument here produced for it may not be conclusive. *Slender* observes to master *Page,* that his *greyhound was out-run at Cotsale* [*Cotswold-Hills* in *Gloucestershire ;*] and Mr. *Warton* thinks, that the games, established there by Captain *Dover* in the beginning of *K. James's* reign, are alluded to. But, perhaps, though the Captain be celebrated in the *Annalia Dubrensia* as the *founder* of them, he might be the *reviver* only, or some way contribute to make them more famous; for in *The Second Part of Henry IV.*

1600, Justice *Shallow* reckons among the *Swinge-bucklers*, " *Will Squeele*, a *Cotsole man*."

In the first edition of the imperfect play, *Sir Hugh Evans* is called on the title-page, the *Welch Knight;* and yet there are some persons who still affect to believe, that all our author's plays were originally published by *himself.* FARMER.

Queen Elizabeth was so well pleased with the admirable character of Falstaff in *The Two Parts of Henry IV.* that, as Mr. Rowe informs us, she commanded Shakspeare to continue it for one play more, and show him in love. To this command we owe *The Merry Wives of Windsor;* which, Mr. Gildon says, [*Remarks* on Shakspeare's Plays, 8vo. 1710,] he was very well assured our author finished in a fortnight. He quotes no authority. The circumstance was first mentioned by Mr. Dennis. " This comedy," says he, in his Epistle Dedicatory to *The Comical Gallant* (an alteration of the present play,) 1702, " was written at her [Queen Elizabeth's] command, and by her direction, and she was so eager to see it acted, that she commanded it to be finished in *fourteen days;* and was afterwards, as tradition tells us, very well pleased at the representation." The information, it is probable, came originally from Dryden, who from his intimacy with Sir William Davenant, had an opportunity of learning many particulars concerning our author.

At what period Shakspeare new-modelled *The Merry Wives of Windsor* is unknown. I believe it was enlarged in 1603.
MALONE.

It is not generally known, that the first edition of *The Merry Wives of Windsor*, in its present state, is in the valuable folio, printed 1623, from whence the quarto of the same play, dated 1630, was evidently copied. The two earlier quartos, 1602, and 1619, only exhibit this comedy as it was originally written, and are so far curious as they contain Shakspeare's first conceptions in forming a drama, which is the most complete specimen of his comick powers. T. WARTON.

# PERSONS REPRESENTED.

Sir John Falstaff.
Fenton.
Shallow, *a country Justice.*
Slender, *cousin to* Shallow.
Mr. Ford, } *two gentlemen dwelling at* Windsor.
Mr. Page, }
William Page, *a boy, son to* Mr. Page.
Sir Hugh Evans, *a Welch parson.*
Dr. Caius, *a French physician.*
*Host of the Garter Inn.*
Bardolph, }
Pistol, } *- followers of* Falstaff.
Nym, }
Robin, *page to* Falstaff.
Simple, *servant to* Slender.
Rugby, *servant to* Dr. Caius.

Mrs. Ford.
Mrs. Page.
Mrs. Anne Page, *her daughter, in love with* Fenton.
Mrs. Quickly, *servant to* Dr. Caius.

*Servants to* Page, Ford, *&c.*

*SCENE,* Windsor; *and the parts adjacent.*

*Jul.* O me, unhappy!           *[Faints.*
*Pro.* Look to the boy.
*Val.* Why, boy! why, wag! how now? what is
    the matter?
Look up; speak.
*Jul.*         O good sir, my master charg'd me
To deliver a ring to madam Silvia ;[9]
Which, out of my neglect, was never done.
*Pro.* Where is that ring, boy?
*Jul.*            Here 'tis : this is it.
                  *[Gives a ring.*
*Pro.* How! let me see :
Why this is the ring I gave to Julia.
*Jul.* O, cry you mercy, sir, I have mistook ;
This is the ring you sent to Silvia.
              *[Shows another ring.*
*Pro.* But, how cam'st thou by this ring? at my
    depart,
I gave this unto Julia.
*Jul.* And Julia herself did give it me ;
And Julia herself hath brought it hither.
*Pro.* How! Julia!
*Jul.* Behold her that gave aim to all thy oaths,[1]
And entertain'd them deeply in her heart :
How oft hast thou with perjury cleft the root?[2]

rio's speech in page 197; and all is right. Why then should Julia
faint? It is only an artifice, seeing Silvia given up to Valentine,
to discover herself to Proteus, by a pretended mistake of the
rings. One great fault of this play is the hastening too abruptly,
and without due preparation to the denouëment, which shews
that, if it be Shakspeare's, (which I cannot doubt,) it was one of
his very early performances. BLACKSTONE.
 [9] *To* deliver *a ring to madam Silvia ;*] Surely our author wrote—
" *Deliver* a ring," &c. A verse so rugged as that in the text
must be corrupted by the players, or transcriber.
 [1] *Behold her that* gave aim *to all thy oaths,*] Gave encouragement, a phrase in archery.
 [2] *How oft hast thou with perjury cleft the* root?] i. e. of her
heart. An allusion to *cleaving the pin* in archery.

O Proteus, let this habit make thee blush!
Be thou asham'd, that I have took upon me
Such an immodest rayment; if shame live¹
In a disguise of love:
It is the lesser blot, modesty finds,
Women to change their shapes, than men their
    minds.
   *Pro.* Than men their minds! 'tis true; O hea-
    ven! were man
But constant, he were perfect: that one error
Fills him with faults; makes him run through all
    sins:
Inconstancy falls off, ere it begins:
What is in Silvia's face, but I may spy
More fresh in Julia's with a constant eye?
   *Val.* Come, come, a hand from either:
Let me be blest to make this happy close;
'Twere pity two such friends should be long foes.
   *Pro.* Bear witness, heaven, I have my wish for
    ever.
   *Jul.* And I have mine.

   *Enter* Out-laws, *with* DUKE *and* THURIO.

   *Out.*              A prize, a prize, a prize!
   *Val.* Forbear, I say; it is my lord the duke.
Your grace is welcome to a man disgrac'd,
Banished Valentine.
   *Duke.*         Sir Valentine!
   *Thu.* Yonder is Silvia; and Silvia's mine.
   *Val.* Thurio give back, or else embrace thy
    death;
Come not within the measure⁴ of my wrath:
Do not name Silvia thine; if once again,

---

¹ —— *if* shame live —] That is, *if it be any shame to wear a
disguise for the purposes of love.*
⁴ —— *the measure*—] The reach of my anger.
        9

Milan shall not behold thee.[5]   Here she stands,
Take but possession of her with a touch ;—
I dare thee but to breathe upon my love.—

   *Thu.* Sir Valentine, I care not for her, I ;
I hold him but a fool that will endanger
His body for a girl that loves him not :
I claim her not, and therefore she is thine.

   *Duke.* The more degenerate and base art thou,
To make such means for her as thou hast done,[6]
And leave her on such slight conditions.—
Now, by the honour of my ancestry,
I do applaud thy spirit, Valentine,
And think thee worthy of an empress' love.
Know then, I here forget all former griefs,[7]
Cancel all grudge, repeal thee home again.—
Plead a new state in thy unrivall'd merit,
To which I thus subscribe,—sir Valentine,
Thou art a gentleman, and well deriv'd ;
Take thou thy Silvia, for thou hast deserv'd her.

   *Val.* I thank your grace ; the gift hath made me
       happy.
I now beseech you, for your daughter's sake,
To grant one boon that I shall ask of you.

   *Duke.* I grant it, for thine own, whate'er it be.

   *Val.* These banish'd men, that I have kept withal,
Are men endued with worthy qualities ;
Forgive them what they have committed here,
And let them be recall'd from their exile :
They are reform'd, civil, full of good,

---

  [5] Milan *shall not behold thee.*]    All the editions—*Verona shall
not behold thee.* But from every circumstance, the poet must have
intended ; i. e. Milan, *thy country, shall never see thee again :
thou shalt never live to go back thither.* THEOBALD.

  [6] *To* make such means *for her as thou hast done,*] i. e. to make
such interest for, to take such disingenuous pains about her.

  [7] —— *all former* griefs,] *Griefs* in old language frequently
signified *grievances, wrongs.* MALONE.

And fit for great employment, worthy lord.

*Duke.* Thou hast prevail'd; I pardon them, and
    thee;

Dispose of them, as thou know'st their deserts.
Come, let us go; we will include all jars<sup>8</sup>
With triumphs,<sup>9</sup> mirth, and rare solemnity.

*Val.* And, as we walk along, I dare be bold
With our discourse to make your grace to smile:
What think you of this page, my lord?

*Duke.* I think the boy hath grace in him; he
    blushes.

*Val.* I warrant you, my lord; more grace than
    boy.

*Duke.* What mean you by that saying?

*Val.* Please you, I'll tell you as we pass along,
That you will wonder what hath fortuned.——
Come, Proteus; 'tis your penance, but to hear
The story of your loves discovered:
That done, our day of marriage shall be yours;
One feast, one house, one mutual happiness.

                      [*Exeunt.*<sup>1</sup>

---

<sup>8</sup> —— include *all jars*—] i. e. *shut up*, or *conclude.*

<sup>9</sup> *With* triumphs,] *Triumphs* in this and many other passages
of Shakspeare, signify Masques and Revels, &c.

<sup>1</sup> In this play there is a strange mixture of knowledge and ig-
norance, of care and negligence. The versification is often excellent, the allusions are learned and just; but the author con-
veys his heroes by sea from one inland town to another in the
same country; he places the Emperor at Milan, and sends his
young men to attend him, but never mentions him more; he
makes Proteus, after an interview with Silvia, say he has only
seen her picture; and, if we may credit the old copies, he has,
by mistaking places, left his scenery inextricable. The reason of
all this confusion seems to be, that he took his story from a novel,
which he sometimes followed, and sometimes forsook, sometimes
remembered, and sometimes forgot.

 That this play is rightly attributed to Shakspeare, I have little
doubt. If it be taken from him, to whom shall it be given? This
question may be asked of all the disputed plays, except *Titus An-*
*dronicus;* and it will be found more credible, that Shakspeare

might sometimes sink below his highest flights, than that any other should rise up to his lowest.  JOHNSON.

Johnson's general remarks on this play are just, except that part in which he arraigns the conduct of the poet, for making Proteus say, that he had only seen the picture of Silvia, when it appears that he had had a personal interview with her.   This, however, is not a blunder of Shakspeare's, but a mistake of Johnson's, who considers the passage alluded to in a more literal sense than the author intended it.   Sir Proteus, it is true, had seen Silvia for a few moments; but though he could form from thence some idea of her person, he was still unacquainted with her temper, manners, and the qualities of her mind.   He therefore considers himself as having seen her picture only.——The thought is just, and elegantly expressed.   M. MASON.

# MERRY WIVES

## OF

# WINDSOR.

---

## ACT I.

*SCENE I.* Windsor. *Before* Page's *House.*

*Enter Justice* SHALLOW, SLENDER, *and Sir* HUGH EVANS.

*Shal.* Sir Hugh,[1] persuade me not; I will make a Star-chamber matter of it: if he were twenty sir John Falstaff's, he shall not abuse Robert Shallow, esquire.

*Slen.* In the county of Gloster, justice of peace, and *coram.*

*Shal.* Ay, cousin Slender, and *Cust-alorum.*

*Slen.* Ay, and *ratolorum* too; and a gentleman

---

[1] *Sir Hugh,*] This is the first, of sundry instances in our poet, where a *parson* is called *Sir.* Upon which it may be observed, that anciently it was the common designation both of one in holy orders and a knight. *Sir* is the designation of a Bachelor of Arts in the Universities of Cambridge and Dublin; but is there always annexed to the surname;—Sir Evans, &c. In consequence, however, of this, all the inferior Clergy in England were distinguished by this title affixed to their christian names for many centuries. Hence our author's *Sir* Hugh in the present play,—*Sir* Topas in *Twelfth Night, Sir* Oliver in *As you like it,* &c. MALONE.

born, master parson; who writes himself *armigero*;¹
in any bill, warrant, quittance, or obligation, *armigero.*

*Shal.* Ay, that we do; and have done any time
these three hundred years.

*Slen.* All his successors, gone before him, have
done't; and all his ancestors that come after him,
may: they may give the dozen white luces in their
coat.

*Shal.* It is an old coat.

*Eva.* The dozen white louses do become an old
coat well; it agrees well, passant: it is a familiar
beast to man, and signifies—love.

*Shal.* The luce is the fresh fish; the salt fish is
an old coat.²

*Slen.* I may quarter, coz?

*Shal.* You may, by marrying.

*Eva.* It is marring, indeed, if he quarter it.

*Shal.* Not a whit.

*Eva.* Yes, py'r-lady; if he has a quarter of your
coat, there is but three skirts for yourself, in my
simple conjectures: but this is all one: If sir John
Falstaff have committed disparagements unto you,
I am of the church, and will be glad to do my benevolence, to make atonements and compromises
between you.

*Shal.* The Council shall hear it; it is a riot.⁴

---

¹ —— *who writes himself* armigero;] Slender had seen the
Justice's attestations, signed "—jurat' coram me, Roberto
Shallow, *Armigero.*"

² *The luce is the* fresh fish; *the* salt fish *is an old coat.*] Our
author here alludes to the arms of Sir Thomas Lucy, who is said
to have prosecuted him in the younger part of his life for a mis-
demeanor, and who is supposed to be pointed at under the character of Justice Shallow. The text, however, by some carelessness of the printer or transcriber, has been so corrupted, that the
passage, as it stands at present, seems inexplicable.

⁴ *The* Council *shall hear it; it is a riot.*] By the Council is

*Eva.* It is not meet the Council hear a riot; there is no fear of Got in a riot: the Council, look you, shall desire to hear the fear of Got, and not to hear a riot; take your vizaments in that.[9]

*Shal.* Ha! o' my life, if I were young again, the sword should end it.

*Eva.* It is petter that friends is the sword, and end it: and there is also another device in my prain, which, peradventure, prings goot discretions with it: There is Anne Page, which is daughter to master George Page, which is pretty virginity.

*Slen.* Mistress Anne Page? She has brown hair, and speaks small like a woman.

*Eva.* It is that fery verson for all the 'orld, as just as you will desire; and seven hundred pounds of monies, and gold, and silver, is her grandsire, upon his death's-bed, (Got deliver to a joyful resurrections!) give, when she is able to overtake seventeen years old: it were a goot motion, if we leave our pribbles and prabbles, and desire a marriage between master Abraham, and mistress Anne Page.

*Shal.* Did her grandsire leave her seven hundred pound?

*Eva.* Ay, and her father is make her a petter penny.

*Shal.* I know the young gentlewoman; she has good gifts.

*Eva.* Seven hundred pounds, and possibilities, is good gifts.

*Shal.* Well, let us see honest master Page: Is Falstaff there?

*Eva.* Shall I tell you a lie? I do despise a liar, as I do despise one that is false; or, as I despise one

only meant the court of Star-chamber, composed chiefly of the king's council sitting *in Camerâ stellatâ*, which took cognizance of atrocious riots.

[9] —— *your* vizaments *in that.*] *Advisement*, an obsolete word.

that is not true. The knight, sir John, is there; and, I beseech you, be ruled by your well-willers. I will peat the door [*knocks*] for master Page. What, hoa! Got pless your house here!

*Enter* PAGE.

*Page.* Who's there?

*Eva.* Here is Got's plessing, and your friend, and justice Shallow: and here young master Slender; that, peradventures, shall tell you another tale, if matters grow to your likings.

*Page.* I am glad to see your worships well: I thank you for my venison, master Shallow.

*Shal.* Master Page, I am glad to see you; Much good do it your good heart! I wished your venison better; it was ill kill'd:——How doth good mistress Page?——and I love you always with my heart, la; with my heart.

*Page.* Sir, I thank you.

*Shal.* Sir, I thank you; by yea and no, I do.

*Page.* I am glad to see you, good master Slender.

*Slen.* How does your fallow greyhound, sir? I heard say, he was out-run on Cotsale.[5]

*Page.* It could not be judg'd, sir.

*Slen.* You'll not confess, you'll not confess.

*Shal.* That he will not;——'tis your fault, 'tis your fault:——'Tis a good dog.

*Page.* A cur, sir.

*Shal.* Sir, he's a good dog, and a fair dog; Can there be more said? he is good, and fair. Is sir John Falstaff here?

---

[5] *How does your fallow greyhound, sir? I heard say, he was out-run on* Cotsale.] *Cotswold,* in *Gloucestershire,* where there was an annual celebration of games, consisting of rural sports and exercises.

*Page.* Sir, he is within; and I would I could do a good office between you.

*Eva.* It is spoke as a christians ought to speak.

*Shal.* He hath wrong'd me, master Page.

*Page.* Sir, he doth in some sort confess it.

*Shal.* If it be confess'd, it is not redress'd; is not that so, master Page? He hath wrong'd me; indeed, he hath;—at a word he hath;—believe me; Robert Shallow, esquire, saith he is wrong'd.

*Page.* Here comes sir John.

*Enter sir* JOHN FALSTAFF, BARDOLPH, NYM, *and* PISTOL.

*Fal.* Now, master Shallow; you'll complain of me to the king?

*Shal.* Knight you have beaten my men, killed my deer, and broke open my lodge.

*Fal.* But not kiss'd your keeper's daughter?

*Shal.* Tut, a pin! this shall be answer'd.

*Fal.* I will answer it straight;—I have done all this:—That is now answer'd.

*Shal.* The Council shall know this.

*Fal.* 'Twere better for you, if it were known in counsel: you'll be laugh'd at.

*Eva.* *Pauca verba,* sir John, goot worts.

*Fal.* Good worts! good cabbage.[6]—Slender, I broke your head; What matter have you against me?

*Slen.* Marry, sir, I have matter in my head against you; and against your coney-catching rascals,[7] Bardolph, Nym, and Pistol. They carried me to the

---

[6] *Good worts! good cabbage.*] *Worts* was the ancient name of all the cabbage kind.

[7] —— *coney-catching rascals,*] A *coney-catcher* was, in the time of Elizabeth, a common name for a cheat or a sharper.

tavern, and made me drunk, and afterwards picked my pocket.

*Bard.* You Banbury cheese!⁸

*Slen.* Ay, it is no matter.

*Pist.* How now, Mephostophilus?⁹

*Slen.* Ay, it is no matter.

*Nym.* Slice, I say! *pauca, pauca;* slice! that's my humour.

*Slen.* Where's Simple, my man?—can you tell, cousin?

*Eva.* Peace: I pray you! Now let us understand: There is three umpires in this matter, as I understand: that is—master Page, *fidelicet,* master Page; and there is myself, *fidelicet,* myself; and the three party is, lastly and finally, mine host of the Garter.

*Page.* We three, to hear it, and end it between them.

*Eva.* Fery goot: I will make a prief of it in my note-book; and we will afterwards 'ork upon the cause, with as great discreetly as we can.

*Fal.* Pistol,—

*Pist.* He hears with cars.

*Eva.* The tevil with his tam! what phrase is this, *He hears with ear?* Why, it is affectations.

*Fal.* Pistol, did you piek master Slender's purse?

*Slen.* Ay, by these gloves, did he, (or I would I might never come in mine own great chamber again else,) of seven groats in mill-sixpences, and two Edward shovel-boards,¹ that cost me two shil-

---

⁸ *You* Banbury *cheese!*] You are like a Banbury cheese,—nothing but paring.

⁹ *How now,* Mephostophilus?] This is the name of a spirit or familiar, in the old story book of *Sir John Faustus.*

¹ —— *Edward* shovel-boards,] were the shillings of Edward VI; the game of shovel-board, or shuffle-board, was played with them in Shadwell's time,

ling and two pence a-piece of Yead Miller, by these gloves.

*Fal.* Is this true, Pistol?

*Eva.* No; it is false, if it is a pick-purse.

*Pist.* Ha, thou mountain-foreigner!—Sir John and master mine,

I combat challenge of this latten bilbo:[2]
Word of denial in thy labras[3] here;
Word of denial: froth and scum, thou liest.

*Slen.* By these gloves, then 'twas he.

*Nym.* Be advised, sir, and pass good humours: I will say, *marry trap,*[4] with you, if you run the nuthook's humour[5] on me: that is the very note of it.

*Slen.* By this hat, then he in the red face had it: for though I cannot remember what I did when you made me drunk, yet I am not altogether an ass.

*Fal.* What say you, Scarlet and John?[6]

*Bard.* Why, sir, for my part, I say, the gentleman had drunk himself out of his five sentences.

*Eva.* It is his five senses: fie, what the ignorance is!

*Bard.* And being fap,[7] sir, was, as they say, cashier'd; and so conclusions pass'd the careires.[8]

*Slen.* Ay, you spake in Latin then too; but 'tis

---

[2] *I combat challenge of this* latten *bilbo:*] A *latten bilbo* means, I believe, no more than *a blade as thin as a lath—a vice's dagger.* STEEVENS.

[3] —— *labras*] i. e. lips.

[4] ——*marry trap,*] When a man was caught in his own stratagem, I suppose the exclamation of insult was—*marry, trap!* JOHNSON.

[5] —— nuthook's *humour* —] i. e. *if you say I am a thief.*

[6] —— *Scarlet and John?*] The names of two of Robin Hood's companions; but the humour consists in the allusion to Bardolph's *red face.*

[7] *And being* fap,] i. e. drunk.

[8] —— *careires.*] i. e. " and so in the *end* he reel'd about with a circuitous motion, like a horse, *passing a carier.*"

no matter: I'll ne'er be drunk whilst I live again,
but in honest, civil, godly company, for this trick;
if I be drunk, I'll be drunk with those that have the
fear of God, and not with drunken knaves.

*Eva.* So Got 'udge me, that is a virtuous mind.

*Fal.* You hear all these matters denied, gentlemen; you hear it,

*Enter Mistress* ANNE PAGE *with wine;  Mistress*
FORD *and Mistress* PAGE *following.*

*Page.* Nay, daughter, carry the wine in; we'll
drink within.                           [*Exit* ANNE PAGE.

*Slen.* O heaven! this is mistress Anne Page.

*Page.* How now, mistress Ford?

*Fal.* Mistress Ford, by my troth, you are very
well met: by your leave, good mistress. [*kissing her.*

*Page.* Wife, bid these gentlemen welcome:——
Come, we have a hot venison pasty to dinner; come,
gentlemen, I hope we shall drink down all un-
kindness.

       [*Exeunt all but* SHAL. SLENDER *and* EVANS.

*Slen.* I had rather than forty shillings, I had my
book of Songs and Sonnets here:——[9]

*Enter* SIMPLE,

How now, Simple! Where have you been? I must
wait on myself, must I? You have not *The Book of
Riddles* [1] about you, have you?

---

[9] —— *my book of* Songs and Sonnets *here:*] "*Songes and
Sonnettes,* written by the Right Honourable Lord Henry Howard,
late Earle of Surrey, and others." Slender laments that he has
not this fashionable book about him, supposing it might have assisted him in paying his addresses to Anne Page.   MALONE.

[1] —— '*The Book of Riddles* —] This appears to have been a
popular book, and is enumerated with others in *The English
Courtier, and Country Gentleman,*

*Sim.* *Book of Riddles!* why, did not you lend it to Alice Shortcake upon Allhallowmas last, a fortnight afore Michaelmas?[2]

*Shal.* Come, coz; come, coz; we stay for you. A word with you, coz: marry, this, coz; There is, as 'twere, a tender, a kind of tender, made afar off by sir Hugh here;—Do you understand me?

*Slen.* Ay, sir, you shall find me reasonable; if it be so, I shall do that that is reason.

*Shal.* Nay, but understand me.

*Slen.* So I do, sir.

*Eva.* Give ear to his motions, master Slender: I will description the matter to you, if you be capacity of it.

*Slen.* Nay, I will do as my cousin Shallow says: I pray you, pardon me; he's a justice of peace in his country, simple though I stand here.

*Eva.* But this is not the question; the question is concerning your marriage.

*Shal.* Ay, there's the point, sir.

*Eva.* Marry, is it; the very point of it; to mistress Anne Page.

*Slen.* Why, if it be so, I will marry her, upon any reasonable demands.

*Eva.* But can you affection the 'oman? Let us command to know that of your mouth, or of your lips; for divers philosophers hold, that the lips is parcel of the mouth;—Therefore, precisely, can you carry your good will to the maid?

*Shal.* Cousin Abraham Slender, can you love her?

*Slen.* I hope, sir,—I will do, as it shall become one that would do reason.

*Eva.* Nay, Got's lords and his ladies, you must

---

* —— upon *Allhallowmas last, a fortnight afore Michaelmas?*] An intended blunder of Shakspeare's.

speak possitable, if you can carry her your desires towards her.

*Shal.* That you must: Will you, upon good dowry, marry her?

*Slen.* I will do a greater thing than that, upon your request, cousin, in any reason.

*Shal.* Nay, conceive me, conceive me, sweet coz; what I do, is to pleasure you, coz: Can you love the maid?

*Slen.* I will marry her, sir, at your request; but if there be no great love in the beginning, yet heaven may decrease it upon better acquaintance, when we are married, and have more occasion to know one another: I hope, upon familiarity will grow more contempt: but if you say, *marry her*, I will marry her, that I am freely dissolved, and dissolutely.

*Eva.* It is a fery discretion answer; save, the faul' is in the 'ort dissolutely: the 'ort is, according to our meaning, resolutely;—his meaning is good.

*Shal.* Ay, I think my cousin meant well.

*Slen.* Ay, or else I would I might be hanged, la.

### *Re-enter* ANNE PAGE.

*Shal.* Here comes fair mistress Anne:—Would I were young, for your sake, mistress Anne!

*Anne.* The dinner is on the table; my father desires your worships' company.

*Shal.* I will wait on him, fair mistress Anne.

*Eva.* Od's plessed will! I will not be absence at the grace.

[*Exeunt* SHALLOW *and Sir* H. EVANS.

*Anne.* Will't please your worship to come in, sir?

*Slen.* No, I thank you, forsooth, heartily; I am very well.

*Anne.* The dinner attends you, sir.

*Slen.* I am not a-hungry, I thank you, forsooth.

Go, sirrah, for all you are my man, go, wait upon my cousin Shallow: [*Exit* SIMPLE.] A justice of peace sometime may be beholden to his friend for a man :——I keep but three men and a boy yet, till my mother be dead : But what though? yet I live like a poor gentleman born.

*Anne.* I may not go in without your worship : they will not sit, till you come.

*Slen.* I'faith, I'll eat nothing ; I thank you as much as though I did.

*Anne.* I pray you, sir, walk in.

*Slen.* I had rather walk here, I thank you ; I bruised my shin the other day with playing at sword and dagger with a master of fence,[3] three veneys for a dish of stewed prunes ;[4] and, by my troth, I cannot abide the smell of hot meat since. Why do your dogs bark so? be there bears i' the town.

*Anne.* I think, there are, sir ; I heard them talked of.

*Slen.* I love the sport well ; but I shall as soon quarrel at it, as any man in England:——You are afraid, if you see the bear loose, are you not?

*Anne.* Ay, indeed, sir.

*Slen.* That's meat and drink to me now : I have seen Sackerson[5] loose, twenty times; and have taken him by the chain : but, I warrant you, the women have so cried and shriek'd at it, that it pass'd:[6]——but

---

[3] —— *a master of fence,*] *Master of defence,* on this occasion, does not simply mean a professor of the art of fencing, but a person who had taken his *master's degree* in it ; in this art there were three degrees, viz. a *Master's,* a *Provost's,* and a *Scholar's.*

[4] —— *three veneys for a dish,* &c.] i. e. three *venues,* French. Three different set-to's, bouts, (or *hits,* as Mr. Malone, perhaps more properly, explains the word,) a technical term.

[5] —— *Sackerson* ——] *Sackerson,* or *Sacarson,* was the name of a bear that was exhibited in our author's time at Paris-Garden in Southwark.

[6] —— *that* it pass'd :] i. e. all expression.

women, indeed, cannot abide 'em ; they are very ill favoured rough things.

### Re-enter PAGE.

*Page.* Come, gentle master Slender, come; we stay for you.

*Slen.* I'll eat nothing, I thank you, sir.

*Page.* By cock and pye,⁴ you shall not choose, sir : come, come.

*Slen.* Nay, pray you, lead the way.

*Page.* Come on, sir.

*Slen.* Mistress Anne, yourself shall go first.

*Anne.* Not I, sir ; pray you, keep on.

*Slen.* Truly, I will not go first ; truly, la : I will not do you that wrong.

*Anne.* I pray you, sir.

*Slen.* I'll rather be unmannerly, than troublesome ; you do yourself wrong, indeed, la.      [*Exeunt.*

### SCENE II.

#### *The same.*

#### *Enter Sir* HUGH EVANS *and* SIMPLE.

*Eva.* Go your ways, and ask of Doctor Caius' house, which is the way : and there dwells one mistress Quickly, which is in the manner of his nurse, or his dry nurse, or his cook, or his laundry, his washer, and his wringer.

*Simp.* Well, sir.

*Eva.* Nay, it is petter yet :——give her this letter; for it is a 'oman that altogether's acquaintance with mistress Anne Page : and the letter is, to desire and

---

⁴ *By cock and pye,*] This was a very popular adjuration, and occurs in many of our old dramatic pieces.

require her to solicit your master's desires to mistress
Anne Page : I pray you, be gone ; I will make an
end of my dinner; there's pippins and cheese to
come. [*Exeunt.*

## SCENE III.

### *A Room in the Garter Inn.*

*Enter* FALSTAFF, Host, BARDOLPH, NYM, PISTOL,
*and* ROBIN.

*Fal.* Mine host of the Garter,—
*Host.* What says my bully-rook?[7] Speak scho-
larly, and wisely.
*Fal.* Truly, mine host, I must turn away some of
my followers.
*Host.* Discard, bully Hercules ; cashier: let them
wag ; trot, trot.
*Fal.* I sit at ten pounds a week.
*Host.* Thou 'rt an emperor, Cæsar, Keisar,[8] and
Pheezar. I will entertain Bardolph ; he shall draw,
he shall tap : said I well, bully Hector?
*Fal.* Do so, good mine host.
*Host.* I have spoke ; let him follow : Let me see
thee froth, and lime :[9] I am at a word ; follow.
[*Exit* Host.
*Fal.* Bardolph, follow him : a tapster is a good

---

[7] —— *my* bully-rook ?] The spelling of this word is corrupted,
and thereby its primitive meaning is lost. The latter part of this
compound title is taken from the *rooks* at the game of chess.
STEEVENS.

[8] —— *Keisar*,] *Keysar* for *Cæsar*.

[9] —— *Let me see thee* froth, *and* lime:] *Frothing* beer and
*liming* sack, were tricks practised in the time of Shakspeare.
The first was done by putting soap into the bottom of the tankard
when they drew the beer ; the other by mixing *lime* with the
sack (i. e. sherry) to make it sparkle in the glass.

trade: an old cloak makes a new jerkin; a withered servingman, a fresh tapster: Go; adieu.

*Bard.* It is a life that I have desired; I will thrive.

[*Exit* BARD.

*Pist.* O base Gongarian wight![1] wilt thou the spigot wield?

*Nym.* He was gotten in drink: Is not the humour conceited? His mind is not heroick, and there's the humour of it.

*Fal.* I am glad, I am so acquit of this tinder-box; his thefts were too open; his filching was like an unskilful singer, he kept not time.

*Nym.* The good humour is, to steal at a minute's rest.

*Pist.* Convey, the wise it call: Steal! foh; a fico for the phrase![2]

*Fal.* Well, sirs, I am almost out at heels.

*Pist.* Why then, let kibes ensue.

*Fal.* There is no remedy; I must coney-catch; I must shift.

*Pist.* Young ravens must have food.

*Fal.* Which of you know Ford of this town?

*Pist.* I ken the wight; he is of substance good.

*Fal.* My honest lads, I will tell you what I am about.

*Pist.* Two yards, and more.

*Fal.* No quips now, Pistol; Indeed I am in the waist two yards about: but I am now about no waste; I am about thrift. Briefly, I do mean to make love to Ford's wife; I spy entertainment in her; she discourses, she carves,[3] she gives the leer of invitation:

---

[1] *O base* Gongarian *wight, &c.*] A cant term in old bombast plays.

[2] —— a fico *for the phrase!*] i. e. a *fig* for it.

[3] —— *she* carves,] It should be remembered, that anciently the young of both sexes were instructed in *carving*, as a necessary accomplishment.

I can construe the action of her familiar style; and the hardest voice of her behaviour, to be English'd rightly, is, *I am sir John Falstaff's.*

*Pist.* He hath studied her well, and translated her well; out of honesty into English.

*Nym.* The anchor is deep:[4] Will that humour pass?

*Fal.* Now, the report goes, she has all the rule of her husband's purse; she hath legions of angels.

*Pist.* As many devils entertain;[5] and, *To her, boy,* say I.

*Nym.* The humour rises; it is good: humour me the angels.

*Fal.* I have writ me here a letter to her: and here another to Page's wife; who even now gave me good eyes too, examin'd my parts with most judicious eyliads:[6] sometimes the beam of her view gilded my foot, sometimes my portly belly.

*Pist.* Then did the sun on dung-hill shine.

*Nym.* I thank thee for that humour.

*Fal.* O, she did so course o'er my exteriors with such a greedy intention,[7] that the appetite of her eye did seem to scorch me up like a burning glass! Here's another letter to her: she bears the purse too; she is a region in Guiana, all gold and bounty. I will be cheater to them both, and they shall be exchequers to me;[8] they shall be my East and West Indies, and I will trade to them both. Go, bear thou this letter to mistress Page; and thou this to mistress Ford: we will thrive, lads, we will thrive.

---

[4] *The* anchor *is deep:*] Perhaps we may read—*the* author *is deep.*

[5] *As many devils* entertain;] i. e. do you retain in your *service* as many devils as she has angels.

[6] —— *eyliads:*] perhaps we should write *oëillades,* French.

[7] —— *intention,*] i. e. eagerness of desire.

[8] *I will be* cheater *to them both*——] By this is meant *Escheatour,* an officer in the Exchequer.

*Pist.* Shall I sir Pandarus of Troy become,
And by my side wear steel? then, Lucifer take all!
*Nym.* I will run no base humour: here, take the
humour letter; I will keep the 'haviour of reputation.
*Fal.* Hold, sirrah, [*to* ROB.] bear you these letters tightly;⁹
Sail like my pinnace' to these golden shores.——
Rogues, hence, avaunt! vanish like hail-stones, go;
Trudge, plod, away, o' the hoof; seek shelter, pack!
Falstaff will learn the humour of this age,
French thrift, you rogues; myself, and skirted page.
    [*Exeunt* FALSTAFF *and* ROBIN.
*Pist.* Let vultures gripe thy guts! for gourd, and fullam holds,
And high and low beguile the rich and poor;²
Tester I'll have in pouch, when thou shalt lack,
Base Phrygian Turk!
*Nym.* I have operations in my head, which be humours of revenge.
*Pist.* Wilt thou revenge?
*Nym.* By welkin, and her star!
*Pist.* With wit, or steel!
*Nym.* With both the humours, I:
I will discuss the humour of this love to Page.
*Pist.* And I to Ford shall eke unfold,
    How Falstaff, varlet vile,

---

⁹ —— *bear you these letters* tightly;] i. e. cleverly, adroitly.

¹ —— *my* pinnace ——] A pinnace seems anciently to have signified a small vessel, or sloop attending on a larger. A *pinnace* now, is a small vessel with a square stern, having sails and oars, and carrying three masts; chiefly used as a *scout* for intelligence, and for landing of men.

² ——*for* gourd, *and* fullam *holds,*
*And* high *and* low *beguile the rich and poor:*] *Gourds* were probably dice in which a secret cavity had been made; *fullams,* those which had been loaded with a small bit of lead, which, being chiefly made at *Fulham,* were thence called " high and low *Fulhams."* The high *Fulhams* were the numbers, 4, 5, and 6.

His dove will prove, his gold will hold,
And his soft couch defile.

*Nym.* My humour shall not cool : I will incense
Page[3] to deal with poison ; I will possess him with
yellowness,[4] for the revolt of mien[5] is dangerous :
that is my true humour.

*Pist.* Thou art the Mars of malcontents : I
second thee ; troop on. [*Exeunt.*

## SCENE IV.

*A Room in Dr. Caius's House.*

*Enter Mrs.* QUICKLY, SIMPLE, *and* RUGBY.

*Quick.* What : John Rugby !—I pray thee, go to
the casement, and see if you can see my master,
master Doctor Caius, coming : if he do, i'faith, and
find any body in the house, here will be an old
abusing of God's patience, and the king's English.

*Rug.* I'll go watch. [*Exit* RUGBY.

*Quick.* Go ; and we'll have a posset for't soon at
night, in faith, at the latter end of a sea-coal fire.[6]
An honest, willing, kind fellow, as ever servant
shall come in house withal ; and, I warrant you, no
tell-tale, nor no breed-bate :[7] his worst fault is, that
he is given to prayer ; he is something peevish that
way ; but nobody but has his fault ;—but let that
pass. Peter Simple, you say your name is ?

*Sim.* Ay, for fault of a better.

*Quick.* And master Slender's your master ?

*Sim.* Ay, forsooth.

---

[3] *I will* incense *Page, &c.*] i. e. instigate.
[4] —— yellowness,] *Yellowness* is jealousy.
[5] —— *the revolt of* mien —] i. e. *change of countenance.*
[6] —— *at the latter end, &c.*] When my master is in bed.
[7] —— *no breed-*bate :] *Bate* is an obsolete word, signifying
strife, contention.

*Quick.* Does he not wear a great round beard, like a glover's paring knife?

*Sim.* No, forsooth : he hath but a little wee face,[8] with a little yellow beard ; a Cain-coloured beard.[9]

*Quick.* A softly-sprighted man, is he not?

*Sim.* Ay, forsooth : but he is as tall a man of his hands, as any is between this and his head ; he hath fought with a warrener.

*Quick.* How say you?—O, I should remember him ; Does he not hold up his head, as it were? and strut in his gait?

*Sim.* Yes, indeed, does he.

*Quick.* Well, heaven send Anne Page no worse fortune ! Tell master parson Evans, I will do what I can for your master : Anne is a good girl, and I wish——

### *Re-enter* RUGBY.

*Rug.* Out, alas! here comes my master.

*Quick.* We shall all be shent:[1] Run in here, good young man ; go into this closet.  [*Shuts* SIMPLE *in the closet.*]   He will not stay long.——What, John Rugby! John, what John, I say !——Go, John, go enquire for my master; I doubt, he be not well, that he comes not home :——*and down, down, adown-a,* &c.                                         [*Sings.*

### *Enter Doctor* CAIUS.[2]

*Caius.* Vat is you sing? I do not like dese toys ; Pray you, go and vetch me in my closet *un boîtier*

---

8 —— *a little* wee *face,*]   *Wee,* in the north, signifies very little.

9 —— *a* Cain-*coloured beard.*]   Cain and Judas, in the tapestries and pictures of old, were represented with *yellow* beards.

1 *We shall all be* shent :]   i. e. Scolded, roughly treated.

2 *Enter Doctor* Caius.]   It has been thought strange that our author should take the name of *Caius* [an eminent physician, who flourished in the reign of Elizabeth, and founder of Caius College

*verd;* a box, a green-a box; Do intend vat I speak? a green-a box.

*Quick.* Ay, forsooth, I'll fetch it you. I am glad he went not in himself: if he had found the young man, he would have been horn-mad. [*Aside.*

*Caius. Fe, fe, fe, fe! ma foi, il fait fort chaud. Je m'en vais à la Cour,—la grande affaire.*

*Quick.* Is it this, sir?

*Caius. Ouy; mette le au mon* pocket; *Depeche,* quickly:—Vere is dat knave Rugby?

*Quick.* What, John Rugby! John!

*Rug.* Here, sir.

*Caius.* You are John Rugby, and you are Jack Rugby: Come, take-a your rapier, and come after my heel to de court.

*Rug.* 'Tis ready, sir, here in the porch.

*Caius.* By my trot, I tarry too long:—Od's me! *Qu'ay j'oublié?* dere is some simples in my closet, dat I vill not for the varld I shall leave behind.

*Quick.* Ah me! he'll find the young man there, and be mad!

*Caius. O diable, diable!* vat is in my closet?— Villainy! *larron!* [*Pulling* SIMPLE *out.*] Rugby, my rapier.

*Quick.* Good master, be content.

*Caius.* Verefore shall I be content-a?

*Quick.* The young man is an honest man.

*Caius.* Vat shall de honest man do in my closet? dere is no honest man dat shall come into my closet.

*Quick.* I beseech you, be not so flegmatick; hear the truth of it: He came of an errand to me from parson Hugh.

in our University] for his Frenchman in this comedy; but Shakspeare was little acquainted with literary history; and without doubt, from this unusual name, supposed him to have been a foreign quack. Add to this, that the doctor was handed down as a kind of Rosicrucian: Mr. Ames had in MS. one of the " *Secret Writings of Dr. Caius.*" FARMER.

*Caius.* Vell.

*Sim.* Ay, forsooth, to desire her to—

*Quick.* Peace, I pray you.

*Caius.* Peace-a your tongue :—Speak-a your tale.

*Sim.* To desire this honest gentlewoman, your maid, to speak a good word to Mrs. Anne Page for my master, in the way of marriage.

*Quick.* This is all, indeed, la ; but I'll ne'er put my finger in the fire, and need not.

*Caius.* Sir Hugh send-a you ?—Rugby, *baillez* me some paper : Tarry you a little-a while. [*Writes.*

*Quick.* I am glad he is so quiet : if he had been thoroughly moved, you should have heard him so loud, and so melancholy ;—But notwithstanding, man, I'll do your master what good I can : and the very yea and the no is, the French doctor, my master,—I may call him my master, look you, for I keep his house ; and I wash, wring, brew, bake, scour, dress meat and drink, make the beds, and do all myself :—

*Sim.* 'Tis a great charge, to come under one body's hand.

*Quick.* Are you avis'd o'that ? you shall find it a great charge : and to be up early and down late ;— but notwithstanding, (to tell you in your ear ; I would have no words of it ;) my master himself is in love with mistress Anne Page : but notwithstanding that,—I know Anne's mind,—that's neither here nor there.

*Caius.* You jack'nape ; give-a dis letter to sir Hugh ; by gar, it is a shallenge : I vill cut his troat in de park ; and I vill teach a scurvy jack-a-nape priest to meddle or make :—you may be gone ; it is not good you tarry here :—by gar, I vill cut all his two stones ; by gar he shall not have a stone to trow at his dog. [*Exit* SIMPLE.

*Quick.* Alas, he speaks but for his friend.

*Caius.* It is no matter-a for dat :—do not you tell-a me dat I shall have Anne Page for myself ?—by gar, I vill kill de Jack Priest ;³ and I have appointed mine host of *de Jarterre* to measure our weapon :—by gar, I vill myself have Anne Page.

*Quick.* Sir, the maid loves you, and all shall be well : we must give folks leave to prate : What, the good-jer !⁴

*Caius.* Rugby, come to de court vit me :—By gar, if I have not Anne Page, I shall turn your head out of my door :—Follow my heels, Rugby.

[*Exeunt* CAIUS *and* RUGBY.

*Quick.* You shall have An fools-head of your own. No, I know Anne's mind for that : never a woman in Windsor knows more of Anne's mind than I do ; nor can do more than I do with her, I thank heaven.

*Fent.* [*Within.*] Who's within there, ho ?

*Quick.* Who's there, I trow ? Come near the house, I pray you,


*Enter* FENTON.


*Fent.* How now, good woman ; how dost thou ?

*Quick.* The better, that it pleases your good worship to ask.

*Fent.* What news ? how does pretty mistress Anne ?

*Quick.* In truth, sir, and she is pretty, and honest, and gentle ; and one that is your friend, I can tell you that by the way ; I praise heaven for it.


³ —— *de Jack priest ;*] *Jack,* in our author's time, was a term of contempt : So, saucy *Jack,* &c.

⁴ *What, the* good-jer !] *Good-jer* and *Good-year,* were in our author's time common corruptions of *goujere ;* i. e. *morbus Gallicus.*

*Fent.* Shall I do any good, thinkest thou ? Shall I not lose my suit ?

*Quick.* Troth, sir, all is in his hands above : but notwithstanding, master Fenton, I'll be sworn on a book, she loves you :—Have not your worship a wart above your eye ?

*Fent.* Yes, marry, have I ; what of that ?

*Quick.* Well, thereby hangs a tale ;—good faith, it is such another Nan ;—but, I detest,[5] an honest maid as ever broke bread :—We had an hour's talk of that wart ;—I shall never laugh but in that maid's company !—But, indeed, she is given too much to allicholly,[6] and musing : But for you—Well, go to.

*Fent.* Well, I shall see her to-day ; Hold, there's money for thee ; let me have thy voice in my behalf : if thou seest her before me, commend me—

*Quick.* Will I ? i'faith, that we will : and I will tell your worship more of the wart, the next time we have confidence ; and of other wooers.

*Fent.* Well, farewell ; I am in great haste now.
[*Exit.*

*Quick.* Farewell to your worship.—Truly, an honest gentleman ; but Anne loves him not ; for I know Anne's mind as well as another does :—Out upon't ! what have I forgot ? [*Exit.*

---

[5] —— *but,* I detest,] She means—I *protest.*
[6] —— *to* allicholly —] i. e. melancholy.

## ACT II.

*SCENE I.* *Before* Page's House.

*Enter Mistress* Page, *with a letter.*

*Mrs. Page.* What! have I 'scap'd love-letters in the holy-day time of my beauty, and am I now a subject for them? Let me see:       [*Reads.*

*Ask me no reason why I love you; for though love use reason for his precisian, he admits him not for his counsellor:*[7] *You are not young, no more am I; go to then, there's sympathy: you are merry, so am I; Ha! ha! then there's more sympathy: you love sack, and so do I; Would you desire better sympathy? Let it suffice thee, mistress Page, (at the least, if the love of a soldier can suffice,) that I love thee. I will not say, pity me, 'tis not a soldier-like phrase; but I say, love me. By me,*

    *Thine own true knight,*
    *By day or night,*
    *Or any kind of light,*
    *With all his might,*
    *For thee to fight,*       John Falstaff.

What a Herod of Jewry is this?—O wicked, wicked world!—one that is well nigh worn to pieces with age, to show himself a young gallant! What an unweighed behaviour hath this Flemish drunkard

---

7 —— *though love use reason for his* precisian, *he admits him not for his counsellor:*] By *precisian,* is meant one who pretends to a more than ordinary degree of virtue and sanctity. Dr. Johnson wishes to read *physician;* and if that be right, the meaning may be,—a lover, uncertain as yet of success, never takes reason for his counsellor, but, when desperate, applies to him as his physician.

picked (with the devil's name) out of my conversation, that he dares in this manner assay me? Why, he hath not been thrice in my company!—What should I say to him?—I was then frugal of my mirth:—heaven forgive me!—Why, I'll exhibit a bill in the parliament for the putting down of men. How shall I be revenged on him? for revenged I will be, as sure as his guts are made of puddings.

*Enter Mistress* FORD.

*Mrs. Ford.* Mistress Page! trust me I was going to your house.

*Mrs. Page.* And, trust me, I was coming to you. You look very ill.

*Mrs. Ford.* Nay, I'll ne'er believe that; I have to show to the contrary.

*Mrs. Page.* 'Faith, but you do, in my mind.

*Mrs. Ford.* Well, I do then; yet, I say, I could show you to the contrary: O, mistress Page, give me some counsel!

*Mrs. Page.* What's the matter, woman?

*Mrs. Ford.* O woman, if it were not for one trifling respect, I could come to such honour!

*Mrs. Page.* Hang the trifle, woman; take the honour: What is it?——dispense with trifles;—what is it?

*Mrs. Ford.* If I would but go to hell for an eternal moment, or so, I could be knighted.

*Mrs. Page.* What?——thou liest!—Sir Alice Ford!——These knights will hack; and so thou shouldst not alter the article of thy gentry.[8]

---

[8] *What?—thou liest!—Sir Alice Ford!—These knights will hack; and so thou shouldst not alter the article of thy gentry.*] These knights will *hack* (that is, become cheap or vulgar,) and therefore she advises her friend not to sully her gentry by becoming one. Between the time of king James's arrival at Berwick in April 1603, and the 2d of May, he made two hundred and thirty-

*Mrs. Ford.* We burn day-light:⁹—here, read, read;—perceive how I might be knighted.—I shall think the worse of fat men, as long as I have an eye to make difference of men's liking:¹ And yet he would not swear; praised women's modesty: And gave such orderly and well-behaved reproof to all uncomeliness, that I would have sworn his disposition would have gone to the truth of his words: but they do no more adhere and keep place together than the hundredth psalm to the tune of *Green sleeves.* What tempest, I trow, threw this whale with so many tuns of oil in his belly, ashore at Windsor? How shall I be revenged on him? I think the best way were to entertain him with hope, till the wicked fire of lust have melted him in his own grease.—Did you ever hear the like?

*Mrs. Page.* Letter for letter; but that the name of Page and Ford differs!—To thy great comfort in this mystery of ill opinions, here's the twin-brother of thy letter: but let thine inherit first; for, I protest, mine never shall. I warrant, he hath a thousand of these letters, writ with blank space for different names, (sure more,) and these are of the second edition: He will print them out of doubt; for he cares not what he puts into the press, when he would put us two. I had rather be a giantess, and lie under mount Pelion. Well, I will find you twenty lascivious turtles, ere one chaste man.

*Mrs. Ford.* Why this is the very same; the very hand, the very words: What doth he think of us?

seven knights; and in the July following between three and four hundred. It is probable that the play before us was enlarged in that or the subsequent year, when this stroke of satire must have been highly relished by the audience. MALONE.

⁹ *We burn day-light :*] i. e. we have more proof than we want; or, we are wasting time in idle talk.

¹ —— *men's* liking :] i. e. men's condition of body.

*Mrs. Page.* Nay, I know not : It makes me almost ready to wrangle with mine own honesty. I'll entertain myself like one that I am not acquainted withal ; for, sure, unless he know some strain in me, that I know not myself, he would never have boarded me in this fury.

*Mrs. Ford.* Boarding, call you it ? I'll be sure to keep him above deck.

*Mrs. Page.* So will I ; if he come under my hatches, I'll never to sea again. Let's be reveng'd on him : let's appoint him a meeting ; give him a show of comfort in his suit ; and lead him on with a fine-baited delay, till he hath pawn'd his horses to mine Host of the Garter.

*Mrs. Ford.* Nay, I will consent to act any villainy against him, that may not sully the chariness of our honesty.² O, that my husband saw this letter ! it would give eternal food to his jealousy.

*Mrs. Page.* Why, look, where he comes ; and my good man too ; he's as far from jealousy, as I am from giving him cause ; and that, I hope, is an unmeasurable distance.

*Mrs. Ford.* You are the happier woman.

*Mrs. Page.* Let's consult together against this greasy knight : Come hither.          [*They retire.*


*Enter* FORD, PISTOL, PAGE, *and* NYM.

*Ford.* Well, I hope, it be not so.

*Pist.* Hope is a curtail dog³ in some affairs :
Sir John affects thy wife.

*Ford.* Why, sir, my wife is not young.

---

² ——— *the* chariness ——] i. e. the *caution.*
³ ——— *curtail dog* ——] That is, a dog that misses his game ; or is, a dog of small value ;——a *cur.*

*Pist.* He wooes both high and low, both rich and
  poor,
Both young and old, one with another, Ford;
He loves thy gally-mawfry;[4] Ford, perpend.

*Ford.* Love my wife?

*Pist.* With liver burning hot: Prevent, or go
  thou,
Like sir Actæon he, with Ring-wood at thy
  heels:——
O, odious is the name!

*Ford.* What name, sir?

*Pist.* The horn, I say: Farewell.
Take heed; have open eye; for thieves do foot by
  night:
Take heed, ere summer comes, or cuckoo birds do
  sing.——
Away, sir corporal Nym.——
Believe it, Page; he speaks sense.  [*Exit* PISTOL.

*Ford.* I will be patient; I will find out this.

*Nym.* And this is true; [*to* PAGE.] I like not the
humour of lying. He hath wronged me in some
humours: I should have borne the humoured letter
to her; but I have a sword, and it shall bite upon
my necessity. He loves your wife; there's the short
and the long. My name is corporal Nym; I speak,
and I avouch. 'Tis true:——my name is Nym, and
Falstaff loves your wife.——Adieu! I love not the
humour of bread and cheese; and there's the humour of it. Adieu.  [*Exit* NYM.

*Page.* *The humour of it*, quoth 'a! here's a fellow frights humour out of his wits.

*Ford.* I will seek out Falstaff.

*Page.* I never heard such a drawling, affecting
rogue.

*Ford.* If I do find it, well.

---

[4] —— *gally-mawfry;*] i. e. a medley.

*Page.* I will not believe such a Cataian,⁵ though
the priest o' the town commended him for a true
man.

*Ford.* 'Twas a good sensible fellow :⁶ Well.

*Page.* How now, Meg?

*Mrs. Page.* Whither go you, George?—Hark
you.

*Mrs. Ford.* How now, sweet Frank? why art
thou melancholy?

*Ford.* I melancholy! I am not melancholy.—
Get you home, go.

*Mrs. Ford.* 'Faith, thou hast some crotchets in
thy head now.—Will you go, mistress Page?

*Mrs. Page.* Have with you.—You'll come to
dinner, George?—Look, who comes yonder: she
shall be our messenger to this paltry knight.

[*Aside to Mrs.* FORD.

*Enter Mrs.* QUICKLY.

*Mrs. Ford.* Trust me, I thought on her: she'll
fit it.

*Mrs. Page.* You are come to see my daughter
Anne?

*Quick.* Ay, forsooth; And, I pray, how does
good mistress Anne?

*Mrs. Page.* Go in with us, and see; we have an
hour's talk with you.

[*Exeunt Mrs.* PAGE, *Mrs.* FORD, *and Mrs.*
QUICKLY.

*Page.* How now, master Ford?

*Ford.* You heard what this knave told me; did
you not?

⁵ *I will not believe such a* Cataian,] By a Cataian, some kind
of sharper is meant. The Chinese were anciently called Ca-
taians. Their tricks are hinted at in some old histories of Catai.

⁶ *'Twas a good sensible fellow :*] This, and the two preceding
speeches of Ford, are spoken to himself.

*Page.* Yes ; And you heard what the other told me ?

*Ford.* Do you think there is truth in them ?

*Page.* Hang 'em, slaves ; I do not think the knight would offer it : but these that accuse him in his intent towards our wives, are a yoke of his discarded men : very rogues, now they be out of service.

*Ford.* Were they his men ?

*Page.* Marry, were they.

*Ford.* I like it never the better for that.—Does he lie at the Garter ?

*Page.* Ay, marry, does he. If he should intend this voyage towards my wife, I would turn her loose to him ; and what he gets of her more than sharp words, let it lie on my head.

*Ford.* I do not misdoubt my wife ; but I would be loth to turn them together : A man may be too confident : I would have nothing lie on my head : I cannot be thus satisfied.

*Page.* Look, where my ranting host of the Garter comes : there is either liquor in his pate, or money in his purse, when he looks so merrily.—How now, mine host ?

*Enter* Host, *and* Shallow.

*Host.* How now, bully-rook ! thou'rt a gentleman : cavalero-justice,[7] I say.

*Shal.* I follow, mine host, I follow.—Good even, and twenty, good master Page ! Master Page, will you go with us ? we have sport in hand.

*Host.* Tell him, cavalero-justice ; tell him, bully-rook.

*Shal.* Sir, there is a fray to be fought, between

[7] —— cavalero-*justice*,] A cant term.

sir Hugh the Welsh priest, and Caius the French doctor.

*Ford.* Good mine host o' the Garter, a word with you.

*Host.* What say'st thou, bully-rook?

> [*They go aside.*

*Shal.* Will you [*to* PAGE] go with us to behold it? My merry host hath had the measuring of their weapons; and, I think, he hath appointed them contrary places: for, believe me, I hear, the parson is no jester. Hark, I will tell you what our sport shall be.

*Host.* Hast thou no suit against my knight, my guest-cavalier?

*Ford.* None, I protest: but I'll give you a pottle of burnt sack to give me recourse to him, and tell him, my name is Brook; only for a jest.

*Host.* My hand, bully: thou shalt have egress and regress; said I well? and thy name shall be Brook: It is a merry knight.—Will you go on, hearts?

*Shal.* Have with you, mine host.

*Page.* I have heard, the Frenchman hath good skill in his rapier.

*Shal.* Tut, sir, I could have told you more: In these times you stand on distance, your passes, stoccadoes, and I know not what: 'tis the heart, master Page; 'tis here, 'tis here. I have seen the time, with my long sword, I would have made you four tall fellows[8] skip like rats.

*Host.* Here, boys, here, here! shall we wag?

*Page.* Have with you:—I had rather hear them scold than fight.

> [*Exeunt* HOST, SHALLOW, *and* PAGE.

---

[8] —— tall *fellows* —] A *tall fellow*, in the time of our author, meant a stout, bold, or courageous person.

*Ford.* Though Page be a secure fool, and stands so firmly on his wife's frailty,[9] yet I cannot put off my opinion so easily : She was in his company at Page's house ; and, what they made there,[1] I know not. Well, I will look further into't : and I have a disguise to sound Falstaff : If I find her honest, I lose not my labour ; if she be otherwise, 'tis labour well bestowed. [*Exit.*

## SCENE II.

*A Room in the Garter Inn.*

*Enter* FALSTAFF *and* PISTOL.

*Fal.* I will not lend thee a penny.

*Pist.* Why, then the world's mine oyster, Which I with sword will open.—
I will retort the sum in equipage.[2]

*Fal.* Not a penny, I have been content, sir, you should lay my countenance to pawn : I have grated upon my good friends for three reprieves for you and your coach-fellow, Nym ;[3] or else you had looked through the grate, like a geminy of baboons. I am damned in hell, for swearing to gentlemen my friends, you were good soldiers, and tall fellows: and when mistress Bridget lost the handle of her fan,[4] I took't upon mine honour thou hadst it not.

---

[9] —— *and stands so firmly on his wife's frailty,*] i. e. has such perfect confidence in his unchaste wife.

[1] —— *and, what they* made *there,*] An obsolete phrase signifying—what they *did* there. MALONE.

[2] *I will retort the sum in* equipage.] Means, I will pay you again in stolen goods. WARBURTON.

[3] —— *your* coach-fellow, *Nym ;*] i. e. he, who *draws* along with you ; who is joined with you in all your knavery.

[4] —— *lost the handle of her fan,*] It should be remembered, that *fans,* in our author's time, were more costly than they are at present, as well as of a different construction. They consisted of ostrich feathers, (or others of equal length and flexibility,)

9

*Pist.* Didst thou not share ? hadst thou not fifteen pence ?

*Fal.* Reason, you rogue, reason : Think'st thou I'll endanger my soul *gratis ?* At a word, hang no more about me, I am no gibbet for you :—go.—A short knife and a throng ;—to your manor of Pickthatch,¹ go.—You'll not bear a letter for me, you rogue !—You stand upon your honour !—Why, thou unconfinable baseness, it is as much as I can do, to keep the terms of my honour precise. I, I, I myself sometimes, leaving the fear of heaven on the left hand, and hiding mine honour in my necessity, am fain to shuffle, to hedge, and to lurch ; and yet you, rogue, will ensconce your rags,⁶ your cat-a-mountain looks, your red-lattice phrases,⁷ and your bold-beating oaths, under the shelter of your honour ! You will not do it, you ?

*Pist.* I do relent ; What would'st thou more of man ?

### *Enter* ROBIN.

*Rob.* Sir, here's a woman would speak with you.
*Fal.* Let her approach.

### *Enter Mistress* QUICKLY.

*Quick.* Give your worship good-morrow.
*Fal.* Good-morrow, good wife.
*Quick.* Not so, an't please your worship.
*Fal.* Good maid, then.

which were stuck into handles. The richer sort of these were composed of gold, silver, or ivory of curious workmanship.

¹ —— *Pickt-hatch,*] A cant name for some part of the town noted for brothels.

⁶ —— ensconce *your rags,* &c.] A *sconce* is a petty fortification. To *ensconce,* therefore, is to protect as with a fort.

⁷ —— red-lattice *phrases,*] Your ale-house conversation. *Red lattice* at the doors and windows, were formerly the external denotements of an alehouse.

*Quick.* I'll be sworn; as my mother was, the first hour I was born.

*Fal.* I do believe the swearer: What with me?

*Quick.* Shall I vouchsafe your worship a word or two?

*Fal.* Two thousand, fair woman: and I'll vouchsafe thee the hearing.

*Quick.* There is one mistress Ford, sir ;—I pray, come a little nearer this ways :—I myself dwell with master doctor Caius.

*Fal.* Well, on: Mistress Ford, you say,——

*Quick.* Your worship says very true: I pray your worship, come a little nearer this ways.

*Fal.* I warrant thee, nobody hears ;—mine own people, mine own people.

*Quick.* Are they so? Heaven bless them, and make them his servants!

*Fal.* Well: Mistress Ford ;—what of her?

*Quick.* Why, sir, she's a good creature. Lord, lord! your worship's a wanton: Well, heaven forgive you, and all of us, I pray!

*Fal.* Mistress Ford ;——come, mistress Ford,——

*Quick.* Marry, this is the short and the long of it; you have brought her into such a canaries,* as 'tis wonderful. The best courtier of them all, when the court lay at Windsor, could never have brought her to such a canary. Yet there has been knights, and lords, and gentlemen, with their coaches; I warrant you, coach after coach, letter after letter, gift after gift; smelling so sweetly, (all musk) and so rushling, I warrant you, in silk and gold; and in such alligant terms; and in such wine and sugar of the best, and the fairest, that would have won any woman's heart; and, I warrant you, they could never get an eye-wink of her.—I had myself twenty

---

* —— *canaries,*] Probably for *quandaries.*

angels given me this morning; but I defy all angels,
(in any such sort, as they say,) but in the way of honesty:—and, I warrant you, they could never get
her so much as sip on a cup with the proudest of
them all: and yet there has been earls, nay, which
is more, pensioners;[9] but, I warrant you, all is one
with her.

*Fal.* But what says she to me? be brief, my good
she Mercury.

*Quick.* Marry, she hath received your letter; for
the which she thanks you a thousand times: and
she gives you to notify, that her husband will be absence from his house between ten and eleven.

*Fal.* Ten and eleven?

*Quick.* Ay, forsooth; and then you may come
and see the picture, she says, that you wot of;[1]—
master Ford, her husband, will be from home.
Alas! the sweet woman leads an ill life with him;
he's a very jealousy man: she leads a very frampold[2]
life with him, good heart.

*Fal.* Ten and eleven: Woman, commend me to
her; I will not fail her.

*Quick.* Why, you say well: But I have another
messenger to your worship: Mistress Page hath her
hearty commendations to you too;—and let me tell
you in your ear, she's as fartuous a civil modest wife,
and one (I tell you) that will not miss you morning
nor evening prayer, as any is in Windsor, whoe'er
be the other: and she bade me tell your worship,
that her husband is seldom from home; but, she
hopes, there will come a time. I never knew a

---

[9] —— *earls, nay, which is more,* pensioners;] *Pensioners*
were Gentlemen of the band of Pensioners, whose dress was remarkably splendid, and therefore likely to attract the notice of
Mrs. Quickly.

[1] *you* wot *of;*] To *wot* is to know. Obsolete.

[2] ——*frampold* —] Peevish, fretful, or cross.

woman so dote upon a man; surely, I think you have charms, la; yes, in truth.

*Fal.* Not I, I assure thee; setting the attraction of my good parts aside, I have no other charms.

*Quick.* Blessing on your heart for't!

*Fal.* But, I pray thee, tell me this: has Ford's wife, and Page's wife, acquainted each other how they love me?

*Quick.* That were a jest, indeed!—they have not so little grace, I hope:—that were a trick, indeed! But mistress Page would desire you to send her your little page, of all loves;[3] her husband has a marvellous infection to the little page: and, truly, master Page is an honest man. Never a wife in Windsor leads a better life than she does; do what she will, say what she will, take all, pay all, go to bed when she list, rise when she list, all is as she will; and, truly, she deserves it: for if there be a kind woman in Windsor, she is one. You must send her your page: no remedy.

*Fal.* Why, I will.

*Quick.* Nay, but do so then: and, look you, he may come and go between you both; and, in any case, have a nay-word,[4] that you may know one another's mind, and the boy never need to understand any thing; for 'tis not good that children should know any wickedness: old folks, you know, have discretion, as they say, and know the world.

*Fal.* Fare thee well: commend me to them both: there's my purse; I am yet thy debtor.—Boy, go along with this woman.——This news distracts me!

[*Exeunt* QUICKLY *and* ROBIN.

*Pist.* This punk is one of Cupid's carriers:——

---

[3] —— *to send her your little page,* of all loves;] *Of all loves,* is an adjuration only, and signifies *by all means.*

[4] —— *a nay-word,*] i. e. a *watch-word.*

Clap on more sails; pursue, up with your fights;[5]
Give fire; she is my prize, or ocean whelm them
    all !                              [*Exit* PISTOL.

*Fal.* Say'st thou so, old Jack? go thy ways; I'll
make more of thy old body than I have done.   Will
they yet look after thee?   Wilt thou, after the expence of so much money, be now a gainer?   Good
body, I thank thee: Let them say, 'tis grossly done;
so it be fairly done, no matter.

*Enter* BARDOLPH.

*Bard.* Sir John, there's one master Brook below
would fain speak with you, and be acquainted with
you; and hath sent your worship a morning's draught
of sack.

*Fal.* Brook, is his name?

*Bard.* Ay, sir.

*Fal.* Call him in; [*Exit* BARDOLPH.]   Such
Brooks are welcome to me, that o'erflow such liquor.   Ah! ha! mistress Ford and mistress Page,
have I encompassed you? go to; *via!*[6]

*Re-enter* BARDOLPH, *with* FORD *disguised.*

*Ford.* Bless you, sir.

*Fal.* And you, sir: Would you speak with me?

*Ford.* I make bold, to press with so little preparation upon you.

*Fal.* You're welcome; What's your will?   Give
us leave, drawer.                    [*Exit* BARDOLPH.

*Ford.* Sir, I am a gentleman that have spent
much; my name is Brook.

---

*Fal.* Good master Brook, I desire more acquaintance of you.

*Ford.* Good sir John, I sue for yours: not to charge you;[7] for I must let you understand, I think myself in better plight for a lender than you are: the which hath something emboldened me to this unseasoned intrusion; for they say, if money go before, all ways do lie open.

*Fal.* Money is a good soldier, sir, and will on.

*Ford.* Troth, and I have a bag of money here troubles me: if you will help me to bear it, sir John, take all, or half, for easing me of the carriage.

*Fal.* Sir, I know not how I may deserve to be your porter.

*Ford.* I will tell you, sir, if you will give me the hearing.

*Fal.* Speak, good master Brook; I shall be glad to be your servant.

*Ford.* Sir, I hear you are a scholar,—I will be brief with you;———and you have been a man long known to me, though I had never so good means, as desire, to make myself acquainted with you. I shall discover a thing to you, wherein I must very much lay open mine own imperfection: but, good sir John, as you have one eye upon my follies, as you hear them unfolded, turn another into the register of your own; that I may pass with a reproof the easier, sith[8] you yourself know, how easy it is to be such an offender.

*Fal.* Very well, sir; proceed.

*Ford.* There is a gentlewoman in this town, her husband's name is Ford.

*Fal.* Well, sir.

---

[7] ——— *not to charge you;*] That is, not with a purpose of putting you to expence, or *being burthensome.* JOHNSON.

[8] ——— *sith* —] i. e. since.

*Ford.* I have long loved her, and, I protest to you, bestowed much on her; followed her with a doting observance; engrossed opportunities to meet her; fee'd every slight occasion, that could but niggardly give me sight of her; not only bought many presents to give her, but have given largely to many, to know what she would have given: briefly, I have pursued her, as love hath pursued me; which hath been, on the wing of all occasions. But whatsoever I have merited, either in my mind, or in my means, meed,[9] I am sure, I have received none; unless experience be a jewel: that I have purchased at an infinite rate; and that hath taught me to say this:

> *Love like a shadow flies, when substance love*
> *    pursues ;*
> *Pursuing that that flies, and flying what pur-*
> *    sues.*

*Fal.* Have you received no promise of satisfaction at her hands?

*Ford.* Never.

*Fal.* Have you importuned her to such a purpose?

*Ford.* Never.

*Fal.* Of what quality was your love then?

*Ford.* Like a fair house, built upon another man's ground; so that I have lost my edifice, by mistaking the place where I erected it.

*Fal.* To what purpose have you unfolded this to me?

*Ford.* When I have told you that, I have told you all. Some say, that, though she appear honest to me, yet, in other places, she enlargeth her mirth so far, that there is shrewd construction made of her. Now, sir John, here is the heart of my pur-

---

9 —— *meed,*] i. e. reward.

pose! You are a gentleman of excellent breeding, admirable discourse, of great admittance,[1] authentick in your place and person, generally allowed[2] for your many war-like, court-like, and learned preparations.

*Fal.* O, sir!

*Ford.* Believe it, for you know it:—There is money; spend it, spend it; spend more; spend all I have; only give me so much of your time in exchange of it, as to lay an amiable siege[3] to the honesty of this Ford's wife: use your art of wooing, win her to consent to you; if any man may, you may as soon as any.

*Fal.* Would it apply well to the vehemency of your affection, that I should win what you would enjoy? Methinks, you prescribe to yourself very preposterously.

*Ford.* O, understand my drift! she dwells so securely on the excellency of her honour, that the folly of my soul dares not present itself; she is too bright to be looked against. Now, could I come to her with any detection in my hand, my desires had instance and argument[4] to commend themselves; I could drive her then from the ward of her purity,[5] her reputation, her marriage vow, and a thousand other her defences, which now are too strongly embattled against me: What say you to't, sir John?

*Fal.* Master Brook, I will first make bold with your money; next, give me your hand; and last, as I am a gentleman, you shall, if you will, enjoy Ford's wife.

---

[1] —— *of* great admittance,] Admitted to all companies,
[2] —— *generally* allowed —] *Allowed* is *approved.*
[3] —— *to lay an* amiable *siege* —] i. e. a siege of love.
[4] —— instance *and argument* —] *Instance* is *example.*

JOHNSON

[5] —— *the* ward *of her purity,*] i. e. The *defence* of it.

*Ford.* O good sir!

*Fal.* Master Brook, I say you shall.

*Ford.* Want no money, sir John, you shall want none.

*Fal.* Want no mistress Ford, master Brook, you shall want none. I shall be with her, (I may tell you,) by her own appointment; even as you came in to me, her assistant, or go-between, parted from me: I say, I shall be with her between ten and eleven; for at that time the jealous rascally knave, her husband, will be forth. Come you to me at night; you shall know how I speed.

*Ford.* I am blest in your acquaintance. Do you know Ford, sir?

*Fal.* Hang him, poor cuckoldly knave! I know him not:—yet I wrong him, to call him poor; they say, the jealous wittolly knave hath masses of money; for the which his wife seems to me well-favoured. I will use her as the key of the cuckoldly rogue's coffer; and there's my harvest-home.

*Ford.* I would you knew Ford, sir; that you might avoid him, if you saw him.

*Fal.* Hang him, mechanical salt-butter rogue! I will stare him out of his wits; I will awe him with my cudgel: it shall hang like a meteor o'er the cuckold's horns: master Brook, thou shalt know, I will predominate o'er the peasant, and thou shalt lie with his wife.—Come to me soon at night:— Ford's a knave, and I will aggravate his stile;[6] thou, master Brook, shalt know him for a knave and cuckold:—come to me soon at night.     [*Exit.*

   *Ford.* What a damned Epicurean rascal is this! —My heart is ready to crack with impatience.— Who says, this is improvident jealousy? My wife hath sent to him, the hour is fixed, the match

---

[6] —— *and I will aggravate his* stile;] *Add more titles to those he already enjoys.*

9

is made. Would any man have thought this?— See the hell of having a false woman! my bed shall be abused, my coffers ransacked, my reputation gnawn at; and I shall not only receive this villainous wrong, but stand under the adoption of abominable terms, and by him that does me this wrong. Terms! names!——Amaimon sounds well; Lucifer, well; Barbason,[7] well; yet they are devils' additions, the names of fiends: but cuckold! wittol-cuckold![8] the devil himself hath not such a name. Page is an ass, a secure ass; he will trust his wife, he will not be jealous; I will rather trust a Fleming with my butter, parson Hugh the Welchman with my cheese, an Irishman with my aqua-vitæ bottle, or a thief to walk my ambling gelding, than my wife with herself: then she plots, then she ruminates, then she devises: and what they think in their hearts they may effect, they will break their hearts but they will effect. Heaven be praised for my jealousy!—Eleven o'clock the hour;—I will prevent this, detect my wife, be revenged on Falstaff, and laugh at Page. I will about it; better three hours too soon, than a minute too late. Fie, fie, fie! cuckold! cuckold! cuckold! [*Exit.*

---

[7] —— *Amaimon—Barbason,*] The reader who is curious to know any particulars concerning these dæmons, may find them in Reginald Scott's *Inventarie of the Names, Shapes, Powers, Governments, and Effects of Devils and Spirits, of their several Segnories and Degrees.*

[8] —— wittol-*cuckold!*] One who knows his wife's falsehood, and is contented with it:—from *wittan,* Sax. to know.

## SCENE III.

### *Windsor Park.*

#### Enter CAIUS *and* RUGBY.

*Caius.* Jack Rugby!

*Rug.* Sir.

*Caius.* Vat is de clock, Jack?

*Rug.* 'Tis past the hour, sir, that sir Hugh promised to meet.

*Caius.* By gar, he has save his soul, dat he is no come; he has pray his Pible vell, dat he is no come: by gar, Jack Rugby, he is dead already, if he be come.

*Rug.* He is wise, sir; he knew, your worship would kill him, if he came.

*Caius.* By gar, de herring is no dead, so as I vill kill him. Take your rapier, Jack; I vill tell you how I vill kill him.

*Rug.* Alas, sir, I cannot fence.

*Caius.* Villainy, take your rapier.

*Rug.* Forbear; here's company.

#### Enter HOST, SHALLOW, SLENDER, *and* PAGE.

*Host.* 'Bless thee, bully doctor.

*Shal.* Save you, master doctor Caius.

*Page.* Now, good master doctor!

*Slen.* Give you good-morrow, sir.

*Caius.* Vat be all you, one, two, tree, four, come for?

*Host.* To see thee fight, to see thee foin,⁹ to see thee traverse, to see thee here, to see thee there;

---

⁹ —— *to see thee* foin,] To *foin* was the ancient term for making a thrust in fencing, or tilting.

to see thee pass thy punto, thy stock,[1] thy reverse,
thy distance, thy montánt. Is he dead, my Ethio-
pian? is he dead, my Francisco?[2] ha, bully!
What says my Æsculapius? my Galen? my heart
of elder?[3] ha! is he dead, bully Stale? is he
dead?

*Caius.* By gar, he is de coward Jack priest of the
vorld; he is not show his face.

*Host.* Thou art a Castilian[4] king, Urinal, Hector of Greece, my boy?

*Caius.* I pray you, bear vitness that me have stay
six or seven, two, tree hours for him, and he is no
come.

*Shal.* He is the wiser man, master doctor: he is
a curer of souls, and you a curer of bodies; if you
should fight, you go against the hair[5] of your professions; is it not true, master Page.

*Page.* Master Shallow, you have yourself been a
great fighter, though now a man of peace.

*Shal.* Bodykins, master Page, though I now be
old, and of the peace, if I see a sword out, my
finger itches to make one: though we are justices,
and doctors, and churchmen, master Page, we have
some salt of our youth in us; we are the sons of
women, master Page.

*Page.* 'Tis true, master Shallow.

*Shal.* It will be found so, master Page. Master
doctor Caius, I am come to fetch you home. I am
sworn of the peace; you have showed yourself a

---

[1] —— *thy* stock,] Stock is a corruption of *stocata*, Ital. from
which language the technical terms that follow are likewise adopted.

[2] —— *my* Francisco?] He means, my Frenchman.

[3] —— *my heart of elder?*] It should be remembered, to make
this joke relish, that the *elder* tree has *no heart*.

[4] —— *Castilian* ——] An opprobrious term, and perhaps a popular slur upon the Spaniards, who were held in great contempt
after the business of the Armada.

[5] —— *against the* hair, &c.] We now say against the *grain*.

wise physician, and sir Hugh hath shown himself a wise and patient churchman : you must go with me, master doctor.

*Host.* Pardon, guest justice :——A word, monsieur Muck-water.[6]

*Caius.* Muck-vater ! vat is dat ?

*Host.* Muck-water, in our English tongue, is valour, bully.

*Caius.* By gar, then I have as much muck-vater as de Englishman :——Scurvy jack-dog priest ! by gar, me vill cut his ears.

*Host.* He will clapper-claw thee tightly, bully.

*Caius.* Clapper-de-claw ! vat is dat ?

*Host.* That is, he will make thee amends.

*Caius.* By gar, me do look, he shall clapper-de claw me ; for, by gar, me vill have it.

*Host.* And I will provoke him to't, or let him wag.

*Caius.* Me tank you for dat.

*Host.* And moreover, bully,——But first, master guest, and master Page, and eke cavalero Slender, go you through the town to Frogmore. [*Aside to them.*

*Page.* Sir Hugh is there, is he ?

*Host.* He is there: see what humour he is in ; and I will bring the doctor about by the fields : will it do well ?

*Shal.* We will do it.

*Page. Shal. and Slen.* Adieu, good master doctor. [*Exeunt* PAGE, SHALLOW, *and* SLENDER.

*Caius.* By gar, me vill kill de priest; for he speak for a jack-an-ape to Anne Page.

*Host.* Let him die : but, first, sheath thy impatience; throw cold water on thy choler: go about the fields 'with me through Frogmore; I will bring thee where mistress Anne Page is, at a farm-house a feasting : and thou shall woo her: Cry'd game, said I well ?[7]

---

6 —— *Muck-water.*] i. e. drain of a dung-hill.
7 —— cry'd game, *said I well?*] An exclamation of encouragement.

*Caius.* By gar, me tank you for dat : by gar, I love you ; and I shall procure-a you de good guest, de earl, de knight, de lords, de gentlemen, my patients.

*Host.* For the which, I will be thy adversary towards Anne Page ; said I well ?

*Caius.* By gar, 'tis good ; vell said.

*Host.* Let us wag then.

*Caius.* Come at my heels, Jack Rugby.

[*Exeunt.*

## ACT III.

### SCENE I. *A Field near Frogmore.*

#### Enter *Sir* HUGH EVANS *and* SIMPLE.

*Eva.* I pray you now, good master Slender's serving-man, and friend Simple by your name, which way have you looked for master Caius, that calls himself *Doctor of Physick?*

*Sim.* Marry, sir, the city-ward,ᵃ the park-ward, every way ; old Windsor way, and every way but the town way.

*Eva.* I most fehemently desire you, you will also look that way.

*Sim.* I will, sir.

*Eva.* 'Pless my soul! how full of cholers I am. and trempling of mind !—I shall be glad, if he have deceived me :—how melancholies I am !—I will knog his urinals about his knave's costard, when I have good opportunities for the 'ork —'pless my soul! [*Sings.*

ᵃ —— *the* city-ward,] i. e. towards London.

> *To shallow rivers,[9] to whose falls*
> *Melodious birds sings madrigals ;*
> *There will we make our peds of roses,*
> *And a thousand fagrant posies.*
> *To shallow——*

'Mercy on me! I have a great dispositions to cry.

> *Melodious birds sing madrigals :——*
> *When as I sat in Pabylon,——*
> *And a thousand vagram posies.*
> *To shallow——*

*Sim.* Yonder he is coming, this way, sir Hugh.
*Eva.* He's welcome :——

> *To Shallow rivers, to whose falls——*

Heaven prosper the right!—What weapons is he?
*Sim.* No weapons, sir : There comes my master, master Shallow, and another gentleman from Frogmore, over the stile, this way.

*Eva.* Pray you, give me my gown ; or else keep it in your arms.

*Enter* PAGE, SHALLOW, *and* SLENDER.

*Shal.* How now, master parson? Good-morrow, good sir Hugh. Keep a gamester from the dice, and a good student from his book, and it is wonderful.

*Slen.* Ah, sweet Anne Page!
*Page.* Save you, good sir Hugh!
*Eva.* 'Pless you from his mercy sake, all of you!
*Shal.* What! the sword and the word! do you study them both, master parson?

---

[9] *To shallow rivers,* &c.] `This is part of a beautiful little poem, by Marlowe.

*Page.* And youthful still, in your doublet and hose, this raw rheumatick day?

*Eva.* There is reasons and causes for it.

*Page.* We are come to you, to do a good office, master parson.

*Eva.* Fery well: What is it?

*Page.* Yonder is a most reverend gentleman, who belike, having received wrong by some person, is at most odds with his own gravity and patience, that ever you saw.

*Shal.* I have lived fourscore years, and upward; I never heard a man of his place, gravity, and learning, so wide of his own respect.

*Eva.* What is he?

*Page.* I think you know him; master doctor Caius, the renowned French Physician.

*Eva.* Got's will, and his passion of my heart! I had as lief you would tell me of a mess of porridge.

*Page.* Why?

*Eva.* He has no more knowledge in Hibocrates and Galen,—and he is a knave besides; a cowardly knave, as you would desires to be acquainted withal.

*Page.* I warrant you, he's the man should fight with him.

*Slen.* O, sweet Anne Page!

*Shal.* It appears so, by his weapons:—Keep them asunder;—here comes doctor Caius.

*Enter* Host, Caius, *and* Rugby.

*Page.* Nay, good master parson, keep in your weapon.

*Shal.* So do you, good master doctor.

*Host.* Disarm them, and let them question; let them keep their limbs whole, and hack our English.

*Caius.* I pray you, let-a me speak a word vit your ear: Verefore vill you not meet a-me?

*Eva.* Pray you, use your patience: In good time.

*Caius.* By gar, you are de coward, de Jack dog, John ape.

*Eva.* Pray you let us not be laughing-stogs to other men's humours; I desire you in friendship, and I will one way or other make you amends:—I will knog your urinals about your knave's cogscomb, for missing your meetings and appointments.

*Caius.* *Diable!*—Jack Rugby,—mine *Host de Jarterre*, have I not stay for him, to kill him? have I not, at de place I did appoint?

*Eva.* As I am a christians soul, now, look you, this is the place appointed; I'll be judgment by mine host of the Garter.

*Host.* Peace, I say, Guallia and Gaul, French and Welch; soul-curer and body-curer.

*Caius.* Ay, dat is very good! excellent!

*Host.* Peace, I say; hear mine host of the Garter. Am I politick? am I subtle? am I a Machiavel? Shall I lose my doctor? no; he gives me the potions, and the motions. Shall I lose my parson? my priest? my sir Hugh? no; he gives me the proverbs and the no-verbs.—Give me thy hand, terrestrial; so:—Give me thy hand, celestial; so.——Boys of art, I have deceived you both; I have directed you to wrong places; your hearts are mighty, your skins are whole, and let burnt sack be the issue.—Come, lay their swords to pawn:—Follow me, lad of peace; follow, follow, follow.

*Shal.* Trust me, a mad host:—Follow, gentlemen, follow.

*Slen.* O, sweet Anne Page!

[*Exeunt* SHALLOW, SLENDER, PAGE, *and* Host.

*Caius.* Ha! do I perceive dat? have you make-a de sot of us?[1] ha, ha!

*Eva.* This is well; he has made us his vlouting-stog.—I desire you, that we may be friends; and let us knog our prains together, to be revenge on this same scall, scurvy,[2] cogging companion, the host of the Garter.

*Caius.* By gar, vit all my heart; he promise to bring me vere is Anne Page; by gar, he deceive me too.

*Eva.* Well, I will smite his noddles :—Pray you, follow. [*Exeunt.*

## SCENE II.

### *The Street in Windsor.*

#### *Enter Mistress* PAGE *and* ROBIN.

*Mrs. Page.* Nay, keep your way, little gallant; you were wont to be a follower, but now you are a leader : Whether had you rather, lead mine eyes, or eye your master's heels?

*Rob.* I had rather, forsooth, go before you like a man, than follow him like a dwarf.

*Mrs. Page.* O you are a flattering boy; now, I see, you'll be a courtier.

#### *Enter* FORD.

*Ford.* Well met, mistress Page : Whither go you?

*Mrs. Page.* Truly, sir, to see your wife; Is she at home?

*Ford.* Ay; and as idle as she may hang toge-

---

[1] —— *make-a de sot of us?*] *Sot,* in French, signifies *a fool.*
[2] —— *scall, scurvy,*] *Scall* was an old word of reproach.

ther, for want of company : I think, if your husbands were dead, you two would marry.

*Mrs. Page.* Be sure of that,—two other husbands.

*Ford.* Where had you this pretty weather-cock?

*Mrs. Page.* I cannot tell what the dickens his
name is my husband had him of : What do you call
your knight's name, sirrah ?

*Rob.* Sir John Falstaff.

*Ford.* Sir John Falstaff!

*Mrs. Page.* He, he ; I can never hit on's name.
—There is such a league between my good man and
he !—Is your wife at home, indeed ?

*Ford.* Indeed, she is.

*Mrs. Page.* By your leave, sir ;—I am sick, till
I see her.     [*Exeunt Mrs.* PAGE *and* ROBIN.

*Ford.* Has Page any brains ? hath he any eyes ?
hath he any thinking ? Sure, they sleep ; he hath
no use of them.   Why, this boy will carry a letter
twenty miles, as easy as a cannon will shoot point-
blank twelve score.   He pieces-out his wife's inclination ; he gives her folly motion and advantage : and
now she's going to my wife, and Falstaff's boy with
her. A man may hear this shower sing in the wind !
—and Falstaff's boy with her !—Good plots !—they
are laid ; and our revolted wives share damnation together.   Well ; I will take him, then torture my
wife, pluck the borrowed veil of modesty from the
so seeming mistress Page,[3] divulge Page himself
for a secure and wilful Actæon ; and to these violent proceedings all my neighbours shall cry aim.[4]
[*Clock strikes.*] The clock gives me my cue, and
my assurance bids me search ; there I shall find Falstaff : I shall be rather praised for this, than mock-

---

[3] ——so seeming mistress Page,] Seeming is specious.
[4] —— shall cry aim.] i. e. shall encourage.

ed; for it is as positive as the earth is firm, that Falstaff is there: I will go.

*Enter* PAGE, SHALLOW, SLENDER, Host, *Sir* HUGH EVANS, CAIUS, *and* RUGBY.

*Shal.* Page, &c. Well met, master Ford.

*Ford.* Trust me, a good knot: I have good cheer at home; and, I pray you, all go with me.

*Shal.* I must excuse myself, master Ford.

*Slen.* And so must I, sir; we have appointed to dine with mistress Anne, and I would not break with her for more money than I'll speak of.

*Shal.* We have lingered about a match between Anne Page and my cousin Slender, and this day we shall have our answer.

*Slen.* I hope, I have your good will, father Page.

*Page.* You have, master Slender; I stand wholly for you :—but my wife, master doctor, is for you altogether.

*Caius.* Ay, by gar; and de maid is love-a me; my nursh-a Quickly tell me so mush.

*Host.* What say you to young master Fenton? he capers, he dances, he has eyes of youth, he writes verses, he speaks holyday,[5] he smells April and May: he will carry't, he will carry't; 'tis in his buttons;[6] he will carry't.

*Page.* Not by my consent, I promise you. The gentleman is of no having:[7] he kept company with the wild Prince and Poins; he is of too high a region, he knows too much. No, he shall not knit a knot in his fortunes with the finger of my substance:

---

[5] —— *he writes verses, he speaks* holyday,] i. e. his language is curious and affectedly chosen.

[6] —— *'tis in his* buttons;] Alluding to an ancient custom among the country fellows, of trying whether they should succeed with their mistresses, by carrying the *batchelor's buttons* in their pockets.

[7] —— *of no* having;] *Having*; i. e. estate or *fortune*.

if he take her, let him take her simply; the wealth
I have waits on my consent, and my consent goes
not that way.

*Ford.* I beseech you, heartily, some of you go
home with me to dinner: besides your cheer, you
shall have sport; I will show you a monster.—Master doctor, you shall go;—so shall you, master
Page;—and you, sir Hugh.

*Shal.* Well, fare you well:—we shall have the
freer wooing at master Page's.

              [*Exeunt* SHALLOW *and* SLENDER.

*Caius.* Go home, John Rugby; I come anon.

                    [*Exit* RUGBY.

*Host.* Farewell, my hearts: I will to my honest
knight Falstaff, and drink canary with him.

                    [*Exit* Host.

*Ford.* [*Aside.*]    I think, I shall drink in pipe-
wine first with him; I'll make him dance. Will
you go, gentles?

*All.* Have with you, to see this monster.

                          [*Exeunt.*

### SCENE III.

*A Room in* Ford's *House.*

*Enter Mrs.* FORD *and Mrs.* PAGE.

*Mrs. Ford.* What, John! what, Robert!
*Mrs. Page.* Quickly, quickly: Is the buck-basket—
*Mrs. Ford.* I warrant:—What, Robin, I say.

*Enter Servants with a Basket.*

*Mrs. Page.* Come, come, come.
*Mrs. Ford.* Here, set it down.

*Mrs. Page.* Give your men the charge ; we must be brief.

*Mrs. Ford.* Marry, as I told you before, John, and Robert, be ready here hard by in the brew-house ; and when I suddenly call you, come forth, and (without any pause, or staggering,) take this basket on your shoulders : that done, trudge with it in all haste, and carry it among the whitsters* in Datchet mead, and there empty it in the muddy ditch, close by the Thames side.

*Mrs. Page.* You will do it ?

*Mrs. Ford.* I have told them over and over ; they lack no direction : Be gone, and come when you are called. [*Exeunt* Servants.

*Mrs. Page.* Here comes little Robin.

*Enter* ROBIN.

*Mrs. Ford.* How now, my eyas-musket?[9] what news with you ?

*Rob.* My master, sir John, is come in at your back-door, mistress Ford ; and requests your company.

*Mrs. Page.* You little Jack-a-lent,[1] have you been true to us ?

*Rob.* Ay, I'll be sworn : My master knows not of your being here ; and hath threatened to put me into everlasting liberty, if I tell you of it ; for, he swears, he'll turn me away.

*Mrs. Page.* Thou'rt a good boy ; this secrecy of thine shall be a tailor to thee, and shall make thee a new doublet and hose.—I'll go hide me.

*Mrs. Ford.* Do so :—Go tell thy master, I am

* —— *the whitsters* —] i. e. the blanchers of linen.
[9] *How now, my* eyas-musket ?] *Eyas* is a young unfledg'd hawk. *Eyas-musket* is the same as *infant Lilliputian.*
[1] —— *Jack-a-lent,*] A *Jack o' lent* was a puppet thrown at in Lent, like shrove-cocks.

alone.    Mistress  Page,  remember  you  your  cue.
[*Exit* ROBIN.

*Mrs. Page.*  I warrant thee ; if I do not act it,
hiss me.                          [*Exit Mrs.* PAGE.

*Mrs. Ford.*  Go to then ; we'll use this unwholesome humidity, this gross watry pumpion ;—we'll
teach him to know turtles from jays.


*Enter* FALSTAFF.

*Fal. Have I caught* thee, *my heavenly jewel?*
Why, now let me die, for I have lived long enough ;
this is the period of my ambition ; O this blessed
hour !

*Mrs. Ford.*  O sweet sir John !

*Fal.*  Mistress Ford, I cannot cog, I cannot prate,
mistress Ford.  Now shall I sin in my wish : I
would thy husband were dead ; I'll speak it before
the best lord, I would make thee my lady.

*Mrs. Ford.*  I your lady, sir John ! alas, I should
be a pitiful lady.

*Fal.*  Let the court of France show me such another ; I see how thine eye would emulate the dia-
mond : Thou hast the right arched bent of the
brow, that becomes the ship-tire, the tire-valiant, or
any tire of Venetian admittance.

*Mrs. Ford.*  A plain kerchief, sir John : my brows
become nothing else ; nor that well neither.

*Fal.*  Thou art a traitor to say so : thou would'st
make an absolute courtier ; and the firm fixture of
thy foot would give an excellent motion to thy gait,
in a semi-circled farthingale.  I see what thou wert,

---

*Have I caught my heavenly jewel ?*]  This is the first line of
the second song in Sidney's *Astrophel and Stella.*

—— *that becomes the ship-tire, the tire*-valiant, *or any tire of*
Venetian admittance.]  Head-dresses then in fashion, received
or admitted from Venice.

if fortune thy foe were not; nature is thy friend:
Come, thou canst not hide it.

*Mrs. Ford.* Believe me, there's no such thing in
me.

*Fal.* What made me love thee? let that persuade
thee, there's something extraordinary in thee. Come
I cannot cog, and say, thou art this and that, like
a many of these lisping haw-thorn buds, that come
like women in men's apparel, and smell like Buckler's-bury* in simple-time; I cannot: but I love
thee; none but thee; and thou deservest it.

*Mrs. Ford.* Do not betray me, sir; I fear, you
love mistress Page.

*Fal.* Thou might'st as well say, I love to walk
by the Counter-gate; which is as hateful to me as
the reek of a lime-kiln.

*Mrs. Ford.* Well, heaven knows, how I love
you; and you shall one day find it.

*Fal.* Keep in that mind; I'll deserve it.

*Mrs. Ford.* Nay, I must tell you, so you do; or
else I could not be in that mind.

*Rob.* [*within*] Mistress Ford, mistress Ford!
here's mistress Page at the door, sweating, and
blowing, and looking wildly, and would needs speak
with you presently.

*Fal.* She shall not see me; I will ensconce me
behind the arras.

*Mrs. Ford.* Pray you, do so: she's a very tattling
woman.——                    [FALSTAFF *hides himself.*

*Enter Mistress* PAGE *and* ROBIN.

What's the matter? how now?

*Mrs. Page.* O mistress Ford, what have you done?

---

* —— *like* Buckler's-bury, &c.] *Buckler's-bury,* in the time
of Shakspeare, was chiefly inhabited by druggists, who sold all
kinds of herbs, green as well as dry.

You're shamed, you are overthrown, you are undone for ever.

*Mrs. Ford.* What's the matter, good mistress
Page?

*Mrs. Page.* O well-a-day, mistress Ford! having
an honest man to your husband, to give him such
cause of suspicion!

*Mrs. Ford.* What cause of suspicion?

*Mrs. Page.* What cause of suspicion?—Out upon you! how am I mistook in you?

*Mrs. Ford.* Why, alas! what's the matter?

*Mrs. Page.* Your husband's coming hither, woman, with all the officers in Windsor, to search for
a gentleman, that, he says, is here now in the
house, by your consent, to take an ill advantage of
his absence: You are undone.

*Mrs. Ford.* Speak louder.—[*Aside.*]—'Tis not
so, I hope.

*Mrs. Page.* Pray heaven it be not so, that you
have such a man here; but 'tis most certain your
husband's coming with half Windsor at his heels, to
search for such a one. I come before to tell you:
If you know yourself clear, why I am glad of it:
but if you have a friend here, convey, convey him
out. Be not amazed; call all your senses to you;
defend your reputation, or bid farewell to your good
life for ever.

*Mrs. Ford.* What shall I do?—There is a gentleman, my dear friend; and I fear not mine own
shame, so much as his peril: I had rather than a
thousand pound, he were out of the house.

*Mrs. Page.* For shame, never stand *you had rather*, and *you had rather;* your husband's here at
hand, bethink you of some conveyance: in the
house you cannot hide him.—O, how have you deceived me!—Look, here is a basket; if he be of
any reasonable stature, he may creep in here; and

11

throw foul linen upon him, as if it were going to bucking : Or, it is whiting-time,[5] send him by your two men to Datchet mead.

*Mrs. Ford.* He's too big to go in there : What shall I do ?

### *Re-enter* FALSTAFF.

*Fal.* Let me see't, let me see't! O let me see't! I'll in, I'll in ; follow your friend's counsel ;—I'll in.

*Mrs. Page.* What! sir John Falstaff! Are these your letters, knight ?

*Fal.* I love thee, and none but thee ; help me away : let me creep in here ; I'll never——
  [*He goes into the basket ; they cover him with foul linen.*

*Mrs. Page.* Help to cover your master, boy : Call your men, mistress Ford :——You dissembling knight !

*Mrs. Ford.* What John, Robert, John ! [*Exit* ROBIN. *Re-enter* Servants.] Go take up these clothes here, quickly ; where's the cowl-staff ?[6] look, how you drumble ;[7] carry them to the laundress in Datchet mead ; quickly, come.

---

[5] —— *whiting-time,*] Bleaching time ; spring.

[6] —— *the cowl-staff* ?] Is a staff used for carrying a large tub or basket with two handles. In Essex the word *cowl* is yet used for a tub.

[7] —— *how you* drumble :] To *drumble*, in Devonshire, signifies to mutter in a sullen and inarticulate voice. No other sense of the word will explain this interrogation. To *drumble and drone* are often used in connection. HENLEY.

A *drumble* drone, in the western dialect, signifies a drone or humble-bee. Mrs. Page may therefore mean—how lazy and stupid you are ! be more alert. MALONE.

*Enter* FORD, PAGE, CAIUS, *and Sir* HUGH
EVANS.

*Ford.* Pray you, come near : if I suspect without
cause, why then make sport at me, then let me be
your jest ; I deserve it.—How now ? whither bear
you this ?

*Serv.* To the laundress, forsooth.

*Mrs. Ford.* Why, what have you to do whither
they bear it ? You were best meddle with buck-
washing.

*Ford.* Buck ? I would I could wash myself of the
buck ! Buck, buck, buck ? Ay, buck ; I warrant
you, buck ; and of the season too ; it shall appear.⁸
[*Exeunt* Servants *with the basket.*] Gentlemen, I
have dreamed to-night ; I'll tell you my dream.
Here, here, here be my keys : ascend my chambers, search, seek, find out : I'll warrant, we'll un-
kennel the fox :—Let me stop this way first :—so,
now uncape.⁹

*Page.* Good master Ford, be contented : you
wrong yourself too much.

*Ford.* True, master Page.—Up, Gentlemen ; you
shall see sport anon : follow me, gentlemen. [*Exit.*

*Eva.* This is fery fantastical humours, and jealousies.

*Caius.* By gar, 'tis no de fashion o' France : it is
not jealous in France.

*Page.* Nay, follow him, gentlemen ; see the issue of his search. [*Exeunt* EVANS, PAGE, *and* CAIUS.

*Mrs. Page.* Is there not a double excellency in
this ?

⁸ —— *it shall appear.*] Ford seems to allude to the cuckold's
horns. So afterwards : " —and so buffets himself on the forehead, crying, *peer* out, *peer* out." *Of the season* is a phrase of
the forest. MALONE.

⁹ —— *So, now* uncape.] A term in fox-hunting, which signifies to dig out the fox when earthed.

*Mrs. Ford.* I know not which pleases me better, that my husband is deceived, or sir John.

*Mrs. Page.* What a taking was he in, when your husband asked who was in the basket!

*Mrs. Ford.* I am half afraid he will have need of washing; so throwing him into the water will do him a benefit.

*Mrs. Page.* Hang him, dishonest rascal! I would all of the same strain were in the same distress.

*Mrs. Ford.* I think, my husband hath some special suspicion of Falstaff's being here; for I never saw him so gross in his jealousy till now.

*Mrs. Page.* I will lay a plot to try that: And we will yet have more tricks with Falstaff: his dissolute disease will scarce obey this medicine.

*Mrs. Ford.* Shall we send that foolish carrion, mistress Quickly, to him, and excuse his throwing into the water; and give him another hope, to betray him to another punishment?

*Mrs. Page.* We'll do it; let him be sent for to-morrow eight o'clock, to have amends.

*Re-enter* FORD, PAGE, CAIUS, *and Sir* HUGH EVANS.

*Ford.* I cannot find him: may be the knave bragged of that he could not compass.

*Mrs. Page.* Heard you that?

*Mrs. Ford.* Ay, ay, peace:—You use me well, master Ford, do you?

*Ford.* Ay, I do so.

*Mrs. Ford.* Heaven make you better than your thoughts!

*Ford.* Amen.

*Mrs. Page.* You do yourself mighty wrong, master Ford.

*Ford.* Ay, ay; I must bear it.

10

*Eva.* If there be any pody in the house, and in the chambers, and in the coffers, and in the presses, heaven forgive my sins at the day of judgment!

*Caius.* By gar, nor I too; dere is no bodies.

*Page.* Fie, fie, master Ford! are you not ashamed? What spirit, what devil suggests this imagination? I would not have your distemper in this kind, for the wealth of Windsor Castle.

*Ford.* 'Tis my fault, master Page: I suffer for it.

*Eva.* You suffer for a pad conscience: your wife is as honest a 'omans, as I will desires among five thousand, and five hundred too.

*Caius.* By gar, I see 'tis an honest woman.

*Ford.* Well;—I promised you a dinner:—Come, come, walk in the park: I pray you, pardon me; I will hereafter make known to you, why I have done this.—Come, wife;—come, mistress Page; I pray you pardon me; pray heartily, pardon me.

*Page.* Let's go in, gentlemen; but, trust me, we'll mock him. I do invite you to-morrow morning to my house to breakfast; after, we'll a birding together; I have a fine hawk for the bush: Shall it be so?

*Ford.* Any thing.

*Eva.* If there is one, I shall make two in the company.

*Caius.* If there be one or two, I shall make-a de turd.

*Eva.* In your teeth: for shame.

*Ford.* Pray you go, master Page.

*Eva.* I pray you now, remembrance to-morrow on the lousy knave, mine host.

*Caius.* Dat is good; by gar, vit all my heart.

*Eva.* A lousy knave; to have his gibes and his mockeries.

*[Exeunt.*

## SCENE IV.

*A Room in* Page's *House.*

*Enter* Fenton *and Mistress* Anne Page.

*Fent.* I see, I cannot get thy father's love;
Therefore, no more turn me to him, sweet Nan.
　*Anne.* Alas! how then?
　*Fent.* 　　　　　　　Why, thou must be thyself.
He doth object, I am too great of birth;
And that, my state being gall'd with my expence,
I seek to heal it only by his wealth:
Besides these, other bars he lays before me,——
My riots past, my wild societies;
And tells me, 'tis a thing impossible
I should love thee, but as a property.
　*Anne.* May be, he tells you true.
　*Fent.* No, heaven so speed me in my time to
　　　come!
Albeit, I will confess, thy father's wealth
Was the first motive that I woo'd thee, Anne:
Yet, wooing thee, I found thee of more value
Than stamps in gold, or sums in sealed bags;
And 'tis the very riches of thyself
That now I aim at.
　*Anne.* 　　　　　Gentle master Fenton,
Yet seek my father's love; still seek it, sir:
If opportunity and humblest suit
Cannot attain it, why then.——Hark you hither.
　　　　　　　　　　[*They converse apart.*

*Enter* Shallow, Slender, *and Mrs.* Quickly.

　*Shal.* Break their talk, mistress Quickly; my
kinsman shall speak for himself.

*Slen.* I'll make a shaft or a bolt on't :[1] slid, 'tis but venturing.

*Shal.* Be not dismay'd.

*Slen.* No, she shall not dismay me : I care not for that,—but that I am afeard.

*Quick.* Hark ye, master Slender would speak a word with you.

*Anne.* I come to him.—This is my father's choice.

O, what a world of vile ill-favour'd faults Looks handsome in three hundred pounds a year!

                        [*Aside.*

*Quick.* And how does good master Fenton? Pray you, a word with you.

*Shal.* She's coming; to her, coz. O boy, thou hadst a father!

*Slen.* I had a father, mistress Anne ;—my uncle can tell you good jests of him :—Pray you uncle, tell mistress Anne the jest, how my father stole two geese out of a pen, good uncle.

*Shal.* Mistress Anne, my cousin loves you.

*Slen.* Ay, that I do; as well as I love any woman in Gloucestershire.

*Shal.* He will maintain you like a gentlewoman.

*Slen.* Ay, that I will, come cut and long-tail,[2] under the degree of a 'squire.

*Shal.* He will make you a hundred and fifty pounds jointure.

*Anne.* Good master Shallow, let him woo for himself.

*Shal.* Marry, I thank you for it; I thank you for

---

[1] *I'll make a shaft or a bolt on't :*] *To make a bolt or a shaft of a thing* is enumerated by Ray, amongst others, in his collection of proverbial phrases. The *bolt* in this proverb means the *fool's* bolt.

[2] —— *come cut and* long-tail,] i. e. come, *poor*, or *rich*, to offer himself as my rival. The origin of the phrase is not decided.

that good comfort. She calls you, coz: I'll leave you.

*Anne.* Now, master Slender.

*Slen.* Now, good mistress Anne.

*Anne.* What is your will?

*Slen.* My will? od's heartlings, that's a pretty jest, indeed! I ne'er made my will yet, I thank heaven; I am not such a sickly creature, I give heaven praise.

*Anne.* I mean, master Slender, what would you with me?

*Slen.* Truly, for mine own part, I would little or nothing with you: Your father, and my uncle, have made motions: if it be my luck, so: if not, happy man be his dole![1] They can tell you how things go, better than I can: You may ask your father; here he comes.

*Enter* PAGE, *and Mistress* PAGE.

*Page.* Now, master Slender:—Love him, daughter Anne.——
Why, how now! what does master Fenton here? You wrong me, sir, thus still to haunt my house: I told you, sir, my daughter is dispos'd of.

*Fent.* Nay, master Page, be not impatient.

*Mrs. Page.* Good master Fenton, come not to my child.

*Page.* She is no match for you.

*Fent.* Sir, will you hear me?

*Page.* No, good master Fenton. Come, master Shallow; come, son Slender; in:—Knowing my mind, you wrong me, master Fenton.

[*Exeunt* PAGE, SHALLOW, *and* SLENDER.

*Quick.* Speak to mistress Page.

[1] —— *happy man be his dole!*] A proverbial expression.

*Fent.* Good mistress Page, for that I love your
　　daughter
In such a righteous fashion as I do,
Perforce, against all checks, rebukes, and manners,
I must advance the colours of my love,
And not retire : Let me have your good will.
　　*Anne.* Good mother, do not marry me to yond'
　　fool.
　　*Mrs. Page.* I mean it not ; I seek you a better
　　husband.
　　*Quick.* That's my master, master doctor.
　　*Anne.* Alas, I had rather be set quick i' the earth,
And bowl'd to death with turnips.⁴
　　*Mrs. Page.* Come, trouble not yourself : Good
　　master Fenton,
I will not be your friend, nor enemy :
My daughter will I question how she loves you,
And as I find her, so am I affected ;
'Till then, farewell, sir :——She must needs go in ;
Her father will be angry.
　　　　　　　　　[*Exeunt Mrs.* PAGE *and* ANNE.
　　*Fent.* Farewell, gentle mistress ; farewell, Nan.
　　*Quick.* This is my doing now ;——Nay, said I, will
you cast away your child on a fool, and a physician ?
Look on master Fenton :——this is my doing.
　　*Fent.* I thank thee ; and I pray thee, once to-
　　night⁵
Give my sweet Nan this ring : There's for thy pains.
　　　　　　　　　　　　　　　　[*Exit.*
　　*Quick.* Now heaven send thee good fortune ! A
kind heart he hath : a woman would run through
fire and water for such a kind heart. But yet, I
would my master had mistress Anne ; or I would

---

⁴ —— *be set quick i' the earth,*
　*And bowl'd to death with turnips.*] This is a common proverb
in the southern counties.
⁵ —— *once to-night* —] i. e. *sometime* to-night.

master Slender had her ; or, in sooth, I would master Fenton had her : I will do what I can for them
all three ; for so I have promised, and I'll be as good
as my word ; but speciously[6] for master Fenton.
Well, I must of another errand to sir John Falstaff
from my two mistresses ; What a beast am I to
slack it ?[7]                                              [*Exit.*

## SCENE V.

*A Room in the Garter Inn.*

*Enter* FALSTAFF *and* BARDOLPH.

*Fal.* Bardolph, I say,—
*Bard.* Here, sir.
*Fal.* Go fetch me a quart of sack ; put a toast
in't. [*Exit* BARD.] Have I lived to be carried in a
basket, like a barrow of butcher's offal ; and to be
thrown into the Thames ? Well, if I be served
such another trick, I'll have my brains ta'en out,
and butter'd, and give them to a dog for a new
year's gift. The rogues slighted me into the river
with as little remorse as they would have drowned a
bitch's blind puppies, fifteen i' the litter : and you
may know by my size, that I have a kind of alacrity
in sinking ; if the bottom were as deep as hell, I
should down. I had been drowned, but that the
shore was shelvy and shallow ; a death that I abhor;
for the water swells a man ; and what a thing
should I have been, when I had been swelled ! I
should have been a mountain of mummy.

---

[6] —— *speciously* —] She means to say *specially.*
[7] —— *to slack it* ?] i. e. neglect.

*Re-enter* BARDOLPH, *with the wine.*

*Bard.* Here's mistress Quickly, sir, to speak with you.

*Fal.* Come, let me pour in some sack to the Thames water; for my belly's as cold, as if I had swallowed snow-balls for pills to cool the reins. Call her in.

*Bard.* Come in, woman.

*Enter Mrs.* QUICKLY.

*Quick.* By your leave; I cry you mercy: Give your worship good-morrow.

*Fal.* Take away these chalices: Go, brew me a pottle of sack finely.

*Bard.* With eggs, sir?

*Fal.* Simple of itself; I'll no pullet-sperm in my brewage.—[*Exit* BARDOLPH.]—How now?

*Quick.* Marry, sir, I come to your worship from mistress Ford.

*Fal.* Mistress Ford! I have had ford enough: I was thrown into the ford; I have my belly full of ford.

*Quick.* Alas the day! good heart, that was not her fault: she does so take on with her men; they mistook their erection.

*Fal.* So did I mine, to build upon a foolish woman's promise.

*Quick.* Well, she laments, sir, for it, that it would yearn your heart to see it. Her husband goes this morning a birding; she desires you once more to come to her between eight and nine: I must carry her word quickly: she'll make you amends, I warrant you.

*Fal.* Well, I will visit her: Tell her so; and bid

her think, what a man is : let her consider his frailty, and then judge of my merit.

*Quick.* I will tell her.

*Fal.* Do so. Between nine and ten, say'st thou?

*Quick.* Eight and nine, sir.

*Fal.* Well, be gone : I will not miss her.

*Quick.* Peace be with you, sir! [*Exit.*

*Fal.* I marvel, I hear not of master Brook; he sent me word to stay within : I like his money well. O, here he comes.

*Enter* FORD.

*Ford.* Bless you, sir!

*Fal.* Now, master Brook? you come to know what hath passed between me and Ford's wife?

*Ford.* That, indeed, sir John, is my business.

*Fal.* Master Brook, I will not lie to you; I was at her house the hour she appointed me.

*Ford.* And how sped you, sir?

*Fal.* Very ill-favouredly, master Brook.

*Ford.* How so, sir? Did she change her determination?

*Fal.* No, master Brook; but the peaking cornuto her husband, master Brook, dwelling in a continual 'larum of jealousy, comes me in the instant of our encounter, after we had embraced, kissed, protested, and, as it were, spoke the prologue of our comedy; and at his heels a rabble of his companions, thither provoked and instigated by his distemper, and, forsooth, to search his house for his wife's love.

*Ford.* What, while you were there?

*Fal.* While I was there.

*Ford.* And did he search for you, and could not find you?

*Fal.* You shall hear. As good luck would have it, comes in one mistress Page; gives intelligence of Ford's approach; and, by her invention, and Ford's wife's distraction, they conveyed me into a buck-basket.

*Ford.* A buck-basket!

*Fal.* By the Lord, a buck-busket: rammed me in with foul shirts and smocks, socks, foul stockings, and greasy napkins; that, master Brook, there was the rankest compound of villainous smell, that ever offended nostril.

*Ford.* And how long lay you there?

*Fal.* Nay, you shall hear, master Brook, what I have suffered to bring this woman to evil for your good. Being thus crammed in the basket, a couple of Ford's knaves, his hinds, were called forth by their mistress, to carry me in the name of foul clothes to Datchet-lane: they took me on their shoulders; met the jealous knave their master in the door; who asked them once or twice what they had in their basket: I quaked for fear, lest the lunatic knave would have searched it; but fate, ordaining he should be a cuckold, held his hand. Well: on went he for a search, and away went I for foul clothes. But mark the sequel, master Brook: I suffered the pangs of three several deaths: first, an intolerable fright, to be detected with[8] a jealous rotten bell-wether: next, to be compassed, like a good bilbo,[9] in the circumference of a peck, hilt to point, heel to head: and then, to be stopped in, like a strong distillation, with stinking clothes that fretted in their own grease: think of that,—a man of my kidney,—think of that: that am as subject to heat, as butter; a man of continual dissolution and thaw; it was a miracle, to 'scape suffocation. And in the

***

[8] —— *detected* with —] *With* was sometimes used for *of,* or *by.*

[9] —— *bilbo,*] A *bilbo* is a Spanish blade, of which the excellence is flexibleness and elasticity, from *Bilboa,* a city of Biscay, where the best blades are made.

height of this bath, when I was more than half stewed in grease, like a Dutch dish, to be thrown into the Thames, and cooled, glowing hot, in that surge, like a horse-shoe; think of that,—hissing hot,—think of that, master Brook.

*Ford.* In good sadness, sir, I am sorry that for my sake you have suffered all this. My suit then is desperate; you'll undertake her no more.

*Fal.* Master Brook, I will be thrown into Ætna, as I have been into Thames, ere I will leave her thus. Her husband is this morning gone a birding; I have received from her another embassy of meeting; 'twixt eight and nine is the hour, master Brook.

*Ford.* 'Tis past eight already, sir.

*Fal.* Is it? I will then address me ' to my appointment. Come to me at your convenient leisure, and you shall know how I speed; and the conclusion shall be crowned with your enjoying her: Adieu. You shall have her, master Brook; master Brook, you shall cuckold Ford. [*Exit.*

*Ford.* Hum! ha! is this a vision? is this a dream? do I sleep? Master Ford, awake; awake, master Ford; there's a hole made in your best coat, master Ford. This 'tis to be married! this 'tis to have linen, and buck-baskets!—Well, I will proclaim myself what I am: I will now take the lecher; he is at my house; he cannot 'scape me; 'tis impossible he should; he cannot creep into a half penny purse, nor into a pepper-box; but, lest the devil that guides him should aid him, I will search impossible places. Though what I am I cannot avoid, yet to be what I would not, shall not make me tame: if I have horns to make one mad, let the proverb go with me, I'll be horn mad. [*Exit.*

---

* —— *address me* —] i. e. make myself ready.

## ACT IV.

### *SCENE I. The Street.*

*Enter Mrs.* PAGE, *Mrs.* QUICKLY, *and* WILLIAM.

*Mrs. Page.* Is he at master Ford's already, think'st thou?

*Quick.* Sure, he is by this; or will be presently: but truly, he is very courageous mad, about his throwing into the water. Mistress Ford desires you to come suddenly.

*Mrs. Page.* I'll be with her by and by; I'll but bring my young man here to school; Look, where his master comes; 'tis a playing-day, I see.

*Enter Sir* HUGH EVANS.

How now, sir Hugh? no school to-day?

*Eva.* No; master Slender is let the boys leave to play.

*Quick.* Blessing of his heart!

*Mrs. Page.* Sir Hugh, my husband says, my son profits nothing in the world at his book; I pray you, ask him some questions in his accidence.

*Eva.* Come hither, William; hold up your head; come.

*Mrs. Page.* Come on, sirrah: hold up your head; answer your master, be not afraid.

*Eva.* William, how many numbers is in nouns?

*Will.* Two.

*Quick.* Truly, I thought there had been one number more; because they say, od's nouns.

*Eva.* Peace your tattlings. What is *fair*, William?

*Will.* *Pulcher.*

*Quick.* Poulcats! there are fairer things than poulcats, sure.

*Eva.* You are a very simplicity 'oman; I pray you, peace. What is *lapis*, William?

*Will.* A stone.

*Eva.* And what is a stone, William.

*Will.* A pebble.

*Eva.* No, it is *lapis*; I pray you remember in your prain.

Will. *Lapis.*

*Eva.* That is good William. What is he, William, that does lend articles?

*Will.* Articles are borrowed of the pronoun; and be thus declined, *Singulariter, nominativo, hic, hæc, hoc.*

Eva. *Nominativo, hig, hag, hog;*—pray you, mark: *genitivo, hujus:* Well, what is your *accusative case?*

Will. *Accusativo, hinc.*

*Eva.* I pray you, have your remembrance, child; *Accusativo, hing, hang, hog.*

*Quick.* Hang hog is Latin for bacon, I warrant you.

*Eva.* Leave your prabbles, 'oman. What is the focative case, William?

*Will.* O—*vocativo*, O.

*Eva.* Remember, William; focative is, *caret.*

*Quick.* And that's a good root.

*Eva.* 'Oman, forbear.

*Mrs. Page.* Peace.

*Eva.* What is your *genitive case plural*, William?

Will. *Genitive case?*

*Eva.* Ay.

Will. *Genitive,—horum, harum, horum.*

*Quick.* 'Vengeance of *Jenny's* case! fie on her! —never name her, child, if she be a whore.

*Eva.* For shame, 'oman.

*Quick.* You do ill to teach the child such words: he teaches him to hick and to hack,[2] which they'll do fast enough of themselves; and to call horum :—— fie upon you !

*Eva.* 'Oman, art thou lunatics ? hast thou no understandings for thy cases, and the numbers of the genders ? Thou art as foolish christian creatures as I would desires.

*Mrs. Page.* Pr'ythee hold thy peace.

*Eva.* Shew me now, William, some declensions of your pronouns.

*Will.* Forsooth, I have forgot.

*Eva.* It is *ki, kæ, cod ;* if you forget your *kies,* your *kæs,* and your *cods,* you must be preeches.[3] Go your ways, and play, go.

*Mrs. Page.* He is a better scholar, than I thought he was.

*Eva.* He is a good sprag[4] memory. Farewell, mistress Page.

*Mrs. Page.* Adieu, good sir Hugh. [*Exit Sir Hugh.*] Get you home, boy.—Come, we stay too long. [*Exeunt.*

## SCENE II.

### *A Room in* Ford's *House.*

### *Enter* FALSTAFF *and Mrs.* FORD.

*Fal.* Mistress Ford, your sorrow hath eaten up my sufferance : I see, you are obsequious in your love,[5] and I profess requital to a hair's breadth ; not

---

[2] —— *to hick and to hack,*] Perhaps, *to do mischief.*
[3] —— *you must be* preeches.] Must be *breeched,* i. e. flogged.
[4] —— *sprag* —] Or *spackt, apt to learn, ingenious.* REED.
[5] —— *your sorrow hath eaten up my sufferance : I see, you are* obsequious *in your love,*] The epithet *obsequious* refers to the seriousness with which *obsequies,* or *funeral ceremonies,* are performed.

only, mistress Ford, in the simple office of love, but in all the accoutrement, complement, and ceremony of it. But are you sure of your husband now?

*Mrs. Ford.* He's a birding, sweet sir John.

*Mrs. Page.* [*Within.*] What hoa, gossip Ford! what hoa!

*Mrs. Ford.* Step into the chamber, sir John.

[*Exit* FALSTAFF.

*Enter Mrs.* PAGE.

*Mrs. Page.* How now, sweetheart? who's at home beside yourself?

*Mrs. Ford.* Why, none but mine own people.

*Mrs. Page.* Indeed?

*Mrs. Ford.* No, certainly;—Speak louder.

[*Aside.*

*Mrs. Page.* Truly, I am so glad you have nobody here.

*Mrs. Ford.* Why?

*Mrs. Page.* Why, woman, your husband is in his old lunes[6] again: he so takes on[7] yonder with my husband; so rails against all married mankind; so curses all Eve's daughters, of what complexion soever; and so buffets himself on the forehead, crying, *Peer-out, peer-out!*[8] that any madness, I ever yet beheld, seemed but tameness, civility, and patience, to this his distemper he is in now: I am glad the fat knight is not here.

*Mrs. Ford.* Why, does he talk of him?

*Mrs. Page.* Of none but him; and swears, he was carried out, the last time he searched for him,

[6] —— *lunes* —] i. e. lunacy, frenzy.

[7] —— *he so* takes on —] *To take on*, which is now used for *to grieve*, seems to be used by our author for *to rage*.

[8] —— *Peer out!*] That is, *appear horns.*

in a basket : protests to my husband, he is now here ; and hath drawn him and the rest of their company from their sport, to make another experiment of his suspicion : but I am glad the [knight is not here ; now he shall see his own foolery.

*Mrs. Ford.* How near is he, mistress Page ?

*Mrs. Page.* Hard by ; at street end ; he will be here anon.

*Mrs. Ford.* I am undone !—the knight is here.

*Mrs. Page.* Why, then you are utterly shamed, and he's but a dead man. What a woman are you? —Away with him, away with him ; better shame than murder.

*Mrs. Ford.* Which way should he go ? how should I bestow him ? Shall I put him into the basket again ?

*Re-enter* FALSTAFF.

*Fal.* No, I'll come no more i' the basket : May I not go out, ere he come ?

*Mrs. Page.* Alas, three of master Ford's brothers watch the door with pistols,[9] that none shall issue out ; otherwise you might slip away ere he came. But what make you here ?

*Fal.* What shall I do?—I'll creep up into the chimney.

*Mrs. Ford.* There they always use to discharge their birding pieces : Creep into the kiln-hole.

*Fal.* Where is it ?

*Mrs. Ford.* He will seek there, on my word. Neither press, coffer, chest, trunk, well, vault, but he hath an abstract for the remembrance of such places, and goes to them by his note : There is no hiding you in the house.

9 —— *watch the door with* pistols,] This is one of Shakspeare's anachronisms.

*Fal.* I'll go out then.

*Mrs. Page.* If you go out in your own semblance, you die, sir John. Unless you go out disguised,—

*Mrs. Ford.* How might we disguise him?

*Mrs. Page.* Alas the day, I know not. There is no woman's gown big enough for him; otherwise, he might put on a hat, a muffler, and a kerchief, and so escape.

*Fal.* Good hearts, devise something: any extremity, rather than a mischief.

*Mrs. Ford.* My maid's aunt, the fat woman of Brentford, has a gown above.

*Mrs. Page.* On my word, it will serve him; she's as big as he is: and there's her thrum'd hat, and her muffler too:[1] Run up, sir John.

*Mrs. Ford.* Go, go, sweet sir John: mistress Page and I, will look some linen for your head.

*Mrs. Page.* Quick, quick; we'll come dress you straight: put on the gown the while.

[*Exit* FALSTAFF.

*Mrs. Ford.* I would, my husband would meet him in this shape: he cannot abide the old woman of Brentford; he swears, she's a witch; forbade her my house, and hath threatened to beat her.

*Mrs. Page.* Heaven guide him to thy husband's cudgel; and the devil guide his cudgel afterwards!

*Mrs. Ford.* But is my husband coming?

*Mrs. Page.* Ay, in good sadness, is he; and he talks of the basket too, howsoever he hath had intelligence.

*Mrs. Ford.* We'll try that; for I'll appoint my men to carry the basket again, to meet him at the door with it, as they did last time.

---

[1] —— *her* thrum'd *hat, and her* muffler *too:*] The *muffler* was a thin piece of linen, which covered the lips and chin. A *thrum'd* hat was made of very coarse woollen cloth.

11

*Mrs. Page.* Nay, but he'll be here presently : let's go dress him like the witch of Brentford.

*Mrs. Ford.* I'll first direct my men, what they shall do with the basket.   Go up, I'll bring linen for him straight.                                           [*Exit.*

*Mrs. Page.* Hang him, dishonest varlet ! we cannot misuse him enough.

We'll leave a proof, by that which we will do,
Wives may be merry, and yet honest too :
We do not act, that often jest and laugh ;
'Tis old but true, *Still swine eat all the draff.*
                                                           [*Exit.*


*Re-enter* Mrs. Ford, *with two* Servants.

*Mrs. Ford.* Go, sirs, take the basket again on your shoulders ; your master is hard at door ; if he bid you set it down, obey him : quickly, despatch.
                                                           [*Exit.*

1 *Serv.* Come, come, take it up.

2 *Serv.* Pray heaven, it be not full of the knight again.

1 *Serv.* I hope not ; I had as lief bear so much lead.


*Enter* Ford, Page, Shallow, Caius, *and Sir* Hugh Evans.

*Ford.* Ay, but if it prove true, master Page, have you any way then to unfool me again ?—Set down the basket, villain :—Somebody call my wife :——You, youth in a basket, come out here !—O, you panderly rascals ! there's a knot, a ging,² a pack, a conspiracy against me : Now shall the devil be shamed.   What ! wife, I say ! come, come

---

² ——— *a* ging.]   *Ging* was anciently used for *gang.*

10

forth; behold what honest clothes you send forth to
bleaching.

*Page.* Why, this passes!³ Master Ford, you are
not to go loose any longer ; you must be pinioned.

*Eva.* Why, this is lunatics! this is mad as a mad
dog !

*Shal.* Indeed, master Ford, this is not well ; indeed.

### *Enter Mrs.* FORD,

*Ford.* So say I too, sir.——Come hither, mistress
Ford ; mistress Ford, the honest woman, the modest wife, the virtuous creature, that hath the jealous fool to her husband !——I suspect without cause,
mistress, do I ?

*Mrs. Ford.* Heaven be my witness, you do, if you
suspect me in any dishonesty.

*Ford.* Well said, brazen-face ; hold it out.——
Come forth, sirrah.

              [*Pulls the clothes out of the basket.*

*Page.* This passes !

*Mrs. Ford.* Are you not ashamed ? let the clothes
alone.

*Ford.* I shall find you anon.

*Eva.* 'Tis unreasonable ! Will you take up your
wife's clothes ? Come away.

*Ford.* Empty the basket, I say.

*Mrs. Ford.* Why, man, why,—

*Ford.* Master Page, as I am a man, there was one
conveyed out of my house yesterday in this basket :
Why may not he be there again ? In my house I
am sure he is : my intelligence is true ; my jealousy
is reasonable : Pluck me out all the linen.

*Mrs. Ford.* If you find a man there, he shall die
a flea's death.

³ —— *this passes !*] This beyond all bounds.

*Page.* Here's no man.

*Shal.* By my fidelity, this is not well, master Ford; this wrongs you.[4]

*Eva.* Master Ford, you must pray, and not follow the imaginations of your own heart: this is jealousies.

*Ford.* Well, he's not here I seek for.

*Page.* No, nor no where else, but in your brain.

*Ford.* Help to search my house this one time: if I find not what I seek, show no colour for my extremity, let me for ever be your table-sport; let them say of me, As jealous as Ford, that searched a hollow walnut for his wife's leman.[5] Satisfy me once more; once more search with me.

*Mrs. Ford.* What hoa, mistress Page! come you, and the old woman, down; my husband will come into the chamber.

*Ford.* Old woman! What old woman's that?

*Mrs. Ford.* Why, it is my maid's aunt of Brentford.

*Ford.* A witch, a quean, an old cozening quean! Have I not forbid her my house? She comes of errands, does she? We are simple men; we do not know what's brought to pass under the profession of fortune-telling. She works by charms, by spells, by the figure, and such daubery[6] as this is; beyond our element: we know nothing.——Come down, you witch, you hag you; come down I say.

*Mrs. Ford.* Nay, good, sweet husband;——good gentlemen, let him not strike the old woman.

---

[4] ——*this* wrongs *you.*] This is below your character.

[5] —— *his wife's* leman.] *Leman,* i. e. *lover,* is derived from *leef,* Dutch, *beloved,* and *man.*

[6] —— *such* daubery ——] Such *gross falsehood,* and *imposition.*

*Enter* FALSTAFF *in women's clothes, led by*
Mrs. PAGE.

*Mrs. Page.* Come, mother Prat, come, give me
your hand.

*Ford.* I'll *prat* her :——Out of my door, you
witch! [*beats him*] you rag,[7] you baggage, you
polecat, you ronyon![8] out! out! I'll conjure you,
I'll fortune-tell you. [*Exit* FALSTAFF.

*Mrs. Page.* Are you not ashamed? I think, you
have killed the poor woman.

*Mrs. Ford.* Nay, he will do it :——'Tis a goodly
credit for you.

*Ford.* Hang her, witch!

*Eva.* By yea and no, I think, the 'oman is a
witch indeed : I like not when a 'oman has a great
peard ; I spy a great peard under her muffler.

*Ford.* Will you follow, gentlemen? I beseech you,
follow ; see but the issue of my jealousy : if I cry
out thus upon no trail,[9] never trust me when I open
again.

*Page.* Let's obey his humour a little further :
Come, gentlemen.

[*Exeunt* PAGE, FORD, SHALLOW, *and* EVANS.

*Mrs. Page.* Trust me, he beat him most piti-
fully.

*Mrs. Ford.* Nay, by the mass, that he did not ;
he beat him most unpitifully, methought.

*Mrs. Page.* I'll have the cudgel hallowed, and

---

[7] ——*you* rag,] This opprobrious term is again used in *Timon.*

[8] ——*ronyon!*] *Ronyon,* applied to a woman, means, as far
as can be traced, much the same with *scall* or *scab* spoken of a
man. From *Rogneux,* Fr.

[9] —— cry *out thus upon no* trail,] The expression is taken
from the hunters. *Trail* is the scent left by the passage of the
game. *To cry out,* is to *open* or *bark.*

hung o'er the altar; it hath done meritorious service.

*Mrs. Ford.* What think you? May we, with the
warrant of womanhood, and the witness of a good
conscience, pursue him with any further revenge?

*Mrs. Page.* The spirit of wantonness is, sure,
scared out of him; if the devil have him not in fee-
simple, with fine and recovery,[1] he will never, I
think, in the way of waste, attempt us again.[2]

*Mrs. Ford.* Shall we tell our husbands how we
have served him?

*Mrs. Page.* Yes, by all means; if it be but to
scrape the figures out of your husband's brains.  If
they can find in their hearts, the poor unvirtuous fat
knight shall be any further afflicted, we two will still
be the ministers.

*Mrs. Ford.* I'll warrant, they'll have him publickly shamed: and, methinks, there would be no period[3] to the jest, should he not be publickly shamed.

*Mrs. Page.* Come, to the forge with it then,
shape it: I would not have things cool.    [*Exeunt.*

## SCENE III.

### *A Room in the Garter Inn.*

#### *Enter* Host *and* Bardolph.

*Bard.* Sir, the Germans desire to have three of
your horses: the duke himself will be to-morrow at
court, and they are going to meet him.

*Host.* What duke should that be, comes so se-

---

[1] —— *if the devil have him not in* fee-simple, *with* fine *and*
recovery,] *Fee-simple* is the *largest estate,* and *fine and recovery*
the *strongest assurance,* known to English law.

[2] —— *in the way of* waste, *attempt us again,*] Make further
attempts to ruin us, by corrupting our virtue.

[3] —— *no period —*] i. e. perhaps, *no proper catastrophe.*

cretly? I hear not of him in the court: Let me
speak with the gentlemen; they speak English?

*Bard.* Ay, sir; I'll call them to you.

*Host.* They shall have my horses; but I'll make
them pay, I'll sauce them: they have had my
houses a week at command; I have turned away my
other guests: they must come off;[4] I'll sauce them:
Come. [*Exeunt.*

## SCENE IV.

### *A Room in* Ford's *House.*

*Enter* PAGE, FORD, *Mrs.* PAGE, *Mrs.* FORD, *and*
*Sir* HUGH EVANS.

*Eva.* 'Tis one of the pest discretions of a 'oman
as ever I did look upon.

*Page.* And did he send you both these letters at
an instant?

*Mrs. Page.* Within a quarter of an hour.

*Ford.* Pardon me, wife: Henceforth do what thou
   wilt;
I rather will suspect the sun with cold,
Than thee with wantonness: now doth thy honour
   stand,
In him that was of late an heretick,
As firm as faith.

*Page.*     'Tis well, 'tis well; no more.
Be not as extreme in submission,
As in offence;
But let our plot go forward: let our wives
Yet once again, to make us publick sport,
Appoint a meeting with this old fat fellow,
Where we may take him, and disgrace him for it.

---

4 —— *they must come* off;] *To come off, is, to pay.*

*Ford.* There is no better way than that they
spoke of.

*Page.* How! to send him word they'll meet
him in the park at midnight! fie, fie; he'll never
come.

*Eva.* You say, he has been thrown into the
rivers; and has been grievously peaten, as an old
'oman; methinks, there should be terrors in him,
that he should not come; methinks, his flesh is pu-
nished, he shall have no desires.

*Page.* So think I too.

*Mrs. Ford.* Devise but how you'll use him when
he comes,
And let us two devise to bring him thither.

*Mrs. Page.* There is an old tale goes, that Herne
the hunter,
Sometime a keeper here in Windsor forest,
Doth all the winter time, at still midnight,
Walk round about an oak, with great ragg'd horns :
And there he blasts the tree, and takes the cattle ;⁵
And makes milch-kine yield blood, and shakes a
chain
In a most hideous and dreadful manner :
You have heard of such a spirit; and well you know,
The superstitious idle-headed eld⁶
Received, and did deliver to our age,
This tale of Herne the hunter for a truth.

*Page.* Why, yet there want not many, that do fear
In deep of night to walk by this Herne's oak :
But what of this ?

*Mrs. Ford.* Marry, this is our device ;
That Falstaff at that oak shall meet with us,
Disguised like Herne, with huge horns on his head.

⁵ —— and takes *the cattle ;*] To *take*, in Shakspeare, signifies
to seize or strike with a disease, to blast.

⁶ —— *idle-headed* eld —] *Eld* seems to be used here for—the
olden time ; or perhaps for *old persons.*.

*Page.* Well, let it not be doubted but he'll come,
And in this shape : When you have brought him
 thither,
What shall be done with him ? what is your plot ?
 *Mrs. Page.* That likewise have we thought upon,
 and thus :
Nan Page my daughter, and my little son,
And three or four more of their growth, we'll dress
Like urchins, ouphes,[7] and fairies, green and white,
With rounds of waxen tapers on their heads,
And rattles in their hands ; upon a sudden,
As Falstaff, she, and I, are newly met,
Let them from forth a saw-pit rush at once
With some diffused song ;[8] upon their sight,
We two in great amazedness will fly :
Then let them all encircle him about,
And, fairy-like, to-pinch the unclean knight ;[9]
And ask him, why, that hour of fairy revel,
In their so sacred paths he dares to tread,
In shape profane.
 *Mrs. Ford.*  And till he tell the truth,
Let the supposed fairies pinch him sound,[1]
And burn him with their tapers.
 *Mrs. Page.*  The truth being known,
We'll all present ourselves ; dis-horn the spirit,
And mock him home to Windsor.
 *Ford.*  The children must
Be practised well to this, or they'll ne'er do't.
 *Eva.* I will teach the children their behaviours ;

[7] —— *urchins, ouphes,*] The primitive signification of *urchin*
is a hedge-hog. Hence it comes to signify any thing little and
dwarfish. *Ouph* is the Teutonick word for a *fairy* or *goblin.*
 [8] *With some* diffused *song ;*] i. e. wild, irregular, discordant.
 [9] *And, fairy-like,* to-pinch *the unclean knight ;*] This use of
*to* in composition with verbs, very common in Gower and Chaucer,
was not quite antiquated in the time of Shakspeare.
 [1] —— *pinch him* sound,] i. e. *soundly.*

and I will be like a jack=an=apes also, to burn the
knight with my taber.

*Ford.* That will be excellent.    I'll go buy them
vizards.

*Mrs. Page.* My Nan shall be the queen of all
        the fairies,
Finely attired in a robe of white.

*Page.* That silk will I go buy;—and in that
        time
Shall master Slender steal my Nan away,    [*Aside.*
And marry her at Eton.——Go, send to Falstaff
        straight.

*Ford.* Nay, I'll to him again, in name of Brook:
He'll tell me all his purpose: Sure, he'll come.

*Mrs. Page.* Fear not you that: Go, get us pro-
        perties,²
And tricking for our fairies.³

*Eva.* Let us about it: It is admirable pleasures,
and fery honest knaveries.

               [*Exeunt* PAGE, FORD, *and* EVANS.

*Mrs. Page.* Go, mistress Ford,
Send Quickly to Sir John, to know his mind.

                   [*Exit Mrs.* FORD.

I'll to the doctor; he hath my good will,
And none but he, to marry with Nan Page.
That Slender, though well landed, is an idiot;
And he my husband best of all affects:
The doctor is well money'd, and his friends
Potent at court; he, none but he, shall have her,
Though twenty thousand worthier come to crave
        her.                 [*Exit.*

---

  ² —— *properties,*] *Properties* are little incidental necessaries
to a theatre, exclusive of scenes and dresses.

  ³ —— tricking *for our fairies.*] To *trick,* is to dress out.

## SCENE V.

### *A Room in the Garter Inn.*

#### *Enter* Host *and* SIMPLE.

*Host.* What would'st thou have, boor? what, thick-skin? speak, breathe, discuss; brief, short, quick, snap.

*Sim.* Marry, sir, I come to speak with sir John Falstaff from master Slender.

*Host.* There's his chamber, his house, his castle, his standing-bed, and truckle-bed; 'tis painted about with the story of the prodigal, fresh and new: Go, knock and call; he'll speak like an *Anthropopha-ginian*[4] unto thee: Knock, I say.

*Sim.* There's an old woman, a fat woman, gone up into his chamber; I'll be so bold as stay, sir, till she come down; I come to speak with her, indeed.

*Host.* Ha! a fat woman! the knight may be robbed: I'll call.——Bully knight! Bully sir John! speak from thy lungs military: Art thou there? it is thine host, thine Ephesian,[5] calls.

*Fal.* [*above.*] How now, mine host?

*Host.* Here's a Bohemian-Tartar tarries the coming down of thy fat woman; Let her descend, bully, let her descend; my chambers are honourable: Fye! privacy? fye!

#### *Enter* FALSTAFF.

*Fal.* There, was, mine host, an old fat woman, even now with me; but she's gone.

---

[4] —— *Anthropophaginim* —] i. e. a cannibal.
[5] —— *thine* Ephesian,] This was a cant term of the time, the meaning of which is not known.

*Sim.* Pray you, sir, was't not the wise woman of Brentford?

*Fal.* Ay, marry, was it, muscle-shell; What would you with her?

*Sim.* My master, sir, my master Slender, sent to her, seeing her go thorough the streets, to know, sir, whether one Nym, sir, that beguiled him of a chain, had the chain, or no.

*Fal.* I spake with the old woman about it.

*Sim.* And what says she, I pray, sir?

*Fal.* Marry, she says, that the very same man, that beguiled master Slender of his chain, cozened him of it.

*Sim.* I would, I could have spoken with the woman herself; I had other things to have spoken with her too, from him.

*Fal.* What are they? let us know.

*Host.* Ay, come; quick.

*Sim.* I may not conceal them, sir.

*Fal.* Conceal them, or thou diest.

*Sim.* Why, sir, they were nothing but about mistress Anne Page; to know, if it were my master's fortune to have her, or no.

*Fal.* 'Tis, 'tis his fortune.

*Sim.* What, sir?

*Fal.* To have her,—or no: Go; say, the woman told me so.

*Sim.* May I be so bold to say so, sir?

*Fal.* Ay, sir Tike; who more bold?

*Sim.* I thank your worship: I shall make my master glad with these tidings.            [*Exit* Simple.

*Host.* Thou art clerkly,[6] thou art clerkly, sir John: Was there a wise woman with thee?

*Fal.* Ay, that there was, mine host; one that hath taught me more wit than ever I learned before

---

6 —— *clerkly,*] i. e. scholar-like.

in my life : and I paid nothing for it neither, but was paid for my learning.⁷

*Enter* BARDOLPH.

*Bard.* Out, alas, sir! cozenage! meer cozenage!

*Host.* Where be my horses ? speak well of them, varletto.

*Bard.* Run away with the cozeners : for so soon as I came beyond Eton, they threw me off, from behind one of them, in a slough of mire ; and set spurs, and away, like three German devils, three Doctor Faustuses.

*Host.* They are gone but to meet the duke, villain ; do not say, they be fled ; Germans are honest men.

*Enter Sir* HUGH EVANS.

*Eva.* Where is mine host ?

*Host.* What is the matter, sir ?

*Eva.* Have a care of your entertainments : there is a friend of mine come to town, tells me, there is three couzin germans, that has cozened all the hosts of Readings, of Maidenhead, of Colebrook, of horses and money. I tell you for good-will, look you ; you are wise, and full of gibes and vlouting-stogs ; and 'tis not convenient you should be co-zened : Fare you well. [*Exit.*

*Enter Doctor* CAIUS.

*Caius.* Vere is mine *Host de Jarterre ?*

*Host.* Here, master doctor, in perplexity, and doubtful dilemma.

---

⁷ —— *I paid nothing for it neither, but was* paid *for my learn-ing.*] He alludes to the beating which he had just received. To *pay,* in our author's time, often signified to *beat.*

*Caius.* I cannot tell vat is dat: But it is tell-a me, dat you make a grand preparation for a duke *de Jarmany* : by my trot, dere is no duke, dat de court is know to come: I tell you for good vill: adieu.

[*Exit.*

*Host.* Hue and cry, villain, go:—assist me, knight; I am undone: fly, run, hue and cry, villain! I am undone!

[*Exeunt* Host *and* BARDOLPH.

*Fal.* I would, all the world might be cozened; for I have been cozened, and beaten too. If it should come to the ear of the court, how I have been transformed, and how my transformation hath been washed and cudgeled, they would melt me out of my fat, drop by drop, and liquor fishermen's boots with me; I warrant, they would whip me with their fine wits, till I were as crest-fallen as a dried pear. I never prospered since I forswore myself at *primero.*[8] Well, if my wind were but long enough to say my prayers, I would repent.—

*Enter Mistress* QUICKLY.

Now! whence come you?

*Quick.* From the two parties, forsooth.

*Fal.* The devil take one party, and his dam the other, and so they shall be both bestowed! I have suffered more for their sakes, more, than the villainous inconstancy of man's disposition is able to bear.

*Quick.* And have not they suffered? Yes, I warrant; speciously one of them; mistress Ford, good heart, is beaten black and blue, that you cannot see a white spot about her.

*Fal.* What tell'st thou me of black and blue? I was beaten myself into all the colours of the

8 —— *primero.*] A game at cards.

rainbow; and I was like to be apprehended for the witch of Brentford; but that my admirable dexterity of wit, my counterfeiting the action of an old woman, deliver'd me, the knave constable had set me i' the stocks, i' the common stocks, for a witch..

*Quick.* Sir, let me speak with you in your chamber: you shall hear how things go; and, I warrant, to your content. Here is a letter will say somewhat. Good hearts, what ado here is to bring you together! Sure, one of you does not serve heaven well,[9] that you are so crossed.

*Fal.* Come up into my chamber.      [*Exeunt.*

## SCENE VI.

*Another Room in the Garter Inn.*

*Enter* FENTON *and* Host.

*Host.* Master Fenton, talk not to me; my mind is heavy, I will give over all..

*Fent.* Yet hear me speak: Assist me in my pur-
          pose,
And, as I am a gentleman, I'll give thee
A hundred pound in gold, more than your loss.

*Host.* I will hear you, master Fenton; and I will, at the least, keep your counsel.

*Fent.* From time to time I have acquainted you

---

[9] *Sure one of you does not serve heaven well,* &c.] The great fault of this play is the frequency of expressions so profane, that no necessity of preserving character can justify them. There are laws of higher authority than those of criticism. JOHNSON.

It is more to be regretted, that many of these expressions, omitted in the folio edition, on account of the Stat. 3 Jac. I. ch. 21, have been restored by the illaudable industry of subsequent editors. C.

With the dear love I bear to fair Anne Page ;
Who, mutually, hath answer'd my affection
(So far forth as herself might be her chooser,)
Even to my wish : I have a letter from her
Of such contents as you will wonder at ;
The mirth whereof so larded with my matter,
That neither, singly, can be manifested,
Without the show of both ;—wherein fat Falstaff
Hath a great scene : the image of the jest
                    [*Showing the letter.*
I'll show you here at large.   Hark, good mine host:
To-night at Herne's oak, just 'twixt twelve and
        one,
Must my sweet Nan present the fairy queen ;
The purpose why, is here ; in which disguise,
While other jests are something rank on foot,[1]
Her father hath commanded her to slip
Away with Slender, and with him at Eton
Immediately to marry : she hath consented :
Now, sir,
Her mother, even strong against that match,
And firm for doctor Caius, hath appointed
That he shall likewise shuffle her away,
While other sports are tasking of their minds,
And at the deanery, where a priest attends,
Straight marry her : to this her mother's plot
She, seemingly obedient, likewise hath
Made promise to the doctor ;—Now thus it rests :
Her father means she shall be all in white ;
And in that habit, when Slender sees his time
To take her by the hand, and bid her go,
She shall go with him : her mother hath intended,
The better to denote her to the doctor,
(For they must all be mask'd and vizarded,)

---

[1] *While other jests are something rank on foot,*] i. e. while
they are hotly pursuing other merriment of their own.

That, quaint in green,[1] she shall be loose enrob'd,
With ribbands pendant, flaring 'bout her head ;
And when the doctor spies his vantage ripe,
To pinch her by the hand, and, on that token,
The maid hath given consent to go with him.

*Host.* Which means she to deceive ? father or
  mother ?

*Fent.* Both, my good host, to go along with
  me :
And here it rests,—that you'll procure the vicar
To stay for me at church, 'twixt twelve and one,
And, in the lawful name of marrying,
To give our hearts united ceremony.

*Host.* Well, husband your device ; I'll to the
  vicar :
Bring you the maid, you shall not lack a priest.

*Fent.* So shall I ever more be bound to thee ;
Besides, I'll make a present recompense. [*Exeunt.*

## ACT V.

### SCENE I. *A Room in the Garter Inn.*

#### Enter FALSTAFF and Mrs. QUICKLY.

*Fal.* Pr'ythee, no more prattling :—go.——I'll
hold :[3] This is the third time ; I hope, good luck
lies in odd numbers. Away, go ; they say, there is
divinity in odd numbers, either in nativity, chance,
or death.—Away.

*Quick.* I'll provide you a chain ; and I'll do what
I can to get you a pair of horns.

---

[1] —— quaint *in green,*] —— may mean fantastically drest in
green. *Quaintness,* however, was anciently used to signify *grace-
fulness.*

[3] —— *I'll* hold :] I'll *keep* the appointment.

*Fal.* Away, I say ; time wears : hold up your head,
and mince.[4]                    [*Exit Mrs.* QUICKLY.

### *Enter* FORD.

How now, master Brook ? Master Brook, the matter will be known to-night, or never.   Be you in the
Park about midnight, at Herne's oak, and you shall
see wonders.

*Ford.* .Went you not to her yesterday, sir, as you
told me you had appointed ?

*Fal.* I went to her, master Brook, as you see,
like a poor old man : but I came from her, master
Brook, like a poor old woman.   That same knave,
Ford her husband, hath the finest mad devil of jealousy in him, master Brook, that ever governed
frenzy.   I will tell you.——He beat me grievously, in
the shape of a woman ; for in the shape of man,
master Brook, I fear not Goliath with a weaver's
beam ; because I know also, life is a shuttle.   I am
in haste , go along with me ; I'll tell you all, master
Brook.   Since I plucked geese,[5] played truant, and
whipped top, I knew not what it was to be beaten,
till lately.   Follow me : I'll tell you strange things
of this knave Ford : on whom to-night I will be revenged, and I will deliver his wife into your hand.——
Follow :  Strange things in hand, master Brook !
follow.                              [*Exeunt.*

---

⁴——*hold up your head, and* mince.] To *mince* is to walk,
with affected delicacy.
⁵ —— *Since I* plucked geese,] To strip a living goose of his
feathers, was formerly an act of puerile barbarity.

## SCENE II.

### *Windsor Park.*

*Enter* PAGE, SHALLOW, *and* SLENDER.

*Page.* Come, come ; we'll couch i' the castle-ditch, till we see the light of our fairies.—Remember, son Slender, my daughter.

*Slen.* Ay, forsooth ; I have spoke with her, and we have a nay-word,⁶ how to know one another. I come to her in white, and cry, *mum ;* she cries *budget ;*⁷ and by that we know one another.

*Shal.* That's good too : but what needs either your *mum,* or her *budget ?* the white will decipher her well enough.—It hath struck ten o'clock.

*Page.* The night is dark ; light and spirits will become it well. Heaven prosper our sport ! No man means evil but the devil, and we shall know him by his horns. Let's away ; follow me. [*Exeunt.*

## SCENE III.

### *The Street in Windsor.*

*Enter Mrs.* PAGE, *Mrs.* FORD, *and Dr.* CAIUS.

*Mrs. Page.* Master Doctor, my daughter is in green : when you see your time, take her by the hand, away with her to the deanery, and despatch

---

⁶ —— *a nay-word,*] i. e. a watch-word.

⁷ —— mum ; *she cries,* budget ;] These words appear to have been in common use before the time of our author. " And now if a man call them to accomptes, and aske the cause of al these their tragical and cruel doings, he shall have a short answer with *mum budget,* except they will peradventure allege this, &c." *Oration against the unlawful Insurrections of the Protestants,* bl. l. 8vo. 1615, sign. C. 8. REED.

it quickly: Go before into the park; we two must go together.

*Caius.* I know vat I have to do; Adieu.

*Mrs. Page.* Fare you well, sir. [*Exit* CAIUS.] My husband will not rejoice so much at the abuse of Falstaff, as he will chafe at the doctor's marrying my daughter: but 'tis no matter; better a little chiding, than a great deal of heart-break.

*Mrs. Ford.* Where is Nan now, and her troop of fairies? and the Welch devil, Hugh?

*Mrs. Page.* They are all couched in a pit hard by Herne's oak,⁸ with obscured lights; which, at the very instant of Falstaff's and our meeting, they will at once display to the night.

*Mrs. Ford.* That cannot choose but amaze him.

*Mrs. Page.* If he be not amazed, he will be mocked; if he be amazed, he will every way be mocked.

*Mrs. Ford.* We'll betray him finely.

*Mrs. Page.* Against such lewdsters, and their
        lechery,
Those that betray them do no treachery.

*Mrs. Ford.* The hour draws on; To the oak, to the oak! [*Exeunt.*

## SCENE IV.

*Windsor Park.*

*Enter Sir* HUGH EVANS, *and Fairies.*

*Eva.* Trib, trib, fairies; come; and remember your parts: be pold, I pray you; follow me into

⁸ —— *in a* pit *hard by* Herne's oak,] An *oak,* which may be that alluded to by Shakspeare, is still standing close to a *pit* in Windsor forest. It is yet shown as the *oak of Herne.*
                                                                STEEVENS.

the pit; and when I give the watch-'ords, do as I
pid you; Come, come; trib, trib.          [*Exeunt.*

## SCENE V.

*Another part of the Park.*

*Enter* FALSTAFF *disguised, with a buck's head on.*

*Fal.* The Windsor bell hath struck twelve; the
minute draws on : Now, the hot-blooded gods assist
me :—Remember, Jove, thou wast a bull for thy
Europa; love set on thy horns.—O powerful love!
that, in some respects, makes a beast a man; in
some other, a man a beast.—You were also, Jupiter,
a swan, for the love of Leda;—O, omnipotent
love! how near the god drew to the complexion of
a goose?—A fault done first in the form of a beast;
—O Jove, a beastly fault! and then another fault
in the semblance of a fowl; think on't, Jove; a
foul fault.—When gods have hot backs, what shall
poor men do? For me, I am here a Windsor stag;
and the fattest, I think, i' the forest: Send me a
cool rut-time, Jove, or who can blame me to piss
my tallow? Who comes here? my doe?

*Enter Mrs.* FORD *and Mrs.* PAGE.

*Mrs. Ford.* Sir John? art thou there, my deer?
my male deer?

*Fal.* My doe with the black scut?—Let the sky
rain potatoes; let it thunder to the tune of *Green
Sleeves;* hail kissing-comfits, and snow eringoes;
let there come a tempest of provocation, I will
shelter me here.                    [*Embracing her.*

*Mrs. Ford.* Mistress Page is come with me,
sweetheart.

*Fal.* Divide me like a bride-buck, each a haunch:

9

I will keep my sides to myself, my shoulders for the fellow of this walk," and my horns I bequeath your husbands. Am I a woodman?' ha! Speak I like Herne the hunter?—Why, now is Cupid a child of conscience: he makes restitution. As I am a true spirit, welcome!      [*Noise within*.

*Mrs. Page.* Alas! what noise?

*Mrs. Ford.* Heaven forgive our sins!

*Fal.* What should this be?

*Mrs. Ford.*
*Mrs. Page.*   }   Away, away.     [*They run off*.

*Fal.* I think, the devil will not have me damned, lest the oil that is in me should set hell on fire; he would never else cross me thus.

*Enter Sir* HUGH EVANS, *like a satyr;* Mrs. QUICKLY, *and* PISTOL; ANNE PAGE, *as the Fairy Queen, attended by her brother and others, dressed like Fairies, with waxen tapers on their heads.*

*Quick.* Fairies, black, grey, green, and white,
You moon-shine revellers, and shades of night,
You orphan-heirs of fixed destiny,[*]
Attend your office, and your quality.

---

° —— *my* shoulders *for the* fellow *of this* walk,] A *walk* is that district in a forest, to which the jurisdiction of a particular keeper extends. To the keeper the *shoulders* and *humbles* belong as a perquisite.

' —— *a woodman?*] A *woodman* was an attendant on the officer, called *Forrester*. It is here, however, used in a wanton sense, for one who chooses female game as the objects of his pursuit.

* *You* orphan-*heirs of fixed destiny,*] Dr. Warburton corrects *orphan* to *orphans*; and not without plausibility, as the word *orphes* occurs both before and afterwards. But, I fancy, in acquiescence to the vulgar doctrine, the address in this line is to a part of the *troop*, as mortals by birth, but adopted by the fairies: *orphans* in respect of their real parents, and now only dependent on *destiny* herself. FARMER.

Fuseli del.                                                     Bromley sc.

I think the devil will not have me damned,
lest the Oil that is in me should set hell on fire

Published by F & C Rivington Jan: 27 1803.

Crier Hobgoblin, make the fairy o-yes.

*Pist.* Elves, list your names; silence, you airy
    toys.

*Cricket,* to Windsor chimnies shalt thou leap:
Where fires thou find'st unrak'd, and hearths un-
    swept,
There pinch the maids as blue as bilberry:[3]
Our radiant queen hates sluts and sluttery.

*Fal.* They are fairies; he, that speaks to them,
    shall die:
I'll wink and couch: no man their works must eye.
        *[Lies down upon his face.*

*Eva.* Where's *Pede?*—Go you, and where you
    find a maid,
That, ere she sleep, has thrice her prayers said,
Raise up the organs of her fantasy,[4]
Sleep she as sound as careless infancy;
But those as sleep, and think not on their sins,
Pinch them, arms, legs, backs, shoulders, sides, and
    shins.

*Quich.* About, about;
Search Windsor castle, elves, within and out:
Strew good luck, ouphes, on every sacred room;
That it may stand till the perpetual doom,
In state as wholesome, as in state 'tis fit;
Worthy the owner, and the owner it.
The several chairs of order look you scour
With juice of balm, and every precious flower:

---

3 —— as bilberry:] The *bilberry* is the *whortleberry.*
4 —— *Go you, and where you find a maid,*—
   *Raise up the organs of her fantasy,*] Mr. Malone supposes
the sense of the passage, collectively taken, to be as follows:—
" Go you, and wherever you find a maid asleep, that hath thrice
prayed to the Deity, *though,* in consequence of her innocence,
she sleep as soundly as an infant, elevate her fancy, and amuse her
tranquil mind with some delightful vision; but those whom you
find asleep without having previously thought on their sins, and
prayed to heaven for forgiveness, pinch, &c."

Y

Each fair instalment, coat, and several crest,
With loyal blazon, evermore be blest !
And nightly, meadow-fairies, look, you sing,
Like to the Garter's compass, in a ring :
The expressure that it bears, green let it be,
More fertile-fresh than all the field to see ;
And, *Hony soit qui mal y pense,* write,
In emerald tufts, flowers purple, blue, and white ;
Like sapphire, pearl, and rich embroidery,
Buckled below fair knight-hood's bending knee :
Fairies use flowers for their charactery.[5]
Away ; disperse : But, till 'tis one o'clock,
Our dance of custom, round about the oak
Of Herne the hunter, let us not forget.
    *Eva.* Pray you, lock hand in hand ; yourselves
        in order set :
And twenty glow-worms shall our lanterns be,
To guide our measure round about the tree.
But, stay ; I smell a man of middle earth.[6]
    *Fal.* Heavens defend me from that Welch fairy !
lest he transform me to a piece of cheese !
    *Pist.* Vile worm, thou wast o'erlook'd even in thy
        birth.[7]
    *Quick.* With trial-fire touch me his finger-end :
If he be chaste, the flame will back descend,
And turn him to no pain ; but if he start,
It is the flesh of a corrupted heart.
    *Pist.* A trial, come.
    *Eva.* Come, will this wood take fire ?
             *[They burn him with their tapers.*
    *Fal.* Oh, oh, oh !

---

    [5] —— *charactery.*] For the matter with which they make
letters.
    [6] —— *of* middle earth.] *Earth,* or *world,* from its imaginary
situation in the *midst,* or *middle* of the Ptolemaic system.
    [7] —— o'er-look'd *even in thy birth.*] i. e. *slighted* as soon as
born.

*Quick.* Corrupt, corrupt, and tainted in desire !
About him, fairies ; sing a scornful rhyme ;
And, as you trip, still pinch him to your time.

*Eva.* It is right ; indeed he is full of lecheries
and iniquity.


SONG. *Fye on sinful fantasy !*
*Fye on lust and luxury !*
*Lust is but a bloody fire,*
*Kindled with unchaste desire,*
*Fed in heart ; whose flames aspire,*
*As thoughts do blow them, higher and higher.*
*Pinch him, fairies, mutually ;*
*Pinch him for his villainy ;*
*Pinch him, and burn him, and turn him about,*
*Till candles, and star-light, and moon-shine be out.*


*During this song, the fairies pinch* Falstaff. *Doctor*
Caius *comes one way, and steals away a fairy in*
*green ;* Slender *another way, and takes off a fairy*
*in white ; and* Fenton *comes, and steals away*
Mrs. Anne Page. *A noise of hunting is made*
*within. All the fairies run away.* Falstaff *pulls*
*off his buck's head, and rises.*


*Enter* PAGE, FORD, *Mrs.* PAGE, *and Mrs.* FORD.
*They lay hold on him.*


*Page.* Nay, do not fly ; I think, we have watch'd
you now ;
Will none but Herne the hunter serve your turn ?

*Mrs. Page.* I pray you, come ; hold up the jest
no higher :——
Now, good sir John, how like you Windsor wives ?
Y 2

See  you these, husband ?  do not these fair yokes
Become the forest better than the town ?[8]

*Ford.* Now, sir, who's a cuckold  now ?—Master
Brook, Falstaff's a knave, a cuckoldly knave; here
are his horns, master Brook: And, master Brook,
he hath enjoyed nothing of Ford's but his buck-
basket, his cudgel, and twenty pounds of money;
which must be paid to master Brook; his horses
are arrested for it, master Brook.

*Mrs. Ford.* Sir John, we have had ill luck; we
could never meet.  I will never take you for my love
again, but I will always count you my deer.

*Fal.* I do begin to perceive that I am made an
ass.

*Ford.* Ay, and an ox too; both the proofs are
extant.

*Fal.* And these are not fairies ?  I was three or
four times in the thought, they were not fairies : and
yet the guiltiness of my mind, the sudden surprize
of my powers, drove the grossness of the foppery
into a received belief, in despite of the teeth of all
rhyme and reason, that they were fairies.  See now,
how wit may be made a Jack-a-lent, when 'tis upon
ill employment.

*Eva.* Sir John Falstaff, serve Got, and leave your
desires, and fairies will not pinse you.

*Ford.* Well said, fairy Hugh.

*Eva.* And leave you your jealousies too, I pray
you.

*Ford.* I will never mistrust my wife again, till
thou art able to woo her in good English.

---

[8] *See you these, husband? do not these fair* yokes
*Become the forest better than the town ?*] Mrs. Page's meaning
is this.  Seeing the horns (the types of cuckoldom) in Falstaff's
hands, she asks her husband, whether those yokes are not more
proper in the *forest* than in the *town;* i. e. than in his own family.
THEOBALD.

*Fal.* Have I laid my brain in the sun, and dried it, that it wants matter to prevent so gross o'er-reaching as this? Am I ridden with a Welch goat too? Shall I have a coxcomb of frize?[9] 'Tis time I were choked with a piece of toasted cheese.

*Eva.* Seese is not good to give putter; your pelly is all putter.

*Fal.* Seese and putter! have I lived to stand at the taunt of one that makes fritters of English? This is enough to be the decay of lust and late-walking, through the realm.

*Mrs. Page.* Why, sir John, do you think, though we would have thrust virtue out of our hearts by the head and shoulders, and have given ourselves without scruple to hell, that ever the devil could have made you our delight?

*Ford.* What, a hodge-pudding? a bag of flax?

*Mrs. Page.* A puffed man?

*Page.* Old, cold, withered, and of intolerable entrails?

*Ford.* And one that is as slanderous as Satan?

*Page.* And as poor as Job?

*Ford.* And as wicked as his wife?

*Eva.* And given to fornications, and to taverns, and sack, and wine, and metheglins, and to drinkings, and swearings, and starings, pribbles and prabbles?

*Fal.* Well, I am your theme: you have the start of me; I am dejected; I am not able to answer the Welch flannel: ignorance itself is a plummet o'er me;[1] use me as you will.

---

[9] —— *a coxcomb of* frize?] i. e. a fool's cap made out of Welch materials. Wales was famous for this cloth.

[1] Ignorance *itself is a* plummet o'er me:] i. e. serves to point out my obliquities. This is said in consequence of Evans's last speech. The allusion is to the examination of a carpenter's work by the *plummet* held over it; of which line Sir Hugh is here represented as the lead. HENLEY.

*Ford.* Marry, sir, we'll bring you to Windsor, to one master Brook, that you have cozened of money, to whom you should have been a pander : over and above that you have suffered, I think, to repay that money will be a biting affliction.

*Mrs. Ford.* Nay, husband, let that go to make amends :
Forgive that sum, and so we'll all be friends.

*Ford.* Well, here's my hand ; all's forgiven at last.

*Page.* Yet be cheerful, knight : thou shalt eat a posset to-night at my house ; where I will desire thee to laugh at my wife, that now laughs at thee : Tell her, master Slender hath married her daughter.

*Mrs. Page.* Doctors doubt that : if Anne Page be my daughter, she is, by this, doctor Caius' wife.
[*Aside.*

*Enter* SLENDER.

*Slen.* Whoo, ho ! ho ! father Page !

*Page.* Son ! how now ? how now, son ? have you despatched ?

*Slen.* Despatched !—I'll make the best in Glocestershire know on't ; would I were hanged, la, else.

*Page.* Of what, son ?

*Slen.* I came yonder at Eton to marry mistress Anne Page, and she's a great lubberly boy ; If it had not been i' the church, I would have swinged him, or he should have swinged me. If I did not think it had been Anne Page, would I might never stir, and 'tis a post-master's boy.

*Page.* Upon my life then you took the wrong.

*Slen.* What need you tell me that ? I think so, when I took a boy for a girl : If I had been married to him, for all he was in woman's apparel, I would not have had him.

*Page.* Why, this is your own folly. Did not I tell you, how you should know my daughter by her garments?

*Slen.* I went to her in white, and cry'd *mum,* and she cry'd *budget,* as Anne and I had appointed ; and yet it was not Anne, but a post-master's boy.

*Eva.* Jeshu! Master Slender, cannot you see but marry boys?

*Page.* O, I am vexed at heart: What shall I do?

*Mrs. Page.* Good George, be not angry: I knew of your purpose; turned my daughter into green; and, indeed, she is now with the doctor at the deanery, and there married.

### Enter CAIUS.

*Caius.* Vere is mistress Page? By gar, I am cozened; I ha' married *un garçon,* a boy; *un paisan,* by gar, a boy; it is not Anne Page: by gar, I am cozened.

*Mrs. Page.* Why, did you take her in green?

*Caius.* Ay, be gar, and 'tis a boy: be gar, I'll raise all Windsor. [*Exit* CAIUS.

*Ford.* This is strange: Who hath got the right Anne?

*Page.* My heart misgives me: Here comes master Fenton.

### Enter FENTON and ANNE PAGE.

How now, master Fenton?

*Anne.* Pardon, good father! good my mother, pardon!

*Page.* Now, mistress? how chance you went not with master Slender?

*Mrs. Page.* Why went you not with master doctor, maid?

10

*Fent.* You do amaze her :[1] Hear the truth of it.
You would have married her most shamefully,
Where there was no proportion held in love.
The truth is, She and I, long since contracted,
Are now so sure, that nothing can dissolve us.
The offence is holy, that she hath committed :
And this deceit loses the name of craft,
Of disobedience, or unduteous title ;
Since therein she doth evitate and shun
A thousand irreligious cursed hours,
Which forced marriage would have brought upon
   her.
 *Ford.* Stand not amaz'd : here is no remedy :——
In love, the heavens themselves do guide the state ;
Money buys lands, and wives are sold by fate.
 *Fal.* I am glad, though you have ta'en a special
stand to strike at me, that your arrow hath glanced.
 *Page.* Well, what remedy ? Fenton, heaven give
   thee joy !
What cannot be eschew'd, must be embrac'd.
 *Fal.* When night-dogs run, all sorts of deer are
   chas'd.
 *Eva.* I will dance and eat plums at your wedding.
 *Mrs. Page.* Well, I will muse no further :——
   Master Fenton,
Heaven give you many, many merry days !——
Good husband, let us every one go home,
And laugh this sport o'er by a country fire ;
Sir John and all.
 *Ford.* Let it be so :——Sir John,
To master Brook you yet shall hold your word ;
For he, to-night, shall lie with mistress Ford.[3]
        [*Exeunt.*

---

[1] —— amaze *her :*] i. e. confound her by your questions.
[3] Of this play there is a tradition preserved by Mr. Rowe, that
it was written at the command of Queen Elizabeth, who was so
delighted with the character of Falstaff, that she wished it to be

diffused through more plays; but suspecting that it might pall by continued uniformity, directed the poet to diversify his manner, by shewing him in love. No task is harder than that of writing to the ideas of another. Shakspeare knew what the Queen, if the story be true, seems not to have known—that by any real passion of tenderness, the selfish craft, the careless jollity, and the lazy luxury of Falstaff must have suffered so much abatement, that little of his former cast would have remained. Falstaff could not love but by ceasing to be Falstaff. He could only counterfeit love, and his professions could be prompted, not by the hope of pleasure, but of money. Thus the poet approached as near as he could to the work enjoined him; yet having, perhaps, in the former plays, completed his own idea, seems not to have been able to give Falstaff all his former power of entertainment.

This comedy is remarkable for the variety and number of the personages, who exhibit more characters appropriated and discriminated, than perhaps can be found in any other play.

Whether Shakspeare was the first that produced upon the English stage the effect of language distorted and depraved by provincial or foreign pronunciation, I cannot certainly decide.* This mode of forming ridiculous characters can confer praise only on him who originally discovered it, for it requires not much of either wit or judgment: its success must be derived almost wholly from the player, but its power in a skilful mouth, even he that despises it, is unable to resist.

The conduct of this drama is deficient; the action begins and ends often, before the conclusion, and the different parts might change places without inconvenience; but its general power, that power by which all works of genius shall finally be tried, is such, that perhaps it never yet had reader or spectator who did not think it too soon at the end. JOHNSON.

* In *The Three Ladies of London*, 1584, is the character of an *Italian* merchant, very strongly marked by foreign pronunciation. Dr. *Dodypoll*, in the comedy which bears his name, is, like *Caius*, a French physician. This piece appeared at least a year before *The Merry Wives of Windsor*. The hero of it speaks such another jargon as the antagonist of Sir Hugh, and like him is cheated of his mistress. In several other pieces, more ancient than the earliest of Shakspeare's, provincial characters are introduced. STEEVENS.

## END OF VOLUME FIRST.

C. Baldwin, Printer,
New Bridge-street, London.

3°

Check Out More Titles From HardPress Classics Series In this collection we are offering thousands of classic and hard to find books. This series spans a vast array of subjects – so you are bound to find something of interest to enjoy reading and learning about.

Subjects:
Architecture
Art
Biography & Autobiography
Body, Mind &Spirit
Children & Young Adult
Dramas
Education
Fiction
History
Language Arts & Disciplines
Law
Literary Collections
Music
Poetry
Psychology
Science
…and many more.

Visit us at www.hardpress.net

CPSIA information can be obtained
at www.ICGtesting.com
Printed in the USA
BVHW062209270819

556849BV00013B/1586/P